MW00461039

Gray Raiders
of the Sea

Chester G. Hearn

Gray Raiders of the Sea

How Eight Confederate Warships Destroyed the Union's High Seas Commerce

INTERNATIONAL MARINE PUBLISHING
Camden, Maine

Published by International Marine Publishing

10 9 8 7 6 5 4 3 2 1

Library of Congress Cataloging-in-Publication Data

Hearn, Chester G.
    Gray raiders of the sea : how eight Confederate war-
ships destroyed the Union's high seas commerce / Chester G. Hearn III.
      p.   cm.
    Includes bibliographical references and index.
    ISBN 0–87742–279–6
    1. United States—History—Civil War, 1861–1865—
Naval   operations.   2. Confederate   States   of
America.   Navy—History.   I. Title.
    E596.H43   1992
    973.7'57—dc20   91–18618
                                                        CIP

TAB BOOKS offers software for sale. For information and a
catalog, please contact TAB Software Department, Blue
Ridge Summit, PA 17294-0850.

Questions regarding the content of this book should be addressed to:

International Marine Publishing
P.O. Box 220
Camden, ME 04843

Edited by J. R. Babb and Tom McCarthy

Text design by Joyce C. Weston
Printed and bound by Fairfield Graphics, Fairfield, Pennsylvania.

Printed on acid-free paper.

To Ann, whose love and patience
have made this work possible

Contents

List of Illustrations

Illustrations may be found following page 192.

Acknowledgments

A great deal of time has gone into the preparation of this book, especially in gathering source material from museums, libraries, and government archives. The staff at the Library of Congress and the National Archives was most helpful in guiding me through daunting masses of documents and microfilms.

The little library in Milton, Pennsylvania has been immensely helpful in locating needed documents and providing copies through national library sources. Much of the credit goes to Suzanne Edwards and Mary Harrison, who prior to my request had little experience with a project of this size. Credit and thanks go also to Evelyn Burns, research specialist at the Brown Library in Williamsport, Pennsylvania.

The United States Army Military History Institute, at Carlisle, Pennsylvania, also helped in many ways. John F. Slonaker's staff in the Historical Reference Branch provided primary source assistance and helped in the development of a full and useful bibliography. Mike Wieny and Randy Hackenberg of the Institute's imaging center helped locate and acquire many of the images used in this book.

Guy Swanson's staff at the Museum of the Confederacy in Richmond, Virginia, was especially helpful in locating the journals and diaries of the men who served aboard the *Shenandoah* and the *Nashville*.

Chuck Haberlein at the United States Naval Imaging Center in Washington, D.C. provided many of the book's illustrations. I went back to him several times for advice and assistance in finding the best images in his immense files covering the Civil War.

I would also like to thank Dave Zullo, Ron Van Sickle, Terry Murphy, James McLean, and Bob Younger's staff, who were aware that I was writing a book on the Confederate cruisers and provided about 80 primary and secondary sources, mostly first editions.

I am also grateful to my son, Chet, who showed me how to use a computer, and to my former secretary, Mrs. Sharon Callenberger, who knows more about computers than I will ever learn.

I especially want to thank James Babb of International Marine Publishing, who had enough confidence in this work to provide patient editorial assistance in preparing the final manuscript. Jim's encouragement was instrumental in giving me the confidence to retire and continue writing, something I had postponed for nearly 35 years.

Introduction

D URING the Civil War, the only force opposing the United States Navy on the high seas was eight Confederate cruisers. Their mission was to dismantle the American carrying trade and force wealthy shippers to press the federal government for a peaceful settlement. Manned by a handful of resolute Confederate officers, they very nearly succeeded.

Denied access to their own ports by the strangling Union blockade, the cruisers were forced to live apart from the land, relying on their own resources and the largesse of friendly foreign powers. Five of the cruisers had numerous deficiencies. The *Sumter*, a converted packet steamer, was small and slow. The *Nashville*, a rickety sidewheeler too flimsy for heavy guns, was fast under steam but slow under sail, and dangerous in heavy seas. The *Georgia*, *Tallahassee*, and *Chickamauga* carried only token sails and were completely dependent on coal obtained from neutral countries—a crippling handicap given that international law prevented their coaling in any one country more frequently than every 90 days.

More successful were the vessels built in England under the able supervision of James Dunwoody Bulloch. The *Alabama*, *Florida*, and *Shenandoah* were masterpieces of design and technology, fast under sail or steam, self-contained and self-sufficient, capable of staying at sea for long periods without refueling. Captained by daring officers, they menaced Union merchant shipping around the world. In time, no vessel registered to the flag of the United States felt safe on the high seas.

In the summer of 1861, when Raphael Semmes took the first Confederate raider to sea, the oceans were filled with ships flying the Stars and Stripes. Since 1846, American merchant traffic had tripled, threatening to eclipse Great Britain's domination of the world's maritime commerce. European shippers looked on in dismay as swift and efficient American ships took over high-profit cargoes, leaving their own ships rotting in port or carrying bulk cargoes at reduced rates. With a strong commercial presence in virtually every port of the world, the American carrying trade in 1860 looked indestructible.

Suddenly there was war between the states. First the *Sumter* and then the *Nashville* were at sea, capturing, looting, and burning American shipping. If the upstart American merchant fleet could not be destroyed by lower freight rates, perhaps it could be destroyed by the Confederate cruisers. Contrary to the public position of the Queen's Foreign Minister, English citizens were more than willing to accept Confederate gold and cotton in return for cruisers, blockade runners, arms, ammunition, and supplies. If that was not enough, Englishmen manned the cruisers, fired the guns, boarded prizes, looted the cargoes, and struck the matches that burned the American interloper to the waterline. Union agents documented British complicity in what was termed "piracy" by both the government and the American public.

For two years Confederate commanders swept the seas of Union shipping with little interference from the American Navy. In time, prizes became scarce. To minimize their losses, American shippers began liquidating their fleets. Some sold their vessels to English merchants at bargain-basement prices. Others changed their registries to Brazil, Italy, Uruguay, Chile or any other country that would protect their interests and save their ships from the torch.

With the American carrying trade no longer a threat, the British policy of benign neglect toward Confederate commerce destroyers tightened. Neutrality laws were now strictly enforced, and the Confederate shipbuilding program in England and France was dismantled. Fuel became harder to find; repairs were refused unless essential to the safety of the ship. Cruiser commanders, whose visits to remote ports were once celebrated with gala balls and banquets, now found themselves ignominiously hurried back to sea.

Most of the deck officers were Southern-born professionals who had served in the United States Navy. The junior officers and seamen of the *Alabama*, *Florida*, and *Shenandoah* were originally Englishmen, but with desertions common in every port, the crews eventually comprised a mix of nationalities who joined for high wages and the promise of fortunes in prize money. By the end of 1863, crews faced the reality that the distribution of prize money would remain a dream. Despite this, devotion and respect led most crews to continue to serve their Confederate officers.

The task of the Confederate commanders was as hopeless as the Confederacy itself, and their existence as arduous. Faced with corroded boilers and a heavy Union blockade, Raphael Semmes was forced to abandon the *Sumter* at Gibraltar. The *Georgia* and the *Nashville* were poorly suited to commerce raiding and decommissioned. The cruises of the *Tallahassee* and the *Chickamauga* ended when they were unable to obtain coal. The *Alabama* remained at sea so long that her powder deteriorated—a deficiency that would prove fatal in her fight to the death with the USS *Kearsarge*. The *Florida* was rammed and captured in a neutral port of a nation too weak to protect her neutrality. Only the *Shenandoah* survived. Unaware of the war's end, James I. Waddell destroyed the American whaling fleet in the Bering Sea, then sailed 23,000 miles back to Liverpool to surrender to England. By then, the once impressive American carrying trade had been driven from the sea.

More than half the American merchant fleet disappeared during the Civil War. The Confederate cruisers destroyed 110,000 tons of shipping. In contrast, frightened shippers sold another 800,000 tons to foreign owners. No record exists to account for the hundreds of vessels that sought shelter under the protection of foreign registries. Many that remained under the Stars and Stripes were old or rotting vessels foreigners did not want.

Eventually the United States sued Great Britain through an international court of arbitration for damages caused by Confederate cruisers having English antecedents. In 1872, the Geneva Tribunal awarded the United States $15.5 million in gold. For the British, it was a cheap price to pay to recover commercial dominance of the seas.

Of all the strategies employed by the Confederacy, destruction of American maritime wealth was one of the few that succeeded. Eight vessels did it all. The Confederate cruisers offer a separate history of bravery, courage, innovation, isolation, success, and final disappointment. No military force faced such unequal odds, not even the Confederate armies.

ONE

Setting the Stage

W HEN South Carolina seceded from the Union on December 20, 1860, the Confederate States of America did not exist. In the following seven weeks, six more southern states left the Union, adopted a provisional constitution creating a confederacy of states, and elected their first and only president, Jefferson Davis.

After the fall of Fort Sumter on April 14, 1861, four more states joined the new Confederacy, an infant government pledged to the preservation of states' rights and to the agrarian traditions of her people. The South's objective was to secure independence, but firing on Fort Sumter precipitated a war that made this unlikely: The small population, minimal manufacturing capability, and complete lack of a navy gave the South little with which to fight.

By contrast, the Union Navy entered the war with 42 ships on active commission, and with another 48 vessels that could be mobilized quickly. It emerged four years later as the strongest naval power in the world, eclipsing even the mighty British Navy—at least for a short while—in both the quality and quantity of armed vessels.

But while the Union concentrated enormous funds on building up its navy—whose major goal was to blockade the southern coast and prevent supplies from entering the South—it lost much of its civilian merchant fleet to the only hostile force the South managed to place upon the high seas—the commerce raiders. This little force of eight ships and four converted tenders—with never more than two cruisers afloat at any one time—caused a sharp decline in American merchant shipping that extended deep into the 20th century.

By 1860, the American carrying trade had grown at a rate both envied and feared by the British—the preeminent maritime power of the age. Yankee vessels were faster, manned more efficiently, and carried cargo more cheaply. Worldwide trade had increased 300 percent in the years preceding the war, and 70 percent of that trade was carried in American bottoms.

The Southern strategy of destroying American commerce was seen merely as a way to shorten the war, but maritime interests in Britain recognized it as an opportunity to eliminate an imposing competitor, and were eager to help the South acquire the ships it needed. Without British assistance, the Confederate commerce raiders could not have been built.

After his inauguration on February 18, 1861, President Jefferson Davis appointed as naval secretary Stephen R. Mallory, an experienced administrator with a lifelong interest in ships and the sea. As a senator from Florida Mallory had been chairman of the Committee on Naval Affairs, where he gained a knowledge of ship design and naval ordnance that would later influence his strategic planning as naval secretary.[1] He also authored a policy that forced the early retirement of many old-line naval officers, and this won him few friends among the officer corps. Despite this, President Davis had complete confidence in his new secretary. No other man in the Confederacy understood naval affairs more thoroughly than Mallory, and for the next four years he exercised almost complete control over the Confederate Navy.[2]

When Mallory took office as Confederate Naval Secretary on March 18, 1861, he found himself less administrator than creator: The South's tiny and unimposing navy—acquired mostly by the individual states at the Union's expense—consisted of but 10 ships carrying a combined firepower of 15 small guns. The largest ship, the *Robert McClellan*, boasted five guns and a crew of 35. He also inherited from the states a ragtag mixture of coasting vessels and harbor craft—some tugs, a few pilot boats, revenue cutters, captured slavers, an ex-pirate, and a forfeited merchantman.

Ample ship timber stood in Southern forests, but the skilled workmen who could fashion it into masts and frames worked in Northern shipyards. Even during peacetime the agricultural South produced insufficient iron to satisfy internal demand; most metal products had come from the North. Only one machine shop could produce a reliable marine engine; only one foundry south of the Potomac River could cast or forge a gun of large caliber and acceptable quality. The only shipyard in the South capable of producing heavy warships, the Gosport Navy Yard in Norfolk, was partly damaged in April 1861 by its own Union forces before it could be occupied by the Confederates. The few Southern workshops capable of building machinery or producing arms supplied the army.[3]

In contrast, within four months after the fall of Fort Sumter the Union Navy under Secretary Gideon Welles had under construction 47 frigate, sloop, and gunboat hulls ranging from 500 to more than 2,000 tons. Thousands of workmen in a score of factories were manufacturing engines and boilers, deck gear, and ordnance. Compared with Welles, Mallory faced a seemingly impossible task.[4]

If the South was to break the strangling cordon of Union ships that prevented supplies from reaching its ports, it needed ships powerful enough and plentiful enough to contend with the Union fleet. The huge amount of guns, ordnance, and supplies captured by the Confederates at the Gosport Naval Yard provided Mallory with the opportunity he needed, and restoration began immediately on three damaged vessels left behind by retreating Union forces.

The 20-gun sailing sloops-of-war *Germantown* and *Plymouth*, and the 40-gun, 3,200-ton, twin-engined *Merrimack* were raised and moved to drydock. The two sailing sloops were restored, but the Confederates had neither the time nor the money to waste equipping them for sea.[5] Mallory chose instead to concentrate every resource on converting the *Merrimack* to an ironclad—the precursor of a policy to concentrate Southern ship construction almost exclusively on ironclad vessels.

Despite engineering problems, the *Merrimack*, now the Confederate ironclad ram *Virginia*, was highly successful against conventional Union ships off Hampton Roads before her career ended in the classic standoff with the *Monitor*.

Thirteen months after the Confederates took control of Norfolk, Union forces recaptured the navy yard when Major General George B. McClellan brought the Army of the Potomac to the doorstep of Richmond. This action forced the destruction of the now-famous *Virginia*, which had been languishing in Norfolk, on the morning of May 11, 1862.

Early praise for the *Virginia's* accomplishments now turned to sharp criticism of Mallory's shipbuilding policies. The only major Confederate shipyard had produced but one formidable vessel, and now both ship and shipyard were gone. The *Richmond Examiner* blamed Mallory and wrote: "The success of the *Merrimack*, however gratifying it may be, is in fact a severe reflection upon our sloth and inactivity in naval preparation. It proves what we could have done in this department of our operations if we had applied the proper energy. There are several other hulks in the Portsmouth Navy Yard that may be rendered just as formidable to the enemy as the *Merrimack* herself, and 50 gunboats could have been so constructed to give these large war vessels aid and comfort."[6]

The *Examiner* accurately pointed to the navy yard's under-utilization, but failed to consider the inadequacy of the South's resources to design and support a major shipbuilding program. Mallory knew his country's limitations, and geared his policies to practical realities. His naval program was broken down into four major strategies: the domestic construction of ironclads; the commissioning of privateers under letters of marque and reprisal; the purchase or seizure of any vessel that could carry a gun; and the purchase abroad of high seas commerce raiders.

In the early stage of the war, lightly armed Confederate privateers went to sea to prey upon merchantmen trading with Cuba and the West Indies. But when the growing Union Navy tightened its blockade of the South, prizes could no longer be brought into Southern ports, and the slow-sailing privateers could not put to sea without risking capture. As a Confederate strategy, privateering failed the first year of the war.

The Union blockade continued to grow at a rate that far exceeded Naval Secretary Welles's early expectations. By the end of the war, the Union Navy had captured or destroyed an estimated 1,500 Confederate blockade runners. Hundreds were purchased from prize courts, converted to gunboats, and put to work chasing runners. The South had no such supply of vessels to draw upon.[7]

If Mallory lacked ships, he did not lack officers to man them. As early as February 14, 1861, the Confederate Congress authorized Charles M. Conrad, chairman of the Committee on Naval Affairs, to offer equivalent rank and seniority to a number of Southern officers in the Union Navy. Commander Raphael Semmes, a Maryland native who had moved to Mobile 20 years earlier, received his telegram while serving on the Lighthouse Board in Washington:

Montgomery, Feb. 14, 1861
Sir: On behalf of the Committee on Naval Affairs, I beg leave to request that you repair to this place, at your earliest convenience.
Your O.B. Servant
C. M. Conrad

Semmes resigned his commission, packed his belongings, and arrived in Montgomery four days later.

Along with such senior officers from the Old Navy as Captains Lawrence Rousseau, Duncan N. Ingraham, and Victor M. Randolph, Semmes participated in a joint session of military and naval committees formed to evaluate what military resources the South could muster. The meeting concluded that if the Confederacy wanted the materiel of war, it would have to go outside the South to purchase it. On the same day that he appointed Mallory to the Navy Department, President Davis dispatched Semmes to the North and Caleb Huse to Europe to secure arms and ammunition. He gave both men detailed letters of instruction, including specific sources where purchases could be made.[8]

Semmes arrived in New York to find Northern agents and industrialists eager to do business with the South. He observed that, "Some of the men who would thus have sold body and soul to me for sufficient consideration occupied high social position and were men of wealth."[9] Shipments of percussion caps, light artillery, rifles, muskets, powder, and other munitions went forward on a regular basis, with little effort taken to disguise the contents.

On March 13, 1861, Mallory wrote Semmes asking him to select and purchase two steamers of strength and light draft. By now, however, Semmes was being watched by Union agents, and he had to abandon the search. At the end of March, he booked passage back to Alabama aboard one of the New York and Savannah steamers, which still operated on regular schedules, "carrying the Federal flag at the peak and the Confederate flag at the fore." The flag at the fore always indicated the "country" of destination.[10] Semmes returned to Montgomery on April 4, 1861, still with no ship to command.

By June 3, 1861, over 300 Southerners—a fifth of the officer corps— had left the Union navy. The influx of officers occurred so rapidly that Mallory could not find vessels or work for everyone. Officers were asked to "bring with you every ship and man you can, that we may use them against the oppressors of our liberties."[11] The plea made good rhetoric, but not a single Southern officer delivered a Union vessel. Years of loyalty to the U.S. Navy left the Southern officers unable to dishonor the flag they once had served and still respected.

Mallory now had the funds to purchase or build 10 screw steamers of 1,000 tons, armed with at least one 10-inch and four 8-inch guns, but he was unable to buy ships in the United States or Canada, and construction remained his only alternative.[12] New Orleans, which had built shallow-draft paddle steamers for many years, appeared to be the secure location where the South could begin to build its navy.

To head the project, Mallory appointed Commodore Lawrence Rousseau, a Louisiana native who had resigned his commission after 52 years of loyal and honorable service in the U. S. Navy. Although no longer young, he typified the officers of the Old Navy who sacrificed security and pensions to serve their home states. Rousseau, who served as commander of the Louisiana navy until its incorporation by the Confederacy, was already at work trying to build a navy when Mallory appointed him to head the project.

No warship had ever been built at New Orleans. Rousseau found several private shipyards that built good riverboats, but their limited facilities were less well suited to building warships from scratch than to refitting existing ships for war. Although he could not find a single vessel at New Orleans that he considered suitable for conversion, at Mallory's suggestion Rousseau purchased two small steamers languishing among the clutter of hulls anchored in the river. Both vessels enjoyed brief but distinctly different careers in the Confederate Navy.

The *Havana*, a bark-rigged steamer that had carried passengers and freight between Havana and New Orleans, seemed to harbor the most potential. Anxious to get a commerce raider to sea, Mallory placed the ship under the direct command of Raphael Semmes, who immediately set about converting the vessel into a diminutive warship.[13] He had her frames strengthened, the spar deck passenger cabin removed, a berth deck and magazines installed, and bunkers expanded to carry an eight-day supply of coal. Armed with an 8-inch pivot gun mounted between the main and mizzen and four 32-pounders in broadside, she became the CSS *Sumter*, a small but deadly forerunner of the Confederate strategy to destroy the carrying trade of the United States.[14]

The *Marquis de la Habana*, an 830-ton seagoing steamer of Mexican origin that earlier had been seized by the United States as a pirate, was modified and renamed the CSS *McRae*. Although she saw limited duty on the lower Mississippi, defective machinery prevented her from following the *Sumter* to sea.

Rousseau's hard work and diligence at New Orleans brought many ships into service, and for a while Mallory hoped the fleet of powerful ironclads could be built there and sent to sea to smash the growing Union blockade. Aspirations for a naval center at New Orleans ended abruptly the following year, however, when the city surrendered to the Union Navy under Admiral David G. Farragut.

Although the loss of New Orleans was a severe setback, Mallory still had plans to build a fleet of high-seas commerce raiders that would prowl the world's sea lanes destroying Yankee commerce, and presumably lure Welles into sending warships in pursuit, thus weakening the blockade. An adjunct to this strategy was a far more ambitious plan to build impregnable ironclad corvettes that could hold hostage the North's principal port cities.

Encouraged by early Southern military victories, France and Britain realized they had much to gain in a postwar world where their major economic competitor was broken in two. The world's best shipyards flourished in Great Britain, which had strong commercial ties with the South and its cotton industry, and in France, which aspired to control Mexico and had received diplomatic approval to do so from the Confederate government. To implement his plan, Mallory sent special agents abroad to buy or build ships. Of these, by far the most effective was James Dunwoody Bulloch.

Born and raised near Savannah, Georgia, Bulloch became a midshipman on the frigate *United States* in 1839 at the age of 16, and graduated second in his class from the Philadelphia naval school in 1844. In 1853, after 14 years at sea, he resigned from government service to join a private New York company operating a line of mail steamers. For the next eight years he sailed the circuit between New York, Havana, and New Orleans.

Unlike many other naval officers, Bulloch had business training and knew the commercial trade. He was expert in naval affairs, had served on every class of war vessel from a 10-gun schooner to an 80-gun ship of the line, and had a clear understanding of international law. While in the mail service he had supervised the construction of two of the ships he later commanded,[15] which gave him the ability to readily distinguish a good ship from a bad one—a quality not lost on Mallory.

On April 13, 1861, Bulloch was in New Orleans, commanding the United States mail steamer *Bienville*. By some unwritten detente, the postal service between North and South had not been disrupted, except for various nuisance activities from customs officials. When Bulloch learned of the action at Fort Sumter he offered his services to the Confederate government, but insisted that he was honor-bound to the *Bienville*'s owners to return the ship to New York. Local officials pressed Bulloch to sell the vessel. When he refused, they threatened to seize it. Governor Brown requested instructions from President Davis and was told, "Do not detain the *Bienville*; we do not wish to interfere in any way with private property."

While some Confederates complained that Bulloch had unreasonably denied the South possession of a fine steamer, Mallory understood the quality of the man and agreed with his decision. When Bulloch reached New York he found a message waiting for him from Confederate Attorney General Judah P. Benjamin, asking that he "come to Montgomery without delay."[16]

After returning the *Bienville* to New York, Bulloch settled his personal matters and headed south, arriving in Montgomery at midnight on May 7. Early the following morning, Mallory asked him if he would go to Europe. Bulloch replied, "I have no impediments, and can start as soon as you explain what I am to do."[17] These were reckless words for a man with a new wife, a comfortable home, and a bright future in New York City.

Bulloch often visited his half-sister Martha, who lived nearby, to bounce her new baby on his knee. Little Theodore was just old enough to remember his "Uncle Jimmie" when Bulloch packed his bags and sought his fortunes with the Confederacy. After the war, Bulloch remained in Great Britain as a successful businessman, and Theodore grew to become the 26th president of the United States.

Bulloch preferred to command a ship, and accepted the post of Confederate naval procurement agent in England on the condition that he would receive command of one of the first cruisers built. Mallory later reneged on this promise, insisting that no other person could be entrusted with the work Bulloch was performing in Europe.[18]

Of the eight Confederate cruisers, all but two, the *Sumter* and the *Nashville*, came from British shipyards. And of these, the ones that most damaged the American carrying trade were put to sea by Bulloch, including the dreaded *Alabama*, commanded by Captain Raphael Semmes; the CSS *Florida*, commanded first by John Newland Maffitt and later by Charles Manigault Morris; and the CSS *Shenandoah*, commanded by James Iredell Waddell.

Matthew Fontaine Maury added the CSS *Georgia*, also purchased in England, but this vessel could not compare with the ships put to sea by Bulloch. Another four cruisers were armed in the Confederacy and sailed from Southern ports: the first was the CSS *Sumter*, followed by the *Nashville*, the *Tallahassee*, and the *Chickamauga*.

Disregarding the few effective gunboats and ironclads refitted or built along the rivers and estuaries of the South, Mallory's navy *was* the Confederate commerce raiders.

The *Sumter* Goes to Sea

A FTER HIS unsuccessful attempt to purchase a fast steamer in the North, Commander Raphael Semmes returned to Montgomery on April 4, 1861, serving for eight days as chief of the Confederate Lighthouse Bureau until Fort Sumter fell and the war was on. Impatient for sea duty and convinced of the merits of commerce raiding, Semmes urged Mallory to give him command of a suitable vessel.[1]

Mallory showed Semmes a report from Commodore Rousseau, whose Board of Naval Officers had searched New Orleans in vain for ships for the Confederate Navy. Every vessel on the list had been rejected, but Semmes spotted "a small propeller steamer, of five-hundred tons burden, sea-going, with a low-pressure engine, sound, and capable of being so strengthened . . . to carry a battery of four or five guns." He believed he could convert her into an effective commerce raider.[2]

At Semmes' insistence, and against the advice of his naval board, Mallory purchased the steam packet *Havana*, which had arrived at New Orleans shortly before the "announced" Union blockade closed the Mississippi. Semmes sailed for New Orleans to take command of the first real warship to fly the flag of the Confederate States, the CSS *Sumter*.[3]

Although she was "only a dismantled packet-ship full of upper cabins and other top-hamper, furniture, and crockery, but as unlike a ship of war as possible," Semmes saw her possibilities: "Her lines were easy and graceful, and she had a sort of saucy air about her which seemed to say that she was not averse to the service on which she was about to be employed."

Semmes immediately set about rebuilding the *Sumter*, but no warship had ever been fitted out in New Orleans, and suitable workshops, proper materials, and skilled workmen were difficult to find. James Martin of Atlantic Dry Dock, across the river at Algiers, received the contract to convert the *Havana* although he admitted having no experience with warships, and gangs of mechanics set to work immediately. Semmes wrote: "Everything had to be improvised, from the manufacture of a water-tank, to the kids and cans of the berth-deck messes, and from a gun-carriage to a friction-primer. I had not only to devise all the alterations but to make plans, and drawings of them, before they could be comprehended."[4]

Semmes ordered hammocks and bedding, guns, and ammunition; workmen strengthened the main deck to support the battery—four 32 pounders in broadside and an 8-inch pivot gun—and built a berth-deck for the crew, quarters for the officers, and a captain's cabin. The engine, partially above the waterline, was enclosed with wooden beams latticed together with iron bars. The rig was changed to a barkentine to improve efficiency, and new suits of sails were ordered.

As work proceeded, the first of a series of logistical delays surfaced: The cruiser's guns, which had been scavenged from the Gosport Navy Yard and shipped to New Orleans, fell victim to the South's overcrowded railways, and were thrown off the train somewhere along the way to make room for other freight. Semmes sent one of his officers, Lt. Robert T. Chapman, in search of them.

More delays followed. On May 27 the *Sumter* still needed water tanks, a gun carriage for the 8-inch pivot gun, and copper tanks for the powder magazine.

If Semmes had trouble finding supplies, he had none finding crew: he could choose the best from among the horde of experienced seamen marooned in New Orleans by the Union blockade, and some of the South's finest young naval officers began arriving from various points in the Confederacy.

As his executive officer, Semmes selected Lt. John McIntosh Kell, an aristocratic Georgian whom he had first met in 1849. Then a passed midshipman, Kell was being court martialed for resisting petty harassment. Ordered to turn down a senior officer's bed and light his lantern, Kells refused, arguing that if officers could not perform these little tasks themselves, a cabin boy should do them—not a midshipman.

Semmes, a member of the court who had himself practiced law and believed Kell's position to be correct, resigned from the court and acted in Kell's defense. Semmes later reflected: "The relation of counsel and client . . . brought us closer together, and I discovered that young Kell had in him the making of a man. So far from being a mutineer, he had a high respect for discipline, and had only resisted obedience to the order in question from a refined sense of gentlemanly propriety."[5] Although Kell lost his case, the navy reconsidered, and he was later reinstated.

Next in command was Lt. Chapman, who had left his young wife behind for duty on the *Sumter*. On the trip from Mobile to New Orleans, Semmes had taken an instant liking to the young naval officer for his openness, good humor, and ready wit. Later, Semmes frequently sent Chapman on delicate missions where tact, diplomacy, and intelligence were essential.[6]

As third lieutenant, Semmes chose John M. Stribling, a slender, sinewy South Carolinian under whose amiable appearance dwelt a firm, well-trained officer. The position of fourth lieutenant went to 24-year-old William E. Evans, a recent graduate of the Naval Academy who enjoyed a spirited argument and had a penchant for starting them.[7]

Commanding the marine detachment was President Davis's brother-in-law, Lieutenant of Marines Becket K. Howell. Like many of the *Sumter*'s officers, Howell later served on other Confederate cruisers.

Semmes wrote Secretary Mallory that: "I have an excellent set of men on board, though they are nearly all green, and will require some little practice and drilling at the guns to enable them to handle them creditably. Should I be fortunate enough to reach the high seas, you may rely upon my implicit obedience of your instructions, 'to do the enemy's commerce the greatest injury in the shortest time.' "[8]

The *Sumter*'s crew, which consisted of 22 officers, 72 seamen, and 20 marines,[9] found their appetite for action whetted when the privateer sidewheeler *Calhoun*, commanded by Captain John Wilson, brought the first prize into New Orleans on May 17, 1862. For a few weeks the Crescent City was a hub for Confederate privateering. It ended with the arrival of Union warships, which bottled-up the passes into the Gulf of Mexico. When Semmes finally was ready for sea, he found his way blocked by the 21-gun *Brooklyn* and three of the fastest and heaviest steamships in the Union Navy—the 16-gun, 3,765-ton *Powhatan*, the 32-gun, 4,582-ton *Niagara*, and the 52-gun, 3,307-ton *Minnesota*.

The 437-ton *Sumter* was no match for this fleet, but Semmes had no intention of challenging them. His mission was to destroy commerce, and he meant to slip to sea. During trials, however, Semmes found that his new cruiser could do no better than 9 knots—well below the 10.9 knots credited to the *Niagara*. The expanded coal bunkers still could carry no more than eight day's fuel. To conserve coal, Semmes intended to rely upon the sails, but the propeller's drag cost him two knots in a good sailing wind. For the moment, however, these problems were secondary to finding a way through the Union squadron.

Semmes ordered the colors hoisted for the first time on June 3, and spent two more weeks training the crew and working the guns. Local dignitaries invited aboard to observe left filled with enthusiasm and praise. Semmes recorded that his "guests were kind enough to wish me a career full of 'blazing honors.' "[10]

On June 18, under a full moon, the *Sumter* steamed into the swift current of the Mississippi and dropped downriver to a point between Fort Jackson and Fort St. Philip. Standing off the Southwest Pass was the 16-gun sidewheel sloop-of-war *Powhatan*, one of the fastest ships in the Union Navy, commanded by Lt. David Dixon Porter. Off the Pass a L'Outre was Captain Charles H. Poor and the *Brooklyn*, which Semmes erroneously believed to be the faster of the two vessels (although he was correct in assuming that both vessels were faster than the *Sumter*).

At nightfall on June 21, while anchored between the two forts, he received word that the *Powhatan* had left her station in pursuit of two ships.[11] Semmes ordered steam, hoisted the anchor, swung into the current, and hurried down to the Head of the Passes, where the river branches into its three main outlets.

Arriving at 10:30 p.m., Semmes sent a boat to the lighthouse to obtain a pilot, but the keeper ignored the request. Semmes passed the night with mounting agitation, unaware that many of the pilots had northern roots and would not help the Confederacy. As morning dawned, the lookout reported that the *Powhatan* had returned to her station. Although Semmes fumed over his lost opportunity, a race against the speedy sidewheeler may well have ended the *Sumter*'s career before it began.

Frustrated at his inability to secure a pilot, Semmes finally sent Lt. Stribling to the Pilot's Association with a written order stating that, ". . . you [are] to repair on board this ship, with three or four of the most experienced pilots of the bar. . . . If any man disobeys this summons I will not only have his branch taken from him, but I will send an armed force and arrest him on board."[12]

Stribling returned with several unenthusiastic pilots. After listening to a barrage of feeble excuses from their captain, Semmes demanded that one pilot remain on board at all times until the *Sumter* got to sea. He then picked a pilot and dismissed the others.

By now the Union ships had sighted the *Sumter* at the Head of the Passes and doubled their watches. The *Brooklyn* sent a boat ashore to destroy a telegraph station that had been transmitting intelligence on the movements of the blockaders. Semmes retaliated by removing the lighting apparatuses from several lighthouses.[13]

As time passed, Semmes wondered why no attempt had been made to destroy his ship. After nine days he wrote, "The enemy watched me closely, day by day, and bent all his energies toward preventing my escape, but did not seem to think of the simple expedient of endeavoring to capture me with a superior force." Each night he sent a patrol boat down the Southwest Pass to watch for the expected attack and kept his boilers hot, but nothing came of it.[14]

On the morning of June 29 the lookout reported that "the *Brooklyn* was nowhere to be seen." Semmes ordered steam, and in a few minutes the raider sped with the muddy current down the Pass a L'Outre. After four miles the lookout located the *Brooklyn* riding at anchor in her customary berth near the bar. During the night the *Sumter* had dragged anchor, shifting just enough to obscure the enemy behind a clump of trees. Once more, fires were banked and the crew spread awnings to protect themselves from the blistering sun.[15]

The following morning, after stowing fresh provisions and 100 barrels of coal delivered by the riverboat *Empire Parish*, Semmes steamed down the Pass a L'Outre on a routine exercise and stopped at the pilot's station by the lighthouse. A single fisherman in a small boat rowed over to the *Sumter*'s side and hailed the officer of the deck, reporting that the *Brooklyn* had left her post to chase a sail and had passed out of sight. Semmes issued sharp orders, observing that: "the crew, who had been cleaning themselves for Sunday muster, at once stowed their bags, the swinging-booms were gotten alongside, the boats run up and, in ten minutes, the steam was again hissing. . . . The men ran around the capstan in double quick in their eagerness to get up the anchor, and in a few minutes more the ship's head swung off gracefully in the current; the propeller being started, she bounded off like a thing of life on this new race, which was to decide whether we should continue to stagnate in mid-summer in the marshes of the Mississippi or reach those glad waters of the dark blue sea."

When the ship was barely underway, however, the pilot lost his courage and claimed that he knew nothing about the bar of the Pass a L'Outre. In a rage, Semmes demanded that he "take us out, and if he ran us ashore or put us in the hands of the enemy he would swing him to the yardarm as a traitor." While Semmes raged, Kell signalled for another pilot.[16]

Semmes, worried that the *Brooklyn* had hidden in a cove to lure his ship out of the Pass, decided to take his chances with the bar rather than lose another opportunity. By now, the enemy probably had spotted his smoke and was making hurried preparations to intercept. Although Kell said the *Brooklyn* was probably faster by three knots and would surely overtake them, Semmes believed the report of her speed exaggerated. He estimated that both vessels had to travel about the same distance to reach the bar, but he would have help from the four-knot current of the Mississippi.

As Semmes was about to steer into the current and risk the bar, the lookout reported a whaleboat pulled by four strong blacks approaching from the lighthouse. In the stern sat a young pilot, adding the sway of his body to the momentum of the boat with each pull. Semmes noticed that on "the balcony of the pilot's house . . . stood a beautiful woman, the pilot's young wife, waving him on to his duty with her handkerchief . . . and I uncovered my head to my fair country-woman." A few moments later, "the gallant young fellow stood on the horse-block beside me."

The *Sumter* gathered steam, swept by the lighthouse wharf where a cheering crowd had gathered, and safely crossed the bar, slowing only long enough to bring the pilot's boat alongside. As the young man descended, he shook Semmes' hand and said, "Now, Captain, you are all clear; give her H_LL, and let her go!" The first Confederate cruiser was at sea.[17]

As the pilot pulled toward shore, the *Brooklyn* was four miles off and closing fast. Kell reported that, with the help of the current, the *Sumter* was making about 9½ knots. The engineer found the boilers foaming, which he attributed to getting up steam so suddenly, and predicted another half knot once the foaming stopped. In the meantime, the *Brooklyn* continued to gain, with her guns closing on firing range.

Both ships loosed their sails and braced up sharply on the starboard tack. Semmes ordered more steam, and jettisoned a small howitzer and 1,500 gallons of water to lighten ship. Noting that the *Brooklyn* lay slightly to weather, Semmes "resolved at once to hold my wind so closely as to compel her to furl her sails, though this would carry me a little athwart her bows and bring me perhaps a little closer to her."[18]

A rain squall interrupted the chase, shrouding both ships from view. As the storm passed the *Brooklyn* emerged, much closer than before. Semmes told Kell, "I could not but admire the majesty of her appearance, with her broad flowing bows and clean, beautiful run, and her masts and yards as taut and square as those of an old time sailing frigate. The stars and stripes of a large ensign flew out from time to time from under the lee of her spanker, and we could see an apparently anxious crowd of officers on her quarter-deck, many of them with telescopes directed toward us." Fearing capture, Paymaster Henry Myers prepared to throw the public chest and ship's papers overboard. Semmes expected to receive a shot at any moment, but the *Brooklyn* did not fire.

Engineer Freeman raced topside with some good news: the foaming had stopped, adding a few more revolutions to the propeller. And there was more good news: The rain squall was followed by a stiff breeze that slightly favored the *Sumter*. Semmes discovered that he was "eating" his pursuer out of the wind. "I knew," he wrote, "that as soon as she fell into my wake she would be compelled to furl her sails." Thirty minutes later the *Brooklyn* hauled up, abandoned the chase, and returned to her post outside the bar at Pass a L'Outre.[19] The *Sumter* had escaped.

Captain Charles H. Poor, who should have continued to pursue the *Sumter* until she was lost from sight in case she suffered a breakdown, became the "goat" in the incident. Perhaps Poor did not attach proper significance to the cruiser's escape.[20]

The *Sumter*'s first evening on the Gulf was graced by the sudden appearance of the Great Comet of 1861, which soared across the Northern Hemisphere with terrifying brilliance. The crew, already exhilarated by their narrow escape, considered it an omen of continued good luck, and celebrated with a round of grog as the raider set course for Cuba.

With scant coal capacity and heavy union warships stationed along Cuba's northern coast, Semmes could not keep the cruiser off the coast for long. He decided to make a dash at the enemy's merchant ships on the south side of Cuba, take on coal at some nearby port, sail to Barbados, coal again, and then strike for the coast of Brazil. This constant worry over fuel would continue to plague the *Sumter*'s career.

On the morning of July 3 the cruiser reached Cape Corrientes and ran between the Cuban coast and the Isle of Pines, a favorite shelter for early pirates. At 3 p.m. the lookout cried "Sail Ho!" for the first time since crossing the Gulf. Moments later a second vessel appeared, straight ahead. Semmes raised the British colors and stopped and boarded the nearest ship, which proved to be a neutral from Cadiz, Spain.

He released the Spaniard and chased the other sail, which showed no colors, but her American craftsmanship was unmistakable. One blank cartridge from the *Sumter*'s gun brought the Stars and Stripes to her peak. Semmes unfurled the Stars and Bars of the Confederate banner, and sent a prize crew aboard the 607-ton *Golden Rocket*, of Brewer, Maine. Her master, Captain William Bailey, a mild, amiable gentleman, could not conceal his astonishment: "A clap of thunder in a cloudless sky could not have surprised me more than the appearance of the Confederate flag in these waters," he said to Semmes. Semmes replied, "My duty is a painful one to destroy so noble a ship as yours . . . as for yourself, you will only have to do, as so many thousands have done before you, submit to the fortunes of war—yourself and your crew will be well treated on board my ship."[21]

After the prize crew removed what supplies they could use, the incendiaries went to work splintering furniture and cupboards for kindling. Both crews stared silently into the darkness at the outline of the doomed vessel. Then, at 10 p.m. someone exclaimed, "There is the flame! She is on fire!" Leaping quickly up the masts and rigging, a light breeze fanned it into "many threads of flame, twisting and writhing like so many serpents that had received their death wounds." As Captain Bailey looked on, feeling the emotions of every sailor witnessing the last agonies of his vessel, the *Golden Rocket*'s pyre lit up the sea for miles.[22]

Burning the *Golden Rocket* stirred deep emotions in Semmes and Kell as well. These two old navy men had devoted their lives to protecting the American flag. Now they had fired on it and destroyed a pretty ship captained by a kindly gentlemen who struggled to hide his tears. Years later, Kell still remembered the scene, and wrote: "It was a sad sight to a sailor's eyes, the burning of a fine ship. We had not then grown accustomed to the sight with hardened hearts."

The prisoners roamed the deck freely and had their own mess, while Captain Bailey enjoyed the companionship of the wardroom. When he was released, the officers made up a small purse so that Bailey could provide for his immediate needs.

Later, Semmes learned that Bailey, hoping to collect on an insurance policy that protected the ship against piracy, had vociferously denounced the *Sumter*'s men as pirates. Denied indemnification by the insurance company, Bailey took his case to court. After a long litigation, three separate courts upheld the insurance company, stating that the *Golden Rocket*'s destruction was not piracy within the meaning of the insurance policy.[23]

Early next morning, while cruising within sight of Cuba's southern coast, the lookouts sighted two more sails. A blank cartridge fired from a 32-pounder brought both ships into the wind and American colors to their peaks. Semmes sent separate boarding parties to retrieve the masters and their papers. Both vessels had just sailed for British ports from Trinidad-de-Cuba with cargoes of sugar and molasses. Their neutral cargoes saved the 200-ton brig *Cuba* and the 245-ton brig *Machias* from destruction. Putting prize crews aboard, Semmes took both ships in tow and steamed toward the Cuban port of Cienfuegos.

At the time the *Sumter* sailed from New Orleans, England and France had issued Proclamations of Neutrality that prohibited belliger-

ents from bringing prizes into their ports. Spain had not declared herself, however, and Semmes hoped that his two prizes would be
adjudicated and awarded. Under international law, the cargoes were the
legal property of their neutral owners, but the ships were fair prizes for
their captors. Semmes could not forget that the incentive for a crew
serving aboard a Confederate cruiser was acquiring prize money.

During the trip to Cienfuegos, the cruiser's speed was so reduced
that Semmes cut the tow ropes and instructed the prize crews to follow
him into port.[24] The next morning the *Cuba* had vanished. During the
night, her men overwhelmed the prize crew under Midshipman
Hudgins and forced their surrender. Months passed before Semmes
learned their fate.

On the evening of July 5, as the *Sumter* arrived off the Cienfuegos
lighthouse, lookouts reported two sails to the southeast. Semmes altered course and intercepted two more sugar traders, the 284-ton *Ben
Dunning* and the 192-ton *Albert Adams*. Prize crews boarded both vessels with orders to stand off the Cienfuegos light until daybreak. With
their cargoes covered by neutral Spanish manifests, Semmes could not
burn the two brigantines, but he noted that, "I could perceive that my
crew were becoming enamored of their business, pretty much as a veteran fox-hunter does in view of the chase."[25]

As the eastern sky brightened on July 6 and Semmes prepared to
move his three prizes into Cienfuegos, he noticed a column of smoke
coming down the river. A young officer climbed up the rigging and reported that "there is a small steam tug coming down, with three vessels
in tow, two barks and a brig . . . they all have American colors set."

Knowing he could not molest them within Spanish jurisdiction,
Semmes ordered a jack hoisted to signal for a pilot. Men went aloft and
arranged the yards to give the ship the appearance of a merchant vessel.
Acting independently, prize masters on the captured vessels raised
their jacks for a pilot, making the deception complete. The three American vessels continued on, unsuspecting, and lazily shaped a course
seaward in the light breeze.

A pilot jumped aboard the *Sumter* and asked her captain if he
wished to go up to town. He was astonished when Semmes replied that
he intended to capture the vessels the tug had just towed to sea as soon
as they cleared territorial waters. When the pilot confirmed that the
vessels were about five miles from shore, Semmes ordered steam and
the *Sumter* raced after the unsuspecting traders. Down came the Spanish colors and up went the Confederate banner, followed by a blank
charge from the pivot gun. All three ships came into the wind and surrendered to boarding parties. As Semmes predicted, they carried neu-

tral cargoes of sugar. Prize crews took charge of the 429-ton bark *West Wind* of Westerly, Rhode Island, the 463-ton bark *Louisa Kilham* of Boston, and the 300-ton brigantine *Naiad* of New York, and joined the small flotilla poised outside the entrance to Cienfuegos.[26]

When the *Sumter* and her six trophies attempted to enter the harbor, she was stopped by musket fire from a small fort guarding the entrance. Sentinels motioned the prizes, still flying the American flag, to proceed upriver to town. The *Sumter* anchored, and Lt. Evans rowed to the fort to ask for an explanation. A Spanish officer who met Evans confessed that he had never seen a Confederate flag and feared that a pirate had entered the harbor to hold the town under tribute. Later that afternoon, Semmes received a visit from the commandant, who offered his apologies and on behalf of the governor of Cienfuegos granted permission for the ship to proceed to the city.[27]

A week had passed since the *Sumter* ran the blockade, and she had only a one-day supply of fuel remaining. Anxious to get back to sea, Semmes sent Lt. Chapman in search of coal, then he opened discussions with the governor regarding the disposition of the prizes.

Since the Spanish government had not yet clarified its position on the adjudication of prizes, Semmes hoped that Spanish ports could be used by Confederate cruisers throughout the war. In a carefully worded statement, Semmes explained that excluding the prizes of both belligerents from neutral ports, in the context of the present war, would be a great injustice to the Confederate States. Union ships had easy access to their own ports, but the U.S. had blockaded all Southern ports. This prevented Confederate commerce raiders from bringing prizes to home ports for adjudication and forced them to rely on friendly nations, such as Spain. Semmes reasoned that although the cargoes were neutral and belonged to Spanish subjects, the ships themselves were fair prizes belonging to the Confederate States. He asked that a local and independent agent retain the prizes while courts studied his request.[28]

The governor of Cienfuegos, unable to respond on such heady international affairs, passed the letter through channels to Madrid. In 1861, communications from home governments took weeks to reach colonial officials. At the time of the *Sumter's* arrival at Cienfuegos, neither Semmes nor the governor knew that on June 17 Queen Isabella had issued a proclamation based upon the same neutral policies as those of Great Britain and France. These were specific concerning the limited rights of privateers, but less so on the rights and privileges extended to the commissioned cruisers of belligerents. Since the *Sumter* was legally a warship, all European proclamations of neutrality could be broadly interpreted. Semmes, who took advantage of every loophole, proved to be a worthy adversary for colonial officials uncertain of their government's neutral policies. However, he could not manipulate the governor of Cienfuegos.[29]

Semmes later learned that Spain had adroitly sidestepped the whole diplomatic issue by returning the vessels to the owners on the grounds that they had been captured inside Spanish territorial waters. Semmes knew this was untrue and hoped privately that when the Confederacy won her independence, Cuba would be annexed and the island divided into two new Confederate states.[30]

Unable to wait for a decision, Semmes left prize agent Senor Don Mariano Diaz of Cienfuegos in charge of the disposition of the seven ships, including the missing *Cuba*. He left instructions for her master, Midshipman Hudgins, purchased 100 tons of coal, and bought fresh provisions. At 11 p.m. on July 7, 1861 the *Sumter* headed back to sea.[31]

Semmes, expecting United States Consul Richard W. Shufeldt to make a strong effort to recover them, retained all the prisoners from the eight prizes. Even if the consul succeeded, without crews the vessels would lay idle for months.

The *Sumter* enjoyed a good start, capturing eight enemy vessels in the first five days of her cruise. Never again would the euphoric crew enjoy such good hunting in so short a time. Union warships, already under steam and circling the island, would find the raider gone. The search had only begun, however, as had the legal arguments and complications with foreign governments. Semmes soon learned that no government wanted his prizes, and his only alternative was the torch. During the months ahead he learned to survive in a world of nations that had not yet decided how to cope with his peculiar form of warfare.

A Scarcity of Game

For six days the *Sumter* bucked heavy winds, slowing progress and foiling Semmes' plan to take on coal in Barbados. Down to two days' fuel, he turned south to bring the wind on his beam, loosed his topsails, and headed for the Dutch island of Curacao. With fires banked and propeller uncoupled to minimize drag, Semmes noted in his journal: "Heavy sea all night, ship rolling and tumbling about, though doing pretty well. The propeller revolves freely, and we are making about five knots." On the following day, July 14, the watch reported a sail on the horizon, but the sea was too rough to attempt a chase.[1]

Like Lord Nelson, Semmes suffered from chronic seasickness, and the turbulent weather forced him to his hammock. At one point, while attempting to go on deck to order a course change after the ship was swept by particularly heavy seas, he lost consciousness and fell down a companionway. Semmes considered seasickness an embarrassing weakness for a sailor, but he was determined to live on at sea without compromising his devotion to duty.[2]

Over the next two days, as the ship approached the Spanish Main, the weather moderated, but one difficulty replaced another. A strong westerly equatorial current forced the *Sumter* to furl her sails and continue under steam. On the afternoon of July 16, she rounded the northwest tip of Curacao and arrived off the pretty town of Santa Ana, which lay just off the Venezuelan coast and enjoyed a prosperous free trade in American and European goods with the mainland. At nightfall a pilot climbed aboard, but refused to enter the harbor until morning.

When United States Consul Moses Jesurun discovered an enemy cruiser standing outside the harbor, he called at the Government House and accosted Governor J. D. Crol, demanding that the "pirate" should not be permitted to enter the harbor. He warned that Secretary of State Seward would be furious, and that the Government might expect "to have the stone and mortar of his two forts knocked about his ears . . . by the ship of war of the Great Republic."

The threat had the desired affect upon His Excellency, who dispatched a pilot to the ship with a message that "the Governor could not permit the *Sumter* to enter, having received recent orders from Holland to that effect."

With only one day's coal remaining, Semmes sent Lt. Chapman to shore with a letter explaining in detail the rights of belligerents according to international law, and asked if Holland had adopted a different rule.[3]

After waiting two hours for an answer, Semmes instructed Kell to give the gun crew a little target practice. "Accordingly, the drum beat to quarters, a great stir was made about the deck as the guns were cast loose, and pretty soon, Whiz! went a shell, across the windows of the council-chamber, which overlooked the sea; the shell bursting like a clap of rather sharp, ragged thunder. . . . By the time we had fired three or four shells, all of which burst with beautiful precision, Chapman's boat was seen returning, and thinking we had exercise enough, we ran out and secured the guns."[4]

With a broad smile, Chapman presented Governor Crol's permission to enter port, and the *Sumter* steamed slowly to her berth through a fleet of bumboats, whose gingham-garbed owners climbed on board to exchange oranges and bananas for what coins and trade goods the crew could muster.

Although the cruiser had been at sea less than a month, her engine and boilers needed repairs, and the foretopmast had sprung during rough weather. Kell made the necessary arrangements with port authorities, and repairs got underway, giving the crew a welcome bit of shore liberty. Semmes issued paroles to the sailors captured off the coast of Cuba and released them. By July 24 the ship had been refitted, repainted, caulked, and overhauled, and its bunkers filled with 115 tons of good English coal. When the ship returned to sea a week later, new additions to the crew included a platoon of monkeys and parrots.

On shore, Consul Jesurun learned from Confederates on liberty that the cruiser was headed for Mona Passage, a commercial crossroad that ran between Santo Domingo and Puerto Rico. Speculating that the ship would soon return to Curacao for coal and supplies because freedom of entry there had been established, he notified his superiors.

Jesurun was among the first of many U.S. consuls to plague Semmes, but he was also among the first to suffer Semmes' talent for misdirection. Only Kell enjoyed the captain's confidence; everyone else was either uninformed or misinformed—which sent many Union warships off his track. During his many visits from officials and sympathizers, Semmes rarely missed an opportunity to mislead his visitors about his intentions. Expecting to be watched as he left Santa Ana, he headed north until out of sight, then changed course, steaming eastward along the Venezuelan coast.

At dawn the lookout sighted a sail not far from the port of Laguaya. After a brief chase the 180-ton New York schooner *Abby Bradford* hove to and surrendered to the boarding officer. Kell estimated the value of the prize and her cargo of flour and provisions at $25,000. Although no effort had been made to cover the contents with neutral certificates, Semmes suspected that a Venezuelan merchant owned the cargo.

Semmes didn't want to burn the prize; he needed money, and still hoped that some foreign government would hold his captures until the courts could settle the matter of ownership.[5] Since the *Bradford* was headed there already, he decided to tow the vessel to Puerto Cabello and try for admission. The *Sumter* and her prize entered the small town, whose chief commodity was inactivity, on the morning of July 26.

Semmes sent a letter to the governor asking permission to place the *Abby Bradford* in the hands of the Venezuelan government until the matter could be settled by Confederate courts. Because the cargo was perishable, he asked for approval to sell the goods locally and deposit the proceeds with a prize agent. A bureaucratic scramble ensued, followed by a reply that the issue must be referred to higher authorities.

Puerto Cabello depended on trade with the Northern states, and United States Consul E. A. Turpin, who had his fingers in many local enterprises, convinced the governor that the proper course of action was to conform with European neutral practices and order the *Sumter* to depart within 24 hours, relinquishing any claim to the prize.

Realizing that the North held imposing commercial leverage over most South American nations, Semmes decided to take the *Bradford* back to sea. After buying fresh provisions, he ordered his quartermaster to sail the prize to New Orleans and report to Commodore Rousseau for further orders, cautioning him to keep to the west of the passes and away from Union blockaders.[6] He also sent a report to Secretary Mallory, who was completely in the dark regarding the *Sumter*'s activities.

But the *Abby Bradford* never reached New Orleans. She was captured just off the coast of Louisiana by the USS *Powhatan*, under the command of Lt. David Dixon Porter, an old shipmate of Semmes'. After interrogating the prize crew and studying the captured dispatches, Porter felt he had enough intelligence to closely estimate the *Sumter*'s location, and took his fast sidewheeler in hot pursuit, reporting somewhat optimistically to Secretary Welles that Semmes "is in a position now where he can't escape, if properly looked after. He is out of coal and out of credit."[7]

After separating from the *Bradford*, the *Sumter* headed back to sea and overhauled the 295-ton bark *Joseph Maxwell*, of Philadelphia. Captain Davis, his wife, and a crew of nine had recently discharged most of their cargo at La Guayra and intended to unload the remainder at Puerto Cabello. Leaving the bark beyond the marine league—the three-mile limit—Semmes put Davis aboard the *Sumter* and steamed back into the harbor, hoping to sell the captured prize and its contents back to its owners. If that failed, he planned to unload the neutral merchandise, turn it over to the local owner, and retain the *Joseph Maxwell*.

Paymaster Myers accompanied Captain Davis to shore to strike a deal. By then, the local consul had become involved, and Semmes received a written command to bring the *Maxwell* in until the Venezuelan courts could determine whether she had been captured within the territorial waters. Semmes noted that "this insolence was refreshing. I scarcely knew whether to laugh or to be angry at it."[8]

Since the governor refused to negotiate, Semmes released Davis and his wife at Puerto Cabello, but retained their crew, and steamed out of the harbor, determined to hold the prize. Placing Midshipman Hicks aboard as prizemaster, Semmes directed him to take the *Joseph Maxwell* to Cienfuegos, on the south side of Cuba.

Semmes had not yet seen Spain's proclamation of neutrality, however, and was unaware that the *Maxwell* could be seized after entering a Cuban port. Upon reaching Cienfuegos, Hicks was ordered to leave. A short distance out of port he mistook a Spanish vessel for a Union warship and, in an attempt to avoid capture, ran the prize aground. Hicks and his crew abandoned the bark and rowed back to Cienfuegos in an open boat.[9]

For the next few days the *Sumter* sailed easterly through waters seldom travelled by merchantmen. On July 30 she reached Trinidad and entered Port of Spain. Paymaster Myers hurried to shore in search of coal while Semmes arranged for the discharge of prisoners. Although British hospitality at Port of Spain was cordial, the colony's attorney general spent hours deliberating whether coal was contraband. After concluding that steam was essential to the movement of the ship and without it she could be blockaded by the enemy, the Provincial Council ruled that coal could be purchased. Unfortunately for the *Sumter*, the coal was inferior and expensive, and four days were lost loading it by hand. Six more days were lost when Kell discovered advanced corrosion in the boilers. The *Sumter* finally steamed out of the harbor on August 5 and headed eastward.

For several weeks Union Naval Secretary Welles had been pressured by influential shipowners such as Cornelius Vanderbilt to take action against the *Sumter* and the small number of privateers that had been pestering Northern shipping. Although Welles believed it unwise to divert ships from the blockade, by July 13 he had sent the seven-gun screw-steamer *Iroquois*, commanded by James S. Palmer, in search of the privateer *Jefferson Davis*, with instructions to keep an eye open for the *Sumter*. Under mounting pressure, Welles further depleted the blockading squadron six days later by ordering Commander Gustavus H. Scott to take the 13-gun steamship *Keystone State* and destroy the *Sumter*.

This order came on the heels of an appeal from Milton S. Latham, banker and senator from California, who reminded Welles that the *Northern Light*, which carried more than $2,000,000 in gold, would be passing through the same area where the raider had been reported. Welles sent out an escort to find the *Northern Light*, and Scott continued to track Semmes, finally striking his trail in the West Indies. He steamed into Trinidad—about two weeks late.[10]

By now the wooden sidewheeler *Powhatan* had joined the chase under a confident and aggressive David Dixon Porter. Porter acutely understood the damage a commerce raider could cause, and how difficult it was to capture such a ship once at sea. His famous father, Commodore David Porter, was himself a noted commerce raider who had destroyed the British whaling fleet in the Pacific Ocean in 1813 while captain of the frigate *Essex*.

Porter stopped at Cienfuegos, learned of the fate of the *Joseph Maxwell*, and hurried to Curacao. There he began receiving the false information that Semmes planted at every port he visited. By sifting through and analyzing this screen of confusion, Porter was able to divine a reasonably accurate image of the Confederate commander's intentions—their two vessels actually passed within 40 miles of one another one dark night. But for every 100 tons of coal the *Sumter* burned, the *Powhatan* burned 700, and her old boilers began to weaken under the strain, forcing Porter to give up the chase—fortunate for Semmes but not for the Confederacy: Porter would later go on to win at Vicksburg the laurels he sought in the Caribbean.

On August 6 the *Sumter* entered the Atlantic Ocean and cruised along the northern coast of South America toward Brazil, making slow progress against the two-knot current and stiff southeasterlies. The only ship sighted had been a Dutch brig off the coast of British Guiana. Faced with dwindling coal supplies and increasing headwinds, Semmes reversed course, ordered the fires banked, and hoisted the sails. The *Sumter* entered the French penal settlement of Cayenne on August 15 to the discharge of cannon celebrating the birth of Napoleon.

Semmes sent Paymaster Myers and Lt. Evans to town to pay their respects to the governor and ask permission to purchase coal, but they were not allowed to land without first submitting to a five-day quarantine. An influential Union consul who lived in Cayenne and enjoyed a prosperous business supplying the French garrison with fresh beef convinced local authorities to refuse port privileges to the Confederates. A port official informed Semmes there was no coal to be purchased and that his visit was unwelcome.[11]

Semmes sailed westward toward Dutch Guiana, hoping to find a friendlier neutral colony. On the evening of August 18 the *Sumter* dropped anchor at the shallow, bar-strewn mouth of the Surinam River. Just before dark, the lookout reported a distant steamer headed directly for them. The vessel had the cut of a warship, but in the evening twilight Semmes could not determine her nationality. He called the men to quarters and prepared the ship for action. At about 10 p.m. the steamer dropped anchor about three miles away, still too distant to reveal her intentions. Semmes allowed the crew to get some rest, but maintained a close vigil throughout the night.

Dawn revealed the stranger underway and standing toward them, and the crew hurried to quarters. Pulses beat rapidly as the strange ship continued to close, still with no colors flying. Semmes recorded the next events: "Desiring to make the stranger reveal her nationality to me first, I hoisted the French colors. . . . To my astonishment, and no little perplexity, up went the same colors on board the stranger! I was alongside a French ship of war, pretending to be a Frenchmen myself! Of course, there was but one thing to be done, and that was to haul down the French flag and hoist my own."[12]

The Frenchman, an old sidewheel steamer that had run short of coal while carrying convicts to Cayenne, received a local pilot, and the *Sumter* followed the *Vulture* up the channel to Paramaribo, joining three American brigantines and two Dutch men-of-war already at anchor in the harbor.

Although she had been at sea less than three weeks since her overhaul in Trinidad, the frail little cruiser needed still more repairs and more coal. Two months of sailing had convinced Kell that the *Sumter* carried too much fresh water. He wanted to remove two large tanks and enlarge the bunkers to increase his steaming range from eight to 12 days. Despite strong arguments from American Consul Henry Sawyer, Governor R. F. Lansberge granted permission to use the port's facilities, and the people of Surinam offered open hospitality.

Consul Sawyer, not to be thwarted, contacted all the coal merchants of Paramaribo and proposed to purchase their entire supply. One document addressed to Van Praag Brothers read: "Understanding that you have coal for sale, I most respectfully request and beg of you, in the name of the United States of America, not to sell a pound to that rascally steamer sailing under the name of *Sumter*." The appeal failed. Many of the merchants personally visited the ship, offering to sell coal, and Semmes filled his bunkers.[13]

Barbadian newspapers received at Paramaribo reported that the *Keystone State* had visited there on July 21 in search of the *Sumter*. Semmes speculated that the false information he had planted at Curacao had probably led the Union warship back to Cuba. From another article he learned that the Union consul at Havana had promptly notified his government when the *Sumter* entered Cienfuegos early in July, and two heavy steamers, the *Niagara* and the *Crusader*, had been hurriedly dispatched to Cienfuegos. So far, they all had followed a cold trail.

On August 29 a rumor circulated in town that two Union cruisers lay in ambush just out of sight beyond the bar. Semmes knew he had been in one place too long, and on the following day steamed back to the mouth of the river. Having left word in Paramaribo that he was bound for Barbados to search for the *Keystone State*, Semmes stood north until out of sight and then changed course for Brazil.

Meanwhile, Commander Palmer on the USS *Iroquois* was still hunting among the islands in the Caribbean, convinced that the raider had snuggled into some hidden cove. Porter headed for Surinam with the *Powhatan*, expecting that Semmes would be forced to return for coal and supplies. Commander Scott, learning that Semmes had been seen in the Guianas, pushed the *Keystone State* hard, hoping to intercept. From Key West, Secretary Welles added the powerful USS *Niagara* to the hunt. Four large warships searched the area where the *Sumter* had been, but she was no longer there.[14]

Although he had eluded capture, Semmes had little to show for the past four weeks. On September 3 he noted in his journal: "We have lost twenty-three days of valuable time—but this time can scarcely be said to be wholly lost . . . since the display of the flag of the young Republic in Cayenne and Paramaribo has had the most excellent effect."

No doubt he believed what he wrote, but his visit to Paramaribo had incited so much diplomatic furor that the Dutch granted a major concession to the United States. Hereafter, all Dutch ports were closed to Confederate privateers, and the warships of both belligerents were permitted to remain in port only 24 hours, and could purchase only enough coal for 24 hours' cruising. This gave the Confederates even fewer ports to enter, and gave the Federals fewer ports to watch.

Semmes exacerbated the situation when he ignored the 90-day rule and coaled at the Dutch colonies of Curacao and Paramaribo within a four-week span. Alert Union consuls vigorously protested this violation and won their point. Semmes had taken a chance and knew the risks, but he had underestimated the consequences.[15]

But Semmes was by nature a risk taker. Growing impatient after waiting for a pilot through the night off the entrance to Sao Luis de Maranhao (Maranham), Brazil, on September 6, he decided to take his chances and run the shallows without one. He crossed the shoals and the irregular middle ground of the Meio without incident and was already congratulating himself that the danger was past when the ship ran "plumb upon a sand bank and stopped! She went on at full speed, and the shock, to those standing on deck, was almost sufficient to throw them off their feet. . . ."[16]

As soon as the ship struck, the engineer stopped the engines. With a strong tide running seaward and the engines reversed, she slid off the bar and back into deep water. The false keel had taken the shock, starting a leak, but the ship wasn't seriously damaged. A nearby fisherman who claimed to know the bottom volunteered to come on board, and with his help the *Sumter* steamed safely into port and anchored off Sao Luis.

September 7 was a day of celebration for the citizens of Sao Luis, the anniversary of their independence from Portugal. The merriment was not enjoyed by the men of the *Sumter*, whose country still fought for independence, and whose flag remained unrecognized among the powers of the world. From a distance they watched and listened.

Semmes felt ill, probably due to the lingering effects of seasickness, and registered at the Hotel Porto in Maranham. The owner, a Senor Porto, had once followed the sea, and he and Semmes soon became friends. Thwarted in earlier attempts to call upon the local president, Semmes' new friend managed to arrange an interview, warning that Union Consul W. H. McGrath had moved to prevent the *Sumter* from coaling. "Never mind!" Porto said, during an afternoon ride through the countryside. "I know all that is going on at the palace, and you will get all the coal and everything else you want." Porto's prediction proved correct. His meeting with the president yielded free access to the markets, allowing Semmes to purchase every commodity except munitions.[17]

By September 15 the *Sumter* had been repaired, painted, coaled, and provisioned. Out of cash, Semmes managed to borrow $2,000 from J. Wetson, a prosperous engineer and millwright from Texas who now lived in Sao Luis. Five weeks had passed since last taking a prize, and Semmes was desperate to capture a vessel that carried enough cash to replenish the empty paymaster's chest. A few degrees to the north lay the equatorial calm belt—a good place to lie in wait for unsuspecting merchant ships passing through one of the ocean's great crossroads.

Four days after the *Sumter* steamed out of Sao Luis, Porter, despite Semmes' false trails, arrived with the *Powhatan*. He had taken risks in getting here, running through the dangerous Sao Luis channel in fog so thick that even the natives beached their boats and kept to shore. Shortly after arriving, Porter located the man who had piloted the *Sumter* back to sea. The native stared in disbelief at the Union officer and said, "You must have had the devil for a pilot . . . Even the little *Sumter* struck coming in and came near to leaving her bones."

Porter found a cold reception in the slave-owning country of Brazil, paying $22 a ton for coal compared with $17.50 paid by Semmes a few days earlier. Nevertheless, in his brief stay Porter managed to gather and pass on to the Navy Department a great deal of intelligence about the raider. He reported that Semmes would no longer try to take his prizes into foreign ports, but instead would burn them. He also stated that the *Sumter*'s well-disciplined crew was becoming discontented, with 15 men in irons when the cruiser left Sao Luis.[18]

On September 25, after 10 unproductive days in the doldrums, the cry of "Sail Ho!" finally broke the monotony on the *Sumter*. Under steam and flying the Stars and Stripes, the raider overhauled the 244-ton *Joseph Park* of Boston, a Maine-built brigantine whose master had noted in the ship's log: "We have a tight, fast vessel, and so we don't care for Jeff. Davis." He had taken no precaution to disguise ownership, but he had left Pernambuco six days earlier in ballast, unable to obtain a cargo because the merchants of that city had received word of the *Sumter*'s presence at Maranham.[19]

Rather than burn the vessel, Semmes decided to use her as a scout, thereby extending his search horizon by eight miles. He put Lt. Evans and a small crew aboard, warning Evans to take the *Park* to a Confederate port if the ships became separated.[20]

For four days the two ships drifted about the crossing without sighting a single sail. Having read a letter sent to the *Park*'s captain advising him to avoid the customary sea lanes, Semmes concluded that all merchant ships had received similar warnings. Discouraged, he removed the prize crew from the *Joseph Park* and allowed his gun crews to enjoy a little target practice before burning her. For Semmes, the calm belt had been an unexpected disappointment, and he continued to sight only neutral sails. He learned from the master of the English brig *Spartan*, who had recently sailed from Rio de Janiero, that all the Yankee ships were laid-up for want of freight.[21]

During this period David Dixon Porter continued his search, and on October 8 came close to catching the elusive *Sumter*. The *Pow-hatan*'s watch spotted a distant light flickering across an exceptionally dark sea. Porter began pursuit, but the light disappeared. Years later, while reading her itinerary, Porter concluded that the mysterious light was indeed the *Sumter*, and that the ships were within 75 miles. When Semmes read the report of the *Powhatan*'s cruise, he concurred, but placed the two ships within 40 miles.[22]

After an uneventful month in the doldrums, on October 27, as Kell prepared for the regular Sunday muster, a lone lookout reported a distant sail. After a long chase, a single blank cartridge brought her into the wind—the 200-ton schooner *Daniel Trowbridge* of New Haven, outward bound from New York to Demerara. Her hold bulged with beef, pork, canvased hams, ship-bread, fancy crackers, cheese, flour, all of the very best quality. The raider's crew plundered the *Trowbridge* for three days before burning her, welcoming the change in their diet from moldy, worm-eaten bread and the toughest and leanest of "old horse," to an unlimited supply of culinary luxuries.[23]

After 45 days at sea the *Sumter* had overhauled 15 neutrals and captured and burned only two prizes, but Semmes did not consider this a failure. From ship's masters and newspapers he learned that the American merchant marine had begun to stagnate: ships could not find cargoes abroad; insurance rates had increased; ships now took long, circuitous detours to avoid capture. Semmes, certain that he was profoundly affecting American shipping, now realized that if he wanted prizes he would eventually have to cross the ocean.

On November 9 the *Sumter* dropped anchor at Fort de France on the western face of Martinique, one of the outer islands of the volcanic chain that separates the Caribbean from the Atlantic. Semmes developed an amiable relationship with Governor Maussion de Cande, a rear admiral in the French Navy. When acting U.S. Consul John Campbell attempted to persuade the collector of customs to prevent the *Sumter* from purchasing coal or any other necessity, the governor interceded on Semmes's behalf.

Kell paroled the prisoners and released them to the Union consul. The crew was given shore leave, but this soon deteriorated into a drunken binge, fights, and desertions. The officers spent endless hours retrieving men from bars and bordellos and apologizing to local officials. This would become standard practice, repeated at nearly every port.[24]

On November 13 the *Sumter* filled her water tanks and steamed across the bay to St. Pierre, the island's commercial center. The collector of customs now made every effort to be cordial, and the *Sumter* began coaling that afternoon. Although Semmes disliked prolonged stays in busy ports, the vessel needed attention again, and Kell hired the well-equipped facilities at St. Pierre to replace the foreyard and patch the boilers.

Rumors circulated in the city that a Union frigate had stopped frequently at Trinidad and St. Thomas. Semmes had heard similar talk in every port, but this was no rumor. Word of the *Sumter's* arrival at Martinique had spread by mail steamer to St. Thomas—a free port with the reputation for being a base of operations for the Union Navy. At 2:30 p.m. on November 14, the 8-gun steam sloop *Iroquois* appeared off the north end of the island. Her captain, Commander James S. Palmer, hoped to pounce on the unsuspecting *Sumter* as she left port. Palmer tried to cloak his ship's identity behind Danish colors and closed gun ports, but there was no concealing the lines of a warship from the old navy men of the *Sumter*. Semmes noted that "the very disguise only made the cheat more apparent."[25]

During the afternoon, as the two adversaries studied each other through telescopes, the *Iroquois* ran into the harbor to communicate with Consul Campbell. Palmer chose not to anchor. He knew that once at anchor, international law would prevent him from going back to sea for 24 hours. After a long discussion with Campbell, Palmer steamed out of the harbor and posted his vessel about two miles off the entrance, cruising slowly back and forth until dark.

At 1:30 a.m. the officer of the deck jarred Semmes awake. The *Iroquois* had entered the harbor and was headed directly toward them. Semmes called the crew to quarters, and in a few minutes the ship was cleared for action. Semmes described the scene:

> It was moonlight, and the movements of the enemy could be distinctly seen. He came along under low steam, but so steadily and aiming so directly for us that I could not doubt that it was his intention to board us. The men were called to "repel boarders"; and for a moment or two a pin might have been heard to drop on the *Sumter's* deck, so silent was the harbor and so still was the scene on board both ships. Presently, however, a couple of strokes on the enemy's stem gong were heard and, in a moment more, he sheared a little and lay off our quarter, motionless. . . . This operation, much to my astonishment, was repeated several times during the night.[26]

When word of the illegal maneuvers reached the governor, he dispatched the French steam warship *Acheron* with orders for Commander Palmer either to anchor or to retire beyond the marine league. Palmer reluctantly returned to a position outside the three-mile limit, but crept back inside the league each night to keep the raider under close surveillance and to send boats ashore to exchange intelligence with Consul Campbell. Palmer also devised a signal system to warn Campbell if the raider changed position or attempted to escape. If Semmes tried to pass to the north or south, a nearby American merchant schooner telegraphed his every move. Semmes, failing to force the removal of the signal lights, began to study them, resolving to use them to his advantage.

Each morning, Semmes protested these violations of French neutrality to the governor, but Palmer knew the criticism he would receive if the smaller, slower, more lightly armed *Sumter* escaped, and the rewards he was likely to receive if he destroyed her. He continued to accept the risk and maintained a vigilant, de facto blockade.

Martinique's citizens, not wishing to miss the spectacle of a fight at sea, gathered daily at various points along the harbor and placed wagers on the outcome. Semmes encouraged them to believe that a fight was imminent, and the crowd's enthusiasm for the expected duel caused further restlessness among the Union warship's crew, already on edge from their nightly patrols. On the *Sumter*, the crew maintained regular watches and enjoyed a full night's rest, leaving matters of escape to the captain.

And escape had a new urgency. In town there were rumors that more American gunboats were on the way. "Fortune had favored us, thus far," wrote Semmes, "but we must now help ourselves. The *Iroquois* was not only twice as heavy as the *Sumter*, in men and metal, but she had as much as two or three knots . . . the speed of her. We must escape . . . unseen of the enemy, and as the latter drew close in with the harbor every night, in fraud of the promise he [Palmer] had made, and in violation of the laws of war. This would be difficult to do. Running all these reasons rapidly through my mind, I resolved to make the attempt without further delay.[27]

Throughout the period the skies had been clear and the moon bright. Semmes waited for a dark night, and continued to study the signals from the Union schooner.

A Harbinger of Disaster

EARLY in the evening of November 23, Executive Officer Kell quietly collected the *Sumter's* crew, who were ashore on liberty. As night fell across the smooth water of the bay, steam hissed in the *Sumter's* boilers, and the crew quietly hoisted the anchor and cut the stern cables. Off in the distance could be seen the faint outline of the *Iroquois*, but the *Sumter* melted into the shadows against the backdrop of the island as Semmes ordered the ship slow ahead. Passing within a few yards of the French warship, the *Acheron's* crew looked on with surprise and gave a soft cheer as the cruiser gathered speed.

Semmes stationed an officer to watch the Yankee schooner and report any signals sent to the *Iroquois*. In a short time, the officer came running aft, saying, "I see them, sir! I see them! Look, sir, there are two red lights, one above the other, at the . . . mast head!" Semmes understood the signal: the *Sumter* was underway and heading south.[1]

Near the southern end of town a towering cliff rose from shore, casting a long shadow far into the bay. The *Sumter* stayed to the south, hugging the dark shoreline until Semmes observed that the *Iroquois* was under steam and moving rapidly toward the point where Palmer expected the two ships to intersect. Picking the proper moment, Semmes changed course and doubled back to the north end of the island. The *Sumter's* engines overheated, forcing her to lie opposite Saint Pierre for 20 minutes until they cooled. He later wrote: "It is safe to say that the next morning, the two vessels were one hundred and fifty miles apart! . . . The signals were of vast service to me."

Semmes' luck had held. The USS *Dacotah* arrived off Martinique the following day. Eight ships had joined the hunt, but the *Sumter* was gone.[2]

When word of the escape reached Washington, Secretary Welles exploded and ordered James C. Palmer relieved of command. After reviewing the facts, however, Welles rescinded the order and four months later reinstated Palmer. Three months later, Welles promoted him to captain and gave him command of the flagship *Hartford*, a nice reward for an officer who only a few months earlier had been fighting to preserve his honor and career. Before the war ended, Palmer was promoted to commodore, and shortly afterward to rear admiral.[3] The only break in an otherwise unblemished career occurred on the night of November 23, 1861, when Raphael Semmes disappeared into the night and left him alone and embarrassed.

The following day Semmes entered the Atlantic Ocean and set course for Europe, hoping for better hunting along the trade routes on the opposite side of the ocean. Although worried by the increasing number of Union warships on his track, his principal concern was the deteriorating condition of his ship. Semmes hoped that in Europe he could obtain a better one.

After two days of rough weather, the cry of "Sail Ho!" finally came, and in towering ocean swells, the *Sumter* steamed after a three-masted square-rigger twice her size. Semmes fired a blank cartridge, signalling the vessel to lie to, and sent over a boarding party. Captain Joseph T. Brown, part owner and master of the 1,083-ton *Montmorenci* of Bath, Maine, came aboard and presented Semmes with wine and cigars, a gesture intended to defuse any hostile intentions. The huge cargo of coal, bound for St. Thomas, a popular coaling stop for the U. S. Navy, was protected by British certification, and Semmes could not burn the vessel without violating a potential ally's neutrality.

Under a ransom bond of $20,000, which covered the value of the ship only and not its neutral cargo, Semmes released the *Montmorenci*—the first of many vessels so bonded. If the Confederacy won her independence, the bond's sum would be added to the spoils of war and a portion distributed among the crew as prize money.[4]

A day later the lookout sighted a ship under gleaming white cotton canvas—an American ship's trademark—and for two hours Semmes chased the 121-ton schooner *Arcade*. The boarding party found her a poor prize—she carried frugal provisions for her small crew and a cargo of barrel staves bound for Guadaloupe—and put her to the torch. The staves made an impressive fire that lighted up the sea for several hours after dark. When Semmes discovered that a fine spyglass removed from the *Arcade* had been awarded to her master, Alexander P. Smith, for saving lives on the sinking steamship *Central America*, he returned it to its owner.[5]

On December 3, approximately 400 miles southeast of Bermuda, the lookout reported a ship approaching dead ahead under American colors. Semmes hoisted the French flag and, under sail, gradually shortened the distance, waiting until their bows crossed before firing a blank charge. The surprised vessel hauled up her courses, backed the main topsail, and hove to. The 1,100-ton ship *Vigilant*, a sleek new vessel from Bath, Maine bound for the guano island of Sombrero, carried little of value beyond a few New York newspapers dated November 21, which reported the *Iroquois* had the *Sumter* cornered at Martinique. With little to salvage, Semmes burned the *Vigilant* and turned eastward, setting a course for Cadiz, Spain.[6]

The North Atlantic in December is a miserable place for ships, and December of 1861 seemed worse than most. A stiff easterly gale halted progress, and bilge pumps worked around the clock as a cold rain beat against reefed sails and huge waves broke over the bow. On December 8 the watch reported a distant vessel, but thick weather obscured her markings. Fearing an enemy warship, Semmes got up steam, raised the funnel, and hoisted the American colors. The stranger did the same. As the two vessels drew closer, Semmes recognized it as a whaling bark.

Twelve days out of New Bedford and bound for the Pacific whaling grounds, the *Eben Dodge* had been severely battered by the recent gale and leaked badly. Before burning her, the prize crew removed a welcome supply of boots, flannels, pea jackets, and other warm clothing for the thinly clad crew of the *Sumter*. Now 22 more prisoners crowded the cruiser's deck, bringing the total to 43. To maintain security, Semmes placed half the prisoners in single wrist irons, alternating each day with the other half. The captives submitted without complaint, seeming to understand the necessity of the precaution. Ten Negroes taken from the *Vigilant* were freed and given duties aboard the cruiser.[7]

Back under sail, the *Sumter* struggled for the next two days with erratic winds, fierce at times, but with no consistent direction. The barometer, after fluctuating for several days, began a sharp descent, followed by gale winds of increasing force. Black storm clouds pierced by lightning raced across the sky, driving squalls of blinding rain. Still the barometer dropped. Semmes ordered close reefs in the topsails and trysails, leaving just enough canvas to steady the ship, and ordered topgallant yards sent down.

Although late in the season for a hurricane, Semmes knew he was in one: "As the night closed in, an awful scene presented itself. The aspect of the heavens was terrific. . . . A streaming scud which you could almost touch with your hand was meanwhile hurrying past, screeching and screaming like so many demons as it rushed through the rigging. The sea was mountainous, and would now and then strike the little *Sumter* with such force as to make her tremble in every fibre of her frame. . . ." After going below to get some rest, Semmes was shaken awake by the old quartermaster, "looking himself like the demon of the storm," who reported that the starboard bow-port was stove in and "the gun-deck is all afloat with water." Semmes raced for the deck, but Kell had already gotten some planks and constructed an effective barricade.[8]

When the wind subsided on December 13, Semmes estimated the hurricane's diameter at 400 miles, with the vortex passing close to the ship as it blew north. The hull was severely strained and leaking, and Kell recruited help from among the prisoners to man the pumps.

On December 28 the *Sumter* entered the great highway of European maritime traffic, where sails of every nation dotted the sea. Semmes wanted to show the Confederate flag, and over the next six days his boarding crews inspected the documents of 19 ships, but failed to find a single American among them. The British vessel *Richibucto*, of Liverpool, provided a bundle of recent English newspapers. Great Britain mourned the death of Prince Albert; the *Trent* Affair raged in diplomatic circles; and a Yankee clipper, the *Harvey Birch*, had been burned in the English Channel by the CSS *Nashville*. The presence of another Confederate cruiser came as unexpected but welcome news to the lonely crew of the *Sumter*.[9]

With nothing but foreign ships passing, the leak worsening, and only four days' fuel remaining, the *Sumter* headed for Spain, 500 miles away, entering Cadiz on the morning of January 4, 1862, the Confederate flag fluttering from the *Sumter*'s peak. Semmes wrote, "A number of the merchant ships of different nations hoisted their flags in honor of the *Sumter* as she passed; and one Yankee ship—there being three or four in the harbor—hoisted hers, as much to say, 'You see we are not afraid to show it.'"[10]

It did not take Spanish officials long to find ways to abbreviate the raider's stay. Ebenezer S. Eggleston, the acting United States consul, persuaded the military governor to order the ship out of the harbor within 24 hours. Semmes responded with one of his classic letters, clearly defining in fluent legalistic jargon his rights as a belligerent. After stating his entitlements he added that, "my ship is in a crippled condition . . . damaged in her hull, is leaking badly, is unseaworthy, and will require to be docked and repaired before it will be possible for her to proceed to sea. I am therefore constrained by force of circumstances . . . to decline obedience to the order which I have received until the necessary repairs can be made." He concluded by reminding the military governor that he had on board 43 American prisoners to be turned over to the local consul "without unnecessary delay." The governor telegraphed the message to Madrid. Within a few hours, Semmes received permission to land the prisoners, but it was not until January 12 that the Spanish government consented to the repairs.[11]

The *Sumter* moved to the well-equipped navy yard at Carraca, about eight miles east of Cadiz, and the following day was out of the water with her bottom exposed for examination. The propeller sleeve was damaged, but the grounding at Maranham had caused only light damage. A section of the false keel had been knocked off, small amounts of copper plating were stripped away, and one of the planks indented. The hull looked sound and tight.

A weak power easily intimidated by the United States, Spain feared war and the possible loss of her colonies, especially Cuba. Spanish officials agreed to allow the repairs but, influenced by Union Consul Eddleston, they would not agree to refurbish the boilers or allow any improvements. Semmes also lost part of his crew to the consul's influence. Eggleston housed the deserters in comfortable quarters, and despite Semmes' protests, the Spanish government refused to assist in their recovery.[12]

Eight men had now deserted, one had been discharged for sleeping on duty, and two Confederate officers had suffered the indignity of being searched by Spanish police. For the rest of his career at sea, Semmes avoided Spanish ports.

Six months at sea and 16 prizes had netted only $1,000; Semmes was bankrupt. He wired William L. Yancey, the Confederate commissioner in London, for $20,000 to purchase coal and other supplies. After two weeks he received Yancey's acknowledgment, but no cash.

With orders from the governor to "depart within six hours," he sent one more protest, but prepared to leave. In the end, the governor reconsidered and granted another 24-hour stay, but Semmes, who had just enough coal on board to make Gibraltar, already had steam up and on January 17 returned to sea.[13]

The *Sumter* passed the Pillars of Hercules and made Gibraltar light at dawn. Lookouts spotted several sails lingering dead ahead waiting for a breeze to carry them through the strong current that rushes into the Mediterranean from the Atlantic. Through telescopes, they located two American ships, always distinguishable by their long, tapered masts, graceful spars, and brilliantly white canvas. Semmes hoisted the Confederate colors, fired the pivot gun, and brought the nearest into the wind, the 322-ton bark *Neapolitan*, of Kingston, Massachusetts, bound from Messina to Boston with 50 tons of sulphur.

Although her papers named the British house of Baring Brothers as owners of the cargo, Semmes believed that contraband destined for the enemy—sulphur was a major component of gun powder—could be destroyed regardless of ownership. When Semmes told him that his ship would be burned, Master Andrew Burditt raged with disbelief, arguing that the shield of Baring Brothers gave him absolute protection from Confederate raiders.

By burning the *Neapolitan*, Semmes overstretched his authority and used questionable judgment, especially since he counted upon a friendly reception at Gibraltar.[14] Although the character of the cargo was clearly in dispute, the matter could only have been settled in a prize court. Nonetheless, the flames' fiery spectacle was watched with great interest and mixed reaction from both sides of the Mediterranean.

The 18th and final prize captured by the *Sumter* was the 141-ton Maine bark *Investigator*, which, in light winds, failed to reach the charmed marine league and surrendered. Her cargo of iron ore carried the British seal, and Semmes placed the ship under ransom bond. From Captain Charles G. Carver, Semmes collected only $51. Combined with the $86 taken from the *Neapolitan*, this represented all the *Sumter*'s ready cash.[15]

With coal running low and several miles to cover before dark, the *Sumter* turned about and headed for Gibraltar. Soon after dropping anchor, Semmes visited the port admiral to report his arrival, and he and his officers received a cordial reception from military and civilian authorities. Governor General Sir William J. Codrington offered the facilities of the base to the Confederate staff.

Repairs to the ship had to await funds from London. On January 24 Semmes wrote Confederate Commissioner James M. Mason that the "want of funds have deprived me of the power of scouring the Mediterranean, the whole of which sea I could have swept without molestation in from fifteen to twenty days. . . ." When the necessary credits were finally made available through Fraser, Trenholm and Company of Liverpool, which also had offices in Charleston, South Carolina, 16 days had elapsed. Since the ship could not leave until the boilers were repaired, Semmes contented himself with a few days of leisure on shore.[16] Meanwhile, the Union Navy arrived.

The *Kearsarge* and the *Tuscarora*—fast, new, and heavily armed screw steamers—took stations in the bay where they could observe every movement on the *Sumter*. Each day one vessel placed itself in the Bay of Algeziras, a Spanish anchorage directly across from Gibraltar. Although the atmosphere in the harbor was tense, the sailors of the two services fraternized on shore. Semmes wrote: "They talked and laughed and smoked and peeled oranges together, as though there was no war going on."[17]

While visiting Semmes, Captain Sir Frederick Warden of the British Navy suggested that the *Sumter* could escape by taking advantage of the 24-hour rule while the *Kearsarge* rode at anchor in the same neutral port. Semmes remarked "that it was useless for us to discuss the rule here, as the enemy's ships had adroitly taken measures to avoid it." When Warden asked why, Semmes replied, "By stationing one of his ships in Gibraltar and another in Algeziras. If I go to sea from Gibraltar, the Algeziras ship follows me, and if I go to sea from Algeziras, the Gibraltar ship follows me."[18]

The *Tuscarora*, under Commander T. Augustus Craven, had just entered Spanish waters from Southampton, England, having spent the past several weeks trying to capture the CSS *Nashville*. In contrast to Semmes' reception at Cadiz, the *Tuscarora* lingered at Algeziras for six weeks without the least hint of displeasure from the Spanish government. At times the *Kearsarge*, under Captain Charles W. Pickering, exchanged stations with the *Tuscarora*.

The Union squadron blockading the *Sumter* continued to grow with the arrival of the USS *Ino* and the sailing sloop-of-war *Constellation*, an old warrior upon which Semmes served during the Seminole war. Eventually, three more warships joined in. Semmes still made no plans to escape, but enjoyed the satisfaction of knowing that his little cruiser had prevented seven Union warships from being usefully deployed elsewhere.[19]

While in Gibraltar, Semmes became instant friends with Colonel Arthur J. L. Freemantle of the Coldstream Guards, who later travelled to the Confederacy and placed himself beside General James Longstreet during the battle of Gettysburg. One afternoon Freemantle called upon Semmes with a pair of horses, and together they rode to the pinnacle of The Rock. The day was clear and the view breathtaking. A British signalman, posted in a quaint little house near the very tip of the Rock, commented to Semmes: "We had a fine view of your ship the other day, when you were chasing the Yankee." He pointed seaward and added, "The latter was hereaway when you set fire to her."

"Are there many Yankee ships passing the Rock now?" Semmes asked.

"No. Very few since the war commenced."

"It would not pay me then, to cruise in these seas?"

"Scarcely," the signalman replied.[20]

Two days later a Spanish naval lieutenant called upon Semmes to protest the burning of the *Neapolitan*, claiming that the vessel had been captured within Spanish jurisdiction. The officer came from the fortress of Ceuta, on the African shore opposite Gibraltar, and delivered the complaint on behalf of the admiral commanding the fort. When Semmes demanded to know upon whose testimony the charge was made, he was told Horatio J. Sprague, the United States consul at Gibraltar. After listening to the Spanish officer's case, Semmes said, "I do not recognize the right of your Admiral to raise any question with me as to the capture of the *Neapolitan*. The capture of that ship is an accomplished fact, and if any injury has been done thereby to Spain, the Spanish government can complain of it to the government of the Confederate States."[21]

Semmes had come to Gibraltar to purchase coal and install new boilers, but British authorities refused to allow the installation of new machinery, and Consul Sprague had managed to convince the local coal merchants not to sell him coal. While he considered his alternatives, an English ship carrying coal arrived. Learning of the *Sumter's* difficulty, the master approached Semmes and struck a deal. The next morning, as the cruiser weighed anchor to receive the promised coal, a boat from the English ship brought a message that the price of coal had doubled during the night. Blaming Sprague, Semmes declined.

On February 10 Semmes telegraphed the English Secretary of Foreign Affairs in London explaining his difficulties and appealing for assistance. A week later the application came back rejected. Frustrated, Semmes decided to buy coal in another port and have it delivered to Gibraltar.[22]

Paymaster Myers and Tom Tate Tunstall, a Southerner who had been United States consul at Cadiz before the war and was anxious to serve the Confederacy, booked passage on the French steamer *Villa de Malaga*, a packet ship that circulated between several ports along the Mediterranean coast.

Their objective was to debark at Cadiz, where Tunstall was still well connected, purchase a load of coal, and return with it by chartered ship. At an interim stop at Tangier, a small Moroccan town on the opposite side of the Strait of Gibraltar, Myers and Tunstall strolled into town sightseeing while the ship loaded freight and landed a few passengers. As they returned from their walk, both men were unceremoniously taken prisoner by Moroccan soldiers, an act that Semmes later learned had been instigated by Acting Consul Judge James De Long, a resident of the town.

A strange treaty existed that gave Christian powers both civil and criminal jurisdiction over their citizens when on Moroccan soil. The Moroccan officials could not distinguish between citizens of the United States and citizens of the Confederate States and simply followed De Long's instructions.

Semmes failed to obtain their release, although Tunstall was still technically a United States citizen, and both were shackled in irons and placed aboard the USS *Ino* by De Long, assisted by 40 armed members of the crew and a small force supplied by Moroccan authorities.

The seizure led to repercussions, however. Tangier's large foreign colony recognized the action's illegality and assailed Lieutenant Commanding Josia P. Creasy of the *Ino* with a shower of stones. De Long later lost his post as interim consul, too late to save Myers and Tunstall. On March 6 they sailed to Boston on the merchant vessel *Harvest Home* and were imprisoned in Fort Warren. Eventually they both received paroles as prisoners of war.[23]

Still without coal and with his ship's corroded boilers precluding escape, Semmes decided to assign a small crew to the *Sumter* and proceed with a number of his officers to London. Abandoning the little cruiser was a difficult decision for Semmes. With all her shortcomings, the *Sumter* had performed a valuable service against a formidable enemy, tying up capital ships from the blockading squadron and allowing Southern blockade runners to slip through the cordon.

On April 7, having received authority from Confederate commissioner Mason in London, Semmes paid off what was left of the crew with the funds intended for repairs. Of 92 enlisted men aboard when the *Sumter* left New Orleans, only 46 remained—and these soon melted away with "snug little sums in their pockets."[24]

On April 11 Semmes turned over the *Sumter* with sufficient funds and provisions for 10 months to Midshipman Richard F. Armstrong, along with Acting Master's Mate Joseph G. Hester and a crew of 10 enlisted men. Then, with Kell and several other officers, he booked passage on a mail steamer bound for Southampton. Shortly after Semmes reached England, he recalled Armstrong and replaced him with Midshipman William Andrews. For six months the *Sumter* lay harmlessly at anchor, watched diligently by Union warships.

Welles' warships were forced to maintain their blockade because British authorities either failed or refused to intern the *Sumter* and her crew—an infraction of international law. But in a war where no one seemed to follow the rules, little illegalities like this were common— especially when they caused Britain's primary maritime competitor inconvenience and expense.

Early in the war, Britain's maritime coalition recognized an opportunity to reduce the growing American merchant fleet, and encouraged liberal treatment of Confederate commerce raiders. In 1862, hoping to establish precedents that would circumvent some of the specific agreements of the Declaration of Paris, which modified Britain's ability to bully other nations with small navies, Her Majesty's foreign policy remained loose and liberal, flexing in her favor whenever an opportunity offered exploitation.[25]

Conditions continued to deteriorate aboard the *Sumter*. On October 15, 1862, after Acting Master's Mate Hester was caught stealing, he shot and killed Midshipman Andrews, and was taken into custody by British authorities at Gibraltar. At the request of the Confederate government, the British agreed to return Hester to the South for a proper trial, providing the United States permitted Her Majesty's warship to pass through the blockade. When the vessel reached Bermuda, however, Secretary of State Seward refused to allow the British ship to pass. Disgusted with the entire matter and feeling that they had provided more than enough assistance in satisfying justice, the British settled the issue by turning Hester loose in Bermuda.[26]

Although still uninterned, the *Sumter* had become a problem for the British, and they wanted her gone. At auction on December 9, the *Sumter* was purchased for $19,500 as a merchant vessel by the Liverpool firm of Melchir G. Klingender & Company, secretly representing Fraser, Trenholm and Company and acting on instructions from James Dunwoody Bulloch. Although Bulloch realized the *Sumter* was not an ideal blockade runner, he needed vessels and this seemed the only way to get the ship out of Gibraltar and back into Confederate service.

Legally, the sale did not exempt the *Sumter* from capture. By her antecedents, she remained a fair prize if caught, and the United States Navy continued its vigil. Finally, on February 6, 1863, the *Sumter* escaped to sea into a howling gale.[27]

Rechristened the *Gibraltar* and refitted to carry cargo at Liverpool, she ran the blockade in July, 1863, and entered Wilmington, North Carolina. As a runner, she had many deficiencies, including her bulky shape and slow speed. Five months passed before she could escape. Shortly after the war ended, the old, seaworn *Sumter* foundered in the North Sea, surviving obscurity by dint of a brief cruise under the Confederate flag and the command of Raphael Semmes.[28]

Semmes achieved celebrity status and was promoted to captain for his work on the *Sumter*, but this was overshadowed and nearly forgotten when he took command the following August of the dreaded CSS *Alabama*—the most successful of all the Confederate cruisers.

During the *Sumter's* six-month cruise, Semmes had hoped for sympathy and cooperation from foreign admiralty courts, but received none. He had captured 18 American vessels, but burned only seven, sparing those with neutral cargoes. By the time he returned to sea as the captain of the *Alabama*, Semmes had become a hardened realist, and he ruthlessly used the torch. He had learned how to fight the war aboard the *Sumter*, and he had learned to fight it with unparalleled efficiency.

Compared with later damage by new and more powerful cruisers, the *Sumter's* actual injury to American shipping meant little, but the fear and alarm in the minds of both foreign and American shippers meant a great deal. Northern ships lay idled in ports, waiting for the *Sumter* to move away from the area. The *Sumter* and a few early privateers made insurance companies nervous enough to raise rates, although not enough to drive shippers from the sea. She also tied up Union warships needed for blockade duty.

Semmes later recorded: "The expense to my Government of running the ship was next to nothing, being only $28,000, or about the price of one of the least valuable of her prizes." John McIntosh Kell remembered the *Sumter* as "Frail and unseaworthy at best, her career was a marvel . . . no ship of her size, her frailness, and her armament ever played such havoc on a powerful foe."[29]

With all her inadequacies, the *Sumter* proved a harbinger of disaster, one which Union Naval Secretary Welles failed to appreciate.

The CSS *Nashville*

BETWEEN the beginning and the end of the *Sumter's* brief cruise, the only other Confederate threat on the high seas was the fast but frail *Nashville*. Her career lasted only four months, and she took only two prizes, yet her unexpected arrival in Great Britain coincided with some alarming news: The United States had just violated Her Majesty's neutrality by stopping the British mail steamer *Trent* on the high seas and removing two Confederate commissioners. During the peak period of anti-American sentiment that followed, the *Nashville* enjoyed the excitement of being the Confederate Navy's sole European representative—until the *Sumter* spectacularly took two prizes in full view of Gibraltar in early January.

Constructed in 1853 as a coastal trader and passenger liner, the speedy 1,200-ton wooden sidewheeler *Nashville* was in mint condition—with a fresh overhaul and new boilers—when she arrived at Charleston, South Carolina, just in time to witness the outbreak of the Civil War.

As a warship she was thoroughly inadequate. Like most sidewheelers, she was a poor performer under sail. Her decks were so flimsy that they shook whenever one of her light 6-pounders was fired. Nevertheless, she was seized by the Confederacy, and Naval Secretary Mallory added her to a very short list—three vessels—of potential candidates for conversion to a commerce raider.[1]

Initially she was purchased by a consortium of Charleston businessmen led by C. H. Stevens, who hoped to commission the *Nashville* as a privateer. But Mallory had other plans for the *Nashville*. Charged by President Davis with the important mission of getting Confederate commissioners John Slidell to France and James M. Mason to Great Britain to obtain recognition for the Confederate government—and if possible, European intervention in the war—Mallory rejected the application for letters of marque, and purchased the vessel for $100,000.

Refitting the *Nashville* for her mission started immediately. She was lightened, decreasing her draft and increasing her top speed to 16½ knots—much faster than her Union counterparts.[2] On September 27, 1861, Lieutenant Robert B. Pegram took command.[3] Finding her unarmed, he borrowed two small English-made 6 pounders from the governor of South Carolina and mounted them in pivot.

By the time Mason and Slidell arrived for their dash to Europe, Union authorities had uncovered the plan and deployed four warships off Charleston's harbor to snare the *Nashville*. Pegram felt uncomfortable risking the capture of his important passengers, and made frequent reconnaissances of the enemy's position, waiting for the right moment to escape.

Becoming impatient with Pegram's caution, Mason and Slidell decided to charter the fast steamer *Gordon* to transport them to Havana. The *Gordon* had been one of the more successful Confederate privateers, but as the blockade tightened her captain found it impossible to bring prizes into port, and he had been reduced to simple charters on inland waters at $200 a day. The $10,000 charter fee offered by the commissioners was too lucrative to ignore.

Friday night, October 11, the *Gordon* slipped through the blockade during a heavy downpour, reaching Cardenas, Cuba, on Wednesday. From there, Mason and Slidell boarded a train to Havana and booked passage on the British Royal Mail steamer *Trent*.[4]

On October 26, under cover of night, Pegram and a crew of 40 escaped through the blockade and headed for Bermuda. Upon their arrival four days later, Union Consul Charles M. Allen sent a telegram to Secretary Welles stating that: "*Nashville* has escaped from Charleston. Is coaling at Bermuda. Will be there till 6th instant. Is lightly armed. Has large amount of treasure. Her destination is Liverpool."[5]

With the *Nashville*'s light armament, Pegram wanted no part of Union warships, and set a course across a section of the North Atlantic seldom frequented by other vessels. For two weeks he and his small crew battled strong headwinds, high seas smashed into the wheelhouses, bulwarks washed away, and part of the hurricane deck was ripped apart.[6]

While the men of the *Nashville* fought the North Atlantic, another drama was being enacted by Union Captain Charles Wilkes of the 14-gun screw steamer *San Jacinto*. Wilkes, who had explored the Antarctic for the navy in 1838, had more recently been in the Caribbean searching for Semmes and the *Sumter*. While coaling in Cienfuegos, Cuba, he received word that two Confederate diplomats were about to board the British mail packet *Trent* at Havana, on the opposite side of the island. For the moment, the ambitious captain forgot the *Sumter* and launched a personal mission that would endure in history as the *Trent* Affair.

On November 8, acting without orders, Wilkes intercepted and boarded the *Trent* in the Bahama Channel and forcibly removed Mason, Slidell, and their secretaries while his marines held outraged British passengers and officers at bay with leveled muskets and fixed bayonets.[7] Wilkes hustled his prisoners over to the *San Jacinto* and headed for Boston, arriving there on November 19.

On the same day that Wilkes reached Boston, the *Nashville* and her weather-worn crew approached the western coast of Ireland and sighted the 1,482-ton clipper ship *Harvey Birch*, bound from Le Havre to New York in ballast. Captain Nelson of the clipper never suspected that the approaching sidewheeler was an enemy and continued on course, expecting to cross bows and exchange the customary civilities. When the Confederate flag unfurled and the gun ports popped open, however, an astonished Nelson lowered the Stars and Stripes, uncertain of his exact status or immediate future.[8]

Pegram ordered Nelson to board the *Nashville* with the clipper's papers, and after a short interview sent an officer to the *Harvey Birch* with instructions to collect the prisoners and their personal belongings, remove the navigational instruments, and burn the ship. In his report Pegram stated: "Before she was lost to our sight her masts had gone by the board and she had burned to the water's edge."[9] He granted the officers and passengers freedom of the deck, but he clapped the crew in irons. Nelson claimed the clipper was worth $65,000.

Pegram anchored off the English port of Southampton on November 21 and released 41 prisoners and passengers. Word of the first Confederate capture in the North Atlantic shipping lanes made sensational news. The following day the London *Times* printed: "Great excitement has been created here by the arrival in our waters this morning of a steamer of war bearing the flag of the Confederate States of America."[10] Shippers planning commercial voyages to the United States ordered their vessels to remain in port.

Six days later, on November 28, news of the *Trent* Affair reached England, and bitter anti-Union feeling erupted across Great Britain at the thought of the upstart United States violating the sanctity of its vessels. The press raged at the affront, demanding an immediate apology from the Lincoln administration. Truculent instructions from the British government to Foreign Minister Lord John Lyons were printed verbatim in the newspapers, demanding that he sever diplomatic relations with the United States within seven days if corrective action had not been taken.

Across the Atlantic, Naval Secretary Gideon Welles, delighted by the affair, sent Wilkes a note of appreciation: "I congratulate you on your safe arrival, and especially do I congratulate you on the great public service you have rendered in the capture of the rebel emissaries. . . ."[11] The House of Representatives further bolstered Wilkes' substantial ego by unanimously passing a resolution of commendation. Stimulated by the government's lead, the Northern press made Wilkes a brief national hero. But by then, Secretary of State Seward privately expressed deep misgivings about the affair, and his own diplomatic corps argued vehemently against the resolution. Welles began to regret his hurried praise.

As the United States rethought its position on the *Trent* Affair, the incident monopolized the columns of British newspapers until December 14, when the announced illness of the Prince Consort shifted the public's interest. Two days later Prince Albert died, requesting on his deathbed that the heated and threatening style of diplomatic correspondence being directed at the United States be tempered. In a token of respect, the *Nashville* was one of the first foreign ships to lower her colors.

The press ignored the prince's dying request and, after the funeral, began publishing details of war preparations: 8,000 troops embarked for Canada; talk of intervention filled the streets; emissaries of Great Britain, France, and Spain held secret diplomatic discussions on the question of recognizing the Confederacy's independence.[12]

While matters of great importance were being discussed at high levels of government, Pegram concentrated on solving his own problems. The Atlantic gales had so battered the *Nashville* that she needed a thorough overhaul. On December 5 Pegram received permission to take his vessel into drydock at Southampton, with the condition that she be restored to original operating order only—no additional strengthening or increase of armament.

Two weeks earlier, the British had honored a similar request from the USS *James Adger* with the same restrictions, but there was one difference: The *Nashville* was placed in drydock with another vessel, making it impossible for her to leave until work on both ships had been completed. Unfortunately, this delayed her departure.[13]

Since leaving Charleston, Pegram had never been satisfied with the crew. Small, unexplained problems occurred with frequency. When several crew members deserted after an unsuccessful attempt to burn the ship, Pegram began to manifest signs of paranoia, trusting no one and suspecting that every difficulty he encountered resulted from a hidden conspiracy.[14]

While the *Nashville* underwent repairs and the British press continued to talk of war, Welles issued orders to Commander T. Augustus

Craven of the USS *Tuscarora* to avenge the burning of the *Harvey Birch*: "This wanton destruction of the property of our merchants upon the high seas requires punishment and must receive immediate attention. You will therefore proceed without delay to the English coast, and ascertain whether the *Nashville* is at Southampton . . . making it a primary object to seize that vessel whenever you can do so without invading the neutral rights or jurisdiction of England, or any other state."[15]

Craven dashed across the storm-swept Atlantic and steamed into Southampton on January 8, 1862, arriving exactly at the moment Pegram completed preparations to leave. Seeing that the port had two exits, Craven anchored the *Tuscarora* inside the harbor, about a mile from the *Nashville*, and asked for assistance from another Union warship. While he waited for help to arrive, an officer and three men went ashore to organize a signal system and spy upon the *Nashville*.[16] With steam up and the crew on constant alert, Craven maintained a vigil over the increasingly nervous and indecisive Pegram.

One day after the *Tuscarora*'s arrival, news came that the United States, yielding to diplomatic pressure, had released Mason and Slidell into the care of Lord Lyons. The British were delighted—especially the cabinet, who were relieved that they would not have to carry out their threats of war. Secretary of State Seward's lengthy apology to Lord Lyons mollified the British press, and the *Trent* Affair dropped as a heated public issue. The United States had lost face, but the Confederacy had lost her best opportunity for European intervention. During the balance of the war, no other issue brought Great Britain so close to war.

Weeks passed as the *Nashville* and the *Tuscarora* continued their standoff, and the British gradually grew weary of the two adversaries exploiting the Queen's hospitality. Officials warned both commanders that, according to international rules of neutrality, if either vessel left port, the other must wait 24 hours before following—and stationed the frigate *Dauntless* nearby to enforce the rule.

Neither ship made a move, and intense arguments developed among Captain Charles G. E. Patey of the Royal Navy and Pegram and Craven over the nature of the 24-hour rule.[17] Defining first start as the vessel that first tripped her anchor, Patey asked that each captain advise him in advance of the time they intended to depart. Complaining that this interpretation gave the *Nashville* an unfair advantage, Craven imagined his situation hopeless, but continued to maintain his vigil in the hope that another Union warship would join him before the *Nashville* could escape.[18]

Pegram remained in port, however, unmoved by the advantage

awarded him by the British, and Craven notified Patey that he was leaving. Pleased to be rid of one problem, Patey did not realize that Craven intended to skirt the 24-hour rule to prevent the *Nashville's* escape. Craven explained his scheme in a report to Welles: "I intend being absent no more than twenty-four hours and on returning to my anchorage shall immediately repeat my notice to depart again."[19]

In addition to clarifying the 24-hour rule, The Queen's Foreign Office redefined a belligerent's rights to occupy her ports. Under certain circumstances—the 90-day rule being one—a belligerent may apply for permission to coal, provision, or make repairs. A time limit would be established by local maritime officials after which the visiting vessel must leave. This change permitted port authorities to demand that both Pegram and Craven depart, one immediately and one 24 hours later.

Pegram, fearing that Craven would wait outside the harbor and attack as the *Nashville* headed out to sea, appealed to the Duke of Somerset for concessions:

> My ship not being originally designed to cross the Atlantic, much less as a war vessel, I have not been able to strengthen her sufficiently to sustain the two light 6-pounder guns which had been put on board her, and to leave within the fatal delay specified in the above order would be to subject me to inevitable capture. . . . Your grace cannot fail to perceive from these orders that my movements are made subordinate to those of the *Tuscarora* and that the commander of that vessel is absolutely empowered to force me into a collision with him on his own terms. If it is indeed true that I am bidden to abandon the asylum whose hospitable shelter I have not abused, and I am thus with my weak ship and slender crew to be placed at the mercy of a powerful man of war with which it would be madness to attempt to cope, I have no alternative but to obey this peremptory order, but I here enter my solemn protest against it in the name of common humanity and that of the government which I have the honor to represent.[20]

Although Pegram had shown no such consideration when he burned the helpless *Harvey Birch*, the British did listen to his plea and reversed their decision on which ship would leave first, giving the advantage back to the *Nashville*. Disgusted, Craven notified Welles that his usefulness at Southampton had ended. "This final decree . . . renders my presence here perfectly idle and useless . . . I see nothing better for me to do than go in pursuit of the *Sumter*, which is still in the neighborhood of Gibraltar. . . ."[21]

At 5 p.m. on February 3, escorted by the British frigate *Shannon*, the *Nashville* steamed arrogantly past the *Tuscarora's* shotted guns and headed out to sea. To guarantee that Craven would not to attempt to follow until 24 hours had elapsed, the *Shannon* took up a position alongside the Union vessel. Bitter over the whole affair, Craven wrote Welles: "The whole transaction appears to me, sir, to have a strong impress of collusion on the part of the authorities to effect the escape of the privateer. I had no sooner anchored here than my arrival was made known at Southampton by telegraph; then, and not till then, did the *Nashville* leave Southampton. The British squadron communicated the fact by signal to the *Shannon*, lying near me, and that ship was at once got underway to convoy the *Nashville* out. . . ."[22]

Craven failed to mention a deeper insult. As the *Nashville* steamed by, he received a taunting message from the celebrating Pegram, inviting him to give chase if he thought he could catch the speedy *Nashville*. Craven ignored the challenge, waited 24 hours, and headed for Gibraltar.[23]

Once at sea, Pegram set a direct course for a Southern port. Forced into Bermuda for coal and minor repairs caused by constant northerly gales, he arrived at St. George on February 20 and met Captain J. Pender, owner of the schooner *Pearl*, who had run the blockade at Beaufort, North Carolina, but had grounded on the northern tip of Bermuda. Pender offered to pilot the *Nashville* safely into Beaufort, and Pegram eagerly accepted the offer.[24]

On February 24 the *Nashville* steamed out of St. George and headed for Beaufort. Two days later, Pegram captured the schooner *Robert Gilfillan*, en route from Philadelphia to Santo Domingo with a cargo of assorted provisions. The master, who mistook the oncoming *Nashville* as the USS *Keystone State*, invited the landing party aboard and entertained them with stories of Yankee triumphs in the war. The party ended when boarding officer John H. Ingraham ordered the *Gilfillan's* master to "Haul down your flag and take your papers aboard my ship immediately. . . . That vessel is the Confederate States steamer *Nashville* and you are my prisoner."[25] With the sea too rough to transfer loot, the officers and crew climbed on board the *Nashville* with their personal belongings and watched their schooner burn. Pegram logged the second and final capture of an erratic voyage during which the commerce raider had spent most of her career safe in port.

At daylight on February 28 the USS *State of Georgia*, on patrol off Beaufort inlet, sighted the *Nashville* about three miles inshore, flying the American flag. As the ships closed, Commander James F. Armstrong withheld fire, disarmed by the Confederate vessel's resemblance to the *Keystone State*. As soon as Pegram passed the slower ship, he hauled down the American flag, brazenly hoisted the Stars and Bars, and sped rapidly away. Armstrong maneuvered to present his broadside and fired 21 shots, all falling short. In a display of false bravado, Pegram replied with one shot from the harmless 6-pounder.[26] At 7 a.m., the *Nashville* passed Fort Macon and moored safely alongside the railroad wharf at Morehead City.

The *Nashville*'s return to a Confederate port ended her brief career as a Confederate cruiser. Her infamy as a raider stirred the Northern press and fueled a national indignation toward Secretary Welles for having only one blockader covering a port that required at least five. Under public pressure for his dismissal, Welles hurried instructions to Captain John Marston of the USS *Roanoke*, stating that, "The Department is unable to learn what measures you can take to keep the *Nashville* in Beaufort, but they should be characterized by energy. . . ."[27] Another pamphleteer published a legal brief implicating the British in the destruction of the *Harvey Birch*, arguing that the *Nashville*'s guns were made in England. This allegation withstood nine years of debate and marked the beginning of a lengthy list of claims against Great Britain that remained unsettled until the Geneva Tribunal in 1872.[28]

Originally purchased by Mallory to carry Mason and Slidell to Europe, the *Nashville* became a decoy when the commissioners grew impatient and chartered the *Gordon*, but the principal purpose of her mission remains unclear. Some believe that the *Nashville* sailed to Great Britain primarily to convince European powers that the Confederate States had a navy on the high seas. By burning the *Harvey Birch*, Pegram added credibility to the South's status as a belligerent, but the demonstration failed to impress the British. The small, lightly armed sidewheeler presented a pathetic example of naval power and, despite the *Trent* incident, accomplished nothing towards achieving the Confederate government's objective—diplomatic recognition.[29]

But several precedent-setting actions resulted from the *Nashville*'s visit to Great Britain: While at Southampton, the cruiser secured belligerent status for Confederate warships in the face of high-level Union protests; she proved the safety of neutral ports. Most important was a statement by Lord John Russell, British Foreign Secretary, that the *Nashville* was not a "pirate" under the terms of Britain's Foreign Enlistment Act of 1819, but a regularly commissioned ship of war with rights to a safe port and use of repair facilities. Russell's interpretation established an 18-month-long liberal policy that became the basic foundation for the postwar arbitration known as the *Alabama* Claims.[30]

When Pegram and the *Nashville* arrived in Beaufort, he learned that his ship had been sold as a blockade runner to Fraser, Trenholm and Company, the Liverpool commercial banking firm based partly in Charleston that played an important role in virtually every financial transaction made in Europe. It was a job she was much better suited for than commerce raiding. Chased from port by the approach of General Ambrose Burnside's forces, the *Nashville* fled to Georgetown, South Carolina, and for the next several months carried cotton to Nassau and arms into the Confederacy as the *Thomas L. Wragg*. After a dash into the mouth of Georgia's Great Ogeechee River in July, she was bottled up for eight months by three Union gunboats, and eventually recommissioned as the privateer *Rattlesnake*—still considered dangerous because of her speed.

Among the Union gunboats watching for the *Rattlesnake* was the monitor *Montauk*, under Commander John L. Worden, who planned to move upriver and destroy the sidewheeler, but was unable to pass the barrier of stakes and torpedoes below Fort McAllister. On February 27, 1863, discovering that the *Rattlesnake* had moved downriver during the night and grounded just below the fort, and knowing that she would float free by high tide the next morning, Worden moved up to the barrier with three gunboats and halted directly under the guns of Fort McAllister. Paying no attention to the steady bombardment from the fort, Worden concentrated on shelling the *Rattlesnake*, whose superstructure he could see from across a swampy point. Thick fog and clouds of smoke obscured vision, but Worden saw a fire blazing at the point where his shells fell and knew he had hit the ship. A short time later he heard a gun explode, followed by the detonation of an entire magazine. When the fog rose, only some fragments of hull remained of the raider that had once been the CSS *Nashville*.[31]

"What's New in Palermo?"

WHILE Semmes labored to get the *Sumter* down the Mississippi and out to sea, James Dunwoody Bulloch arrived in Liverpool to help create a Southern navy. Of the many agents Mallory sent to Europe to purchase arms and ships, Bulloch surpassed them all in capability and resourcefulness. During his years in the United States Navy, he had traveled the major sea-lanes, entered the principal harbors of the Western Hemisphere, learned proper military protocol, and studied advances in naval gunnery and armament. As a merchant shipper, he had learned the techniques of handling money, bills of exchange, and contracts and shipping manifests. He was a man of ingenuity, finesse, and unusual intelligence, and he conducted his business with the British with a full understanding of the logistical and diplomatic problems confronting the South.

It did not take long for United States Secretary of State William H. Seward to discover Bulloch's abilities, and he notified State Department officials abroad to keep Bulloch under close surveillance. For four years Bulloch and Thomas H. Dudley, the excitable Union consul at Liverpool, actively engaged in a deadly game of cat and mouse. Dudley employed a large staff of spies to infiltrate and undermine Bulloch's schemes, but Bulloch consistently thwarted his best efforts.

Liverpool, with an astounding density of 66,000 persons per square mile, and Birkenhead, across the Mersey River, were at the center of the explosive growth in the English Midlands fueled by the industrial revolution. Both sides of the mile-wide Mersey estuary swarmed with maritime activity: hundreds of ships, barges, and ferries competed for space; thousands of sailors passed through. Both banks teamed with docks and shipyards — an ideal place for Bulloch to build a Confederate Navy.

On June 5 1861, the day after his arrival in Liverpool, Bulloch called upon Charles K. Prioleau of Fraser, Trenholm and Company, the Confederate's commercial banking firm in Europe. Although at the time Bulloch arrived the bank had received no funds for the purchase or construction of ships, Prioleau arranged for the firm to accept responsibility for any orders Bulloch wished to place.

With financial headaches removed, Bulloch engaged F. S. Hull, a member of one of Liverpool's leading law firms, to learn how far he could stretch Britain's Foreign Enlistment Act, which prohibited the outfitting of warships for belligerent powers. The lawyers felt that under the as yet untested law, a ship could be legally built, regardless of intended use, as long as the vessel was not equipped for war within British waters. This meant no guns, gun carriages, or ammunition. Bulloch therefore was careful that all building contracts omit any reference to the ship's ultimate use or destination—a policy which ultimately prevented the seizure of the *Florida* and the *Alabama*.[1]

With Prioleau's assistance, Bulloch searched Britain's harbors for suitable vessels. He wanted a ship that could cruise under steam or sail for long periods independent of foreign ports for repairs and supplies. This meant a wooden vessel, which, unlike ships built of iron, could be repaired by any good ship's carpenter. It would have large coal bunkers—uncommon because they sacrificed passenger and cargo space, and it would sail well, which meant having a propeller that could be uncoupled and lifted to prevent drag. He found ships for sale of every description, but none met his requirements. Before the end of June, he gave up his search to buy a vessel and contracted to build one with the firm of William C. Miller and Sons of Liverpool.[2]

Bulloch chose his shipbuilder carefully. Miller and Sons had many years of experience in the design and construction of wooden ships capable of carrying heavy armament and large crews. From several designs that could be modified to meet his requirements, Bulloch selected a fast dispatch gunboat of the Royal Navy, making only two changes: He lengthened the ship to provide more space for coal and supplies, and expanded the sail area to increase her speed. Messrs. Fawcett, Preston and Company, also of Liverpool, subcontracted to build and install the engines. Fraser, Trenholm and Company backed all the financial arrangements, and the shipyard agreed to start construction immediately.

To disguise the vessel's intended use he named her *Oreto*, told the workmen the ship was being built for an Italian owner in Palermo, and hired John Henry Thomas, local agent for the firm of Messrs. Thomas Brothers of Palermo, to supervise the construction details and act as registered owner.

The disguise went undetected until the following October when United States Minister to England Charles Francis Adams heard rumors, originating with the workmen, some of whom suspected the ship's ultimate use, that the ship might be intended for the Confederacy.[3] By November, Adams had accumulated enough information to feel confident that Confederate ships were being built in England, although he had no evidence of any vessel receiving arms.

Typical of the flow of intelligence into Adams' office was the following dispatch from Consul Thomas Dudley, at Liverpool: "The Oritis [sic] a screw gunboat is fitting out in one of the docks at this place, she is built of iron and is 700 tons. She is reported for the Italian Government, but the fact of the machinery being supplied by Fawcett and Preston and other circumstances connected with it made me suspicious, and causes me to believe she is intended for the South."[4]

Dudley had reason to be suspicious: The local Italian consul stated that he did not believe his government was building any warships in England. Then Dudley heard a rumor that the Oreto had loaded two gun carriages, and notified Adams without taking time to confirm it. Adams sent a protest to British Foreign Secretary Lord John Russell, demanding that the vessel be inspected for warlike intent. As the document circulated through channels, Dudley's agents made a more incriminating discovery: Fawcett, Preston and Company had been paid by Fraser, Trenholm and Company, the Confederacy's recognized bankers. He hurried this new information to Adams and waited for the British to take action.[5]

Lord Russell agreed to investigate the matter. Miller and Sons admitted that the Oreto was built like a gunboat, but confirmed that the owner was Thomas Brothers of Palermo, whom they believed intended to sell the Oreto to the Italian Government. British customs officials, who examined the ship periodically, confirmed that the vessel looked like a gunboat, but that all evidence pointed to Italian ownership. Russell advised Adams that since the ship had neither guns, gun carriages, nor ammunition on board, she had broken no law and could not be seized regardless of ownership.

Dismayed by the British ruling, Dudley's agents continued to search for any evidence that could compel the British to impound the ship. Now convinced that the Oreto would leave port unarmed and receive her armament at some remote rendezvous outside British territorial waters, Dudley launched a search for a companion vessel or tender, which led to the discovery that arms were being loaded on the Bermuda. Jumping to the conclusion that this was the Oreto's companion vessel, he sounded the alarm; Adams notified the United States Navy to shadow the Bermuda and prevent her from arming the Oreto. Once again, Dudley had come close, but not close enough: The arms for the *Oreto* were shipped to Nassau on the *Bahama*, not the *Bermuda*.

On March 22, 1862 the *Oreto* slipped her cables and headed for sea under the command of James A. Duguid, an English captain. For the benefit of Dudley's agents, Bulloch invited a number of ladies on board, conveying the impression that the ship was enjoying another trial run. Just before leaving the harbor, he hustled the visitors ashore in small boats, leaving aboard only one passenger, Mr. John Low, whose instructions came directly from Bulloch, and who was the only person aboard beside the officers who knew that the ship's destination was not Palermo, but Nassau.

During the voyage, Low's principal mission was to befriend the crew, apply soft persuasion, plead the Southern cause, and recruit seamen to serve on the cruiser when she changed colors.[6] Raised by relatives in Aberdeen and Liverpool, Low went to sea at the age of 16. Four years later, he settled in Savannah, Georgia, establishing himself as a bright young ship chandler on West Broad Street. His uncle, Andrew Low, had preceded him to Savannah and become quite wealthy through a combination of businesses—Andrew Low and Company, affiliated with two Liverpool trading firms and a London-based insurance company. Through his uncle, John Low met Bulloch, a friend of the family, and a warm friendship developed despite a 12-year difference in age. When Georgia seceded, Low joined the militia as a private, and was in the process of joining the Army of Northern Virginia when the long arm of Bulloch snatched him from Lee's army and brought him to Great Britain as a master in the Confederate States Navy.[7]

During her 37-day voyage to Nassau, made mostly under sail to save coal, the *Oreto* performed up to expectations. On May 1, three days after arriving in port, Low wrote Bulloch: "I took particular notice as regards the *Oreto*'s speed under steam and canvas, and am happy to report most favourably of her in all respects. . . . I now give you what I have seen her do during the passage: under steam, with smooth water, 10½ knots, and under canvas alone . . . 13½ good. As regards her stability, I do not think there is a stronger vessel of her class afloat; when pitching, you could not see her work in the least, not so much to crack the pitch in the waterway, where I believe a vessel is as likely to show weakness as anywhere else. . . ."[8]

Low carried orders from Bulloch to turn over command of the *Oreto* to Lt. John Newland Maffitt, who was not at Nassau but expected within the week.[9] Maffitt was somewhere on the Confederate blockade runner *Gordon*, a profession at which he excelled, but one that defied schedules. Low checked into the Royal Victoria Hotel to wait, leaving instructions for Captain Duguid to move the ship nine miles down the harbor where it would be out of sight of British customs authorities. By the time Maffitt arrived with a load of Confederate cotton on May 4, Low was snarled in problems initiated by Samuel Whiting, the United States consul at Nassau, who had at first mistaken the *Oreto* for another blockade runner.

Union agents put constant pressure on British officials to search the ship. On May 1 a boarding party from the HMS *Greyhound*, led by Captain Henry D. Hinckley, inspected the *Oreto*. Hinckley found a vessel eminently suited for warlike purposes, but without arms or ammunition, and he released the ship. Having survived the search, Low settled back to wait for Maffitt, but more problems quickly developed: a task force of 12 Union warships had just entered the harbor, led by the heavy cruiser USS *Cuyler*. To the officers of the speedy *Cuyler*, there was no disguising the *Oreto*'s intended purpose.[10]

On May 3 came more unexpected trouble: 20-odd members of the crew, led by Boatswain Edward Jones, succumbed to a generous bribe from Consul Whiting and jumped ship, reporting to Captain Henry McKillop of the HMS *Bulldog* that the *Oreto* was to become a Confederate warship and was in Nassau to receive arms, and that Captain Duguid was an Englishman employed by the South to conceal the ship's intended purpose.

To complicate matters further, the *Bahama* steamed into Nassau with her cargo of arms intended for the cruiser. Among her passengers were several Confederate seamen from the *Sumter*, including Lt. John M. Stribling and Lt. Beckett K. Howell. Fearing that the cargo would become public information, Low had her captain transfer it to storage in a dock-side bonded warehouse.[11]

When Maffitt arrived on May 4, he met privately with Low and calmly digested the lengthy list of problems. Maffitt enjoyed adventure. As a blockade runner, he had been among the best. Realizing that Low had run out of ideas, he decided to take command of the vessel, writing in his journal that night: "As the *Oreto* is in an equivocal position, with no regular Confederate States officer to look out for her interest, I shall give up the *Gordon* and privately assume the entire control, and hasten to sea before the Government authorities become exercised as to her character and ultimate occupation."[12] The following morning he assumed command of the cruiser in the name of the Confederate States Navy, but remained in the background and issued orders through Low until a crew could be recruited.

The Union Navy kept the *Oreto* under constant surveillance. Each day the *Cuyler* crept closer, her officers training glasses upon the helpless ship for any sign of change. Commander McKillop of the HMS *Bulldog* watched both ships. Gradually convincing himself that the *Oreto* was receiving arms in some nefarious manner, McKillop took sudden unilateral action and seized the ship for violating the Foreign Enlistment Act.

Governor Charles J. Bayley promptly disagreed: the ship was under British registry, carried the British flag, and violated no British law. He released the *Oreto* and instructed McKillop not to seize the ship again unless he actually observed munitions being taken on board. Privately, Bayley agreed with McKillop's suspicions and increased the number of customs officials assigned to inspect all supplies loaded on the *Oreto*.[13]

Desperate for a crew, Maffitt wrote to Mallory, requesting that seamen be raised in the South and shipped to Nassau on blockade runners. While waiting for an answer, Commander Hinckley of the HMS *Greyhound*, McKillop's senior officer, returned to Nassau and resumed command of the British squadron.

On June 5, after a few days of close surveillance, he spotted the *Oreto* unloading shells from a boat. According to a statement made by Thomas Robertson of the *Oreto*'s crew, Captain Duguid was physically in the process of boarding shells when he sighted the British vessel approaching and issued sharp orders to get the shells off the ship.

Hinckley seized the ship, placed a prize crew on board, and turned the *Oreto* over to the British Admiralty Court for adjudication. Strangely enough, the second seizure outraged Governor Bayley, who felt it infringed upon the rights of local civil authorities. Hinckley threatened to move the ship to another British port where proper action could be expected—a threat that Bayley interpreted as a personal insult. With the help of the attorney general, he pressured Hinckley into releasing the vessel.[14]

While the governor exchanged blows with Her Majesty's Navy, the *Melita* arrived in Nassau laden with supplies for the Confederate Ordnance Bureau and carrying Raphael Semmes, Lt. John M. Kell, and Surgeon Francis L. Galt, late of the notorious *Sumter*. Although Semmes found a letter waiting from Secretary Mallory ordering him back to England to command the *Alabama*, rumor placed Semmes in charge of the *Oreto*—a timely diversion for Maffitt. Unfortunately this made little difference: Maffit still had no crew.[15]

Meanwhile Consul Whiting demanded to know how Governor Bayley could unilaterally force the *Oreto*'s release in the face of Hinckley's evidence. Certain that the attorney general would rule in favor of the vessel's release and end the issue, Bayley agreed to bring the case to trial. For the third time he ordered the *Oreto* seized for violating the Foreign Enlistment Act, and asked that the trial be conducted as soon as possible. Whiting, believing this was the end of the alleged Confederate warship, wrote a note to Hinckley thanking him for his part in forcing litigation.

Bayley, already annoyed at Hinckley, became livid when the U.S. consul praised Hinckley for attempting to circumvent the governor's authority, and angrily demanded that the United States immediately recall Whiting for insulting and attempting to manipulate civilian authority.[16] Although Seward did not recall Whiting, it is likely that the incident worked against the interests of the United States.

When the trial began, Whiting believed the evidence against the *Oreto* was overwhelming and irrefutable. He became further encouraged when he learned that Semmes had returned to England, interpreting this as an indication that the Confederates had abandoned hope. Even John Low had arranged passage back to Liverpool, leaving only Captain Duguid, his officers, and a few crew members to represent the defense. Whiting never suspected Maffitt, who was known only as the captain of a blockade runner. Throughout the trial, Maffitt spent personal funds for bribes to police, fees for messengers, and monetary inducements for witnesses. With both patience and tact, he persuaded several of Naṣsau's leading merchants to testify that the *Oreto* seemed to be a commercial vessel. Combined with Duguid's innocuous testimony, the court decided that there was nothing irregular about the ship.

Although Hinckley's statement, and those of some crew members, claimed that the vessel contained shot lockers, magazines, and no cargo space, the court ruled that while the vessel may have been designed like a warship, under the terms of the Foreign Enlistment Act it was not a warship because it carried no guns. On August 7 the ship was ordered released.[17]

Whiting was horrified by the decision, and wrote Seward that the judge had accepted the testimony of hired sailors while choosing to ignore that of Commander Hinckley, a British naval officer, that the log book of the *Oreto* had been purposely overlooked by the court, and that no inquiries had been made into the ship's ultimate destination or use. Whiting suspected that the trial had been conducted exclusively by Confederate sympathizers whose intentions from the beginning were to arrange for the vessel's release. Whiting exercised his only remaining alternative and instructed the United States Navy to intercept the *Oreto* the instant it left port.[18]

Several Union warships patrolled the area and more were expected, and Maffitt wasted no time getting the *Oreto* out of Nassau. For crew, Maffitt had young J. Laurens Read, his own stepson, seven officers who had been staying on shore, and only 14 deckhands.[19] Several hours earlier the *Prince Albert* had loaded the guns from the bonded warehouse and started on its way to an uninhabited nearby island. On August 8 the undermanned *Oreto* headed for sea.

Alerted by Whiting, the USS *Cuyler* detected the *Oreto*'s movement and started off in pursuit. Maffitt, recognizing at once that he was being chased, took advantage of neutral water and brought his ship to anchor beside the HMS *Petrel*. After the *Cuyler* circled the *Oreto* several times, Captain Watson of the *Petrel* ordered the Union ship to return to the harbor or leave British territorial waters. The *Cuyler* put to sea, her captain believing that he could capture the Confederate vessel on her way out.[20]

Maffitt had skirted too many blockades to feel threatened by the *Cuyler*. After waiting for the cruiser to get well to sea, he set a course for Charleston, knowing that his movements would be observed. When he saw that the *Cuyler* had taken the same heading, he slipped into the shadow of Hog Island, came to anchor, and watched the Union warship disappear over the horizon.

Maffitt changed course to the south, and finding the *Prince Albert* in its designated location, took it in tow until the following day, when both ships dropped anchor off Green Cay, a small uninhabited island 60 miles south of Nassau. Although the officers and crew of the *Oreto* had escaped, their real ordeal had just begun. Maffitt wrote in his journal: "Now commenced one of the most physically exhausting jobs ever undertaken by naval officers. All hands undressed to the buff, and with the few men we had commenced taking in . . . guns, powder, circles, shell and shot, etc. An August sun in the tropics is no small matter to work in. On the 15th, C. Worrell, wardroom steward, died and we buried him on Green Cay. Several cases of fever appear among the crew. At first I thought it but ordinary cases, originating from hard work and exposure to the sun, but in twenty hours the unpalatable fact was impressed upon me that yellow fever was added to our annoyances. Having no physician on board, that duty devolved upon me, and nearly my whole time, day and night, was devoted to the sick. On the 16th of August all the armament and stores were on board. . . ."[21]

In a simple ceremony on August 17, 1862, Maffitt commissioned the CSS *Florida*. As the flag of a new nation ascended to the peak, her weary crew cheered. For some, it would be their last cheer. Yellow fever spread slowly through the crew, forcing Maffitt to seek refuge in Cuba. A few officers, still on their feet, made a discouraging discovery: After a thorough search of supplies transferred from the *Prince Albert*, no beds, quoins, sights, rammers, or sponges could be found for the guns. The worst was still ahead, but in Maffitt there was no quit.

"I Haven't Time to Die"

AT 1:20 A.M. on August 19 the *Florida* entered the harbor of Cardenas, Cuba, and anchored, her crew decimated by yellow fever. Maffitt communicated his helpless condition to the authorities ashore and received permission from the governor-general to remain as long as necessary. If the *Florida* were to leave port, she would need to add crew, and Maffitt sent Lt. John M. Stribling and Paymaster's Clerk A. Vesterling to Havana to recruit more men and locate medical assistance.

As Yellow Jack continued to take possession of the vessel, Maffitt turned the quarterdeck into a hospital, personally looking after the sick and attending to their comfort.[1] On the afternoon of August 22, while administering medicine, he experienced a sudden chill, followed by pain in the back and loins, dimness of vision, and nausea. Recording in his journal, "The painful conviction was forced upon me that I was boarded by this horrible tropical epidemic," he issued directions for the vessel's care to Acting Master Wyman and Midshipman Bryan, telling them his health was broken to the point that he doubted he could survive. After requesting a physician, he took a warm mustard bath and slipped into his bunk and shortly afterwards into unconsciousness. For seven days he fought death while others around him died.

On August 29 he opened his eyes to three dim figures talking in soft tones in the shadows of his sunlit cabin. The trio included Dr. R. H. Barrett of Georgia and a physician from the Spanish gunboat *Guadalquivir*. Hearing Barrett predict that he doubted the captain could survive beyond noon, Maffitt spoke for the first time in a week, "You're a liar, sir. I have too much to do. I haven't time to die."[2]

During his illness, six crew members had died, including his much-loved stepson, Laurens Read. Only four crewmen could perform their duties. Twelve new seamen recruited at Cardenas were a welcome addition, and Dr. Barrett resigned his post with the government hospital in Havana and signed on the *Florida* as acting assistant surgeon, but the ship was still dangerously undermanned.[3]

On August 30 the governor-general advised Maffitt that the safety of his ship was in jeopardy if he remained at Cardenas. The small city had no protective forts, and already Union warships were patrolling offshore, awaiting the *Florida*'s departure. Shorthanded and in frail health, Maffitt faced the difficult task of sailing.

The following evening, Union commanders mistook a Spanish mail steamer bound for Havana as the *Florida* and sped off in pursuit. Fortunately, several long shots missed the fleeing Spanish steamer, which finally gained refuge at Matanzas. With the Union Navy chasing the wrong vessel, Maffitt seized the opportunity to leave and sailed out of Cardenas at 9:30 p.m., running unmolested along the coast and entering Havana late the following morning.

Semmes' old nemesis, Consul Richard W. Shufeldt, learning of the *Florida*'s arrival, dispatched a hurried message to the bewildered Union squadron,[4] which arrived at Havana the following morning, resumed the blockade, and waited for the unarmed rebel cruiser to emerge.

Maffitt hoped to recruit a crew and purchase the missing parts for his guns in Havana, but yellow fever had driven seamen from the city, and Spanish authorities prevented the Confederate officers from buying the missing hardware. Despite his wretched health, Maffitt concluded that no purpose could be served by remaining at Havana, but he did not know where to go.

A Southerner there suggested the ship be taken to Mobile and offered to serve as pilot, claiming that only a single man-of-war guarded the entrance to Mobile harbor. Maffitt liked the idea. He knew the bars, and if successful, the *Florida* could be properly officered, manned, and equipped. If he remained at Havana, the ship could be doomed to internment or forced to leave the protection of the harbor as soon as the fever subsided. Still unable to walk, Maffitt asked to be carried on deck and seated in a chair. He would sail that night.

The attempt to escape would be risky. Unwilling to risk the chance that his ship might fall into enemy hands and be used against the South, Maffitt ordered Lt. Stribling to set a fuse to the magazine long enough to give every man aboard sufficient time to abandon ship if capture became imminent.

Under a clear and moonless night, the *Florida* slipped her cable and steered quietly past Morro Castle, the old Spanish fort that guarded the harbor's entrance. The dark shapes of Union warships could be seen at their stations, but no sound pierced the night. Running close to shore, Maffitt hid his ship in the land's shadowy backdrop—the tactics of an old blockade runner. In an hour, he was at sea, on course for Mobile.[5]

Back in Washington, Secretary Welles greeted the news of the *Florida*'s third escape with outright annoyance. The Northern press gave him no rest—it was the little *Sumter* giving the *Brooklyn* the slip off the Pass L'Outre all over again. What annoyed Welles most was that not one of his captains became aware of the *Florida*'s escape until the following morning. Later, in a court of inquiry, Welles learned only that the Confederate ship had simply vanished in the night.[6]

At 3 p.m. on September 4, Maffitt sighted Fort Morgan at the entrance to Mobile Bay—and two Union gunboats. Lt. Stribling advised Maffitt to wait until dark; it would be suicide to run their unarmed vessel through all that firepower.

Maffitt disagreed. The lighthouse and channel markers had been removed. With the *Florida*'s deep draft, it would be impossible to get the ship safely through the main shipping channel at night. The dash had to be done in daylight.

When Maffitt had sighted the six-gun USS *Winona* and the 10-gun USS *Oneida*, her 11-inch guns capable of smashing the smaller *Florida* with a few well-placed shots, he did not see the two-gun schooner *Rachel Seaman*. A fourth gunboat, the six-gun USS *Cayuga*, lay out of sight off the western channel. As he approached and spotted the other vessels, Maffitt called for full steam, giving no thought to retreat.

Commanding the Union squadron was George H. Preble, Maffitt's old shipmate. The two had formed a close friendship while serving together as midshipmen on the old *Constitution*. Little did Maffitt realize the blow he was about to deliver to his old friend's career.[7]

Two forts guarded the entrance to Mobile Bay: the huge brickwork Fort Morgan, with its 700 man garrison, and Fort Gaines, three miles to the west across the channel. Inside the bay, watching the inlets from Mississippi Sound, stood Fort Powell, and earthworks still under construction. The trio of forts kept Union warships at a distance and provided cover for inbound blockade runners—a procedure with which Maffitt was completely familiar.

When his lookouts sighted the *Florida*, Commander Preble was in his cabin on the *Oneida* penning a weekly report to Flag Officer David G. Farragut at Pensacola. At first, the deck officer mistook the *Florida* for the USS *Susquehanna*, but as she drew closer, the black smoke pouring from her funnels indicated a full press of steam, and Preble went on deck to see for himself. As she drew nearer, Preble made out the English ensign and pennant, and the cut of the ship resembled an English gunboat, but he sensed something unusual about the boldness of the stranger's approach.

Preble hesitated. The *Trent* Affair still smoldered as a national embarrassment; another incident with the British could bring on a war that Preble wanted no credit for starting. It was not unusual for an English warship to steam along the coast to confirm the presence and effectiveness of the blockade. Sometimes they checked into a Confederate port after obtaining permission from the blockading officer. Preble waited, expecting the oncoming steamer to sheer off and state her business. The *Oneida* held her fire, but Preble ordered the ship maneuvered into the intruder's path.[8]

Still feeble and unable to walk the deck, Maffitt asked Stribling to find a piece of rope and tie him to the quarter rail. He insisted on directing the steerage of the ship and placed Quartermaster J. W. Billups and Boatswain Sharkey at the wheel—two men he trusted to follow his orders until the *Florida* was shot to pieces or sunk. Steaming along at 14 knots under false colors—a strategy as old as naval warfare—the unarmed *Florida* closed rapidly with the *Oneida*.

With the *Florida* within a mile of the *Oneida* and directly on a collision course, Preble made a costly mistake: He reversed his engines to avoid being rammed by what he still believed to be a reckless British ship. Maffitt held his course, coming within 80 yards of the *Oneida* before Preble could maneuver into position to fire a warning shot across her bow. While this drama unfolded, the *Winona* and *Rachel Seaman* loitered passively to port, fully expecting Preble to stop the arrogant "Englishman."[9]

When the two vessels came abeam, Preble fired another warning shot, followed by a full broadside at point-blank range—a stone could have been thrown from one deck to the other. The shot tore through her upper hamper, smashing the boats, sweeping away rigging, and ripping up woodwork, but it was too high to cause serious damage. The *Florida* sped by, shaken but not badly hurt. Maffitt recorded: "Had their guns been depressed, the career of the *Florida* would have ended then and there."[10]

If Preble still harbored doubts of the strange steamer's identity, they ended when Maffitt ordered Stribling to haul down the English colors and raise the Stars and Bars. Preble reloaded and ordered pursuit, determined to recover from his blunder.

The *Oneida*'s broadside had awakened the idle *Winona*, off the port beam, and the *Rachel Seaman*, off the port bow, and shot and shell soon began splashing repeatedly all around the *Florida*. One 11-inch shell crashed through the *Florida*'s starboard hull nine inches above the waterline, decapitating Fireman John Duncan, wounding nine others, and grazing the port boiler before ripping through the port side and exploding harmlessly over the water. Had the fuse been set one second sooner, it would have destroyed the ship. A smaller shell from the *Winona* tore up the pantry, and another exploded near the port gangway. At one point, the ships were so close to each other that marines on the *Oneida* peppered the *Florida* with musket fire.[11]

Unable to fight back, the *Florida* used her only weapon—speed. Maffitt attempted to hoist his sails to wring out an extra knot, but Preble countered by firing shrapnel shells into the rigging. With only a small amount of canvas set, Maffitt sent the crew below, keeping on deck only the officers, himself, and the two men at the wheel. The ship continued to take a beating. Maffitt later wrote, "The loud explosions, roar of shot and shell, crashing spars and rigging, mingled with the moans of our sick and wounded, only increased our determination to enter our destined harbor."[12]

An officer of the *Oneida* later remembered a sole figure on the *Florida*'s quarterdeck, sometimes standing, sometime sitting, seemingly indifferent to the hail of destruction exploding around him. This officer later stated, "Those who longed for his discomfiture could not but admire the steady bearing of the brave man who sat alone on the deck."

As the *Florida* pulled away, Preble called furiously for every bit of additional speed, ordering rosin and other high-temperature combustibles fed to the furnace. He worked the gun crews, adjusting their elevation and exhorting them to fire faster. As the *Florida* continued to maneuver through the hail of fire, Preble realized that she had gradually forced his squadron into a single line, nullifying the *Winona*'s fire and forcing the *Oneida* to veer out of line to bring her guns to bear. With each attempt at a broadside, the *Florida* pulled farther away. By dusk the chase had ended; the *Florida* reached the protection of Fort Morgan's guns. Although the ship had sustained damage and nine men were wounded, only one man had been killed.

It had been a lucky day for Maffitt, but not for Commander Preble. His report to Rear Admiral Farragut was apologetic and failed to identify the mysterious man-of-war. He explained to Farragut that: "observing that she was burning black smoke, I immediately got the *Oneida* underway and stood toward her, signalling to the *Winona* to chase at discretion. . . . When abeam of him, about 100 yards distant, I hailed him, but receiving no answer I fired a shot across his bows. He ranged ahead without stopping, but still thinking he was an English man-of-war, I fired two more shots across his bows, and then directed a shot at him, which unfortunately went over between his fore and main masts. . . . We continued firing at him, assisted by the *Winona* and one of the mortar schooners, but he made sail, and by his superior speed and unparalleled audacity managed to escape. . . ."[13]

A day later, Farragut penned a brief note of censure, erroneously referring to the unidentified gunboat as the No. 290 [CSS *Alabama*], which had been commissioned 3,000 miles away in the Azores. Preble responded with a long letter of explanation, hoping to salvage his injured reputation.[14]

Secretary Welles fumed while the press howled for Preble's head. Bulloch had made fools of American diplomats in England, first with the *Oreto* and then with the *Alabama*. Now the *Florida* [Oreto] had run the blockade in broad daylight and entered Mobile Bay without so much as firing a shot. Welles complained to his diary: "Preble, by sheer pusillanimous neglect, feebleness and indecision, let the pirate steamer *Oreto* run the blockade. She came right up and passed him flying English colors. Instead of checking her advance or sinking her, he fired all around, made a noise, and is said to have hurt none of her English crew. There must be a stop put to the timid, hesitating and, I fear, sometimes traitorous course of some of our officers. Tenderness, remonstrance, reproof do no good. Preble is not a traitor, but loyal. I am sorry for Preble, but shall be more sorry for my country if it is not done. Its effect upon the navy will be more salutary that were he and fifty like him to fall in battle."[15]

The final blow arrived on September 20, when Welles' letter reached Preble: "Upon submitting your letter to the president, I received from him prompt directions to announce to you your dismissal from the service. You will from this date cease to be regarded as an officer of the Navy of the United States:"[16] Five months later, Lincoln rescinded the directive and restored him to the rank of commander, but it was not until 1872, when Maffitt appeared before a Court of Inquiry at Washington, that Preble attained full exoneration.[17]

After being battered and chased for nearly an hour, Maffitt loosened the rope holding him to the quarter rail, rose unsteadily to his feet, and praised Billups and Sharkey for their steadiness when running the Union gauntlet. Steering at half speed up the channel, Maffitt passed Fort Morgan, a chorus of cheers echoing across the inlet and a 21-gun salute booming from the parapet. Her hull and upper works scarred in more than 1,400 places, the *Florida* anchored off Melrose as twilight settled over the bay.

As word spread across the South of the cruiser's dash into Mobile and the difficulties of her escape, praise came in torrents. Even Union Admiral David Dixon Porter, in his *Naval History*, expressed a touch of open admiration: "During the whole war there was not a more exciting adventure than this escape of the *Florida* into Mobile Bay. The gallant manner in which it was conducted excited a great admiration even among the men who were responsible for permitting it. We do not suppose there was ever a case where a man, under all the attending circumstances, displayed more energy or more bravery."[18]

Maffit had run the gauntlet, but he still had serious problems. Several cases of yellow fever forced the ship into quarantine; Lt. Stribling fell ill shortly after entering the harbor. On September 9 Maffitt noted in his journal, "Stribling very ill; will not allow anyone to administer his medicine but me, and I am hardly able to stand . . . case assuming a doubtful phase." The young officer died September 12—a great personal loss to Maffitt. Stribling was buried the following day at Melrose.[19]

During the siege of illness, the only person permitted to join the crew was Assistant Surgeon Frederic Garretson, who replaced the ailing Dr. Barrett. Garretson, a former United States naval officer who had changed his name from Van Biber when entering the Confederate service to protect his family living in Union-controlled Maryland, nursed the crew back to health. The yellow flag of quarantine finally came down on September 30.

On October 3 repairs began, but because of the ship's deep draft and the shallow channel to Mobile, workmen had to be transported 28 miles by water. Weeks passed with little progress. There was a shortage of skilled workmen, and many refused to go on board until a killing frost annihilated any remaining vestiges of the dreaded disease. Ordnance supplies needed to activate the guns took more than three months to arrive. Machinery and equipment that could not be repaired on board had to be disassembled and hauled to Mobile by boat. To make matters worse, rough weather and winter gales in the open bay frequently slowed work, especially on the rigging.[20]

The Confederacy did enjoy one small benefit from the *Florida*'s extended stay at Mobile: Her presence compelled the Union to station a large number of ships to block her escape, thereby depleting resources for duty at other ports.

Also during the *Florida*'s four-month stay, Maffitt collected a crew. He selected officers with care, discarding any undesirables sent to him by the Navy Department. Lt. Dulany A. Forrest reported aboard on October 9 as executive officer to replace Stribling. Three weeks later, Lt. Samuel W. Averett arrived, a man whom Maffitt regarded as "an officer of high standing for this period of service; his frank, manly manner pleases me much." By then, Maffitt considered Forrest a "most unfortunate selection, but 'tis not his fault that heaven has not formed him with brains." He privately arranged a transfer for Forrest and appointed

Averett executive officer.[21] The housecleaning included two officers who had come on board at Nassau: Acting Master Otey Bradford had developed into a malcontent short on ability; his job went to Richard B. Floyd of Georgia. Maffitt dubbed Paymaster Clerk A. Vesterling a "pest" and a "jackass," and filled the post with W. H. Wilson from the District of Columbia.[22]

The officer's roster brightened on October 13 with the arrival of Lt. James L. Hoole, who had seen action at Roanoke Island and still carried a nasty head wound. On November 4, Lt. Charles W. Read reported, fresh from action on the Mississippi. Maffitt, aware of the young man's bravery and coolness at the battle of New Orleans, had applied for him personally. Although somewhat indolent in the absence of excitement, Read thirsted for adventure—a quality ideal for duty aboard the *Florida*. By January the *Florida*'s roster had swollen to 19 officers and 116 men, although many had little sea experience. A few men had come from the Old Navy or the merchant service, but the rest were raw recruits with one common characteristic—they were Confederates, an advantage not enjoyed by commanders of the *Alabama, Georgia,* and *Shenandoah*.

The long delay in sailing made the crew restless, although it gave the officers time to train unskilled men for battle at sea. Discontent aboard ship combined with misguided speculation in Richmond misled Mallory, who was losing patience with the delays, into thinking that his commander preferred the safety of Mobile to the dangers at sea. He decided to make a change, and on December 30 ordered Lt. Joseph N. Barney to Mobile to take command of the *Florida*.

Maffitt, not known for his complacency, complained to Franklin Buchanan, the hero of the CSS *Virginia* (Merrimack) and the Confederacy's first admiral, who recognized the injustice of the situation and was irritated that Mallory had taken this action without first conferring with him. Buchanan dispatched a letter to Mallory accusing the secretary of undermining his authority and praising Maffitt's conduct and effort. Buchanan appealed to President Davis, who happened to be in Mobile at the time. Agreeing with Buchanan, Davis telegraphed Mallory from Mobile, and Maffitt retrieved his lost command.[23]

During his tenure in the United States Navy, Maffitt had never held a high opinion of Mallory—and this did not escape the naval secretary's notice. As chairman of the Naval Affairs Committee, Mallory had created the unpopular Naval Retiring Board, forcing the retirement of many competent officers, including Maffitt. Although later reinstated, Maffitt never had much confidence in Mallory's aptitude as an administrator. Maffitt said little publicly on the issue, but he confided to his journal that, "Mr. Mallory, with characteristic littleness of mind,

has permitted surreptitious naval gossip to operate, with the least mag-
nanimity of soul or manliness of purpose." As time passed, Maffitt
continued to blame him for failing to understand the needs of the
Confederacy.[24]

On January 11 the *Florida* steamed down Mobile Bay and anchored
off Fort Morgan. Repaired and armed with two new rifled pivot guns
firing 110-pound shells; painted like a blockade runner with a mixture
of whitewash and lampblack to make her fade into the night, the Confederacy's newest cruiser was ready for sea. Maffitt went ashore and
climbed the parapet at Fort Morgan to observe and record the position
of Union warships off the channel. In September there had been three.
Now he counted 13, including his old friend the *Oneida*, joined now by
the speedy 10-gun *R. R. Cuyler* and the huge 15-gun flagship *Susquehanna*. Maffitt did not like the odds. Even if he made it to sea, the *Cuyler* could match or exceed his speed.

To keep the restless crew occupied while waiting for a dark, dreary
night to make his escape, Maffitt maneuvered the ship around the Bay.
Twice she grounded, and the men, already grumbling from the delays,
had to unload guns and coal to lighten the ship enough for two tugs to
pull her free. The misfortune almost cost Maffitt the perfect night to
escape.[25]

Mallory's instructions were a little vague and left most of the
cruise to the captain's discretion, although he did suggest that Maffit
try to capture one or two of the fast steamers that regularly transported
California gold to the federal treasury. Uncertain how long the $50,000
in the ship's strong-box would last, Maffitt agreed that a little cache of
extra gold might prove useful. Mallory also suggested that Maffitt destroy his prizes and not attempt to bring them through the blockade to
a Confederate port. American merchant ships had started to make extensive use of British registry to protect their vessels and cargo, and
since Maffitt would be dependent upon foreign ports for supplies, Mallory admonished him not to offend neutrality. In concluding his instructions, he asked Maffitt to "obtain at Mobile two uniform copies of
any small English lexicon or dictionary, one to be retained by you and
the other to be sent to the Department. Whenever in your letters or
dispatches a word is used which may betray what you may desire to
conceal, instead of using that word write the numbers, in figures
within brackets, of the page where it is to be found, and also the number of the word on the page, counting from the top."[26] This simple cod-
ing system had been used by Semmes.

On the evening of January 15 a violent norther erupted, blowing
gale-force winds offshore. Heavy rain mixed with flying spray made vis-

ibility so limited that the pilot could not see to navigate. Maffitt considered the weather perfect for slipping by Union sentinels and kept the crew in readiness. At 2 a.m. the rain subsided, leaving a leaden mist hanging over the water. With the steam throttle cracked open, the *Florida* glided over the chop, gradually gaining momentum as she passed Fort Morgan and headed for the bar.

Three Union warships stood just offshore, anchored in the channel. The *Florida* was bearing directly toward one of the blockaders when the lookout spotted it dead ahead. Maffitt sidestepped the first gunboat and passed undetected. On he went, maneuvering through the squadron, which had apparently decided that the cold, gusty night was too unpleasant for even the *Florida* to sneak out. Directly ahead the lookout reported two more vessels, the *Susquehanna* and the *Cuyler*, spaced about 300 feet apart. Maffitt crept by, but at the last moment, a bright flash of coal dust sent sparks spewing from the funnels. Instantly Coston lights blazed, searching the darkness for the source of the sparks. Signal lights transmitted the *Florida's* position and called the squadron to quarters. Maffitt ordered full steam and all sails set to ride before the gale, and the cruiser sped away. The chase was on.[27]

The fastest gunboat in the Union squadron, the *Cuyler*, lost important time getting underway. Her captain, Commander George F. Emmons, who had gone to bed, came on deck partially dressed to assess the situation before issuing orders. The *Cuyler's* superior speed soon left the rest of the Union fleet behind. Emmons later reported, "We kept the *Oreto* continually in sight, and at daylight were out of sight of land and squadron, having the *Oreto* ahead, distant about five miles, under all sail and steam, with the wind blowing a gale from the N. W., accompanied with a heavy sea . . . Under all sail and steam that I could raise, I continued the chase all day in a combing sea that kept the decks covered with water and the propeller racing part of the time, sometimes gaining and other times losing; carried away topsail yard and had to send it down with the sail; had no substitute. . . . Resorted to every expedient to increase the speed of the vessel, which varied from 11½ to 12½ [knots], and under ordinary circumstances I think would have been sufficient to have overhauled the enemy in a calm . . . From fancying myself near promotion in the morning, I gradually dwindled to a court of inquiry at dark, when I lost sight of the enemy."[28]

Maffitt expected a fast ship to be hard on his heels, but he was startled when a large warship, which he believed to be the USS *Brooklyn*, suddenly appeared ahead. Having few choices, he stayed on course and bluffed his way past the cruiser. "The only evidence she gave of seeing us," wrote Maffitt, "was by showing a light over the starboard gangway, and continued gracefully on . . . taking us for one of their own gunboats."

Far astern, a fleck of sail slowly grew larger as the day lengthened into afternoon. Suspecting it was the *Cuyler*, the ship he most feared, when darkness approached, Maffitt resorted to an old trick from his blockade-running days. He stopped the engine and furled all sails, allowing the *Florida* to drift in the trough of a rough sea, her low-lying hull riding the high swells and blending with the swirling spray. The *Cuyler* sped past and disappeared over the southern horizon, chasing an empty sea.[29]

By the following morning, Emmons was racing toward the Yucatan. Earlier, he had received information from a captured Mobile pilot that the cruiser carried 300 men and planned to meet another Confederate warship off the Mexican coast to supply her with a crew. His hunch proved to be wrong, but his prediction of a future court of inquiry proved to be accurate. When word reached Washington of the *Florida*'s escape, Congress spent a full day condemning a miserable Gideon Welles in particular and his navy in general. Welles responded by threatening to sack 11 captains, beginning with the commodore of the squadron who, like others, slept as the *Florida* stole past his ships.

An editorial in *The New York Times* accused Secretary Welles of incompetence and the navy of a lack of determination in tracking down the cruisers. It asked why George Preble had been dismissed for letting the *Florida* slip into Mobile, while no one had been disciplined for letting the raider slip out. Welles had ample reminders of these lost opportunities over the next year, as daily reports crossed his desk describing the depredations to American commerce by John Newland Maffitt and the CSS *Florida*.[30]

The Hunter Is Loose

For two days Maffitt cruised southward toward the shipping lanes off the Cuban coast, without sighting a single sail. The crew was in fine spirits, and looked forward to mixing with the merchantmen in the West Indies, but Maffitt knew that Union warships prowled the same sea lanes.

Although designed to wage war on commerce and not battle enemy warships, the *Florida*—armed with two 7-inch Blakely rifles mounted in pivot with six 32-pounders in broadside—was a match for many of the Union ships that later hunted her. At 700 tons she was slightly smaller than the CSS *Alabama*, and she was built for speed. In the escape from Mobile, a stiff tailwind had pushed her sleek clipper hull and tall bark rig to 14½ knots. The *Florida* was well suited to the destructive work of high-seas raiding, an occupation her crew of 20 officers and 116 men had yet to learn.

As she rounded the western tip of Cuba on January 19, 1863, lookouts aboard the *Florida* sighted the brig *Estelle*, a New York trader bound from Santa Cruz to Boston heavily laden with honey and molasses. This rich cargo was consigned by Venecia Rodreguez and Company to Homer and Sprague of Boston.[1]

The *Estelle*'s captain, John Brown, had seen the *Florida* coming, but with the American ensign flying from the masthead, he mistook her for a Union gunboat. When a blank charge erupted from the cruiser, Brown quickly changed his mind, brought his ship into the wind, and surrendered to a boarding party led by Lt. Hoole. The Confederates, whose lives often depended on what they could scavenge from prizes, removed the brig's sails, spare rigging, and foretopsail yard, and hurried the *Estelle*'s crew with their personal belongings back to the *Florida*.

Brown claimed that because his cargo, valued at $130,000, was owned by a neutral, his vessel could not be destroyed. Nonetheless, the raider's torchmen disappeared into the hull of his vessel. Soon strands of smoke drifted from open hatchways, building into black clouds that could be seen for 30 miles. Maffitt chose not to loiter.[2]

Determining the disposition of prizes remained in the hands of Confederate commanders, who made their decisions on the spot, often after a cursory inspection of cargo documents, manifests, and registries. No neutral ports admitted Confederate prizes, and Confederate ports were closed by the Union blockade. Burning the prize was often the only alternative. Some neutral cargoes were burned because documents were sloppy. A few cargoes were spared because documents had been cleverly forged. The Confederate commanders often made mistakes, but not with the *Estelle*: She surrendered 10 miles outside Spanish territorial waters, and Boston merchants owned the cargo.

Since leaving Mobile, the *Florida* had run hard under both steam and sail. Maffitt, noting that the boilers consumed coal at an alarming rate and that the crew desperately needed clothing, decided to put into Havana to obtain both. Late on January 20 he entered the harbor. Unaware that the rules of entering port had changed since his last visit, Maffit steamed by a Cuban guard boat signalling for the *Florida* to stop, and came to anchor near the admiralty. At dusk he went ashore to meet with the local Confederate agent, Major Charles Helm, and by midnight had made arrangements to buy supplies and fill the bunkers with Cardiff coal the following morning.

Helm was worried that Maffitt's failure to respond to the guard boat's signal could be interpreted as an insult, and Cuban officials might be unwilling to issue the required permits. Maffitt, with Helm's assistance, called upon the authorities in the morning and apologized for entering port after sundown and without obtaining a required medical inspection. The Cubans accepted Maffitt's apology and granted the necessary permits.[3]

Havana awoke to the news that the *Florida* had returned. Many Cubans had followed the ship's troubled history since the day she struggled out of the harbor flying the pestilent yellow pennant. Boatloads of people, complete with a barge carrying a band that played *Dixie* and *Bonnie Blue Flag*, greeted the ship in a grand display of pro-Confederate sentiment.[4]

U.S. Consul Robert Schufeldt did not join in celebrating the *Florida*'s return. Instead, he dispatched a message to Key West to alert any Union warships in the area, then set about to postpone the *Florida*'s departure to give the navy time to arrive. Schufeldt assailed Spanish authorities for permitting the raider to buy coal and supplies. When news of the *Estelle*'s destruction reached his office, he insisted that her cargo had been Spanish property. When an American merchant ship left port, he demanded that the *Florida* be delayed 24 hours after its departure. Spanish authorities, feeling more kinship with the South, paid little attention to the consul's protests, however, and granted all of Maffitt's requests.[5]

Knowing Havana was not a safe haven, Maffitt departed at daybreak on January 22 and sailed eastward along the Cuban coast, looking for prizes. The Portland, Maine bark *La Coquena* ignored the raider's gun and narrowly escaped capture by making a spirited dash to the safety of the three-mile limit.[6] At noon, the New York brig *Windward*, brimming with molasses loaded at Matanzas, failed to outsail the *Florida* and surrendered after a shot from the cruiser skipped across her bow. Richard Roberts, the captain, complained that Maffitt did not raise the Confederate flag until after his ship had been boarded. Before burning the vessel, Maffitt allowed the captain and his crew to gather their belongings and row to shore in the ship's boats.

With smoke still curling skyward from the smoldering *Windward*, the brig *Corris Ann*, of Machias, Maine, sailed into Maffitt's clutches, and she and her cargo of barrel staves were torched. Her captain, Frederick A. Small, stated that she was captured between Cay Piedras and Cay Mono in the one-mile-wide channel that led into Cardenas. The city's inhabitants watched the blazing wreck drift slowly ashore, preceded by the boats carrying the vanquished crew. For the second time that day, the master of a destroyed vessel accused Maffitt of raiding under British colors.[7] Maffitt ignored the accusation, giving substance to the claim that he willfully violated Great Britain's neutrality.

After a night spent under the Cardenas light making repairs, Maffitt's officers discovered that the expensive coal they had purchased in Havana burned poorly; the engineer could raise only enough steam for five knots. The officers found enough Mobile coal for three days' steaming and suggested that the Cardiff coal "be thrown overboard to make a gangway to the better coal," and that a fresh supply be purchased at "the nearest English port."[8] Maffitt sailed at dawn on January 22 in search of coal.

During the previous two weeks, the *Florida* and the *Alabama* had prowled the same area, at one time passing within 100 miles, unaware of the other's presence. Raphael Semmes, commanding the CSS *Alabama*, had just sunk the USS *Hatteras* in a short engagement in the Gulf of Mexico; the *Florida* had burned three prizes.

Back in Washington, Naval Secretary Welles received all the bad news at once. Worried that the two cruisers might join forces for a strike at some vulnerable point along the New England coast, he tried to deploy his navy to prevent it — a concern perhaps justified, but in the event unnecessary. Maffitt sailed from Cardenas just in time to elude

Rear Admiral Charles Wilkes, who had left Havana on the USS *Wachusett* in hot pursuit. Wilkes issued search-and-destroy orders to the *Santiago de Cuba, San Jacinto,* and *Sonoma,* and then followed with his flagship,[9] but both Maffitt and Semmes seemed to vanish. Once again, the Union Navy reacted to the latest information and converged on the place the Confederate commanders had just left.

Four days after leaving Cardenas, Maffitt entered Nassau—for the second time in a week blundering into a foreign port without asking permission. Informed of his mistake, he called upon Nassau's governor, Charles J. Bayley, to apologize for his oversight, and returned to the *Florida* with a 24-hour permit to coal. While British naval officers and old friends visited the ship, 26 crewmen slipped ashore and deserted. Maffitt was philosophical, referring to the deserters as "our hard cases." Recruiting in a British port violated the Foreign Enlistment Act; nevertheless, six men joined the crew before the *Florida* sailed.[10]

Although Consul Samuel Whiting tried to prevent the raider from coaling, the *Florida* filled her bunkers by 6 a.m. on January 27, and four hours later steamed down the channel. Maffitt anchored outside the harbor and waited for darkness, knowing that Whiting would not fail to observe his movements.

Secretary Welles wanted results. For several days, Rear Admiral Wilkes had been sending urgent directives to the scattered components of his West India Squadron. Wilkes ordered Commander Thomas H. Stevens of the USS *Sonoma* to proceed to Cardenas, and after checking there, to steam up "through the tongue of the ocean, ascertain if the *Oreto* has entered, or has been heard of at Nassau. . . ." On the last leg of his mission, Stevens stumbled upon "a strange sail hoisting English colors." Upon approaching, he suspected that the vessel was the *Florida* and ordered full steam and all sail set, anticipating a long stern chase.[11]

On February 1 Maffitt passed through the Queen's Channel and sighted an enemy steamer churning towards him that he believed to be the 10-gun *Santiago de Cuba.* Unwilling to risk an engagement with a warship at least his equal in firepower, he decided to run, in what became an odd chase. The Union ship gained ground, but each time it reached firing range it inexplicably fell back. In his report to Wilkes, Stevens wrote, "Three times we had the *Oreto* almost under our guns, when the blower belt parted and all that we had gained upon her was lost." For 34 hours this minuet continued over a span of 300 miles before a freshening wind finally filled the *Florida's* sails and swept her over the horizon. Maffitt learned later that his pursuer was not the *Santiago de Cuba* but the small four-gun *Sonoma.* Had the breeze been light, and had the *Sonoma* outsteamed the *Florida,* Maffitt stated that he would have engaged her. If the truth were known, both commanders were probably satisfied that the *Florida* made good her escape.[12]

Two days of hard steaming had bitten deeply into Maffitt's coal supply. Disregarding the shortage, he headed for New England but was turned back at Cape Hatteras by a powerful gale that carried away some rigging. With topside damage and water pouring into the ship through opened deck seams, Maffitt postponed his New England call and headed south.

Sailing southeasterly on February 5 through a dense fog, the lookout suddenly reported a large steamer, with clouds of thick black smoke pouring from her funnels, bearing down upon the *Florida.* As the big ship approached, Maffitt suspected that he was about to be attacked by the huge *Vanderbilt,* a speedy sidewheeler armed with 11-inch guns donated to the navy by wealthy financier Cornelius Vanderbilt. Maffitt parried by cutting his steam and lowering the twin stacks while the crew frantically tried to disguise the ship as a harmless West Indies trader. The warship slowed within hailing distance and carefully scanned the *Florida* as she wallowed in the swells, looking quite innocent. After nosing about for a few minutes, the warship opened her throttle and sped off into the night. Relieved, Maffitt noted in his journal: "To have been rammed by this immense steamer would have closed our career, and we were rejoiced to see her leave us."[13]

At the time of this incident, several Union gunboats were under orders to seek and destroy the *Florida.* One of them, perhaps the *Vanderbilt,* had missed a rare opportunity.

After repairing the ship's rigging, Maffitt resumed the hunt and initiated a six-hour stern chase of a fast clipper ship carrying clouds of canvas. The *Jacob Bell,* returning to New York from Foo Chow, China, surrendered with a cargo of 1,380 tons of choice tea, cassia, camphor, and 10,000 boxes of fire crackers. Valued at $1.5 million, the cargo was the largest captured by a Confederate cruiser during the war. Her 43 persons included two women passengers who, with their "tons of baggage," were lodged into the captain's cabin.[14]

One of the passengers, Mrs. Martha Noyes Williams, later wrote a book condemning Maffitt for her harsh treatment as a captive and accused the Confederate prize crew of plundering her personal baggage. Maffitt later wrote, "Mistaking Mrs. Williams for a lady, I gave her the entire possession of my stateroom and slept on the QR [quarter] deck between the guns." Captain Charles Frisbee, who owed Maffitt no favors for burning his ship, later wrote of Mrs. Williams: "She is an awful woman—a perfect she devil!"

Maffitt referred to Mrs. Frisbee, the other woman from the *Jacob Bell*, as "a very quiet, kind-hearted lady." The two women occupied Maffitt's cabin for five days before he was able to persuade the captain of the Dutch bark *Morning Star* to transport them and the rest of the crew of the *Jacob Bell* to St. Thomas—thereby restoring harmony and discipline to the ship.[15]

The crew spent an entire day removing provisions, baggage, and useful stores from the hold of the prize, which Maffitt claimed were worth $2,000,000 or more, and at 2 p.m. on February 13 set fire to the magnificent clipper.[16] Burning the *Jacob Bell* left a lasting impression upon young Midshipman Terry Sinclair, who wrote: "She rounded to—and as she lay thus with black hull, gilt streak, scraped and varnished masts, and snow white sails, there was a general expression of admiration coupled with regret that such a thing of beauty must be destroyed."[17]

When word of the *Jacob Bell*'s destruction reached Lt. Baldwin of the *Vanderbilt*, he raced toward Martinique, followed by Captain Nichols in the USS *Alabama*. Captain Frisbee had reported that the *Florida* was running short of coal. Since the *Florida* had last coaled in a British port 30 days ago, Baldwin assumed that Maffitt would adhere to the 90-day rule and buy his next load of coal in a French port. Once again, Maffitt played by his own rules, and on February 24 entered the British port of Bridgetown, Barbados.[18]

Inquisitive natives flocked around the cruiser, seeing for the first time a Confederate flag in their harbor. Remembering the desertions at Nassau, Maffitt withheld shore leave and kept all the officers on duty. Nonetheless, he was impressed by the fine reception at the island colony, and recalled a time in 1841 when as a young officer aboard the USS *Macedonian* he had entered this port and found it much less friendly toward the American flag.

Maffitt needed a coaling permit from Governor James Walker. Walker did not believe that the *Florida* was entitled to coal under the 90-day provision, but Maffitt convinced the governor that the ship had been injured by severe weather and, by exception, satisfied the requirement of "dire need." He neglected to inform the governor that a substantial amount of coal had been fed to the boilers during the six-hour chase of the *Jacob Bell*.[19]

The American consul at Bridgetown, Edward Throwbridge, was unaware that the *Florida* had coaled recently at Nassau. His protest to the governor argued that the 100 tons granted Maffitt far exceeded the supply needed to reach her stated destination of Charleston. Governor Walker ignored Throwbridge's complaint but detained the *Florida* for

24 hours to allow two American merchant ships to sail. Maffitt used the extra time to replenish the ship with fresh vegetables and other supplies. When Throwbridge later discovered that Maffitt had violated the 90-day coaling rule, he advised Secretary of State Seward, who then assailed the British Foreign Office through Minister Charles Francis Adams. Seward had a penchant for referring to all Confederate cruisers as pirates—a term most foreign governments considered distasteful. As a result, many of Seward's protests were politely ignored.[20]

During his two days at Bridgetown, Maffitt led an active social life, either being entertained by the governor or hosting officials aboard his ship. When the cruiser departed on the evening of February 25, she became entangled with a merchant ship, due to the inebriated condition of Maffitt and his officers. Maffitt vowed never to let it happen again.

When the *Florida* reached the open sea, 10 new recruits emerged from the hold and joined the crew. While in port, Maffitt dismissed Third Assistant Engineer W. H. Jackson for incompetence. Other engineering officers reported that Jackson, in addition to being useless, was an outright menace to the safety of the ship and had been responsible for damaging the machinery on past occasions.

Having announced at Bridgetown that he intended to cruise off Panama in search of a treasure ship, Maffitt changed course and sailed southeasterly toward the sea lanes off the great hump of Brazil. Rear Admiral Wilkes took the bait and dispatched his squadron to Panama. Wilkes was a man of action. On the same day that Maffitt sailed from Barbados, Wilkes "captured" the British steamer *Peterhoff* off St. Thomas on suspicion of carrying Confederate contraband, despite the fact that the ship held legal clearance to the neutral port of Matamoros. A prize crew took the vessel to Key West for adjudication, and the British press demanded Wilkes' head. They got their wish. Welles removed Wilkes, which appeased the British, but the *Peterhoff* case didn't reach settlement until after the war.[21]

At daylight on March 6 Maffitt lowered the propeller and chased a sail seven miles to windward. At four miles, a single shot brought the 941-ton Boston clipper *Star of Peace* into the wind. The ship was bound from Calcutta to the DuPont munitions works with 1,000 tons of saltpeter to be used against the Confederacy. Maffitt ordered his incendiaries to set a slow fire, allowing the *Florida* time to reach a safe distance. Gun crews shot 22 rounds at the burning clipper but struck her only six times. Five hours later the saltpeter ignited. Maffitt noted that "the fire was really beautiful; the sea lit up for thirty miles around."[22]

One week later, on March 13, the *Florida* captured the schooner *Aldebaran*, out of New York bound for the Brazilian port of Maranham

[Marapanim] with a cargo of flour and New England delicacies. Her captain, Robert Hand, tried to escape, but the cruiser gained steadily; one shot from the forward pivot gun ended the contest. Hand appealed to Maffitt for leniency, claiming that he shared deep sympathies for the Southern cause. Unmoved, Maffitt listened stoically as his crew gathered staples and delicacies from the doomed ship, including brandy, wines, rum, whiskey, and lobster, which had been kept alive in barrels packed with ice and seaweed. Another 30 manacled prisoners crowded the *Florida's* decks to watch as their schooner burned to the waterline.[23]

For the next few days, Maffitt tried to rid the ship of prisoners. He overhauled the British schooner *Laura Ann* but failed to persuade her captain to take a single soul. On March 18 the master of the English brig *Runnymeade*, bound for Scotland from Pernambuco, agreed to take both captains, the mates, and three other prisoners in return for a generous supply of water and provisions. A week later, Maffitt stopped an Australian bark laden with coal for the Cunard Lines. The cargo looked suspicious, but Maffitt settled for dispensing three more captives and released the vessel. In the interim, two prisoners from the captured *Star of Peace* enlisted on the *Florida*, but three weeks elapsed before Maffitt found passage for all the prisoners.[24]

On March 28 the *Florida* entered the mid-Atlantic and cruised the western edge of the Sargasso Sea. With coal running low, Maffitt made a fortuitous capture. After a short chase over a calm sea, the Boston bark *Lapwing* surrendered a bulging cargo of furniture, lumber, and smokeless coal destined for Batavia and Singapore. The crew hefted 10 tons of fuel to the cruiser by bucket. The cache of coal influenced Maffitt's next decision.

For months Maffitt had waited for a prize that he could convert into a tender. The *Lapwing* fell short of expectations, but with a hold full of precious coal, he recognized the value of retaining her. He gave Lt. Averett command of the ship and provided him with three officers and 15 men. Although her main function was to serve as a tender, the *Lapwing* received a 12-pounder for armament.

Averett's instructions were to cruise in parallel with the *Florida*, keeping about eight miles distant. Maffitt counted on her New England lines to deceive any passing trader, while providing the lookouts an expanded view of the ocean. Averett received a signal book and flags, along with two rendezvous points where he could rejoin the *Florida* if the ships became separated.[25]

On March 30, while still in sight of the *Florida*, the *Lapwing* observed a sail dead ahead and signalled back to the cruiser. Averett watched as Maffitt steamed by, but lost contact in the darkness. The *Florida* overhauled the New York bark *M. J. Colcord*, bound for Cape Town with a cargo of mixed goods that resembled a foreign aid program—a gift from the United States to Britain's colony on the southern tip of Africa. While stores were being unloaded, a curious Danish brig sailed to the scene for a closer look. Seizing the opportunity to release his prisoners, Maffitt paid the master of the *Christian* with captured goods to carry all the captives to Santa Cruz.

After burning the *Colcord*, the *Florida* and the *Lapwing* lost contact for two weeks. For both ships, the separation was uneventful. This puzzled Maffitt until he later learned that the *Alabama* had preceded him and swept the area free of shipping. Averett sighted and chased sails but all wore foreign colors. The *Lapwing* proved slow and sluggish, with troublesome leaks. On April 14 the *Florida* reappeared, and for two days the ships drifted together as the crews manhandled more coal from the tender.[26]

On April 16 the two ships resumed the hunt, Averett sailing that afternoon with instructions to rendezvous at Fernando de Noronha, Brazil's isolated penal island. The *Florida* took a different course and on the following day captured and burned the 1,300-ton clipper *Commonwealth of New York*, bound for San Francisco with a huge cargo insured for $370,000.[27]

On April 23 Maffitt captured the Baltimore bark *Henrietta*, bound for Rio de Janeiro with 3,250 barrels of flour, 600 kegs of lard, and thousands of candles. Her master, George Brown, had ignored the war, carrying goods around the world as if he and his ship were exempt from involvement. Brown was an old Downeaster crammed with biblical lore on the merits of slavery and strong on states rights, and his beliefs contrasted sharply with those of his Northern brethern. Maffitt liked the man, but not enough to spare his ship. As flames leapt skyward, the lard sizzled and crackled in the hold, and great greasy clouds of smoke shrouded the ship. Brown watched with strange interest, commenting: "Doesn't she burn pretty? She belongs to Mr. Whitridge. He is a great Union man."[28]

In addition to the crew, the *Henrietta* carried four passengers, identified only as Mrs. Flories and her three children, a daughter of 13 years, a son of seven, and an infant. Maffitt made them his guests and again surrendered his cabin. Fortunately, the plunder from the *Commonwealth* included cans of condensed milk; baby food was scarce aboard a warship.

The following day the *Florida* overhauled another large clipper, the *Oneida*, bound for New York out of Shanghai with tea and China trade goods estimated to be worth $1,000,000. The New Bedford master, Jessie F. Potter, harangued Maffitt for flying the British flag, and his bitterness increased when Maffitt forced him to leave his ship and most of his personal belongings behind. Maffitt distributed two bolts of Chinese silk to each member of the crew as a souvenir; two hours after her capture, flames engulfed the once famous China clipper.

Once again, the *Florida*'s deck overflowed with grumbling prisoners. While the *Oneida* burned, Maffitt chased another sail and overhauled the French bark *Bremontier*, bound from Bordeaux to New Caledonia. Captain Destremeaux protested Maffitt's interference, but agreed to take six of the prisoners to Brazil. He did not agree to accept the 15 men Maffitt thrust upon him, who included Captain Brown, his two officers, and other passengers. Although Brown's report of the incident complimented Maffitt for his courtesy, Potter complained that the French captain "made a claim on me of 400 francs for myself and two mates, board and detention . . . which I had to draw on my owners . . . when landed at Pernambuco."[29]

In the meantime, after roving the ocean for nearly a month, on April 22 the *Lapwing* finally chased and caught her only prize, the Yankee ship *Kate Dyer*. Although nearly twice the *Lapwing*'s size, the *Dyer*'s master surrendered quickly at the sight of a huge muzzle pointed his way. Realizing that most ships considered his puny 12-pounder as a signal gun, Averett had carved a large wooden gun barrel from a chunk of wood, painted it black, and mounted it on wheels. The *Dyer* was saved by her neutral cargo of guano bound for an Antwerp owner. Averett bonded the ship for $40,000, and set off toward Fernando de Noronha to rendezvous with the *Florida*.[30]

An enormous tower of cloud-shrouded granite 200 miles off Cape St. Roque, the penal colony of Fernando de Noronha is a landmark for mariners, and receives many visitors despite its character. Maffitt reached the island ahead of Averett, missing Semmes and the *Alabama* by only a few days. Maffitt did not enjoy the same friendly reception given Semmes by the governor at the time, Major Jose Basilio Pyrrho, who ran a loose prison system on the desolate island.

Basilio had been severely criticized for allowing Semmes to violate Brazil's neutrality. On May 1 a Brazilian mail steamer arrived bringing a new governor, Colonel Antonio Gomez Leal, who suspected that, unless it could be stopped now, the island would become a perpetual base of operations for the Confederate Navy. On May 3 Gomez ordered Maffitt, who had already landed 32 prisoners, to obtain whatever supplies he needed and leave within 24 hours.[31]

Shortly thereafter the *Lapwing* arrived, and the *Florida* towed it to a quiet area to unload more coal. Maffitt placed Acting Master Richard S. Floyd in charge of the tender and her remaining supply of coal, with orders to meet at Rocas Island, midway between the Brazilian mainland and Fernando de Noronha.[32]

On May 6 the *Florida* hailed the Baltimore-bound brig *Clarence*, laden with 10,000 bags of coffee from Rio. The ship looked like a good sailer and attracted the attention of Lt. Read, who had watched with interest the adventures of the *Lapwing*. While 300 bags of the precious beans were being hauled to the *Florida*, Read asked Maffitt to give him command of the prize—but not as a tender: Read wanted to head north and operate as a cruiser. Maffitt looked at the flimsy *Clarence* and wondered whether Read was serious, and if so, whether he should let him go.

In Washington, Secretary Welles faced a dilemma, too: Criticized by the newspapers for lack of action, hounded by irate shippers, and annoyed by visits from alarmed insurance companies, Welles was under heavy pressure to eliminate these "pirates." But deploying more warships in an all-out chase of two or three Confederate cruisers meant weakening the blockade, which would allow more arms to filter into the Confederacy and conflict with his government's overall policy.

Welles faced his critics by deploying just enough warships at foreign ports to maintain a presence, and continued to focus on the blockade. Combating the Confederate cruisers became more of a diplomatic issue than a naval initiative, and as time passed, diplomacy abroad did more to disrupt Confederate plans for a navy than Gideon Welles' gunboats.

"Daring Beyond the Point of Martial Prudence"

W HEN Lieutenant Charles W. Read reported for duty aboard the
Florida at Mobile Bay, Maffitt wrote in his journal, "Mr. Read is
quiet and slow, and not much of a military officer of the deck, but I
think him reliable and sure, though slow." Perhaps this first impression
was influenced by Read's youth, for in a few short months, Maffitt
would write that he was "daring beyond the point of martial prudence."[1]

A June 1860 graduate of the U.S. Naval Academy, Read served only
seven months before resigning to enter the service of his home state of
Mississippi. During the lopsided battle of New Orleans, he had been
one of the few Confederates cited for bravery. Taking command of the
McRae from her fatally wounded captain, young Read continued to
fight the ship until it became permanently disabled. He then retrieved
and returned to action the CSS *Resolute*, which had been run ashore
and abandoned early in the battle by a less courageous commander.
After the Confederate surrender at New Orleans, Read distinguished
himself as gunnery officer of the ironclad ram *Arkansas* in her battle
with Farragut's overwhelming Union fleet at Vicksburg.

Read had watched the lackluster career of the *Lapwing* with interest. When the *Florida* captured the brig *Clarence* off Cape San Roque,
he saw a chance for his own command. Read presented Maffitt with a
bold plan to take 20 men from the *Florida*, including an engineer and a
fireman, enter Hampton Roads, which was clogged with supply ships
and transports, and "cut out a gunboat or a steamer of the enemy. . . . If
it was found impossible to board a gunboat, or a merchant steamer, it
would [still] be possible to fire the shipping in Baltimore."[2]

The *Clarence* seemed ideal for the purpose. She carried 10,000
bags of Brazilian coffee consigned to a Baltimore merchant, and her
genuine registery and clearance papers might get the vessel safely
through the Union blockade at the Chesapeake's mouth and into the
congested inner harbor. After destroying what shipping he could and

escaping to sea with a steamer, Read planned to rejoin Maffitt and together destroy Northern commerce and harass the ports along the un-
defended New England coast.

Maffitt was reminded of a proposal he had once made to Secretary
Mallory to raid and burn the New York Navy Yard. Mallory had rejected the plan as too risky, but Mallory had no say here. Maffit enthusiastically approved the plan, added a brass 6-pounder howitzer to
Read's store of small arms, and stated: "You might make a capture or
two on the way up. You'll be on your own, no orders to hamper you.
Your success will depend upon yourself, and your sturdy heart."[3]

On May 7, 1863, the new confederate cruiser *Clarence* dipped her
new colors, filled her sails, and headed north. Among the many things
going through the mind of her 23-year old commander were Maffitt's
final words of caution: "If you find it impossible to enter Hampton
Roads, you will continue up the coast to Nantucket. The *Florida*
should be there by July 4, unless. . . ." In the hazardous business of commerce destroying, eight weeks can be forever.

The *Clarence*, which turned out to be a mediocre sailer, approached the Windward Islands, but after two uneventful weeks she
had chased many strange sails but captured none. With the brig's larder
depleted, Read overhauled a British bark. When Assistant Engineer
Eugene H. Browne boarded to ask for supplies, her master flew into a
rage that he had been fired upon by what he believed to be a Union
merchant ship. But when Read hoisted the Stars and Bars, the captain
softened: "I'll give you the whole darned ship if you want it," he said,
ordering his steward to break out the stores. Read reciprocated with 300
bags of coffee. The first crisis ended and fresh provisions filled the supply room.[4]

Early in June the *Clarence* approached the American coast, with a
startling transformation in her armament. As Averett had done on the
Lapwing, Read had his men convert surplus spars into an imposing battery of quaker guns, painted black and mounted on wooden carriages.
The crew cut gun ports, placed the guns in position, and rehearsed firing a quaker broadside on command.

On June 6, 250 miles west of Bermuda, the *Clarence* captured her
first prize, the bark *Whistling Wind* of Philadelphia. With a broadside
run out, a puff of smoke spewing from the howitzer, and the Confederate colors fluttering over an unlikely assailant, the *Whistling Wind*'s
master hauled up his courses and waited for the boarding officer. Read
found the bark laden with coal for Admiral Farragut's squadron on the
Mississippi. Gratified that he could destroy supplies bound for the enemy, Read burned the ship.[5]

Early the next morning, the *Clarence* intercepted the schooner *Alfred H. Partridge* of New York, laden with arms and clothing that the master claimed were being shipped to Confederate forces in Texas via the neutral port of Matamoras, Mexico. At first Read doubted the skipper's claim, but he knew that many Northern merchants secretly traded with the South, exchanging a variety of goods for cotton to supply the empty mills of New England. Read bonded the prize for $5,000 and released the ship under the pledge that the bond would be cancelled if the cargo was faithfully delivered "to loyal citizens of the Confederate States." The captain kept his promise.[6]

On June 9 the *Clarence* captured the Boston bark *Mary Alvina*, bound for New Orleans with a cargo of commisary stores for the United States Army. Read burned her after removing what supplies he needed, including some recent newspapers. From these, and from information gathered from prisoners, Read learned that all vessels entering Hampton Roads were being stopped, searched, and prevented from entering unless their cargoes were specifically designated for the federal government. Gunboats watched all vessels, and sentries patrolled the wharves. Although the *Clarence*'s papers were legitimate, Read realized that he would never get past the blockade and "that it was impossible to carry out the instructions of Commander Maffitt."[7]

Unclear as to his next move, Read decided to cruise along the coast and somehow capture a supply ship bound for Fortress Monroe with proper clearance papers. And he wanted a ship faster than the sluggish *Clarence*, but capturing one would require different tactics.

Just off the Virginia Capes on June 12 the lookout reported a sail six miles distant and running before a fair breeze. Read knew the *Clarence* couldn't catch her, and the brass six-pounder couldn't reach her, but he wanted that ship. With gun ports closed, Read hoisted the American flag upside down—the traditional signal of a ship in distress.

From the deck of the bark *Tacony*, in ballast from Port Royal, S.C. to Philadelphia, Captain William Munday peered through a light morning mist at what seemed to be a fellow sailor in serious trouble. But there was something unnatural about the brig. If it were really in trouble, it was close enough to shore for the crew to reach safety in the ship's boats. While intuition warned him to leave her alone, the law of the sea compelled him to offer help. And then there were lucrative salvage claims to consider. Munday eased toward the *Clarence*.

As the two ships drew closer, Munday observed a boat loaded with 10 sailors shove off the *Clarence* and pull toward his ship. As the boat bumped aqainst the *Tacony*, the men scrambled hand over hand to the deck and "presented revolvers at the captain and mate and those on deck and ordered them into their boat and took them to the *Clarence* as prisoners."[8] Read, who had let his reddish mustache grow and looked like an old-time bucaneer, led the boarding party. Learning from the ship's log that the *Tacony* was a much faster sailer than his coffee merchant, he decided to trade vessels and issued orders to transfer his "armament" and flag.

Hardly had the new orders been issued to transfer ships when the schooner *M. A. Schlinder*, in ballast from Port Royal to Philadelphia, approached the scene. For the second time Read took to his boat, and within half an hour had captured the schooner and set it afire.

Meanwhile, Captain George E. Teague of the schooner *Kate Stewart* noticed smoke rising from a burning vessel. As he drew nearer he saw two other vessels, apparently assisting the ship in flames. Read saw him coming, but his six-pounder was still in a boat en route to the *Tacony*. As the *Stewart* came within hailing distance of the *Clarence*, the brig's gun ports popped open to reveal a broadside ready to fire into his ship. Teague jumped to his cabin roof and bellowed through a trumpet, "For God's sake don't shoot! I surrender!"[9] Ordered to bring his papers to the *Clarence*, Teague gazed unbelievingly at the wooden guns that had forced his surrender.

The *Stewart*, which was owned by the same company as the *Tacony*, presented a problem: She carried passengers—20 ladies on their way to Mexico. With too many prisoners on board already, Read decided to bond the *Stewart* for $7,000 and have Teague take all 50 "guests" to shore. He knew that the moment the *Stewart* reached port Teague would warn the Union Navy, but there might be a way to turn this to his advantage. Read boasted privately to Teague that a great fleet of Southern ships would soon strike the Atlantic coast and destroy the Union blockading force.[10] The navy would be searching for ships far more formidable than the little *Tacony*.

Before the morning ended, the converted *Tacony* confirmed her superior sailing qualities by chasing and capturing the brig *Arabella* in less than 30 minutes. The *Arabella* carried a neutral cargo, and Read bonded her for $30,000, expressing regret that he had a few hours earlier bonded the *Kate Stewart*.

At noon Read returned to the *Clarence*, now cast adrift with more than 8,000 bags of coffee still in her hold. What a treat for Confederate troops, used to drinking chicory root and other concoctions, to be able to land her on a Southern shore, but this was impossible. As the ship burned, the pungence of scorched timbers and tarred rigging mixed with the aroma of roasted coffee. Forced to abandon a scheme to enter Hampton Roads, Read headed north for his rendezvous along longitude

70 with the *Florida*—unaware that Maffit had wasted 15 days at Rocas Island waiting for the *Lapwing*.

On Saturday afternoon, June 13, Secretary Gideon Welles noted in his diary that "three vessels were yesterday captured by a pirate craft off Cape Henry and burnt. Sent [Gustavus Vasa] Fox at once with orders to telegraph to New York and Philadelphia, etc., for every vessel in condition to proceed to sea in search of this wolf that is prowling so near to us. . . ." Fox moved quickly. By evening, he had issued pursuit orders to naval commandants from Boston to Hampton Roads.[11]

Meanwhile, the *Tacony*'s former master touched shore at a small harbor on the New Jersey coast and caught the first train to Philadelphia. There he recounted a tale of fire, terror, and piracy to the ship's owners and waiting reporters. The press printed Teague's version of Read's fictional account of the great Confederate fleet poised to ravage the eastern seaboard, further sensationalizing it by including both the dreaded *Alabama* and the now infamous *Florida* in the armada. These rumors drifted into the Navy Office, intensifying the prevailing state of confusion.

The welter of pursuit orders fills more than 80 pages of the Official Records, and includes vessels ranging from warships to converted pleasure yachts. Typical of the messages sent was an order to Admiral Hiram Paulding, commanding the New York Navy Yard: "The privateer *Clarence*, a sailing vessel fitted out by the *Oreto*, made three captures yesterday . . . send what vessels you can in pursuit." Out went the *Tuscarora*, *Dai Ching*, and *Adela*, with a promise from Paulding that, "We hope to get the *Virginia* and *Kittatinny* off tomorrow."[12]

The United States Navy could not be accused of apathy. Within three days, 38 armed ships cruised the coast in search of "the pirates," their commanders in search of prestige and promotion. Unfortunately, organization and planning had been overlooked in the scramble. The ships fanned out at random. As days passed, it became evident that the entire navy was looking in the wrong place. A few steamers executing a proper search within predetermined grids probably would have caught the wooden-gunned *Tacony* within a day or two.

Late on June 14, Secretary Welles heard of Read's change of ships from the owners of the *Tacony*; his navy was chasing the wrong vessel. Because most of his ships were at sea and out of communication, Welles dispatched new orders to hunt for the Confederate: "Charter or seize half a dozen moderate-sized, fast vessels; put on board an officer, a dozen men, plenty of small arms and one or two howitzers. Send them out in various directions. Take any vessel that can be sent to sea within the next forty-eight hours."[13]

The whereabouts of Read and the *Tacony* remained a mystery until June 15 when he captured and burned the brig *Umpire* about 300 miles off the Delaware River. When a suspicious steamer appeared on the horizon, Read stuffed his prisoners into the hold and waited for the vessel to pass. Later that night, a Union warship hailed the bark asking for news about the "piratical *Tacony*." Read trumpeted back, "Yes, we saw her at dusk chasing an East Indiaman." He added a bogus heading and waited, holding his breath until the Union commander accepted the reply and hurried off in pursuit.[14]

Another Union warship unexpectedly appeared through the morning mist and stopped the *Tacony*, her commander raising the same question. Read, now well rehearsed, replied with the same answer but gave different bearings. Once again, the officer took the bait and raced away in the opposite direction.[15] Read knew that the enemy had not yet obtained a good description of his ship. In the next few days, he gave them one.

On June 20 he overhauled the huge packet *Isaac Webb*, with 750 passengers aboard en route to new homes in America. One blank shot from his popgun brought her into the wind. As the crowds on deck gazed down in awe at the row of guns ready at the broadside, Read went on board and talked to the master, knowing that he could not burn the ship. Settling for a $40,000 bond, he was returning to the *Tacony* when the curious skipper of the fishing schooner *Micabar* sailed over to investigate.[16] His curiosity ended when three black-painted barrels poked through the *Tacony*'s gunports. In full view of the *Webb*'s panicked passengers, Read ordered the schooner torched. Many of the immigrants dropped to their knees and raised their voices to heaven, unaware that they had already been spared.

The following day, as Read continued looking for the *Florida*, he captured the fine new clipper ship *Byzantium*, out of Newcastle for New York with a large cargo of coal. Read considered retaining the ship to fuel the *Florida*'s bunkers, but he was beginning to worry that Maffit had encountered misfortune. With regrets, he ordered the match.

Later in the day, the *Tacony* overhauled and burnt the bark *Goodspeed*, returning to New York in ballast from Londonderry. Upon reaching shore, her angry skipper concocted a story that a Union gunboat stood off a mile or two and watched cowardly as Read destroyed his vessel. The press, already faulting the navy, had a field day. Gideon Welles doubted the accusation, but the publicity forced him to undertake a formal, but inconclusive, investigation. It turned out that naval vessels searching for the *Tacony* actually had passed the *Byzantium* and the *Goodspeed* earlier in the day, but they didn't stop to warn the commercial ships of Read's presence.[17]

June 22 was an unfortunate day for New England fishing schooners, which dotted the sea in every direction, attracted by shoals of spawning cod and halibut. Before evening, there would be four fewer of them. Read captured the schooners *Marengo, Florence, Elizabeth Ann, Rufus Choate,* and *Ripple,* sparing only one. He noted in his journal, "The *Florence* being an old vessel I bonded her and placed seventy-five prisoners on her. The other schooners were burned."[18]

Read continued north, keeping a sharp eye out for the smoke of enemy steamers and wondering if the navy had simply decided to ignore him. On June 23 he captured and burned the *Ada* and the *Wanderer,* two more fishing schooners. From recent newspapers and talkative prisoners he learned that the navy now had an accurate description of the *Tacony* and had started to overhaul all ships of her kind. It was time for another change.[19]

The following day he stopped the big clipper ship *Shatemuc,* bound from Liverpool to Boston with hundreds of Irish immigrants. Read boarded the vessel and threatened to burn the ship unless the captain signed a $150,000 bond. The captain, a crusty veteran whose face reddened quickly behind a stream of profanity, looked at the throng of anxious passengers frantically praying for help from above, decided the young sea raider might not be bluffing, and signed the bond.

Read wanted to burn this ship despite the huge passenger list, for the *Shatemuc's* hold contained tons of iron plate and war supplies for the North. He wasted most of the day attempting to capture enough prizes to take off the prisoners, but was finally forced to set the ship free.[20]

That evening, just before dark, the mackerel schooner *Archer* became Read's twentieth prize. Out of ammunition for the howitzer, he had to invent new ways of punishing the enemy. In his diary he noted, "During the night we transferred all our things on board the schooner *Archer.* At 2 a.m. set fire to the *Tacony* and stood west. The schooner *Archer* is a fishing vessel of 90 tons, sails well, and is easily handled. No Yankee gunboat would ever dream of suspecting us. I therefore think we will dodge our pursuers for a short time. It is my intention to go along the coast with a view to burning the shipping in some exposed port and of cutting out a steamer."[21]

By morning only a charred, unidentifiable hulk remained of the *Tacony.* Read had destroyed his trail. While more than 38 Union ships prowled the Atlantic searching for the *Tacony,* and the powerful mayors of large port cities pressured Welles for more action, Read and his crew commissioned the tiny schooner *Archer* as a new Confederate man-of-war. Three cheers and a ration of grog accompanied the raising of the flag.

By the morning of June 26, the *Archer*, looking like any other fishing schooner, lay off Portland, Maine. Read picked up two local lobstermen who had been adrift in a dory throughout the night and fed them a hot breakfast. When Albert T. Bibber and Elbridge Titcomb were told they were prisoners of the Confederate States Navy, they thought it a joke, believing they were the guests of fellow fishermen out for a frolic. They supplied information regarding Portland's defenses, which included the United States revenue cutter *Caleb Cushing*, schooner rigged and mounting a 12- and a 32-pounder. This stirred Read's interest, but when he learned that the fast passenger liner *Chesapeake* lay at a wharf ready to sail for New York in the morning, his attention shifted to the larger vessel.[22]

At sundown the *Archer*, piloted by the helpful lobstermen, crept into the harbor and anchored. For their reward, Bibber and Titcomb were clapped in irons and herded below. Read gathered his officers and informed them of his plans to capture the *Chesapeake*, burn the shipping in the harbor, and during the confusion dash back to sea. But Engineer Browne doubted his ability to manage the engines of the big *Chesapeake* without help from another engineer, and he worried that steam would be down and impossible to raise before morning—leaving the ship under the guns of the fort. Read changed his plan and decided instead to grab the *Caleb Cushing*.

"There's a good offshore breeze blowing," Read told his crew. "After getting beyond the fort, we'll go back and fire the shipping." All knelt for a short prayer. Every man felt the weight of his responsibility, and listened reverently as their captain implored heaven to bless the enterprise and bring independence to the Confederacy. From tired bodies came solemn "Amens."[23]

When the moon set at 1:30 a.m., Read selected three men to take the *Archer* to sea and wait. He and 19 others split into two boats, and with muffled oars rowed silently toward the slumbering *Caleb Cushing*. Good fortune still favored the raiders. The cutter's captain had just died and his successor, Lt. James H. Merryman, was not expected to reach Portland until morning. For one night only, the command fell into the youthful hands of Lt. Dudlay Davenport, a native of the South. Half the crew and three of her officers were on shore liberty. A dozen remained on board, but only two stood deck watch. At that moment, a good night's sleep was important. The cutter was under orders to put to sea in the morning to help track down the *Tacony.*

The two men drowsing on watch sighted Read's boats approaching and hurried below to awaken Davenport. By the time Davenport comprehended that his ship was being boarded, Read was already on the cutter's deck, his pistol leveled at the two men as they returned from the cabin. Nineteen men lined up behind Read, ready to shoot if necessary. "I'll kill you both if you make a sound," Read said. "Don't speak a word." Both men were ironed to the mast; the rest of the crew was captured while they slept in their hammocks. Everything had worked as planned. Read had the cutter, and not a sound had reached shore. But at the very moment they were congratulating each other, the stiff offshore breeze eased, and before the fouled mooring cables could be slipped, the flood tide began. Read discarded any thoughts of firing the shipping: the problem now was survival.[24]

Read placed oarsmen in two small boats, unshackled Titcomb to act as pilot, and towed the *Caleb Cushing* through Hussy Sound seaward against the tide. At dawn the cutter was still within range of Fort Preble, but no one seemed to notice. By early morning, the *Caleb Cushing* was five miles outside the harbor and safely beyond the guns. The breeze freshened enough to raise sail and Read recalled the boats. He felt safe enough to order breakfast for all and invited his old Annapolis classmate, Lt. Davenport, to join him. Between mouthfuls of captured bacon and eggs, Read chided his friend for deserting the South and choosing the wrong side.[25]

While the men in gray enjoyed breakfast on their new flagship, Portland awoke to the stunning news that the revenue cutter had mysteriously departed without orders. Church bells tolled the alarm. People swarmed to the waterfront. "Women and children filled the streets and were rushing hither and thither in aimless fright."[26] Once word spread that Southern-born Davenport had been left in charge of the cutter, everyone concluded that he had either stolen the ship or was somehow involved in a broader conspiracy.

Amid mounting confusion, Port Collector Jedediah Jewett took matters into his own hands. Without authority or instructions, he commandeered the Boston Line sidewheeler *Forest City* and enlisted those of the *Cushing's* crew who had been on shore leave, and who were anxious to get even with Davenport for stealing their ship. Jewett collected 36 men from the 17th Regulars at Fort Preble and hustled them on board with two 12-pounder field howitzers. By 10 a.m., the *Forest City* had a head of steam, and with Jewett barking orders, the newly minted warship sliced through the harbor in pursuit of the *Caleb Cushing*.[27]

The fast propeller steamer *Chesapeake*, impressed into service by Portland's mayor, Jacob McLellan, joined the chase. The local agent for the New York Line protested as he watched his ship armed and manned, and eventually succeeded in detaining the vessel long enough to see her vital parts protected by bales of cotton. With McLellan issuing orders, the steamer joined the pursuit with a detachment of the 7th Maine Volunteers and about 20 zealous citizens armed with squirrel rifles, ancient muskets, and rusty cutlasses. A makeshift battery of two 6-pound field guns were braced to her deck.[28] An unarmed steam tug joined the pursuit at a safe distance, followed by a host of curious spectators in almost anything that would float.

From the deck of the *Caleb Cushing*, then 20 miles at sea and moving slowly under sail, Read saw the smoke from "Admiral-General" Jewett's attack fleet and promptly cleared for action. He had learned how to fight at New Orleans and prepared to do it again. The *Forest City* entered the pursuit several minutes ahead of the *Chesapeake*. As she came into range, Read opened with a 32-pounder that splashed about 50 yards off the *Forest City*'s bow. Three more shots had her bracketed, the last falling close to her waterline. The marksmanship of Read's gunners quieted the enthusiasm of the citizen volunteers, and the *Forest City* back-tracked to confer with McLellan on the faster *Chesapeake*. After a brief council of war, the two commanders decided to get up a full head of steam and ram the cutter before her long gun caused serious damage.[29]

This plan of attack might have proved disastrous for the impromptu Portland navy if Read had done a better job of checking his inventory before breakfast. Although he had 500 pounds of powder in the cutter's magazine, he could find no more than five or six 32-pound shots. Somewhere on board was a reserve shot chest, but Read couldn't find it, and prisoner-guest Davenport refused to reveal its hidden location.

Into the gun went the final rounds. When those were gone, the gun was reloaded with scraps of metal, hardware, and crushed cookware until there was nothing left to fire. Read knew it was the end, but when Browne came on deck with a ball of Dutch cheese from the officer's mess, they decided to make one final gesture, and it was rammed home and fired. Unlike many of the earlier shots, this one struck home, and fragments of cheese splattered the deck of the *Chesapeake*, bewildering her defenders.[30]

As the steamers crept closer, Read ordered everyone into the longboats, remaining behind with a few men long enough to fire the *Cushing*. Three hundred yards away the boats converged to watch the flames leap into her sails. A spark touched the powder, and the Confederate's twenty-second and final prize exploded into flaming splinters. By the time the *Chesapeake* reached the boats to collect their prisoners, Read and his men were waving white handkerchiefs tied to the tips of their oars. During the confusion the *Archer* almost made it safely back to sea. Only vigilance on the part of one of the liberated lobstermen caused her capture after a short chase.[31]

Read and his men, their clothes in tatters after being ripped to pieces by a frenzied crowd in Portland, were hustled off to the protective walls of Boston's Fort Warren, where they were imprisoned for a year before being exchanged as prisoners of war. Read returned to fight again, but not until the war's final days.

Read and his men captured 22 prizes in 21 days, demonstrating just how much damage a few well-led men in a sluggish bark carrying no more firepower than a remounted 6-pound field howitzer could inflict on the Union merchant fleet. Admiral David Dixon Porter caustically wrote in later years: "A single Federal gunboat, under an intelligent captain, would have nipped Read's whole scheme in the bud."[32] Porter must have forgotten his own ineffective search for the *Sumter*, which began in the Gulf of Mexico and extended as far as the coast of Brazil.

Inaccurate reports, false sightings, and exaggerated press coverage created hysteria all along the East Coast. Under pressure, Welles ordered every available ship into the search, but his staff could not differentiate between valid information and nonsense. Operating always on stale information, the vessels usually were two or three days behind the Confederates—and because Read changed vessels three times, they were often looking for the wrong ship. Whether Read was lucky, daring, or just extremely intelligent is moot. The fact remains, at least 38 Union warships steamed frantically up and down the northeastern seaboard, unable to stop a few determined Confederate raiders in a succession of slow, almost unarmed ships.

Catching the Clippers

O N MAY 6, 1863, off Cape San Roque, Maffitt and the *Florida* had captured the *Clarence*, setting the stage for Read's destructive cruise up the East Coast. That same week Stonewall Jackson, one of the Confederacy's most brilliant generals, lay dying at Chancellorsville—and with him much of the Southern hope for independence. General Ulysses S. Grant had crossed the Mississippi, and the fateful Vicksburg campaign was underway. In Richmond, Confederate Naval Secretary Mallory sat down to write this letter to Maffit:

> You are hereby informed that the President has appointed you . . . a commander in the Navy of the Confederate States, to rank from the 29th day of April, 1863, for gallant and meritorious conduct in command of the steam sloop *Florida* in running the blockade in and out of the port of Mobile against an overwhelming force of the enemy and under his fire, and since in actively cruising against and destroying the enemy's commerce.[1]

Unfortunately, "actively cruising" would have to wait: The *Florida* suffered from engine problems that could not be corrected at sea, and Maffit decided to put into the nearest port—Pernambuco, 200 miles to the southwest. When the *Florida* entered port on the morning of May 8, 1863, Governor Joao Silveira de Souza's tranquil life became suddenly complicated. Under heavy pressure from United States Consul Thomas W. Adamson, Governor Silveira sent Maffit a curt letter granting the *Florida* permission for only a 24-hour stay, insinuating that he could use the ship's sails if the engine could not be repaired in time.[2]

Maffitt, suspecting that Adamson had intimidated the governor, decided to deliver his response in person. He found Silveira affable, but very much afraid of the United States government. He warned Maffitt that three Union warships were scheduled to arrive at Pernambuco within the next few days, and he doubted that Brazil could protect the *Florida*. Maffitt stated that he could protect himself, and after lengthy negotiations, convinced Silveira that he needed four days to carry out the repairs, an extension justified under the criteria of "dire need." Maffit departed with a letter allowing him time for repairs, provisioning, and coaling.[3]

Silveira notified Consul Adamson of the change in the *Florida's* status. After all, he was obliged to extend equal privileges to both belligerents. This brought more threats from the consul, who condemned the Brazilian government for tolerating the destruction of American shipping in neutral waters, and showed the governor an incriminating report prepared by prisoners released at Pernambuco. Out of patience, Silveira stated bluntly that the prisoners were landed in the name of humanity, and asked Adamson if he believed they should have been dumped in the sea.[4]

After loading supplies and carrying out temporary repairs, Maffitt headed for Rocas Island and a rendezvous with the wandering *Lapwing* on May 13. On the way, he captured and burnt the Boston clipper *Crown Point*, bound for San Francisco with 1,098 tons of assorted merchandise. Nine recruits joined the *Florida's* crew, filling vacancies created by manning the *Lapwing* and the *Clarence*.[5]

Meanwhile, Acting Master Richard S. Floyd and the *Lapwing* spent 30 days waiting for the *Florida* at an island he erroneously believed to be the designated rendezvous. When supplies ran short, Floyd finally decided to sail to Barbados. On June 20, the seven-man crew set fire to the *Lapwing* and rowed ashore to an enthusiastic reception from the Barbadians. The group later booked passage on a British ship bound for Queenstown, Ireland, and through the efforts of Confederate agents in England, eventually rejoined the *Florida* at Brest, France.[6]

During the *Florida's* long wait at Rocas Island, three men died— one by illness and two by drowning. Late in May, Maffitt finally tired of waiting, convinced that the *Lapwing* had been captured or destroyed, unaware that the tender was huddled behind a nearby island waiting patiently for him. He left a message for Floyd sealed in a bottle and sailed toward Ceara, Brazil, once again in search of coal and provisions.[7]

For more than a month, the *Florida* and the *Alabama* had wreaked havoc on American shipping off the coast of Brazil. Even the CSS *Georgia* stopped for 10 days at Bahia, lending further credence to the rumors of a growing Southern Navy. "But where was the Union Navy?" Brazilians wondered. Only the USS *Mohican* stopped regularly at Bahia, but never when the Confederate cruisers were around.

Still, it was never wise to linger in one area, and Semmes and Maffitt left Brazilian waters at about the same time—Semmes headed toward South Africa, and Maffit headed north. Shortly after leaving Ceara Island on June 6, the *Florida* captured and burnt the 938-ton medium clipper *Southern Cross* of Boston, bound for New York with a cargo of dye-wood.[8]

On June 18, about eight degrees above the equator and well east of the Windward Islands, the 1,038-ton Boston clipper *Red Gauntlet* crossed the *Florida*'s path. The *Red Gauntlet* had sailed for Hong Kong on May 24 with a cargo of ice, coal, and musical instruments. Maffitt put a prize crew on board and kept the big clipper in company for several days while a detail removed coal. The crew enjoyed an experience rare in the tropics: ice at sea.

Presenting consular certificates as proof, Captain A. H. Lucas argued daily that his cargo belonged to British firms. He fully expected Maffitt to bond his ship and was flabbergasted when it was burned. He later reported that Maffitt would bond no more ships as he believed that President Lincoln would not honor bonds. Maffitt may have told Lucas this, but he continued to bond ships. Insured for only $41,000, the *Red Gauntlet*'s owners submitted claims to the Geneva Awards Commission totalling $124,475. Five of the crew volunteered to serve on the *Florida*.[9]

Still tracking eastward, on June 16 the *Florida* captured the Connecticut clipper ship *Benjamin F. Hoxie*, bound for Falmouth, England from the west coast of Mexico with a cargo of logwood and $105,000 in silver bars. Claiming neutral ownership for the cargo, Captain Carey insisted that the ship could not be destroyed. Maffitt examined the ship's papers and formed a different opinion: "The captain claimed this as a neutral cargo, but as her clearance was very irregular, her destination not positive with the crew, I could not permit her to pass without capture. The silver bars, officers, and crew I received on board and burned the vessel."[10]

Maffitt eventually delivered the silver bars to the firm of John T. Bourne, agent for the Confederacy at Bermuda. Bourne discovered that the silver legitimately belonged to an English firm and shipped it to the proper owner, barely avoiding an embarrassing incident with the British government. This did not end the silver episode, however. Captain Carey reported to the *Royal Gazette* of Hamilton, Bermuda that his ship actually carried $400,000 in silver bars, 30 tons of silver ore valued at $500,000, and $7,000 to $8,000 in gold. The difference was never reconciled, and no authority took action on Carey's allegation, implying that the story had been fabricated for the sole purpose of stimulating British opinion against Confederate cruisers.[11]

After burning the *Hoxie*, Maffitt headed toward the coast of the United States to find Read, his deck crowded with prisoners. He overhauled the Italian ship *Due Fratelli* on June 18 and persuaded the master to accept a few prisoners, but he still had 54 on board. The prisoners continued to be a problem until June 27, when the *Florida* captured the whaling schooner *V. H. Hill* of Providence. A poor prize and not worth burning, Maffitt bonded the schooner for $10,000 and crammed every prisoner aboard. Fearing for the safety of his ship, the *Hill*'s captain hurried back to Providence.[12]

When Maffitt captured the packet ship *Sunrise* on July 7, he finally learned of Read's escapades from a stack of recent New York newspapers. More importantly, he learned that Secretary Welles expected the *Florida* and had almost 40 gunboats out combing the seas. Moreover, the coal from the *Red Gauntlet* had proven inferior and the *Florida* could not make full speed. Maffitt referred to the situation as a "sad moment." Just over the port bow lay New York, her harbor packed with helpless merchantmen. With the element of surprise gone, his old dream of a hit-and-run night raid was out of reach.[13] Maffitt reluctantly bonded the *Sunrise* and abandoned his plans to raid the Northeast.

On July 8 the *Florida* still lingered in a choppy sea about 50 miles off Sandy Hook, New Jersey. At noon the lookout reported a four-funnelled sidewheeler bearing down on them. Maffitt studied the approaching steamer and ordered the crew to quarters. The USS *Ericsson*, recently chartered and armed by the navy to search for the *Tacony*, was no match for the *Florida*. When her commander, Joseph N. Miller, realized that the distant warship under British colors might be a Confederate cruiser, he turned around and steamed toward safety.

Maffitt responded by running up the Confederate flag and firing a broadside. The first shot splashed short, ricocheted, and struck the rim of the *Ericsson*'s foretop. The green crew manning the 22-pound Parrott gun panicked and ran for protection behind the bulwarks; the crew tending the two 12-pounder rifled howitzers followed. Only a fortuitous disappearance into a nearby fogbank saved the *Ericsson* from capture.[14] Thus ended the *Florida*'s sole offensive action against an enemy warship.

Maffitt headed eastward and captured the brig *W. B. Nash*, fresh out of New York with 650,000 pounds of lard—which made a brilliantly crackling bonfire. Nearby was the whaling schooner *Rienzi* of Provincetown, her hold packed with whale oil from the South Pacific. Her crew had just seen the flames from the *Nashville*; knowing they were next, and being almost on Provincetown's doorstep, they jumped into their whaleboats and pulled for home. Maffitt sent crew to burn the ship immediately. The flames from the two vessels leapt skyward 200 feet, leaving a red glow that could be seen for 50 miles.[15]

Welles received the news of another Confederate raider's presence off the northeast coast without surprise; it just confirmed Read's story that a Confederate fleet was converging upon the East Coast. He dispatched this telegram to Commodore John B. Montgomery of the Boston Navy Yard: "Send the *Tuscarora*, *Montgomery*, and *Cambridge* off Nantucket and to the eastward immediately. Have the *Aries*, *Shenandoah*, and *Iron Age* ready to move at a moment's notice. From a journal of one of the crew of the *Tacony* it appears Read expected to meet the *Florida* off Nantucket."[16]

As usual, Union naval forces were converging on a Confederate raider's last known position. As usual, the Confederate raider wouldn't be there when they arrived: Maffitt was headed for Bermuda.

Maffitt needed coal and hoped to complete repairs to the English engines at the Queen's shipyard in Bermuda. The commandant of the fort at St. George agreed to exchange salutes with the *Florida*, but Governor George Ord, citing rules laid down shortly after the *Nashville* had been ejected from Southampton, refused to sell government coal or permit the cruiser to use government dockyards.[17] Maffitt managed to obtain permission to use commercial repair facilities, but there was no coal until the next ship arrived. With his legal 24-hour stay extended to 11 days by the coal shortage, Maffitt had extra time to make minor repairs—and socialize on shore.

Maffitt's enjoyment of Bermuda's social life came to an end when the USS *Wachusett* steamed into harbor and anchored nearby. Although the governor interceded and asked the *Wachusett* to move, reminding her commander that, under the neutrality laws, he must allow the *Florida* a 24-hour head start before putting back to sea, her presence made Maffitt nervous. He had also been unable to obtain drydock space, so all work on the engines and hull had to wait. The *Florida* took on fresh provisions, and on July 27 steamed out of the harbor and headed for Europe.[18]

En route to Europe on August 6, the *Florida* captured two large passenger ships, bonding each for $40,000: the clipper ship *Francis B. Cutting*, bound for New York with 230 immigrants and the packet ship *Southern Rights*, also bound for New York, with 400 immigrants. Maffitt wondered what the *Southern Rights*'s Yankee owner had in mind when naming his ship. It was common knowledge that penniless immigrants enlisted in the Union Army soon after reaching port, giving the Union Army an unlimited supply of fresh recruits. Maffitt regretted bonding the *Southern Rights*, convinced that many of her passengers would soon be wearing Yankee blue.[19]

As the *Florida* continued on toward Europe, her engineers reported constant problems with the machinery: The drive shaft was out of alignment; a sleeve leaked; the steam delivery valves operated sluggishly; and the hull's copper sheathing, which had sprung and curled enough to slow the ship, needed to be repaired in a drydock. Maffitt wanted to enter a British port for repairs, but recent changes in Britain's neutrality laws made it impossible: he could not enter a British port until October 26—90 days from the date he left Bermuda. He could either cruise around in circles until the legal time elapsed, or head for a friendly port close enough to England to obtain parts. The engineers convinced him to go elsewhere; of his many alternatives, he picked the French port of Brest. It had adequate docking facilities, and the added advantage of being difficult to blockade with the one ship the Union Navy had available.[20]

Anticipating an extended stay in France, Maffitt took the precaution of making arrangements in advance. In Europe, political attitudes changed constantly, and the whims of Napoleon III were unpredictable. On the night of August 17, Maffitt sent Lt. Averett ashore at Cork, Ireland, with orders to proceed to France and solicit the help of Confederate Commissioner John Slidell in securing permission from the Emperor to dock at Brest. The *Florida's* nocturnal visit did not go unnoticed. An article about it in *The London Times* alarmed American shipping in English ports and alerted all Union warships within calling distance.[21]

To give Averett time to contact Slidell, Maffitt headed back to sea and cautiously resumed the hunt. On August 21, the *Florida* captured and burnt the 868-ton medium clipper *Anglo Saxon*, bound for New York with coal from Liverpool. Maffitt stopped several neutral vessels on the way to Brest in an unsuccessful effort to discharge the prisoners from the prize.

Evan Evans, an English Channel pilot captured aboard the *Anglo Saxon*, protested to the British Consul that Maffitt had no right to remove him from his piloting grounds and deposit him at Brest. Evans may have been unaware of Maffitt's efforts to transfer the prisoners to an inbound merchantman, but his protest caused enough concern for the British to send warships into the English Channel to protect Her Majesty's rights.[22]

The *Florida* arrived at Brest on August 23. Maffitt notified the port authorities that the needed repairs would require at least 18 days. As for himself, his health had broken and he needed a rest. In a report to Secretary Mallory, he stated, "I regret to inform the Department that in consequence of impaired health I shall be under the necessity of applying for a detachment from this vessel."[23] A few days later Commander Matthew Fontaine Maury, responding from Paris, relieved Maffitt "with reluctance," and placed Commander Joseph N. Barney in command.[24]

By odd coincidence, Barney was the same officer Mallory had sent to replace Maffitt at Mobile, only to have those orders revoked by President Davis. Maffitt had little confidence in his replacement, but this meant little since Barney never got to sea. The cruiser languished at Brest for six months. Like his predecessor, Barney's health failed, and on January 5, 1864 he was relieved by Lt. Commanding Charles M. Morris.[25]

Under Maffitt's command, the *Florida* typified what old sea dogs called a "bad-luck ship," surviving a series of catastrophes, ranging from an epidemic of yellow fever to chronic mechanical problems, that would have stopped a less determined or resourceful captain. Maffitt went to sea despite poor health, and the fact that he remained physically effective until reaching Brest is remarkable. Even more remarkable was what he accomplished in his eight months at sea: The *Florida* captured 25 prizes, destroying 19 and bonding six. Captures by the *Lapwing*, *Clarence*, *Tacony* and *Archer*, added another 22 vessels to the ledger, bringing the overall count to 47 prizes.

This destruction did not go unnoticed by American shipping interests, nor by their insurance companies. The real beneficiary of the *Florida*'s depradation was not the Confederacy, however, but the British: British shippers purchased American ships at bargain prices and experienced a rapid resurgence in business; British shipyards boomed with a backlog of orders. While there is no conclusive evidence that the British government conspired to destroy their American rival, there is evidence that Britain could have prevented the *Florida* and other Confederate raiders built in English shipyards from going to sea.[26]

In 1854, Britain passed the Merchant Shipping Act, strict legislation regulating merchant traffic and placing authority in the hands of Her Majesty's Board of Trade. The Foreign Office wielded no influence over this board, nor did the antiquated Foreign Enlistment Act of 1819. If there were culpability within the British government, it rested within the Board of Trade, where individuals could make and influence decisions at levels far removed from the elevated and dignified function of Lord Russell's Foreign Office.

When Bulloch contracted with the Lairds to build the *Florida*, he registered it under the Merchant Shipping Act. By doing so, he provided the Board of Trade with the power to seize the vessel at any time it violated the Act, either before it sailed, on the high seas, or in any colonial port.

Bulloch purchased the vessel as a merchant ship. The Act clearly states that "any person on behalf of himself or any other body of persons, wilfully makes a false declaration . . . to own British ships, or any shares therein, the declarant shall be guilty of a misdemeanor, and the ship . . . be forfeited to Her Majesty." During the Geneva Arbitration, this issue formed an important part of the argument for claims submitted against Britain by the United States.[27]

The *Florida* waited at Brest for five months for repairs to be completed. Doubtless this could have been done more quickly in England. But if Maffitt had done so, the cruiser could have been seized or otherwise detained by the court until the war ended. The fortunes of the South had changed, and the British Foreign Office had initiated policy changes less favorable toward the Confederacy. U.S. Minister Charles Francis Adams kept close score of American vessels destroyed by British-built raiders. Secretary of State Seward piled diplomatic correspondence on the British Foreign Office, constantly protesting Lord Russell's lenient Confederate shipbuilding policies. Seward and Adams both threatened Russell with huge liability suits.

Throughout Europe, the relentless destruction of American ships carrying neutral foreign cargoes caused a subtle change in attitude toward the Confederacy, while in England, people were still puzzling over the strange case of the *Alexandra*.

The Strange Case
of the *Alexandra*

B Y THE summer of 1862, anti-British sentiment in America reached a new high as lurid newspaper accounts continued to detail the depredations of the Confederate raiders *Florida* and *Alabama*—ships built and equipped in Great Britain.

Theoretically, Britain's Foreign Enlistment Act of 1819 prevented its citizens from fitting out, equipping, or arming ships for combat in wars where Britain remained neutral. But Britain had strong ties with the South, which supplied much of the cotton to feed its mighty textile industry. And in the aftermath of the *Trent* Affair—in which the U.S. Navy had the audacity to stop one of Her Majesty's mail steamers on the high seas and remove two confederate diplomats—there was considerable pro-Southern sentiment, both in the public and within the government.

Both raiders had gotten to sea through the capable management of James Dunwoody Bulloch. By complying with the letter of the law rather than with the intent, and with the connivance of sympathetic British officials, Bulloch was able to skirt the Foreign Enlistment Act. Willing British naval contractors disguised the real purchasers of Confederate warships and registered the vessels as merchants: The *Oreto*, which became the *Florida*, was being built for the Italian government; the *Enrica*, which became the *Alabama*, was being built for Spain.

Once these raiders got to sea and shed their disguise, and when the excitement stirred by the *Trent* Affair subsided, the British government began to reconsider its liberal interpretation of the act and adopt a strictly neutral policy. Although this change of attitude coincided with the Confederate failure at Gettysburg and the fall of Vicksburg, the event that ultimately led to the demise of Confederate shipbuilding in Britain was not important land battles, but a relatively obscure court case involving a 300-ton steamer called the *Alexandra*.

Thomas H. Dudley, the American consul at Liverpool, had been relentless in his search for covert Confederate attempts to acquire a navy. Agents and detectives prowled the shipyards, talking to workers, questioning sailors in grog shops—and keeping Bulloch under close surveillance. From this network Dudley received a constant flow of information—some factual, and some cleverly planted by Bulloch. Consequently, Dudley usually found himself a few steps behind the Confederate procurement specialist.

Toward the end of 1862, Dudley believed he had spotted another Confederate cruiser—a small wooden screw steamer under construction in the Liverpool shipyard of Messrs. W. C. Miller and Son. Miller's yard had produced the *Florida*, and the new ship, the *Alexandra*, although much smaller, bore distinct similarities in material and design. Dudley reported the new cruiser to Secretary of State Seward, but felt his case was not yet strong enough under the Foreign Enlistment Act to solicit Her Majesty's intervention.

It was natural for Dudley to suspect that Bulloch was behind the building of the *Alexandra*: every element fit his method of operation. Bulloch, however, never had the slightest control over the vessel, and never issued an instruction in reference to her. The ship was actually built under a contract with Charles K. Prioleau, of Liverpool, at his own risk and expense. Bulloch learned of the project later when Prioleau confided to him "that his purpose was to send her as an unarmed ship to run the blockade into Charleston, if possible, and after her arrival there he meant to present her to the Confederate Government."[1]

At this stage of the war, Prioleau had no reason to be concerned about finishing the ship and getting it to sea. Dozens of vessels had been built or converted to blockade runners without interference from the government. Great Britain enjoyed brisk sales of ordnance to both belligerents, her shipyards were inundated with profitable contracts, and her maritime commerce had expanded rapidly to fill the void left by the demise of American shipping.

While the British enjoyed unusual prosperity, the Queen's ministers began to realize that the North might win the war, and the active Confederate shipbuilding program in Britain could strain relations with a reunified and militarily strengthened United States. Charles Francis Adams, United States Minister to England, had been a persistent critic of British failures to suppress Confederate shipbuilding, and his constant pressure on Foreign Secretary Lord John Russell induced Great Britain to bring a test case to trial.

By late March, 1863, Dudley thought he had sufficient evidence to justify legal action. Three of Dudley's paid agents submitted sworn statements testifying that the *Alexandra* was a new Confederate cruiser. On March 28 Dudley sent a formal request to Samuel Price Edwards, collector of customs, to seize the ship on the grounds that it was "being equipped, furnished, and fitted out in order that such vessel shall be employed in the service of the persons assuming to exercise the powers of Government and called the Confederate States of America, and with the intent to cruise and commit hostilities against the Government and citizens of the United States of America, with which Government Her Majesty the Queen is not now at war."[2]

Minister Adams reinforced Dudley's demands by emphasizing to Lord Russell that "the same individuals who were concerned in the . . . departure of the gunboat #290 [*Alabama*] are now mentioned as directing the outfit of the *Alexandra.*" He insisted that this incident was no isolated violation of British neutrality, but was part of a vast network of Southern naval activity masterminded by Confederate secret agents. Adams pledged to leave no avenue unexplored in bringing this activity to an end. There is little doubt that both Dudley and Adams suspected that Bulloch was the central figure in the affair.[3]

On the question of neutrality, the British ministry faced two contending elements, one being the proper discharge of Britain's international obligations, and the other being the protection of lawful domestic private enterprise. There was sufficient reason to suspect that the *Alexandra* was being built as a gift to the Confederacy by Southern sympathizers in England. On paper, she was the legal private property of Fawcett, Preston, and Company, a reputable British firm. There was no concrete proof of Confederate ownership, and the crucial question concerning the presence of warlike equipage remained ambiguous. Dudley's evidence on this point was imperfect.

Conflicting points of view among British Foreign Office advisors further complicated matters. Customs Collector Edwards claimed that in his judgment the ship was "intended for the Confederate Government," and that special detectives would soon have sufficient evidence to enable the government to act. He recommended to Russell that the *Alexandra* be "unofficially" detained. In a separate investigation conducted by the treasury, inspectors admitted that the ship was more strongly built than "customary in merchant vessels," but violated no rules, there being no law forbidding the construction of specially reinforced vessels.[4]

Finally, two of England's leading legal experts, Roundell Palmer and Robert Phillimore, were consulted. Believing that the ship's structure provided suitable grounds, both recommended that the *Alexandra* be seized. With no precedents to guide legal action on the "intended" use of a vessel, the ambiguity in the Foreign Enlistment Act needed to be tested in court. They expected the owners would bring suit to recover their property and hoped such action would help clarify the rules. If the court sanctioned seizure merely upon suspicion of intent, the entire Confederate construction program could come to an end. Carefully following the advice of counsel, Lord Russell ordered the ship seized on suspicion that her owners intended to use the ship against the United States.[5]

On April 5, 1863 the surveyor of customs at Liverpool ordered the King's Broad Arrow marked on one of her masts, and seized the *Alexandra* under the Foreign Enlistment Act. The vessel was now the property of the Crown, an action that drew considerable public attention. *The Times* described the ship as a fine tidy-looking craft, "nicely coppered and copper fastened," projecting an impression of speed, but with no gunports or shell room. After noting that the engines had not been fitted, the account concluded, "she presents the appearance of a fast schooner-rigged steam yacht."[6]

The following day, Adams expressed to Lord Russell his "lively satisfaction" over the detention of the vessel and promptly promised to provide every assistance in gathering further information to support the seizure. Adams then sent a hurried note to Secretary Seward, advising him that, "I think we may infer from this act that the government is really disposed to maintain its neutrality."[7]

As expected, Fawcett, Preston and Company protested the seizure, claiming that the firm had built the ship as a speculative venture. She was described as a three-masted schooner of under 300 tons with engines upon the screw principle of 60 horsepower, calculated to drive her at a speed of 9 to 10 knots, and designed to be fitted out either as a passenger boat, mailboat, or yacht.[8]

A great deal of procedural confusion ensued in bringing the case to court, exhausting the patience of both Union and Confederate officials. Because local sentiment in Liverpool was heavily influenced by the prosperity of the shipbuilding industry, the government moved the case to London. Although the delay exasperated Northern interests, naval contractors throughout Great Britain hesitated to continue work on contracts for the South until the court ruled on the impounded ship's status. For nearly four months, the issue languished in uncertainty.

Finally, on June 22, 1863, the British Court of Exchequer opened the trial of the *Alexandra* at Westminster, charging Fawcett, Preston and its agents with violating 96 counts of the Foreign Enlistment Act.[9] The Court directed the Crown to prove, first, that the vessel was built for the purpose of being equipped for war; second, that she was intended at some stage of her construction for the service of the Confederate States. As the trial began, it soon became apparent that the government stood little chance of winning. Roundell Palmer was arguing his first case against both Sir Hugh Cairns, one of England's most gifted attorneys, and George Mellish, one of Britain's best trial lawyers. The defense was brilliantly constructed: key witnesses for the prosecution lost credibility under cross-examination; sensitive issues were presented in terms that Englishmen coveted as individual liberties; arguments appealed to national pride, anti-Americanism, and domestic economic interests.

The three important witnesses for the prosecution were spies on the payroll of Consul Dudley, and Sir Hugh Cairns openly criticized testimony given by paid informants. John Da Costa claimed to be a reputable shipping agent and steamboat owner, but Sir Hugh revealed that he was actually "a crimp and a partner in a tug."[10] Next came George Templeton Chapman, one of Dudley's spies who had infiltrated the offices of Fraser, Trenholm and Company for the purpose of taking Prioleau into his confidence and learning his secrets. Despite a long, sworn statement upon which the Crown had relied when seizing the *Alexandra*, Sir Hugh dismantled the evidence to such an extent that Chapman could not "put his finger upon a single fact that could bear upon the case of the *Alexandra*."[11]

The most dubious testimony came from Clarence R. Yonge, Bulloch's former private secretary and the acting assistant paymaster for Semmes at the time the *Alabama* went to sea. Semmes had discharged Yonge in disgrace for embezzlement. Sir Hugh gave the court Yonge's history in capsule form: "How am I to describe this specimen of humanity? The man who began his career by abandoning his wife and child in his native country . . . who then became a deserter, slipping overboard and leaving the ship of which he was an officer, in order that he might by lying pretense of a marriage effect the ruin and plunder the property of a widow, who had the misfortune to entertain him in her country and to be possessed of some property of her own; who succeeded in possessing himself of that property; who brought her over to Liverpool, and who then turned her adrift, penniless, on the streets; . . . who stood there in the witness-box before you, who denied no crime and blushed at no villainy, until, indeed, it was suggested that the victim of his villainy had been a mulatto woman, and not his wife, and then all his feeling of self-respect recoiled, and he indignantly denied the charge." By the time Sir Hugh finished with Yonge, the Crown had lost its case.[12]

After a three-day trial, Judge Sir Jonathan Frederick Pollack told the jury: "If you think the object was to build a ship in obedience to an order, and in compliance with a contract, leaving it to those who bought it to make what use they felt fit of it, then it appears to be that the Foreign Enlistment Act has not been in any degree broken."

Throughout the trial, Pollack had demonstrated a Southern bias that mirrored the sentiment of much of the country. At one point, he suggested from the bench that if the law did not prohibit sale of munitions and muskets, why should ships be an exception? Answering his own question, he advised the court that there was no difference. This statement helped to destroy the Crown's case, as Britain's brisk sale of arms to both belligerents was widely known and accepted.[13]

Only a verdict of acquittal was possible. The chief juror declined a trial transcript, and according to a reporter from Liverpool, "without hesitating for more than a half a minute, returned a verdict against the Crown." The public approved, but Adams called the verdict scandalous. The *Liverpool Daily Courier* heralded the larger issue: "In effect this makes construction and supplying of the *Alabama* and *Florida* . . . as those vessels left our shores, perfectly legal acts."[14]

A few days later, Fawcett, Preston applied for the restoration of the *Alexandra*, only to learn that the Crown had filed an appeal with the House of Lords. The vessel had been placed in dry dock and her exposed planking showed signs of deterioration. Fawcett, Preston suggested that the ship be acquired by the Royal Navy, but the navy did not want the vessel even though the Foreign Office favored the solution for political reasons: The United States would interpret the purchase as a change in British policy toward building Confederate naval vessels. Other British officials suggested that the vessel be sold to Venezuela as a means of overcoming a political impasse, but Lord Russell opposed this action because Venezuela itself was at war.[15]

In April 1864, after the appeal to the House of Lords had failed and a full year after her seizure, Fawcett, Preston finally recovered the *Alexandra*, claiming £6,370 in damages, but settling eventually for £3,700. With legal battles ended, they sold the *Alexandra* to a firm who rechristened her *Mary* and modified her for blockade running.

When Dudley orchestrated the seizure of the *Alexandra*, he opened the eyes of the British government to the profusion of Confederate shipbuilding activities in Her Majesty's shipyards. Two mysterious ironclad cruisers known as the "Laird Rams" were under construction at Birkenhead, identified only as 294 and 295. Their ownership was shrouded in secrecy, but Dudley's spies were compiling evidence to show that the underlying owner of the rams was the Confederate government, and that the conspirator behind the contracts was Bulloch.

Consul Dudley's proof was sketchy, but his assumptions were correct. The rams, powerful seagoing vessels capable of attacking and destroying the Union blockading fleet, were part of a fleet of ironclads under construction in both Great Britain and France.[16] To the Confederacy, the rams represented the last hope of keeping Southern ports open to receive essential war materials. To the British, they represented a future liability if the South failed in her war for independence.

Russell discovered another potential cruiser—an enlarged, higher powered copy of the *Alabama*—on the stocks in the yard of J. and G. Thomson and Company of Glasgow, Scotland. Built under well-disguised ownership, Lt. George T. Sinclair intended to commission the vessel as the CSS *Pampero*.

Work on the ship accelerated during the summer of 1863, and by October, the American consul at Glasgow began clamoring for her detention. Adams pressed Russell for action to prevent the nearly completed ship from sailing, but he was unable to get sufficient evidence to seize her. Union officials tried to find proof that the notorious Captain Maffitt was in Glasgow with a crew and planned to sail as captain. When Russell learned that the vessel had not yet applied for a certificate of registry or a declaration of nationality, he stationed two gunboats alongside until someone in authority stepped forward to make the required disclosure and comply with the Merchant Shipping Act. When no action resulted, Russell authorized the Glasgow customs collector to seize the ship on December 10, 1863, advising his government that seizure would continue until the case came to court. He then deferred the hearing until after the war ended.[17]

Although the South considered the outcome of the *Alexandra* trial a victory for their clandestine cruiser-building program, it actually provoked a change in thinking within the British government. News of the defeats at Gettysburg and Vicksburg convinced Lord Russell that the North ultimately would win the war and reunite the nation, leaving Britain to deal with a war-hardened United States that wavered between being barely tolerant and openly hostile.

Russell detained the "Laird rams," took steps to suppress other Confederate shipbuilding activities, and delayed the release of the *Alexandra* until April, 1864. Despite public opposition, and contrary to his own legal advisors, Russell's action prevented further shipbuilding in Great Britain. In diplomatic matters involving the South, France closely followed Britain's lead. Shortly thereafter, Napoleon III abruptly changed French policy, and Confederate aspirations for an ironclad fleet were defeated forever.

It was about August 18, 1863 when Maffitt made the decision to take the *Florida* to Brest for repairs. Had he entered a British port for that purpose, Russell would probably have found a way to detain him. No record exists, but it is probable that Maffitt was guided or instructed during his brief stop at Cork, Ireland, to seek a French port to repair the *Florida*. Considering the alternatives, Brest proved a good choice.

As for the *Alexandra*, now the *Mary*, she never left the watchful eyes of the United States. On September 10, 1864 the consul at Halifax, Nova Scotia, reported her arrival and stated that he believed she intended to receive arms. Three months later revenue agents at Nassau detained her when they discovered a 12-pound rifled gun and cases of shells in her afterhold. The gun, embossed "Fawcett Preston & Co. 1862," had been loaded on the ship during a recent stop at Bermuda. At Nassau, the court reviewed the case and eventually released the ship. By then, however, the war was over.[18]

Interlude at Brest

T HE *FLORIDA'S* arrival at Brest on August 23, 1863 was an exciting occasion for this fishing port on the tip of the Breton peninsula. Although no salute boomed from French shore batteries to recognize the first appearance of the Stars and Bars in a French port, the towns-people rushed to the waterfront to see the famous Confederate raider that had blazed a trail of smoldering wreckage across the Atlantic. The enthusiastic reception demonstrated a strong sympathy for the Southern cause.

While Maffitt sought permission to repair and refit his ship, word spread of the cruiser's arrival. In Paris, United States Minister to France William L. Dayton protested to the French government that the *Florida* was not a warship but a pirate. Dayton's statements made sensational copy for Parisian papers. Ugly horror stories changed shouts of praise to guarded whispers of innocent mariners swinging from yardarms, as blackguards transferred chests of gold and silver into the bulging hold of the ruthless corsair.[1]

Dayton fanned the flames of public criticism, demanding that the pirate be ejected from France, and public sentiment turned against the *Florida*. French officials, however, ignored the clamor. Maffitt easily received permission from Vice Admiral Count de Gueyton, who was in charge of the port at Brest, to purchase supplies and to engage any of the privately owned facilities he needed to repair the cruiser, so long as he did not increase her armament. De Gueyton, who had followed the *Florida's* sweep of the oceans with uncommon interest, was awed by Maffitt's accomplishments, and dismissed the press coverage as simple commercial sensationalism.[2]

Nevertheless, Maffitt recognized the importance of squelching the unfavorable rumors circulating ashore, and invited Count de Gueyton aboard to observe the ship's discipline and draw his own conclusions. The Vice Admiral was delighted, and agreed to visit the following day. Maffitt hurried back to the ship, ordering haircuts and beard trims for every officer and sailor before they turned to for a marathon field day.

When Count de Gueyton and his official staff ascended the gang-way the following day, they could not have found a nattier crew on a French warship; everything aboard was shipshape and Bristol fashion. As salutes boomed across the harbor, the count expressed satisfaction over the vessel's legitimacy — any hidden doubts implanted by a hostile press vanished after a few hours of Southern hospitality. Count de Gueyton returned to shore and issued an official communique: "The steamer *Florida*, now undergoing repairs at Brest, is not a corsaire as has been first supposed. She belongs to the navy of the Confederate States of America." The message was magic. Once again the citizens of Brest gathered at the waterfront to cheer the weary visitor and her gallant crew.[3]

While Maffitt and de Gueyton were exchanging mutual admiration in Brest, Minister Dayton was in Paris initiating a diplomatic war to have the *Florida* expelled. He expected the French to recognize the ship as a belligerent entitled to the conventional rights offered by neutrals, but claimed that, because her sail had been reported in good condition, she was perfectly safe to go to sea and did not need the shelter of a French port. Dayton applied every diplomatic stumbling block he could contrive to prevent the raider from refitting, and sent a message to Captain John A. Winslow of the USS *Kearsarge*, urging him to hurry over to Brest and "do something" about the *Florida*.

On September 17, 1863, Winslow entered the harbor and anchored beside the raider.[4] This lasted a very short time, as de Gueyton wanted no trouble at Brest and ordered the *Kearsarge* out to sea.

The *Kearsarge*'s arrival at Brest attracted the attention of *The London Times*, which dispatched a correspondent to watch for developments and, if possible, obtain an interview with Maffitt. Privately, *The Times* hoped that the two ships would square off and fight to the finish. Maffitt made it clear that he did not intend to pick a fight. The Union Navy had more than 1,000 vessels; the Confederacy but two — the *Florida* and the *Alabama*. Maffitt would not fight unless forced to blast his way through a Union blockade when he was ready for sea.[5]

Shortly after the *Florida*'s arrival, Maffitt discovered that the commercial docking facilities at Brest were inadequate, and once again called upon de Gueyton, this time for permission to use the extensive government docking and repair facilities. The Vice Admiral granted the request, but insisted that all munitions be removed and that prompt payment be made for the use of the shipyard. Maffitt deposited F40,000 in advance with M. Aumaitre, agent for the *Florida* at Brest, and unloaded the munitions into a barge anchored alongside.

Maffitt's use of the government dockyard invited another barrage of protests from Dayton, but he received only polite replies from French officials. The American consul at Paris, John Bigelow, viewed the matter more optimistically, stating to a colleague: "I hope they will let the *Florida* into the Government Docks. I will engage that she does not get out in four or five months. All her machinery will have to be taken out of her piece by piece and nothing is quite so slow as a French Government work shop of any kind."[6] Time proved Bigelow correct.

Seeking refuge in France began to look like a bad idea. In September, several French ship owners lodged grievances with the Tribunal of Commerce at Marseille for damages to their property caused by the *Florida*. One owner sought damages of F100,000 for losses suffered when the *Florida* forced one of his vessels to carry prisoners to Acapulco. Another owner filed a claim for cargo lost when the raider burned the *W.B. Nash*. The Tribunal asked for seizure.

None of these claims was prompted by United States actions. Both Dayton and Bigelow believed that France would be more inclined toward seizure if the U. S. avoided the issue altogether. A refusal to seize the ship would mean that France recognized the *Florida* as a regularly constituted warship—an action counter to France's stated declaration of neutrality. Bigelow believed that the incident could develop into a great source of national embarrassment.[7]

Bigelow's hope for the *Florida*'s seizure collapsed when the French Minister of Marine refused to accept the claims. When most European maritime countries had signed the Declaration of Paris against privateering, the United States had declined; therefore, damages could not be indemnified for neutral property destroyed on American ships. The ruling generated no repercussions beyond disappointing a few French merchants and Minister Bigelow.

Reference to the Declaration of Paris opened another door for Dayton: privateering. There was a difference between the rights accorded a privateer and those available to a duly constituted man-of-war. Dayton argued that allowing a privateer to refit in a French port was contrary to the position France adopted when she signed the treaty. He also argued that it made no difference if the United States did not sign; a commerce raider was a privateer whether she carried a letter of marque or a commission.

The French, on the other hand, considered the *Florida* a warship holding a legally recognized commission and thereby entitled to make any navigational repairs she wished as long as there was no increase to her armament. They reminded Dayton that since the United States had not signed the Declaration of Paris, it was entitled to no protection from it.[8]

While diplomats argued over international law, repairs to the *Florida* proceeded with surprisingly little interference. The ship remained in the government dockyard for nearly five weeks. From there, it moved into the merchant harbor, where workmen refitted the engine and installed a new blower system to improve the burning of inferior coal.

Work on the *Florida* took months, and nothing went smoothly. Parts had to be shipped from England; French mechanics unfamiliar with the machinery had to be replaced by imported English mechanics. Trial runs revealed new problems that required more delays and more parts. Through all this, the French were patient and seemed willing to give the *Florida* unlimited time—as long as tariffs and other expenses were promptly paid.

Shortly after arriving at Brest, Maffitt inexplicably released 59 members of the crew. (They later landed at Cardiff, Wales, where their unexpected appearance misled the United States consul there to believe they were to be reassigned to a Confederate ironclad.) There is no record of the reason for this action, but the high cost of carrying so many men in port must have been a consideration.[9] Excluding F135,000 for repairs, Assistant Paymasters John R. Davis and Richard Taylor distributed over F300,000 for the crew and for simple maintenance of the ship.

An account left by G. Terry Sinclair, a midshipman on the cruiser, implies another reason for the crew's dismissal: a mutiny may have been brewing. The officers received shore leave and went to Paris, but rumors stirred among the crew that shore liberty for them had been denied. This may have caused a work disruption, but the matter of actual mutiny only came to light 35 years later, leaving doubt of its validity. The *Florida* was watched closely by American agents while at Brest, and no record exists of a mutiny aside from Sinclair's questionable account.[10]

Also during this time, Maffitt suffered a possible heart attack. A specialist from Paris decreed a three-month rest, followed by some leisurely travel. While waiting for his replacement, Commander Joseph N. Barney, to arrive, Maffitt kept to his bunk. Without Maffitt on deck, morale declined. The crew, most of whom had shipped at Mobile, and whose confidence rested entirely with their stricken captain, did not trust the junior officers, taking a special dislike to Lt. Averett. Idleness made them quarrelsome, and the officers struggled to maintain discipline.

When Barney arrived at Brest, he inherited not only an inadequate crew, but the difficulty of trying to fill vacancies without violating French neutrality. This problem was exacerbated by the temporary absence of Bulloch from Liverpool. When Maffitt discharged part of the crew at Brest, he paid each $25 on account and arranged for their passage to Liverpool. In a separate letter, he advised Bulloch that the men were to be paid off by Fraser, Trenholm and Company upon arrival, in hopes that they could be retained for future service in the Confederate Navy. When the men arrived in Liverpool and found Bulloch gone, they suspected duplicity.[11]

Out of cash, the angry crew shifted about Liverpool for five days waiting to be paid. Finally some of them became so disgusted that they brought their problem to U.S. Consul Dudley, who listened sympathetically to their grievances, made them comfortable, and extracted an enormous amount of important intelligence. When he realized that the *Florida* could not return to sea with its present crew, Dudley initiated actions to prevent Barney from enlisting a new one. Knowing that the men had come to Liverpool to be paid, but had not been paid, Dudley inserted this in the *London Daily Post*:

> We the undersigned sailors and firemen of the steamer *Florida*, wish to know if Captain Bulloch, agent of the Confederate States of America, will pay our orders from Captain Maffitt, Commander of the Confederate States steamer *Florida*, as we have now been here five days, and have no means of subsistence. We trust that Captain Bulloch will send his address to 36 Sparling Street. We have all got orders for our wages from Captain Maffitt, amounting to from $60 to $260 each, and we trust that we shall have no further trouble getting our money.[12]

When Bulloch returned from his trip, he paid the wages, but not until September 29 — two weeks late. As Dudley had hoped, the publicity did not go unnoticed by other sailors who might have been tempted to sign aboard a Confederate vessel, encumbering Barney's efforts to obtain experienced replacements. Although the impact of this incident cannot be fully measured, the *Florida*'s shortage of manpower delayed her departure from Brest.

Through Dudley's efforts, Minister to England Charles Francis Adams obtained a roster of the *Florida*'s discharged crew. With some research, he identified several sailors as British subjects and sent the information to Lord Russell, along with a protest citing the flagrant violation of the Foreign Enlistment Act, which prohibited the recruiting of British subjects. He warned that these men were in England to transfer to another Confederate warship, and produced a second roster of 15 men from the *Florida* whom he claimed had specifically requested a transfer to another Confederate ship.[13]

With repairs progressing slowly, Barney applied to the French government for permission to fill the vacancies in his crew. Ruling that replacements were necessary for the navigation of the ship, France approved the request, stipulating that the vacancies could not be filled by French nationals. Dayton's protests were ignored by French officials, although the *Florida* was not permitted to increase her crew beyond the 70 men Barney claimed Maffitt had discharged.

Finding replacements became a difficult and complicated process. Men could not be recruited from French ports, and U.S. agents in Britain, aware of the *Florida's* shortage, made determined efforts to prevent recruitment in England. Union agents in Liverpool and other British ports sought out sailors who might enlist on the *Florida* and paid them full wages to remain at home. Another tactic threatened sailors with prosecution under the Foreign Enlistment Act. Between bribes and threats, seamen and recruiting agents became scarce in Britain.[14]

Barney wanted English-speaking seamen, and the small number recruited in England were insufficient to man the cruiser. Confederate agents gathered the new inductees into small groups, forwarded them to Calais, and arranged their transport to Brest by rail. Most of the sailors did not know they were to be shipped on the *Florida* until they arrived, which helped prevent Union agents from uncovering their destination. The remainder of the crew were Spanish and Italian seamen, unfamiliar with the ship or her machinery. They spoke little English and clashed with their Anglo-American shipmates. Eventually, Barney scavenged enough seamen to operate the ship, although the crew never reached its full complement.[15]

After supervising most of the ship's repairs, Barney developed chronic dyspepsia and asked to be relieved of command—and lost for the second time the opportunity to take the cruiser to sea. According to Surgeon Thomas J. Charlton, the illness resulted from poor diet and excessive confinement; only fresh provisions and exercise would restore his health. On January 5, 1864, Flag Officer Samuel Barron detached Barney and replaced him with Lt. Charles M. Morris, who was in Paris and seeking a command.[16]

When Georgia seceded, Morris had resigned from the U.S. Navy and was appointed a lieutenant in the Confederate Navy, commanding the gunboat *Huntress* at Savannah. When Bulloch began building the Confederate ironclads at Birkenhead, Mallory sent Morris to England to command one of the rams. After the British seized the ironclads, he became available for reassignment. Morris was an experienced and capable officer, but had neither the imagination nor the resourcefulness of Semmes and Maffitt.[17]

Morris' first priority was to get the *Florida* back to sea. After a disappointing trial run around the harbor, he discovered several new problems with the machinery. Engineer Charles W. Quinn reported that if the engine was to stand a long cruise, more parts must be ordered. By now, even the French wanted the ship out of Brest.[18] Morris requested and to his surprise received permission from French authorities to use the facilities at the local arsenal. With help from a competent machine shop, Morris energetically solved many of the remaining problems and finally had the cruiser ready to sail on February 9. Nearly six months had elapsed since Maffitt entered Brest for a quick overhaul. Any of the large English shipbuilding yards could have accomplished the same work in a few weeks, especially those on the Clyde or the Mersey, but with the seizure of the Birkenhead rams, Maffit felt safer in France.[19]

During the *Florida*'s long stay at Brest, lookouts on the *Kearsarge* scanned the *Florida* 24 hours a day, with orders to report any unusual activity to Captain Winslow. The harbor at Brest was open and broad — a difficult place to confine a fast ship. Maffitt had chosen Brest for this very reason. Three channels radiated out from the harbor. Winslow, admitting that he could cover only one at a time, decided that if the *Florida* sailed, he would ignore the 24-hour rule and blast the ship to pieces despite the consequences.[20]

Through spies ashore, Winslow learned that the *Florida* needed further repairs that could not be completed for several weeks. Nonetheless, on October 9 he sent a written challenge, which Barney returned unopened. Edward G. Eastman, the U.S. consul at Queenstown, Ireland, himself a former sea captain, felt that Winslow's challenge had not been strong enough and asked that another attempt be made publicly. Eastman believed that refusing a public challenge would imply cowardice, but he overlooked the cruiser's condition. The *Florida* could not fight (her munitions had been off-loaded), and Barney again disregarded the challenge. No record exists, but Barney probably felt relieved to have a reason to decline an engagement with the more powerful *Kearsarge*.[21]

Vice Admiral Count de Gueyton noticed Winslow's tendency to call his men to quarters every time unusual activity occurred on the *Florida*. Barney suspected that Winslow planned to violate the 24-hour ruling, and de Gueyton threatened to protect the regulation with force. Concern diminished when the French ironclad fleet unexpectedly steamed into Brest. Winslow wrote that it was one of the most powerful naval forces he had ever seen. A few days later he learned that work on the *Florida* would not be completed for at least a month, and on October 31 the *Kearsarge* steamed out of the harbor in search of the CSS *Georgia*, which had just been reported.[22]

Winslow returned to Brest on November 7 after learning that the *Georgia* had entered Cherbourg. He stationed the *Kearsarge* off one of Brest's three channels and wrote Welles for assistance in guarding the other two. Welles feared the diplomatic repercussions of establishing a blockade of French ports, however, and sent no help. Meanwhile, Winslow waited and watched, prepared to go after the *Florida* or the *Georgia*, whichever moved first.[23]

French warships shadowed the *Kearsarge* constantly, watching for any violation of neutrality. Welles sent a message reporting another Confederate cruiser operating in the English Channel; an old British warship, commissioned CSS *Rappahannock*, had just sailed into Calais. Now Winslow had three raiders to watch, and still no help. A few days later he learned that the *Rappahannock* had been pierced for eight guns, but had not yet been armed. He knew the vessel would be coming out to receive her ordnance on some remote island, or at sea, and attempted to position the *Kearsarge* to intercept any of the three cruisers, regardless of which moved first.[24]

The *Kearsarge* put to sea on December 5, never wandering far from Brest, entering port occasionally to obtain provisions and collect information on the *Florida's* progress. Constant cruising had begun to wear down the Union warship, however, and by the end of January, the *Kearsarge* needed extensive repairs. On January 23, 1864, Winslow abandoned his vigil and steamed for Cadiz, Spain. His timing was bad. When he returned to Brest on February 19, the *Florida* had sailed, and to his dismay, so had the *Georgia*. The sudden disappearance of both ships gave rise to speculation that the Confederate cruisers planned to combine forces and attack the *Kearsarge*. While the thought worried Winslow, the rumor was untrue.[25] Winslow's luck eventually changed, but not until June 19, 1864. His adversary then would be Raphael Semmes and the *Alabama*, back from a long, hard voyage to the Far East. As for the *Florida*, he never saw her again.

THIRTEEN

The *Florida* Under Morris

O N FEBRUARY 9, 1864, Vice Admiral Count de Gueyton informed Lt. Morris that the *Florida*'s extended stay at Brest must end, and gave him 24 hours to leave. The *Kearsarge* had gone, and it was safe to leave, but Morris was still shorthanded, the new recruits were inexperienced, and the gun carriages were worn and nearly useless.[1] Nevertheless, on February 10, the *Florida* headed back to sea.

After nearly six months of continuous repairs, Morris still was dissatisfied with the *Florida*'s performance. Shortly after leaving Brest she was struck by a strong gale, and could make only eight knots under power, although her boilers consumed coal at a prodigious rate. Morris hoisted sail and banked the fires, determined to avoid having to take on coal in a European port, where he was almost certain to be reported to the Union.

Morris did not have far to look for an explanation for his ship's poor efficiency. On February 16 a fireman went on deck after opening the lower blow cock, and forgot to return to close it. Water gradually drained from the boiler, causing it to overheat, damaging the smoke box. Chief Engineer Charles W. Quinn entered the fire room just in time to save the boilers from permanent damage. The starboard furnace overheated, creating a three-inch bulge in the arch and burning the tips of 26 tubes.[2]

On February 19 the *Florida* rendezvoused off Belle Isle with a steam tug carrying ordnance supplies, including new carriages and slides for the pivot guns, and various arms and munitions that had been ordered from time to time by the preceding three commanders. Morris wrote Flag Officer Barron, "I have met Captain Tessier, and have all on board that was expected, and hope to be off by daylight."[3] The *Florida* sailed south toward Madeira.

The raider's unexpected disappearance launched a search by every Union vessel in Europe. Reports of sightings drifted into consular offices from the North Atlantic to Africa. Once again, the Union navy reacted to every report and scattered the fleet in all directions. Although some of the claimed sightings may have been honest mistakes, Confederate agents intentionally planted inaccurate reports among known Union agents.[4] One rumor caught the attention of Commander George H. Preble, aboard the 700-ton sailing sloop-of-war *St. Louis* at Lisbon. Anxious to atone for his unfortunate experience with Maffitt at Mobile, Preble set all sail for Madeira, arriving at Funchal Roads on February 22. The raider wasn't there, but Preble wouldn't have long to wait.[5]

Morris arrived at Funchal on February 26, and was surprised to see the *St. Louis*. Normally, Morris would be unconcerned by a Union vessel that carried only sail, but he had come to Funchal for coal. With bunkers down to 30 tons limiting his steaming range, the *St. Louis* could prove troublesome.

The American consul at Funchal had just died, and Preble appointed Robert Bayman to the vacancy. The new consul immediately pressured local authorities to deny the *Florida* coal or provisions. Morris confronted an obstinate governor who "positively refused to let me have coal, water, or bread, and the captain of the port gave me a verbal order to leave . . . which I declined doing without . . . coal." After a second appeal Port Captain Joaquin Pedro de Castelbrance, who was anxious to get rid of Morris, replied, "The said governor has ordered me to communicate to you that he agrees that you shall take the necessary biscuit and water and 20 tons coal to enable you to proceed to the high seas, at the same time requiring that you quit this port by to-morrow evening."[6]

Meanwhile, Preble, in an effort to head off an international incident, found it necessary to unload his guns to prevent his patriotic crew from shooting at the enemy anchored nearby.[7] Although this probably prevented a diplomatic debacle, Secretary Welles harshly criticized Preble for disarming his ship in the presence of an enemy.[8] Preble felt his action justified because he believed, and correctly so, that Morris would not fight. Morris had excercised a pivot gun and found it unmanageable. Moreover, the *Florida* had just been repaired, and her commander would not want to risk damaging his ship with so few friendly ports available.[9]

On February 29 Morris sent a second message to the governor appealing for another 20 tons of coal, stating that without it he would be unable to reach another port.[10] The governor shot back a refusal accompanied by a warning that if Morris did not accept the 20 tons, that, too, would be withdrawn. Morris loaded his meager ration and sailed that evening, slipping quietly by the vigilant *St. Louis*. Preble had reshotted his guns, suspecting that if the *Florida* departed at night, she might fire a salvo as she passed. Despite a sharp lookout, when the moon rose after midnight the Union sloop's lookouts reported the *Florida* gone.[11]

Morris sailed for Tenerife to fill bunkers, leaving word behind that he was heading for Cadiz. This did not fool Preble, who again divined the *Florida's* heading. On their way back to sea on March 6, after coaling at Tenerife, the *Florida's* lookout sighted the *St. Louis* approaching. Morris again chose not to fight, but he may have lost an opportunity: In the calm winds, the *Florida* would have been much more maneuverable than the *St. Louis*. Morris still did not trust his guns, however.[12]

For the next three weeks the *Florida* sailed west, gradually edging southward. Neutral ships passed daily, but no American merchantmen. Morris conducted daily gunnery drill, and the crew constructed new carriages for the big pivot guns. Work details scraped and painted until the ship sparkled like new, and gradually discipline improved.

Finally on March 29 the *Florida* captured her first prize since August 21, 1863, the Boston ship *Avon*, bound for the Howland Islands with 1,600 tons of guano. After being stripped of valuables and used for target practice, the ship was burned. Fourteen of her 17-man crew elected to enlist with the cruiser. Five days later Morris stopped the English bark *Francis Milly*, bound for London, and negotiated passage for the remaining prisoners.[13]

For the next four weeks, the *Florida* cruised a section of the Atlantic that once had been crowded with homeward-bound American commerce. Now, however, only one of the many vessels boarded was American—and she had just been transferred to British registry.[14] When he steamed into Saint-Pierre, Martinique on April 26, Morris had little to show for two months at sea except empty bunkers, an empty larder, and a disillusioned crew.

For five days the *Florida* loaded supplies while half the crew enjoyed shore leave. Six sailors failed to return. Desertions were common after a long voyage, as the charms of grog shops and brothels took their toll. Such losses seldom affected the efficiency of a ship, as the most unreliable men usually are the ones who fail to return. Morris, however, could hardly afford to lose anyone.[15]

Morris then lost two officers to illness. Second Lt. James L. Hoole had been suffering with a chronic lung disorder for nearly four months, and Surgeon Carlton considered him unfit for duty. Second Assistant Engineer John C. Lake showed signs of secondary syphilis and resigned. Two of the remaining engineering officers reported sick, and Morris struggled to find ways to keep the ship under steam.[16]

On April 30, the *Florida* returned to sea with a fresh supply of coal and a greatly diminished purse. Cruisers counted on prizes to replenish their coin, and prizes had become hard to find. Admiral James L. Lardner, commander of the West Indies Squadron, learned of Morris's visit to Martinique and his cash problems. Worried that the raider would go after a treasure ship, the Union commander dashed off in the *Powhatan*, chasing rumors between St. Thomas and Martinique. By then, the *Florida* was off Bermuda, 1,000 miles away.[17]

Morris hoped to solve two problems at Bermuda: acquire cash to keep the ship supplied, and engineers to keep it running. Two days before reaching Bermuda, Acting Chief Engineer Quinn had discovered another near disaster with the after boiler. In his report he stated: "At present you have a dissatisfied set of engineers. As for myself, I am not satisfied with the assistance I have got at present, especially when I have got engineers who are not satisfied with the vessel and who desire to leave as soon as possible. . . . I can not put the same trust and confidence in them that I ought and would wish for, especially having so many accidents since leaving Brest."

When the *Florida* entered Bermuda on May 12, Surgeon Charlton urged that Lt. Averett, who suffered from chronic vertigo resulting from overwork, be relieved. Morris agreed, and realizing that sending his first officer would lend credibility to the appeal, prepared dispatches for Averett to carry to Mallory at Richmond urgently requesting both funds and engineering personnel. Morris included Quinn's report and put Averett on a blockade runner for Wilmington, North Carolina.[18]

Competence in the engine room had declined to the point where the engines could be operated on only one watch. The engineers had to travel constantly between the fire rooms and the engine room to make sure the men performed their work. Quinn had done his best, but he was frequently ill, and Assistant Engineer Daniel McWilliams complained of poor health and skulked at his duties. Undermanned and out of cash, Morris abandoned a planned raid along the northeastern coast and hoped that British officials at Bermuda would grant him enough time for men and money to arrive from Mallory.[19]

On the evening of May 12 the *Florida* returned to sea and cruised slowly toward the northeast, never straying far from Bermuda. On May 18, seven weeks since her last capture, the raider overhauled the 198-ton schooner *George Latimer* of Baltimore, bound for Pernambuco with a cargo of bread, flour, and lard—exactly what the *Florida* needed. After stripping her supplies and taking her captain and crew prisoner, Morris burned the vessel. Three sailors signed on as crew; the remainder were transferred to the British ship *Nourmahal* three weeks later.[20]

Fresh food in the larder helped boost morale, but a month passed before the *Florida* captured another prize: the 338-ton hermaphrodite brig *William C. Clarke* of Machias, Maine, bound for Mantazas with a cargo of lumber. Although the captain testified that the cargo belonged to Spanish merchants, he could produce no supporting documents. So many American ships had gone to the trouble of obtaining false foreign documentation that Morris found it difficult to believe a captain would fail to obtain proper registration for a legitimately owned neutral cargo. After burning the brig, Morris returned to Bermuda and released the prisoners at St. George.[21]

Chief Engineer Quinn continued to struggle with mechanical difficulties ranging from "the injurious shake and jerk in the propeller screw" to "the Kingston blow valve to the after boiler" being carried away. Mechanical problems were so serious that Quinn wanted to put the ship in drydock. The valve, five feet below the waterline, could not be repaired at sea, and Quinn believed that the valve sheets had been sprung, reducing the boilers' ability to withstand steam pressure.[22]

After some difficulty, Morris received permission to use British facilities on Inland Island for five days to make the necessary repairs.[23] Although a drydock was unavailable, divers repaired the propeller and valve, and the crew scraped and cleaned the hull. Anticipating the arrival of funds, Morris had the bunkers cleaned to receive a new supply of coal.[24]

Morris returned to Bermuda on June 19 to find that Mallory had received his message and forwarded replacements: Lt. Thomas K. Porter and First Assistant Engineer William Ahern were waiting to join the cruiser; Chief Engineer Wingfield S. Thompson and Second Assistant Engineer John B. Brown reported for duty just prior to sailing. A fifth engineer, Charles H. Collier, had been delayed. With all-new officers on hand, the entire remaining engineering department resigned with the exception of Quinn, who had fallen ill. Morris sent him home.

Morris also received a sight draft from Mallory for $50,000, to be drawn on Fraser, Trenholm and Company, Liverpool. Because Major W. S. Walker, the Confederate agent in Bermuda, could not supply gold, Morris was able to obtain only $42,000 from a Colonial bank, but this was enough to send him to sea. With specie in the strongbox, full bunkers, a full larder, and a healthy staff of engineers, Morris looked ahead with renewed enthusiasm.[25]

On June 27 Morris steamed out of the harbor but remained close to Bermuda, still hoping to receive the missing engineer on an incoming runner. His crew had changed noticeably. To fill vacancies, 30 men had been recruited illegally on shore. Only First Class Fireman James Butler, who had been captured on the Confederate ironclad *Atlanta* and had recently escaped from the U.S., joined the crew legally.[26]

On July 1, still cruising off Bermuda, the *Florida* captured the bark *Harriet Stevens* of New York, bound from Portland, Maine to Cienfuegos with a cargo of lumber, shooks, heads, and spars. A far more valuable commodity aboard was 312 pounds of gum opium, which was worth its weight in gold in the Confederacy. After firing a few practice rounds at the *Harriet Stevens*, Morris ordered her burned, transferred the prisoners to a passing Danish bark, and steamed back to St. Georges in search of a blockade runner to take the much-needed medicine to the Confederacy. Morris was able to transfer the opium to the blockade runner *Lillian*, but later in the day suffered the humiliation of being ejected from port for illegally attempting to receive additional coal from a tug.[27]

The *Florida*'s extended stay in Bermuda had again invoked the wrath of the United States. Minister Charles Francis Adams complained to British Foreign Secretary Russell that Great Britain was again ignoring its own neutrality laws. For several days the *Florida* had cruised six miles off the island, stopping every ship headed for harbor—behavior that would never have been tolerated from a Union warship. Adams got the usual answer that the matter would be investigated, and expected little satisfaction. This time he was wrong. Russell found that some of Her Majesty's colonies applied looser interpretations of the Foreign Office's new policies on neutrality than the Home Government wished. Slowly this changed, and Confederate raiders began to lose their favored treatment in colonial ports.[28]

On July 3 Morris stumbled into a bit of luck when he stopped the British ship *T. H. A. Pitt* from New York. To replace the still-missing Engineer Collier, William H. Jackson, a passenger on the *Pitt* who had been chief engineer on the blockade runner *Greyhound*, signed on as acting second assistant engineer. For the first time since leaving Brest, Morris felt satisfied with his crew. It was time to head for the enemy's home waters.[29]

On July 8 the *Florida* entered U.S. coastal waters and captured the 330-ton New Bedford whaling bark *Golconda*, homeward bound from a two-year voyage with 1,800 barrels of whale oil. Morris burned the ship and the oil, for which the owners later claimed $169,195.92 in damages.[30]

The following morning Morris captured the New York supply schooner *Margaret Y. Davis*, returning from Port Royal in ballast. No sooner had the vessel been set afire than the watch reported another sail. Morris called for steam and overhauled the British schooner *William Clarke*, out of New York bound for Harbor Island. Determined to get something for his trouble, Morris talked the captain into taking the officers and boat steerers from his last two prizes in exchange for a quantity of pilfered supplies.[31]

The day had not yet ended when the lookouts sighted a steamer towing a bark not far from Cape Charles. After spotting the approaching *Florida*, the steamer cast off and sped for safety—too fast to catch. The bark was not so lucky. The prize proved to be the 549-ton *Greenland* from Brunswick, Maine, loaded with 900 tons of anthracite coal, Philadelphia to Pensacola. Chief Engineer Thompson examined the cargo and regretted that anthracite "was of no use for our furnaces." Morris learned that he had unsuccessfully chased the steamer *America*, which was sure to make port and report the *Florida*'s location. Morris, however, was not quite ready to scurry off to safety; he torched the *Greenland* and headed for the capes of Delaware.[32]

July 10 proved to be the pinnacle of the *Florida*'s career as a commerce raider. The busiest day of her short life began at 3 a.m., about 35 miles off the eastern shore of Maryland, with the capture of the 469-ton bark *General Berry* of Kennebunk, Maine, bound for Fortress Monroe with 1,202 bales of hay and straw for Union mounts. She made an impressive bonfire at dawn.[33]

About three hours later, the *Florida* overhauled the 559-ton bark *Zelinda* of Eastport, Maine, in ballast, Mantanzas to Philadelphia. Before Morris had time to burn her, the lookouts reported another sail. He instructed the prize crew to follow the *Florida* and chased the third victim. A shot from the pivot gun brought the New York schooner *Howard* into the wind. The homeward bound schooner carried fresh fruit from San Salvador, a commodity that would have been greatly appreciated by the *Florida*'s crew. To everyone's disappointment, English merchants owned the cargo, forcing Morris to bond the ship for $6,000. The low value placed on the schooner reflected her master's willingness to absorb the 62 prisoners then crowding the cruiser's decks. As the *Howard* sailed away, her new passengers watched the *Zelinda* go up in flames.[34]

After overtaking the English schooner *Lane*, which was laden with more "neutral" fruit, the *Florida*'s lookouts sighted a steamer standing southward, and Morris hurried to cut her off. The stranger began pulling away, but she was in range of the pivot gun. Three shots later, the new 810-ton propeller steamer *Electric Spark* surrendered. Bound to New Orleans from New York with the United States mail, the ship also contained a valuable cargo, 43 passengers and a crew of 36.

The *Electric Spark*, whose modern engine developed enough thrust to maintain a constant cruising speed of 12 knots, was a superior vessel to the *Florida*, and Morris wanted her. First, however, he had to deal with disposing of her 79 prisoners. Morris doubled back to recapture the schooner *Lane*, which had become a speck in the distance, and placed Lt. Sardine A. Stone aboard the *Electric Spark* with orders to follow. It took a two-hour chase and a blast from the windward gun to halt the angry Englishman.[35]

After much negotiation, Morris convinced the *Lane's* captain to carry the prisoners as far as the Delaware breakwater, 73 miles away. To make room on the schooner, Morris purchased the deck cargo of fruit for $720 in gold and transferred it to the *Florida*. Because several of the prisoners were officers in the service of the United States, Morris authorized the issue of paroles. The *Lane*, her decks crammed with passengers, finally got underway and sailed directly to New York, arriving there on July 12.[36]

At first, Morris intended to put a prize crew aboard the *Electric Spark* and run the blockade at Wilmington. But this would mean transferring engineers and firemen from the *Florida*. Two of his best men went to look at the *Spark's* machinery and returned baffled. Reluctantly, Morris decided to destroy the ship rather than risk leaving his cruiser shorthanded in return for a longshot gamble.

With the *Lane* still in sight, Morris decided to sink the *Spark* rather than burn her. By opening her air ports and allowing her to fill inconspicuously with seawater, he hoped to convince the *Lane's* passengers that the *Spark* would soon fly the Confederate flag as a warship. Morris regretted sinking this prize. While her 19-foot draft was too deep for blockade running, she would have made an excellent cruiser. Morris was prudent in scuttling her, but the more resourceful Maffitt might have tried to find a way to save the $175,000 ship for the Confederacy.[37]

The mail transferred from the *Spark* contained no important dispatches, but Morris recovered $12,000 in postage stamps, $1,305 in American greenbacks, $219 in gold and $460 in New Orleans notes. The rest of the cargo, which the owners later valued at $800,000, went down with the ship. Aside from a few valuable personal items gleaned from letters and packages, the balance of the mail was heaved overboard.[38]

The escape of the steamer *America* altered Morris' plan to continue up the coast and raid the fishing fleet. Although he hoped they would waste time and resources searching for the *Electric Spark*, he knew that cruisers stationed at Philadelphia and New York soon would be after him. A shortage of coal further increased his vulnerabilty, and on the morning of July 11 Morris headed for Tenerife in the Canary Islands. A lone fatality marred the mission. Midshipman William B. Sinclair, whose boat swamped when returning the prize crew from the

Electric Spark, drowned trying to save a crewman who could not swim, and for this act of heroism, received a posthumous citation that eventually was read on every ship in the Confederate Navy.[39]

As Morris predicted, when the *America* reached port on July 9 and spread the news of a Confederate raider off the coast, Welles ordered to sea every available warship from Portland, Maine to Hampton Roads, Virginia. Early intelligence correctly pinned down the *Florida's* location on July 1 as off Cape Henry and headed up the coast, then off Cape May, still on the same heading. As the hunt expanded, conflicting reports filed into the naval office; ships ranged the entire coastline, often chasing each other as they crossed paths. The chase collapsed into a confused mass of directives that accomplished nothing beyond frustrating Welles and his captains.[40] As late as August 24 Union warships still reported on their attempts to locate the *Florida.*

The disappearance of the *Electric Spark* worried Welles. Captain Daniel B. Ridgely of the USS *Shenandoah* thought that both ships were hiding around one of the Bahama cays, a good place to obtain supplies and plan future operations. Welles, however, suspected that the *Electric Spark* had been moved to the French islands in the Gulf of St. Lawrence and directed Lt. Commander William Mitchell to take the USS *Ascutney* and search there. No one in the Navy Department seems to have considered that the *Spark* had been scuttled, which was exactly what Morris had hoped.[41]

The threat of raids along the northeast coast brought back vivid memories of the *Archer,* and the people of Maine insisted upon protection. Following a false report of a suspicious steamer off the coast, Maine Governor Samuel Corry telegrammed Welles, "You can not be too quick in getting out gunboats to look after this craft and her consort. . . ."[42]

During the *Archer's* raid on Portland, A. L. Drayton had been captured and imprisoned at Fort Warren along with Read and the rest of the crew. Drayton disliked prison and turned informant, stating that he sincerely wished for the restoration of the Union. He passed himself off as an officer on the *Florida* and convinced Welles of his sincere desire to assist in capturing the cruiser. He claimed to have knowledge of the time and location of the *Florida's* next rendezvous with her tender. Earlier, he had predicted the cruiser's summer raid along the coast, which added credence to his other stories. This satisfied Welles, and he ordered the prisoner released.

Convinced that Drayton knew the *Florida's* recognition signal and next destination, Welles assigned him to the navy as a pilot aboard the USS *Ticonderoga,* and ordered Captain Charles Steedman to take the warship wherever Drayton felt it should go in order to intercept the raider. While it is unlikely that Drayton possessed any knowledge of the *Florida*'s destination then or at any other time, his guess that the cruiser would be in the vicinity of Rocas Island on August 25 was close, for when she left Tenerife on August 4, she maintained a course to the southwest and arrived at Bahia on October 4. Drayton's actual value to the Union navy will never be known, as the *Ticonderoga* arrived at the appointed site 11 days late.[43]

Drayton's motives remain a mystery, but there is doubt that he intended to become a traitor. It is more likely that he tired of prison and hatched the whole scheme to be set free. His action did nothing to harm the Confederacy, and by engaging the attention of a Union warship for several months in an unproductive search, he probably did the Confederacy a small service.

Once out of the mainstream of the northeastern shipping lanes, the *Florida* sighted nothing but neutral ships on her voyage to Tenerife. To those ships she hailed and stopped, Morris passed off the *Florida* as a Union warship. When he arrived at Santa Cruz on August 4, the United States finally became aware of her true location. By the time notification reached Welles, it was September.

The *Florida* left Santa Cruz with 148 tons of coal and fresh provisions, and headed southwest, hoping to pick up some prizes as she recrossed the ocean. Eighteen uneventful days elapsed before Morris captured the *Southern Rights* of Richmond, Maine, with 18,000 sacks of rice belonging to English merchants. Morris bonded the clipper for $35,000, and during the next 15 days sighted another 12 ships, but none were American.[44]

Two months of boredom and no shore leave sparked dissension in the crew. Several officers were disliked; Lt. Thomas K. Porter in particular seemed to have gained the crew's unanimous hatred. A feud between the foreign element and their British and American counterparts continued to fester, the Greeks, Italians, and Spaniards claiming unequal treatment. A note written to Morris on September 11 implied that a mutiny was imminent.[45]

An investigation led to the confinement of several crew members, who Morris tried on charges of mutinous behavior. Two other men were charged with sodomy. On September 20 he acquitted eight men, but the two sodomists were fined three months pay and discharged. Thus ended the first serious episode of misconduct aboard the *Florida*, but Morris recognized the underlying cause of the problem to be a long uneventful cruise with no shore liberty. He was tired of the boredom himself and set a course for Bahia.[46]

On September 26 the *Florida* captured and burned her final prize, the Baltimore bark *Mandamis*, which was in ballast. This was another indication of the increasing difficulty Yankee skippers encountered in acquiring cargoes—a difficulty due to the activities of the Confederate cruisers.[47]

On October 4, Morris entered Bahia. After nearly eight months at sea, the *Florida* had captured only 13 prizes, bonding two. Of the 11 ships destroyed, six were captured during a three-day raid along the U.S. coast.

The poor showing is not a reflection upon Morris' ability as a commander. Morris had stopped as many ships as Maffitt; unlike Maffitt, he found most American-built carriers under foreign flags with well-documented cargoes. Morris was more conservative and took fewer chances than Maffitt, and there is every likelihood that Maffitt would have made another strike at the U.S. coast once he discovered better hunting there.

A few weeks after Morris left the coast, the CSS *Tallahassee* made a quick pass through the New England shipping lanes and netted 33 prizes, most of them small vessels. All it took was a daring skipper.[48]

The *Tallahassee* and the *Chickamauga*

WHEN Morris and the *Florida* left the coast of the United States for the safety of the open sea on July 11, 1864, another Confederate cruiser was being fitted out at Wilmington, North Carolina. She became a ship of many names, but she started her career as the *Atlanta*. She and her sistership *Edith* were both launched into the Thames in March 1864 by the J. and W. Dudgeon Company of Cubitt Town Yard, Millwall. Both vessels started and ended their careers as blockade runners, interrupted briefly by service as commerce destroyers.

The twin vessels were designed by Captain T. E. Symonds of the Royal Navy to represent the most recent technology in marine engineering and construction. Twin propellers powered by two separate 100-horsepower steam engines drove the *Atlanta* to 17 knots; by reversing one screw, she could turn on her center. Overall, she was 220 feet long, with a 24-foot beam and 14 foot depth of hold. Although the iron vessel displaced 700 gross tons, unburdened she drew only 9 feet of water.

With her speed and her low, gray-painted silhouette, broken only by two smokestacks and two sparsely rigged masts, she was an ideal blockade runner. As a cruiser, however, she left much to be desired. She was totally dependent on coal for mobility, and was designed for runs that seldom exceeded 1,000 miles.[1]

Between April and July 1864, the *Atlanta* logged four successful trips carrying war supplies to the South between Bermuda and Wilmington. During one of these trips, Commander Albert G. Clary of the USS *Keystone State* reported to Secretary Welles that he had chased the *Atlanta* into Bermuda at a speed of 11.5 knots, but she was "not even altering her course to avoid us, although we were running to head her off."[2]

In the summer of 1864, while at a Wilmington wharf unloading beef and bacon for Lee's army, the *Atlanta* caught Mallory's eye. He approached the firm of Peters, Stevenson and Wilson Company and purchased her for $125,000, well above the ship's original cost of $85,000. On July 15 work commenced on her conversion to a cruiser.[3]

Within a week, the former blockade runner received three guns: a rifled 32-pounder forward, a rifled 100-pounder amidships, and a heavy Parrott aft—not a large battery, but few merchant ships carried cannon. And she had another weapon: speed. When commissioned, CSS *Tallahassee* may have been the fastest warship afloat.

On July 23, 1864, Secretary Mallory named John Taylor Wood commander of the *Tallahassee*. Jefferson Davis, Wood's uncle by marriage, had personally appointed Wood a lieutenant in the Confederate Navy on October 4, 1861, and had since followed the young man's career. Between assignments, Wood served on Davis's personal staff.

Although he came from a traditional army family, Wood joined the United States Navy on April 7, 1847, and entered the Naval Academy at Annapolis in June. He graduated second in his class in 1853, married, and eventually became a respected instructor at the academy. These years were spliced with a generous amount of sea duty, but his professional interests were the science of gunnery, seamanship, and naval tactics.

When war erupted between the states, Wood sold his farm in southern Maryland, buried his silver, and with a few personal belongings, moved his family to Richmond. At 32 years of age, with no job and a young family, he arrived at the doorstep of Jefferson Davis.

After receiving his lieutenancy, Wood went to work on the CSS *Virginia* (Merrimack) at Portsmouth, where he trained gunners and transformed ordinary seamen into first-rate crews for the special brand of service aboard the novel ironclad. Under the eyes of Commodore Franklin Buchanan, Wood fought those guns against the Union's largest warships until the final standoff with the *Monitor*.[4]

When Commander Wood arrived at Wilmington late in July, the *Tallahassee* was nearly ready for sea. His hand-picked crew of 120 officers and men were volunteers from the James River Squadron, many of whom had served under him on the *Virginia*. Although familiar with river craft, few had sea experience. Mallory sent Lt. William H. Ward as executive and boarding officer, John W. Tynan as chief engineer, and Charles L. Jones as paymaster. For 10 days Wood drilled the crew, established discipline, and practiced gunnery. By August 4 he felt they were ready for sea.[5]

Following a technique used by blockade runners, Wood steamed down the Cape Fear River to Smith's Island and moored to a buoy directly under the protection of Fort Fisher. Located at the mouth of the river, Smith's Island formed two entrances about six miles apart: New

Inlet, protected by Fort Fisher, and Old Inlet, guarded by Fort Caswell. With a full load of coal, the *Tallahassee's* draft had increased from 9 to 13.5 feet, making the deeper New Inlet channel Wood's best choice.

That night, at high tide and under a moonless sky, the cruiser headed down the channel.[6] Wood wrote: "Everything was secured for sea. The lights were all carefully housed, except the binnacle, which was shaded; fires were cleaned and freshened, lookouts were stationed, and the men were at their quarters. The range lights were placed; these, in the absence of all bouys and lights, were necessary in crossing the bar, and were shown only when vessels were going in and out. The Mound, a huge earthwork, loomed up ahead, looking in the darkness like a black cloud resting on the horizon."[7]

After steaming a short distance, the ship's bow grounded on a bar known as the Rip. Wood lost two hours pulling free and postponed the run until August 5, but his luck then was no better: He grounded so firmly that three steamers working in unison barely pulled him free.

Old Inlet had been his second choice, but Wood decided to try it. On the morning of August 6 the *Tallahassee* crossed to a point below Smithville and waited until dark. At 10 p.m. the moon dropped below the horizon and patches of heavy black clouds hung in the sky. A shadowy mist rose from the sea, blotting out the few sparsely spread stars, and Wood crept quietly down Old Inlet. As the ship bumped over the bar, the crew waited anxiously until the leadsman found deep water. The ocean—and a gauntlet—lay ahead.

Union warships stood just offshore for many miles surrounding the mouth of the Cape Fear River, deployed in an inner cordon of slower ships and an outer line of fast steamers. The *Tallahassee's* firepower meant nothing in the face of so many Union guns. Wood instead relied upon the cover of darkness and his speed. Turning to Chief Engineer Tynan beside him on the bridge, he said, "Open her out, sir . . . let her go for all she is worth." Tynan, who had been with Wood on the *Virginia*, headed for the engine room, ordering that every combustible from pork fat to pine knots be thrown into the fires for quick heat and extra steam. As the raider's speed increased, sparks flew from the funnels, alerting the Union lookouts.[8]

Two blockaders loomed ahead, signalling to each other as Wood approached. While racing between them, the *Tallahassee* passed so close to one ship that Wood could hear the deck officer shouting commands to the aft gun crew: "Run out! Elevate! Steady! Stand clear!" The gun erupted and a shell streaked between the cruiser's twin stacks and arced off into the night. Union rockets pierced the darkness, and another blockader opened fire, sending a shell on target but high. The

Tallahassee, by now skimming across the water at 15 knots, was saved once again by her low freeboard. Wood passed by three more Union vessels unobserved, wisely holding his fire and letting them believe that another runner, and not a cruiser, had broken through the blockade.[9]

Still ahead, patrolling 50 miles offshore, were Union ships stationed to intercept outbound runners at daylight. Wood had been heading east, outlined plainly against the horizon, when he discovered a warship under steam and sail five miles off his stern in full chase, and another off the bow. Wood altered course to the north, putting both pursuers on his beam and forcing them into the wind, nullifying the extra speed from their spread of canvas.

When Engineer Tynan opened the throttles, the enemy faded from sight. Wood later recorded: "It was at times like this that the ship and engines proved themselves reliable; for had a screw loosened or a journal heated we should have been lost." A third steamer hove into view later in the afternoon, but Wood barely altered his course. Unexpectedly, a fourth Union warship emerged suddenly from the darkness, bearing hard to cut off the speeding *Tallahassee*. After Wood failed to answer a challenge, the enemy opened with several shots, all of which missed. Wood stayed on course and left the last of his pursuers far behind. Within 24 hours he had evaded 11 of the 50 ships comprising the Wilmington blockading squadron.[10]

Mallory had given Wood almost unlimited latitude in pursuing his mission, asking only that he adhere to international law and respect the neutral rights of friendly nations. Ahead beckoned the northeastern seaboard, one of the few stretches of the Atlantic where American commerce still felt safe to carry cargoes. Wood looked forward to good hunting.

For three days the *Tallahassee* steamed north through the Gulf Stream, along the way stopping several vessels, all under foreign registries and flying British colors. Finally, at first light on August 11, only 80 miles off Sandy Hook, Wood sighted an American coasting schooner. Hoisting the Stars and Stripes, he chased and captured the *Sarah A. Boyce*, in ballast from Boston to Philadelphia. After bringing aboard the captain, crew, and the ship's valuables, Wood elected to scuttle the *Boyce* by chopping holes in her hull rather than risk detection by lighting a fire.[11]

Standing 20 miles off New York, Wood spotted a pilot boat, noting with amusement that the captain was probably in search of a fee. Wood, flying the Stars and Stripes, posed as a ship in search of a pilot. A large man in a black suit with a high hat and a sparkling gold watch chain descended into a small boat and made his way slowly toward the ship. The pilot stepped aboard the raider, eagerly assisted by the Confederate crew, glanced at the armament and then at the flag, which Wood had changed to the Stars and Bars, and said, "My God! What is that? What ship is this?" "A more astonished man never stood on deck of a vessel," Wood recorded. "He turned deadly pale, and drops of perspiration broke from every pore." Informed that the *James Funk* was now the prize of the CSS *Tallahassee*, Master Robert Yates grieved that his beautiful pilot boat would be destroyed.[12]

Temporarily at least, Wood had other plans. He transferred two officers and 20 men to the *Funk* with instructions to overhaul enemy ships and pilot them to the *Tallahassee*, where Wood could decide their fate. The ruse worked so well that the brigs *Carrie Estelle* and *A. Richards*, and the bark *Bay State*, fell easy prizes, crowding the cruiser's deck with 40 prisoners and piles of baggage. Later in the day, Wood captured the schooner *Carroll*, which he bonded for $10,000, and paroled his haul of prisoners for safe conveyance to shore.[13]

At dusk, another pilot boat cautiously approached the *Tallahassee*'s circle of bobbing prizes. The suspicious captain, finally convinced that all was not well, sped away under full sail. Engineer Tynan opened the engines and the raider surged after the fast pilot boat. To gain speed, Wood even raised his ineffectual sails. Once within range, the bow guns opened and after the third shot, the *William Bell* luffed her sails and surrendered.

Wood empathized with the pilot boat's distraught master, James Callahan, but rejected his plea to bond the boat for $30,000. Wood considered sparing the vessel in exchange for a pilot to guide the cruiser up the East River, where he intended to set fire to ships, shell the navy yard, and escape through Hell's Gate into Long Island Sound. The pilots refused.

Finally, Wood, knowing that his presence would no longer be secret once the paroled prisoners reached shore, burned the prizes.[14]

August 12 was equally busy. Wood captured six prizes, including the 989-ton packet ship *Adriatic*, carrying 170 German immigrants to new homes in America. When told their ship would be burned, the passengers were terrified. "It was some time before they could comprehend that we did not intend to burn them also," noted Wood.

Although he suspected the men would enlist in the Union army soon after debarking, he transferred the Germans to the *Suliote*, a bark captured earlier and bonded as a cartel. He also bonded the 222-ton schooner *Robert E. Packer*, en route from Baltimore to Richmond,

Maine, with a cargo of lumber. Master Joseph E. Marson did not resist when Wood loaded prisoners from the schooners *Atlantic* and *Spokane* and the brig *Billow*, all of which had been captured earlier in the day.

Wood scuttled the *Billow* in the morning, but all the remaining ships met a fiery end, with the large *Adriatic* illuminating "the water for miles, making a picture of rare beauty," as she burned to the water's edge.

By coincidence, the *Billow* never sank. While searching for the *Tallahassee*, the USS *Grand Gulf* stumbled onto the floating brig and towed her to port.[15]

Recognizing the need to shift cruising grounds, Wood set a course for New England. Nearing Boston on August 13, Wood captured the 789-ton bark *Glenarvon*, bound for New York from Glasgow with a cargo of iron. Wood removed a stock of provisions, including chickens and pigs, loaded the prisoners, and scuttled the vessel: "We watched the bark as she slowly settled, strake by strake, until her deck was awash, and then her stern sank gradually out of sight until she was in an upright position, and one mast after another disappeared with all her sail set, sinking as quietly as if human hands were lowering her into the depths. Hardly a ripple broke the quiet waters."[16]

While Captain James Watts dejectedly watched his ship sink slowly beneath the sea, one of the *Glenarvon's* lady passengers tirelessly upbraided Wood. The wife of a retired sea captain, she "came on board scolding and left scolding, and never tired." Wood attempted to pacify her by offering his cabin, which she scornfully rejected; harmony aboard the raider was not restored until a passing Russian ship agreed to take the couple. As she stepped off the *Tallahassee*, ". . . she snatched her bonnett from her head, tore it to pieces, and threw it into the sea."[17]

August 13 ended with the capture of the schooner *Lamont Du Pont* of Wilmington, Delaware, laden with coal from Cape Breton, Nova Scotia, to New York. To a Confederate, any vessel bearing the name Du Pont—the manufacturor of Union munitions—invited destruction. As the *Tallahassee* sped northward up the coast of Maine, Master L. C. Corson watched his ship burn until it faded from sight.

The following day brought a mixture of heavy seas and pockets of fog. Coal was consumed at an alarming rate. The sudden appearance of the 547-ton ship *James Littlefield* in an open patch of sea at first seemed an act of Providence. Her hold contained anthracite from Cardiff, Wales, but rough weather made a transfer at sea impossible. With regret, Wood scuttled the ship and continued north.

On August 15, the *Tallahassee* captured six small schooners, ranging from 39 to 148 tons. Wood scuttled all but the *Sarah B. Harris,* which he saved to convey prisoners to Portland.

Wood captured four more small schooners on August 16, along with the 283-ton bark *P. C. Alexander.* The captain of one of the schooners, which had been busily fishing when the raider steamed up, protested that he was only a poor fisherman and should be spared. Wood replied: "But you are the very fellows we are looking for." One at a time, Wood torched all five vessels, clearly in sight of horrified onlookers on Matinicus Island at the mouth of Penobscot Bay.[18]

On August 17 four more small schooners and the 286-ton brig *Neva* joined the *Tallahassee's* growing list of Yankee prizes. Wood bonded the brig for $17,500 and loaded her with prisoners. Two small fishing schooners, *Diadem* and *D. Ellis,* bound for Harwich, Massachusetts, carried 505 barrels of neutral-owned mackerel and were set free, despite their destination.

With only 40 tons of coal left in the bunkers, the raid north had reached an end. But when Wood encountered a Nova Scotia pilot-fisherman on August 18 who offered to guide him into the neutral port of Halifax, he decided to refuel quickly and return to sea.

The *Tallahassee's* seven-day raid did not go unnoticed by Union Naval Secretary Gideon Welles. On August 12 he noted in his diary: "Have news this evening that a new pirate craft, the *Tallahassee,* has appeared off New York, burning vessels. Steamers ordered off in pursuit." Three days later he recorded that "Depredations by the piratical Rebel *Tallahassee* continue. We have sixteen vessels in pursuit, and yet I feel no confidence in their capturing her."

When the raider arrived at Halifax, U.S. Consul Mortimer M. Jackson immediately dispatched the information to Welles, then took steps to prevent the *Tallahassee* from coaling while Welles got word to his warships. Welles hurried instructions to Commodore Paulding about the *San Jacinto,* which had just arrived at New York in quarantine, to sail immediately for Halifax; he was "disappointed and astonished" to find the steamer still in port the following morning.[19]

The *Tallahassee* arrived at Halifax preceded by a reputation for lawless behavior. Lurid accounts from released prisoners appeared in the New York papers, detailing how they had been robbed of personal items, exposed to the weather, and deposited in overcrowded ships with no means of sustenance.

Wood, however, was a strict disciplinarian who had kept his crew under control. He had been cautioned by Mallory to treat his prisoners deferentially. They were to be fed, provided with adequate shelter, and returned safely to shore at the first opportunity. The only incident brought to his attention by a prisoner involved a stolen watch. This was promptly returned and the crew member punished.

Northern propaganda found believing readers, and Wood found British Admiral Sir James Hope very disagreeable on the subject of supplying coal. Local citizens thronging the dock held different views, however, and there were a thousand on hand to greet Paymaster Charles L. Jones as he rowed ashore to contact B. Wier and Company, Confederate agents in Halifax. Jones recorded: "As I stepped from the boat it was with great difficulty that I could get away from the crowd who showed in their manner the greatest interest in our cause." He and several other officers enjoyed a ball sponsored by a local regiment and attended by British officers, a mingling of uniforms seldom seen after three years of war.[20]

After an unproductive visit with Admiral Hope, Wood called on Lieutenant Governor Richard Graves MacDonnell to request permission to purchase a full load of coal. Although the meeting was cordial, MacDonnell cited the Queen's Proclamation of Neutrality, which restricted a belligerent from obtaining more coal than that necessary to reach the nearest home port.

Consul Jackson continued to pressure the governor, insisting that the *Tallahassee* be detained for violating international law by loading munitions of war while in port. Wood had not obtained munitions, but MacDonnell found himself in the uncomfortable position of acting as intermediary between Jackson and the *Tallahassee*'s captain. From his perspective, the best solution was to order the cruiser to sea as quickly as possible.[21]

Wood called upon the governor the following day and learned that he "must leave at once." Admiral Hope, who had been instructed to determine exactly how much coal the *Tallahassee* required to return to Wilmington, sent three British officers for the stated purpose of seeing the new twin-screw propulsion system. Wood suspected that their real mission was to learn how much coal he had on board and the approximate rate of consumption.

Shortly after this visit, the governor sent a note to Wood restricting the purchase of coal to 100 tons, and then dispatched Admiral Hope to enforce the order. The admiral complied with vigor, sending an inspector backed by 11 armed boats that surrounded the *Tallahassee* during the coaling process. Because the boats had come from a ship under quarantine for smallpox, Wood succeeded in compelling MacDonnell to recall the boats, but not Hope's inspector.[22]

On August 19 Wood, hoping to give Consul Jackson the impression he would be in port at least another day, advised the governor that 80 tons of coal had been loaded, but he would need an extension to complete the replacement of the mainmast. The governor granted the request, but Wood, who expected to see Union warships arriving at any moment, had no intention of staying longer. With the help of Confederate agent Weir, he filled the bunkers with 40 more tons of coal and hired Jock Fleming, one of Halifax's best harbor pilots, to take the *Tallahassee* to sea. Together they studied the charts and decided to try a small and obscure eastern inlet filled with shoals and numerous sharp turns—made navigable only by the twin-screw *Tallahassee*'s ability to turn in her own length. "Don't be 'feared; I'll take you out all right," the pilot promised. Wood remembered the words when he later wrote, "As he spoke he brought his hand down on my shoulder with a thud that I felt in my boots."[23]

Wood ordered the ship underway on the next tide. At 1 a.m. on August 20, under cover of clouds, the *Tallahassee* headed for the inlet. In exactly one hour, the cruiser reached the open sea and turned south into a fresh headwind. Certain that Consul Jackson would take the bait, Wood had let it leak the previous day that he intended to attack the northern fishing fleet in the Gulf of St. Lawrence. When the USS *Pontoosuc* arrived at Halifax at 6:15 a.m. and found the *Tallahassee* gone, Commander George A. Stevens promptly weighed anchor and steamed north in hot pursuit. Continuing to act on Jackson's erroneous information, Secretary Welles continued to dispatch warships to the Gulf of St. Lawrence for the next week.[24]

The *Tallahassee*'s unfriendly treatment by Halifax officials came as a blow to Secretary Mallory. Until now, Southern cruisers in British ports had received the same privileges as Union warships. Indeed, Confederate commanders had often enjoyed preferential treatment: coaling frequently, extending their legal length of stay, and covertly recruiting British subjects.

But official British attitude toward the South had changed; these little favors had suddenly stopped. In fact, allowing the *Pontoosuc* to leave port in pursuit of the *Tallahassee* less than 24 hours after she departed violated the Queen's neutrality as much as allowing a Confederate warship to acquire an excessive supply of coal. Lieutenant Governor MacDonnell justified this by stating, "It was clear that a cruiser reported to have captured or destroyed between thirty or forty vessels in about twelve days, and said to have a speed exceeding by five knots that of the *Alabama*, was the most formidable adversary which the Federal commerce had yet encountered." He was deeply concerned that as little as five tons of additional coal could impose "a heavy loss to Federal shipping."[25]

Wood now had few options: Without a full load of coal he could not continue his raids along the coast; an outbreak of yellow fever precluded a voyage to Bermuda; even if he captured a collier, he could not transfer coal at sea. His only other alternative was to head home. On his trip back to Wilmington, he burned his final prize, the tiny 127-ton brig *Roan*.

Nearing the coast of North Carolina on August 25, the *Tallahassee* outdistanced two pursuing Union steamers of the outer blockading squadron. At nightfall, Wood called the crew to quarters and put the vessel under full steam, headed for New Inlet along the shoreline just outside the breakers, in the fashion of blockade runners. Suddenly the USS *Monticello* appeared ahead; Wood tried to pass to the inside, but the Union ship was almost in the surf. Wood then turned sharply seaward, plunging between two more enemy gunboats, who wasted time exchanging signals.

The Union ships, convinced they had a blockade runner in their midst, opened fire. When Wood fired back, they hesitated: blockade runners never returned fire; this might be one of their own ships. Wood reloaded and fired again, supported now by the big guns from Fort Fisher. The *Tallahassee* sped through the water at 14 knots and swept over the bar to safety, coming to anchor under the protective guns of Fort Fisher at 10:30 p.m. on August 26. Wood mustered the crew and offered prayers of thanksgiving for their safe return. At sunrise, the *Tallahassee* hoisted the Confederate flag, exchanged a 21-gun salute with the fort, and steamed up to an enthusiastic reception at Wilmington.

Within a few days, President Davis ordered Wood to Richmond. Without him as her champion, the *Tallahassee* became the target of political fighting. North Carolina's governor, Zebulon Vance, complained that Wood had only irritated the enemy, increasing the "swarm of enemy gunboats" patrolling off the coast. General W.H.C. Whiting, Wilmington's military commander, argued that the *Tallahassee* was unsuitable as a warship and that her men and guns should be deployed in naval batteries to defend the entrance of the Cape Fear River. He added that seven of the fastest blockade runners were lost as a direct result of the raider's exploits, stating that the cruiser had commandeered all the hard coal for her mission, leaving only inferior and smoky soft coal for the runners.[26]

Wood recommended that the *Tallahassee* be retained as a cruiser, but it took Davis and Mallory's intervention to get Governor Vance to agree. With her name changed to CSS *Olustee*, Lt. William H. Ward took her for a brief cruise along the North Atlantic coast and destroyed six vessels.[27]

At this same time, a new Confederate cruiser made ready for sea. The *Tallahassee*'s sistership *Edith* had become the CSS *Chickamauga*, under the command of Lt. John Wilkinson. The two ships were often confused in Union reports. The *Tallahassee*'s (renamed *Olustee*) second raid coincided with the cruise of the *Chickamauga*. At first, Union naval intelligence could not distinguish one vessel from the other, and for a while failed to recognize that two raiders, not one, were cruising the seaboard shipping lanes.

Almost all the difficulties experienced by John Taylor Wood on the *Tallahassee* were relived by Wilkinson on the *Chickamauga*. An experienced and successful blockade runner, he had early misgivings about the *Chickamauga* and wrote, "She was more substantially built than most of the blockade runners, and was very swift, but altogether unfit for a cruiser, as she could only keep to sea while her supply of coal lasted."[28] Although he admitted that destroying the commerce of the United States had some virtues, he had little appetite for burning coastal traders and fishing schooners.

Over a month lapsed before Wilkinson penetrated the blockade and reached the open sea. Earlier attempts had resulted in grounding on bars or beating a quick retreat from Union vessels occupying the inshore channels. Finally, on October 26, the *Chickamauga* approached the bar just after nightfall, grounded, backed off, tried again, and eventually cleared.

She was spotted almost immediately. A shower of rockets arced through the darkness, and Union forces opened fire. The USS *Dumbarton*, under Lt. H. Brown, led the chase, followed by two other Union warships. Brown hurled shells at the raider, but discovered that the two vessels in his rear were firing at him. He signaled them to stop, but they were slow to respond, suspecting another Confederate trick. Wilkinson did no shooting, concentrating instead on maximizing his speed, and soon outdistanced his pursuers. The following day, Brown reported that the *Tallahassee* had escaped, not the *Chickamauga*.[29]

During the next five days, Wilkinson headed north, bagging six prizes near New York, among them the bark *Mark L. Potter* of Bangor, Maine, on October 30; and the barks *Emily L. Hall* and *Albion Lincoln*, and the ship *Shooting Star*. Wilkinson loaded all his prisoners onto the older *Albion Lincoln* and burned the other two vessels. Although ordered by Wilkinson to proceed to Fortress Monroe, the *Lincoln*'s captain went to New York and raised the alarm.[30]

On November 4, Secretary Welles finally learned that a new raider, the *Chickamauga*, was burning ships off Long Island. Not knowing the full extent of this new incursion, he sent a telegram to Rear Admiral Porter: "It is reported that four privateers are out of Wilmington. Three have actually committed depredations, namely, *Tallahassee*, *Chickamauga*, and *Olustee*."[31] By November 5, Welles and Porter had issued pursuit orders to nine warships.

Meanwhile, Wilkinson had captured and scuttled the schooners *Goodspeed* and *Otter Rock* off Block Island, and the following day bonded and released the bark *Speedwell*. Captured newspapers warned Wilkinson that his escape from Wilmington had been reported, and that Union vessels had entered the hunt.[32] By the time gunboats converged upon Wilkinson's last reported position, the *Chickamauga* was off St. George, Bermuda, looking for coal.

Wilkinson encountered the same difficulties coaling in Bermuda that Wood had found at Halifax; Britain's new policies on neutrality were being rigidly enforced. To extend his stay in port, Wilkinson was forced to sabotage his own condenser. This allowed him enough time to bribe a customs officer with a large supply of alcohol and obtain more than the permissable supply of coal.

Unfortunately, the strategy worked against him. About 65 men, including a gunner, deserted. The governor refused to help recover the men, leaving Wilkinson desperately shorthanded. The customs officer recovered from his binge and stopped further delivery of coal. Frustrated and undermanned, Wilkinson started back to Wilmington on November 15.[33]

Arriving off the coast on the night of November 18, the *Chickamauga*'s pilot became lost, admitting that he did not recognize the coast at all. Wilkinson took over the pilot's work himself. Concealed by fog, he maneuvered the vessel down the coast, running just outside the breakers, and came to anchor just before dawn, under the protective guns of Fort Fisher, to await high water to clear the bar.

Just as daybreak thinned the surrounding fog, four of the inshore blockaders sighted the *Chickamauga*. Thinking they had spotted a grounded runner, the USS *Clematis*, *Wilderness*, *Cherokee* and *Kansas* began firing and moved in for the kill. Fort Fisher returned the fire, and to the surprise of the Union vessels, guns roared from the *Chickamauga*. When the shooting ceased at 7:30, not a single shell from either side had hit its target. Wilkinson cleared the bar without difficulty and safely entered the Cape Fear River.[34]

In three weeks, the *Chickamauga* had captured but seven ships; the *Olustee* had captured four. The *Tallahassee* captured most of the 55 prizes taken in 1864 by the Confederate cruisers. Aside from bolstering Southern morale during a period when most war news was bad news, the prizes had little strategic value. As Governor Zebulon Vance had predicted, the vessels were more important to the cause as runners, bringing supplies to a war-torn country, than as raiders. And by focusing Union attention on the importance of capturing Fort Fisher, the Wilmington raiders proved a costly strategy. When Federal forces stormed Fort Fisher, the *Chickamauga* participated in the final battle, retreated upriver to Wilmington, and was burned by her crew.

The *Olustee* was reconverted to a blockade runner and renamed the *Chameleon*. Captain John Wilkinson took command with the single purpose of running food from Bermuda to feed Lee's starving army. Wilkinson escaped, but returned to find both Charleston and Wilmington occupied by Union forces. He withdrew across the Atlantic, reaching Liverpool the day Lee surrendered.[35] The British Government seized the vessel and turned it over to the United States, who later sold it to Japan.[36]

John Taylor Wood escaped from the Confederacy after accompanying Jefferson Davis' entourage deep into the South after Appomattox. Strangely enough, he settled in Halifax, Nova Scotia, and soon became a leading citizen, establishing a partnership in a merchant commissioning house with his old friend and blockade runner John Wilkinson.

Northern reporters, knowing that he was still an unreconstructed Rebel, continued to follow Wood's colorful career as a successful Nova Scotian businessman. At a gala affair Wood threw to celebrate the purchase of a ship, a local reporter noted: "We understand that although Mr. Wood's invitations to the excursion were generally circulated among the business men of Halifax, he intentionally omitted our popular [U.S.] Consul, Judge Jackson." The Judge may have become accustomed to being snubbed, but it's doubtful that he ever became accustomed to the Confederate flag fluttering over Wood and Company.[37]

Never Trust the Enemy

WHEN A suspicious-looking steamer entered the port of Bahia, Brazil at dusk on October 4, 1864, Commander Napoleon Collins of the USS *Wachusett* dispatched a small boat to investigate. The boat's officer, claiming to be from the British ship *Curlew*, hailed the stranger: "What ship is that?" When the cry came back *"Florida,"* the boat hurried back to report. Collins immediately ordered steam and cleared for action—an unnecessary precaution as it turned out: The Confederate commander had not spotted the Union cruiser.

Although his ship was one of the few vessels Secretary Gideon Welles kept at sea specifically to destroy Confederate commerce raiders, Collins was here more by accident than by design. When he entered port on September 26, he knew nothing of the *Florida's* whereabouts. Now, a few days later, she shared the same harbor.

The following morning, Charles Morris awoke to find that the ship anchored nearby was not a British steamer, but the USS *Wachusett*. Still, he wasn't worried: It was not uncommon for Union and Confederate ships to share neutral ports, where international law prevented belligerents from attacking one another.[1] Morris expected this to be just another game of cat-and-mouse, but the captain of the *Wachusett* was a different breed of cat. To Commander Collins, the *Florida's* arrival was a wonderful opportunity to advance his career—or have it destroyed like other Union captains who rose in the morning to find a carefully guarded raider had vanished in the night.

Later that morning, Morris had a cordial meeting with Antonio Joaquim da Silva Gomes, president of the Province of Bahia. The president granted Morris 48 hours to coal, provision, and make minor repairs—this despite earlier warnings from United States Consul Thomas F. Wilson of serious diplomatic repercussions should Brazil aid the *Florida*.

The consul had promised da Silva the United States would not violate Brazilian neutrality by engineering an "incident," however, and Morris assured him that he would precipitate no hostilities.[2] When he returned to the ship, Morris found a Brazilian engineer sent to ascertain the extent of the repairs. Based on his report that the freshwater condenser could not be repaired in the allotted time, da Silva granted Morris another two days.[3]

To further ease the president's concerns, a Brazilian admiral suggested the *Florida* be moved closer to shore and his own ships anchored between the two adversaries. This suited Morris; he and his crew had been at sea for 61 days. With the port's neutrality protected by Brazilian warships and his own ship safe, he granted part of the crew a long-deserved shore leave.[4]

While the port watch was ashore enjoying a 12-hour liberty, a boat from the *Wachusett* came alongside carrying Consul Wilson with a message for Morris. Lt. Porter received the letter, but finding it incorrectly directed to "Captain Morris" of the "sloop *Florida*," he returned it, stating that the letter would be received when properly addressed.

The next morning Mr. L. de Videky attempted to deliver the same letter to Morris. Again, Morris refused to read it on the grounds that it was improperly addressed. This did not dissuade de Videky from informing Morris of its contents—an open challenge for the *Florida* to fight the *Wachusett*. Morris told de Videky that he had come to Bahia for a different purpose; nevertheless, "I would neither seek nor avoid a contest with the *Wachusett*, but should I encounter her outside of Brazilian waters, would use my utmost endeavors to destroy her."

Since the *Florida's* arrival, Consul Wilson had spent most of his time aboard the *Wachusett* with Collins, plotting ways to end the raider's career. Because the *Florida's* speed virtually assured her successful escape should Morris decide to leave, Wilson pressured Collins to capture or destroy the raider in port. Although Collins was as anxious as Wilson to destroy the *Florida*, he was unwilling to violate international law. Wilson decided to take matters into his own hands.[5]

Without the knowledge or approval of Collins, Wilson recruited Lester A. Beardslee, the *Wachusett's* first lieutenant, along with Paymaster William W. Williams and Surgeon M. King, into a conspiracy to hire a steam tug to ram the anchored *Florida*. Wilson found a tug available for charter at 2 a.m. on October 6, but a closer inspection in the daylight revealed it to be too frail for the job. A search for a larger steamer turned up no candidates, and the group gave up in disgust. Their disappointment doubled when they returned to their ship to find two Brazilian warships at anchor between the *Wachusett* and the *Florida*.[6]

For two days now Wilson had barely slept, but if he felt fatigue, it did not dampen his resolve to destroy the raider. He went right back to work pressuring Collins, who finally agreed to call his officers together and hear their opinions. Wilson was very persuasive. With one exception, all agreed that an immediate attempt should be made to sink the *Florida* before she could leave port.

Caught between pressure from the consul and the consensus of his officers, Collins made, or at least accepted, the decision to attack. Wilson remained with the ship to keep an eye on Collins and avoid the outrage of the Brazilian government. Collins permitted no one to go ashore for fear a crew member would reveal the plan.[7]

When the port watch returned from liberty, Morris and several of his officers joined the starboard watch and went ashore. With the *Florida* safe under the protection of the Brazilian Navy, he decided to check into a hotel and leave his troubles behind for a few hours, unaware of the plot unfolding as he slept.

At 3 a.m. on October 7, the *Wachusett* slipped her cable and glided undetected past the Brazilian warships. Collins called for full steam and his vessel surged forward toward the slumbering *Florida*, just over half a mile away. The *Florida*'s deck officer, Acting Master Thomas T. Hunter, spotted the *Wachusett* and sent the quartermaster to awaken Lt. Porter. By the time Porter reached the deck, the Union warship was 20 yards from impact. Everyone braced themselves for the collision.[8]

With a full head of steam, the *Wachusett* struck the *Florida* on the starboard quarter, cutting down her bulwarks and carrying away the mizzenmast and main yard. Collins backed off. Two guns fired from his broadside; pistol shots flashed between the ships.

The Brazilian government had ordered the *Florida*'s guns unloaded upon entering harbor, and Porter knew he could not hold off an armed warship with pistols. When he announced his intention to surrender, 15 men jumped overboard and swam for shore. Only six succeeded; the remaining nine were shot in the water.

Over the strident protests of Lt. Porter, Collins took 12 officers and 58 crewmen prisoner, releasing one civilian who had been captured on the *Mondamis*. The officers were paroled and given the freedom of the ship; the enlisted men were placed in double irons.

Collins knew he could not remain in Bahia after violating Brazilian neutrality. Finding the *Florida* surprisingly undamaged and in no danger of sinking[9], he ordered a hawser attached, placed Beardslee in charge of the prize, and headed for sea.

If Collins held any hope that his actions might be ignored by the Brazilian government, they ended when the fort lobbed a few shells in his direction. Shortly afterwards he sighted a Brazilian sloop of war towed by a paddle gunboat in slow pursuit. He ordered all sail set on both ships.[10]

At 3:30 the hotel proprietor woke Morris and informed him "that there was some trouble on board the *Florida*, as he had heard firing and cheering in the direction of the vessel, but on account of the darkness was unable to discern anything." Morris jumped into his clothes and dashed to the landing, and a boat hurried him to the admiral's vessel.[11]

When lookouts aboard the Brazilian corvette *Dona Januaria* first spotted the *Wachusett* under way, Commander Gervasio Macebo had sent an officer to order her back to her anchorage. The officer returned waving a piece of paper showing that Collins had agreed, and it appeared to Macebo that the *Wachusett* was returning to her anchorage. When she passed, however, he saw that she had the *Florida* under tow.

Although the *Wachusett* was directly off the corvette's bow and the guns could not be brought to bear, Macebo fired a few rounds, then ordered full pursuit. The *Dona Januaria* was a sailing ship, however; with little wind to fill her sails, Macebo signalled the steamer *Paraense* for a tow. Trailing behind came the yacht *Rio de Contes*, another slow sailing vessel.

The *Wachusett* and her prize had little trouble extending their three-mile lead, and soon slipped below the horizon. At noon, Macebo returned to port and apologized to his president for the inability of his small squadron to overtake the *Wachusett*:

> I trust your excellency will believe that when I left this port it was with the decided determination of sacrificing every consideration, present and future, to fight her, notwithstanding the small amount of force on which I could reckon, in order to vindicate the insult offered to the sovereignty of the country in thus taking by main force the steamer *Florida*.[12]

It's fortunate for Macebo that his small force could not overtake the *Wachusett*. There is little doubt that the better-armed Union warship and her well-trained gunners could have sunk the Brazilian fleet while suffering little damage. It seems fortunate for Collins as well: had he done so, he would have been in an even worse diplomatic mess.

On the other hand, if Morris had accepted Collins' challenge, it's likely he would have prevailed. The *Florida* carried a heavier broadside, and all her guns were rifled. Many of Collins' guns were smoothbores, good for close action only. The faster *Florida* could have outmaneuvered her opponent and pounded her at long range. Morris knew his advantages, but his mission was the destruction of commerce, and he refused to engage an enemy ship unless forced at sea.[13]

Which ship would have prevailed was now moot, however. The *Florida* was gone and Morris was stranded in Bahia with four other officers and 71 men and no money to pay them. Although Morris strongly protested his ship's capture to President da Silva Gomes, there was little the Brazilian government could do. Brazil had not officially recognized the Confederacy, and Morris had to receive the president's reply through the newspapers.

Morris finally managed to secure passage to London for all the men and most of the officers on the English bark *Linda*. He and Paymaster Taylor booked berths on an English mail steamer, hoping to reach London and arrange for the crew's settlement or reassignment before they arrived.[14]

For Collins, the capture of the *Florida* was an unexpected burden. He had intended to ram her, reverse his engines, and clear for sea, leaving the stricken raider behind to sink at anchor. Like most hurriedly conceived plans, something went wrong; when something goes wrong in the navy, there must be someone to blame. This time the blame fell upon Lt. Commander Lester A. Beardslee.

To allow the ship to slip anchor noiselessly, Beardslee had been ordered to unshackle the anchor chain and attach it to a long hawser. Collins believed Beardslee had attended to the matter, but when the ship accelerated on her ramming run, the still-shackled anchor was discovered. By then it was too late to stop, and the anchor's drag deprived the *Wachusett* of full momentum.[15]

With the anchor incident vivid in his mind, Collins found reason to blame Beardslee for everything else that went wrong. In a statement to Welles, Collins accused him of confusing the crew by issuing an order to "stand by to repel boarders" when there were no boarders, and at a time when he had ordered the *Wachusett* to back away. He claimed that despite orders "not to fire our large guns unless the *Florida* first fired hers, and not then until we had swung so as to be certain of hitting her," Beardslee had fired the guns when they were not bearing, and the shot had splashed harmlessly into the harbor.

Despite all this Collins placed Beardslee in charge of the prize crew aboard the *Florida*. By the time Welles received the list of charges, Collins' own career was in deep trouble. There is no record that Beardslee, who continued to serve in the navy, ever faced a court martial.[16]

For 23 days the *Wachusett* and the *Florida* sailed north, reaching St. Bartholomew, West Indies, on October 29. The Union ship put into port for supplies, but because of the *Florida's* uncertain legal status,

Collins kept her at sea, with orders to Beardslee "to keep within sight of each other's lights."[17]

The rift between Collins and Beardslee now reached a climax. When the *Wachusett* left port in the morning, the *Florida* was nowhere to be seen. An enraged Collins spent several hours searching for her, threatening to fire on the ship when he found it. Beardslee, claiming he had drifted off during the night and was never farther than nine miles from the island, was outraged when he learned that Collins had considered firing on him. His reply to Collins read:

> Should the *Wachusett* at any time begin firing at this United States steamer I should most certainly be led to the belief that the Confederates aboard of the *Wachusett* had captured the vessel and that my duty to my country called upon me to destroy her. I shall most certainly return a shell from the *Wachusett* with both broadsides of this ship, which are in readiness, and if I shall have made a mistake none of us probably will live to rectify it, as I shall sink this ship, if I cannot the *Wachusett*.[18]

After the threat to exchange broadsides, Collins' behavior became even more bizarre. He seemed obsessed with the idea that the Confederates either would take over the *Wachusett* or recapture the *Florida*. Since leaving Bahia, he had held his prisoners in irons. Coxswain Henry Norman had been manacled to a stanchion with his hands behind him for having a key to the *Florida*'s irons in his pocket; Fireman John Brogan had been stuffed into a sweatbox for having a suspicious discussion with a shipmate. Before leaving St. Bartholomew, Collins moved the *Florida*'s swords and colors, along with Dr. Charlton and 18 Confederate prisoners, to the *Kearsarge*, which happened to be in port.[19]

Collins next sailed for coal into St. Thomas, where he permitted another 18 prisoners to escape. In fact, Collins seemed so anxious to be rid of them that he chased them to shore in an armed boat, even though the *Wachusett* was under a flag of quarantine for carrying a possible case of smallpox.

This was another serious diplomatic error for Collins. The Dutch, furious when they learned their quarantine laws had been broken, collected the prisoners and shipped them to Bermuda, sending a protest to the U. S. government along with a bill for $500 for transportation.

Now Gideon Welles got involved, and snapped off a letter to Collins asking for more details. By now, Collins knew he was in trouble and changed his story, writing Welles that he had not authorized the release of the prisoners. When he realized what had happened, he had dispatched two armed boats to retrieve them. According to Collins' revised story, the prisoners reached shore first and made good their escape.[20]

After leaving St. Thomas, the *Wachusett* and the *Florida*, which had been left outside the port, continued on uneventfully to Newport News, Virginia, arriving there on November 12. Beardslee told the remaining Confederate prisoners that they would be released if they agreed to take an oath of allegiance to the United States. All refused, and they were sent to Fort Warren in Boston.

On January 19 Lt. William H. Woodman, USA, approached Lt. Porter with a letter from Secretary Welles offering to parole the prisoners and give each of them $20 for food and transportation if they would leave the United States within 10 days. They all agreed, but found themselves thrust upon the street without a cent. Porter finally obtained a draft to be paid at Liverpool and booked passage to England. By the time Welles discovered that the men had been released without funds, they were out of the country.[21]

When the remaining members of the *Florida*'s crew arrived in Britain, Morris reassigned those who wished to continue in service to the *Rappahannock*, a converted dispatch-boat purchased from the Royal Navy to be fitted as a cruiser. When this vessel became bottled-up at Calais, many of the men transferred to the CSS *Stonewall*, a formidable new ironclad that came too late for the Confederacy. When she arrived at Nassau on May 6, 1865, Captain Thomas J. Page learned of Lee's surrender and sold the ship to the Cuban government for $16,000, paid off the officers and crew, and left them to their individual destinies.[22]

Two days after arriving at Newport News, the *Florida* was stripped of her instruments, armament, personal articles, and papers. Assistant Secretary Gustavus Fox issued instructions that she "be anchored in a very safe place, clear of the fleet, as it is a season of heavy gales." Acting Master Jonathan Baker received command of the vessel, with instructions to maintain the ship until the government could determine her status.[23]

On November 19 the *Florida* was damaged in a suspicious collision with the *Alliance*, an army transport just getting underway. Before the collision, water had been rising in the bilges at the rate of five inches per hour; the collision increased the rate of rise to eight inches. Admiral David Dixon Porter ordered Baker to move the ship to a position where it could be protected by the USS *Atlanta*.[24] When Baker reported that the leak had worsened, the admiral told him to keep all the steam pumps running and to make sure the deck pumps could be used if they were needed. Despite Porter's precautions, on the morning of November 28 the *Florida* sank in nine fathoms of water.[25]

Since October 7 the Brazilian government had been trying through diplomatic channels to recover the captured raider and return her to the Confederacy. As late as December 12, 1864 the Brazilian legation was still demanding an answer from Secretary of State Seward. On December 26 Seward finally advised Brazil's minister that the ship had sunk:

> The *Florida* was brought into American waters and was anchored under naval surveillance and protection at Hampton Roads. While awaiting the representation of the Brazilian Government, on the 28th of November she sank, owing to a leak which could not be . . . stopped. The leak was at first represented to have been caused, or at least increased, by a collision with a war transport. Orders were immediately given to ascertain the manner and circumstances of the occurrence. . . . In the meantime it is assumed that the loss of the *Florida* was a consequence of some unforeseen accident which cast no responsibility upon the United States.[26]

Seward even denied that Brazil's neutrality had been violated. To him, the *Florida* was a pirate, and belonged to "no nation or lawful belligerent, and therefore that the harboring and supplying of these piratical ships and their crews in Brazilian ports were wrongs and injuries for which Brazil justly owes reparation to the United States. . . ."[27]

Brazil was most offended, however, by the bad faith demonstrated by Consul Wilson and Commander Collins, who had reneged on their promise not to attack the *Florida* in port. When Wilson disappeared along with the *Wachusett* after the incident, the affair looked like premeditated treachery to Brazilian officials.

Although Seward refused to admit that the attack had been treacherous or that the officers involved had been guilty of lying, he conceded that the *Wachusett* had acted without authority, and that President Lincoln would "suspend Captain Collins, and direct him to appear before a court martial." Wilson's head also rolled. Seward dismissed him from the service after finally admitting "that he [Wilson] advised and incited the captain and was active in the proceedings."[28]

In the interim, a court of inquiry delving into the sinking of the *Florida* exonerated Acting Master Baker. According to the testimony of Engineer William Lannau and Fireman James Halkier, the *Florida*'s pumps had kept the leak under control until 10:30 p.m. on November 27, when Lannau discovered a sudden increase in the rate of leakage, which he attributed to an unexpected bursting of a sea cock. He stated that the damage was neither a deliberate act nor carelessness on the part of his men, since he had known all the men for over six months and could vouch for their competence and fidelity.[29]

Fireman Halkier, who had been on duty by himself, testified that the steam pump stopped operating shortly after 11:00 p.m. The water had risen to the fireroom floor when he called Lannau. After making hurried repairs, the pump still failed to work properly. Lannau, realizing that the ship was sinking, tried to start the main engines to move her onto a shoal, but the rising water put out the fires. After finding several of the deck pumps inoperable, he signaled the *Atlanta* for help. By the time extra men arrived, it was too late.

The court ruled that the *Florida* sank "owing to the giving out of the steam or donkey pump on the night of her sinking, to the neglect of the fireman on watch to call the engineer on time, and to the fact that some of the deck pumps were out of order." In other words, it was an unavoidable accident.[30]

Questions about the sinking remained unanswered, however. The sudden increase in the volume of leakage combined with the abrupt failure of pumps that had been in good working order a few hours earlier was too conveniently coincidental. Porter had given Baker explicit orders to ensure that the deck pumps were in good operating condition, yet they became unserviceable at the very moment they were needed. Even more puzzling was the inactivity of the nearby *Atlanta*, which did nothing to prevent the ship from sinking. The court of inquiry never pursued either line of questioning.[31]

The puzzle wasn't solved until some years after the war, when Admiral Porter admitted that he had placed an engineer aboard the *Florida* with the following orders: "Before midnight open the sea cock—and do not leave the Engine room until the water is up to your chin—at sunrise that Rebel Craft must be a thing of the past." With the object of a diplomatic flap now gone, the United States government privately rejoiced over the loss—whether the sinking was accidental or intentional.[32]

Seward kept his promise to Brazil. Commander Napoleon Collins was court martialed for "violating the territorial jurisdiction of a neutral government." In his defense, United States Minister to Brazil James Watson Webb admitted "that he had ordered one or more of the commanders of our men-of-war to attack any of the rebel cruisers in any of the ports of Brazil, or to run them down, and that he (Webb) would make it all right with Brazil."

As early as May 1863, Webb had sent a letter to Seward stating that he had explored the attitude of the Brazilian Minister of Foreign Affairs and believed ". . . if we should sink these pirates in Brazilian waters, the government of Brazil would secretly rejoice over the act, and be content with a handsome apology."[33]

Doubtless Consul Wilson was well aware of this when he persuaded Collins to take illegal action. With such assurances, it is no wonder a Union commander felt some security in violating international law. But in a report to Seward, Webb regretted he had not known the *Wachusett*'s commander better before he became involved in such a sensitive mission. Any other captain would have sunk the vessel as soon as it was out of port; Collins had been foolish to take the cruiser back to the United States.[34]

Despite Webb's testimony, there was no saving Collins. On March 23, 1865 he pleaded guilty, requesting "that it may be entered on the records of the courts that the capture of the *Florida* was for the public good." The following sentence was read aboard the USS *Baltimore* in the Washington Navy Yard on April 7, 1865:

> And the accused having pleaded guilty to the said charge, the court doth sentence the accused, the said Commander Napoleon Collins, of the Navy of the United States, to be dismissed. . . .[35]

With Collins' dismissal, Brazil showed signs of being mollified, as Webb had promised. As early as September 1865, the promised "handsome" apology was being discussed and seemed no more complicated than firing a salute to the Brazilian flag. This was finally carried out by the USS *Nipsic* on July 21, 1866—now a mere formality, as diplomatic difficulties had already been reconciled.[36]

With the repaired relations came reinstatement for Napoleon Collins. On September 17, 1866, Secretary Welles advised him that the "sentence of the court is not approved, and you will await the further orders of the Department." Two years had passed. If Welles or Seward felt any obligation to Collins, they were slow in fulfilling it.[37]

The *Florida*'s cruise spanned two years and represented one of the Confederacy's most profitable military investments. She had taken 60 prizes, of which 46 were destroyed, 13 bonded, and one recaptured. At the Geneva Tribunal of 1872, owners of 43 vessels destroyed by the *Florida* and her tenders filed claims totalling $4,617,144—more than ten times the total cost for her two-year cruise.[38]

Indirect damage is less easily quantified. One estimate pegs the navy's cost to search for the raiders at $3,325,000, a figure several times greater than the cost of *all* the Confederate cruisers.[39] Premiums on war-risk insurance covering ships and their cargoes rose from pennies to $9 per $100 of insured value. On some routes, overall insurance rates rose as much as 15 times prewar rates. As a result, American merchant tonnage declined from 5,219,181 tons in 1860 to 1,674,516 tons in 1864.[40]

Yet because she spent the equivalent of half her cruise in port, the *Florida*'s threat was often more implied than overt. She could not be supplied by the Confederacy or fully provisioned from prizes, and thus depended on the cooperation of foreign governments and careful adherence to their policies on neutrality. But as 1864 approached, neutral nations became increasingly disenchanted with the South and its policy of commerce destruction. With growing awareness that the South could not win the war and the prospects of being held accountable by a unified and militarily powerful United States, Morris and other Confederate commanders found neutral nations less cooperative.

The cruise of the *Florida* and her formidable sister the *Alabama* occupied the attention of five major powers for two years. All were relieved when both ships were finally destroyed—but the cruise of the *Alabama* had a much different ending.

The Mysterious No. 290

WHEN Naval Secretary Mallory needed an agent in Great Britain to build his navy, he could not have selected a more energetic or capable one than James Dunwoody Bulloch. When he arrived in Liverpool on June 4, 1861, Bulloch started to work immediately. Before the end of the month, he signed a contract with William C. Miller and Sons to construct the *Florida*. On August 1 he engaged the famous Birkenhead shipyard of John Laird Sons to build the *Alabama*, the most powerful of all the Confederate cruisers.[1]

Laird's was a fortuitous selection; Bulloch quickly developed a warm friendship with the owners, John and William Laird, who took an unusual personal interest in the project. Since 1829, the Lairds had been moving slowly toward the construction of composite and iron-hulled vessels, a trend accelerated by the growing popularity of steam and the scarcity of good ship timber.

By mid-century, an iron ship could be built faster and at less expense than one of wood; nevertheless, Bulloch insisted on a wooden ship. Unlike an iron vessel, a wooden ship could be easily repaired at sea by a ship's carpenter; major repairs could be handled by almost any drydock. Wooden decks were more resilient and stronger than metal decks, especially under the strain of heavy ordnance. Despite the timber shortage, the Lairds used only the best-quality material. A vessel's keystone is the sternpost, bored and sleeved to support the screw shaft and subjected constantly to severe mechanical loads. During two years of strenuous service, the Laird timbers never failed.[2]

Unlike the *Florida*, a copy of a fast British dispatch gunboat, the *Alabama* was an all-new design. Drawing on his 22 years' experience with naval and commercial vessels, Bulloch spent endless hours attending to details as he sought to create a cruiser capable of sustaining itself independent of foreign ports. Extra space was allotted belowdecks for stores, provisions, repair parts, and tools. Iron bunkers stored 350 tons of coal, enough for 12 days' steaming. Special condensing apparatuses on the boilers supplied fresh water daily.

Largest of all the Confederate cruisers at 1,040 tons displacement and built to the highest standards and with the latest innovations specified for Royal Navy ships,[3] the *Alabama* was 220 feet long with a 32-foot beam; her sleek coppered hull drew 15 feet fully loaded.[4] Her two horizontal engines, nominally rated at 300 horsepower, developed 1,000 horsepower during trials. Although the *Alabama* was meant to avoid enemy warships and concentrate on merchant shipping, she would have teeth: a 7-inch 100-pounder rifled Blakely gun; an 8-inch smoothbore 68-pounder; and six 6-inch 32-pounders. Bark-rigged, with long lower masts to provide oversized fore and aft sails, all-wire rigging, and a retractable screw to eliminate drag, she was fast under steam and fast under sail—the perfect raider, needing no home but the sea.[5]

Bulloch agreed to pay the Lairds £47,500 in five installments of £9,500 each, the last payment to be made following acceptable trial runs. Considering the ship's quality, this seemed a bargain to Bulloch, and the Lairds yard laid its 290th keel.

As he had done with the *Florida*, Bulloch took steps to disguise the ship's ownership to throw off Union spies and protect the Queen's neutrality, and never intimated to the Lairds just how he intended to use the vessel. As expert builders, the Lairds could not have overlooked the vessel's warlike characteristics, but there is no record of the issue ever being raised. That issue was left to American consul Thomas H. Dudley.[6]

When Bulloch arrived in Liverpool, he regarded his mission as most secret; only a few highly placed officials in the Confederate government knew of his assignment. To his surprise, he found himself continuously watched by United States agents. The reason soon became clear. He wrote Mallory:

> By far the greatest perplexity that has cramped my individual movements has arisen from a cause which you will doubtless be shocked to learn and which has occasioned me the utmost astonishment as well as chagrin. Almost simultaneously with my arrival in England there came in due course of mail a New York paper, I think the *Times*, with nearly half column of telegrams, purporting to have been sent from Montgomery via Petersburg, Va., on the 19th of May, in which my departure for Europe, with the precise service assigned me, the total amount of money furnished, and even the banks and bankers through whom the credits were to be arranged, was as minutely detailed as if the particulars had been furnished direct from the Treasury Department or from the pages of my instructions, and this, before either the money or the orders had reached me.[7]

A deadly game ensued between two remarkably different adversaries. Bulloch, prematurely bald with heavy, gray-flecked mustaches and sideburns that made him appear older than his 38 years, was open, cheerful, highly intelligent, and aristocratically charming. Dudley's sharp, thin features revealed a driven, strongly opinionated individual violently opposed to slavery and the South.

Bulloch had bested him once already. Dudley blamed the *Florida*'s escape on his own inability to provide the British government with a case strong enough to detain the vessel. Dudley resolved that, no matter what, No. 290 would never fly the Stars and Bars.[8]

Bulloch's legal labyrinth masking the 290's ownership made Dudley's work frustrating and difficult. To build a case, Dudley hired British detective Matthew Maguire, and soon the dockyards of Liverpool swarmed with Union spies buying information from seamen and workers employed at the Laird shipyard. Maguire managed to slip aboard the 290 and provide Dudley with a report describing the interior of the mysterious warship. This failed to slow work on the vessel, however, and the Lairds took no special precaution to conceal her construction. Customs agents maintained a regular vigil over the ship's progress and, finding nothing illegal in her character, the No. 290 slid down the blocks on May 15, 1862 with a new name, the *Enrica*.[9]

Soon after the *Enrica* hit the water, two tugs arrived and towed the vessel to the graving-dock, where a huge derrick began inserting the engines and boilers. Behind schedule, the Lairds pushed the work forward. Finally, on June 15 the ship weighed anchor for her first trial run.[10]

Dudley, remembering the *Oreto* and her fictitious Palermo destination, was not fooled. But he had no proof that any British law had been broken—and Bulloch intended to keep it that way. To comply with Britain's Foreign Enlistment Act, the *Enrica* could not be armed in Her Majesty's territorial waters; she would have to rendezvous with a tender far at sea. Through an agent, Bulloch purchased the 350-ton bark *Agrippina* for £1,400 at the end of May, and moved her to the London docks to load guns, ordnance, clothing, stores, and 350 tons of coal. While Dudley's spies roamed the Liverpool waterfront, the *Agrippina* and her boastful, hard-drinking captain, Alexander McQueen, attracted no unusual attention along the wharves of London.[11]

Bulloch now needed a crew. As a British vessel, the *Enrica* required a captain holding a Board of Trade certificate. From several applicants, Bulloch selected Matthew J. Butcher to command the ship and authorized him to enlist a crew for a voyage to the West Indies. Butcher, who knew that his destination was elsewhere, gave them no hint of the vessel's intended service. Bulloch assigned Lt. John Low, who had just returned from delivering the CSS *Florida* to Nassau, as first officer; Master's Mate George Townley Fullam became second officer; David H. Llewellyn was appointed surgeon; J. McNair, chief engineer; and Clarence R. Yonge, paymaster. When the *Enrica* finally sailed, the officers, crew, and ship seemed distinctly British. The only American among the officers was Yonge, who later proved to be one of Bulloch's few mistakes in judging character.[12]

When Bulloch sent the *Florida* to sea on March 22, Secretary Mallory had implicitly promised him command of the *Alabama*. In the interim, however, Bulloch had opened negotiations with the Lairds for construction of two ironclad rams intended to destroy the Union blockade. Mallory, who considered the completion of this project crucial, now felt Bulloch was too valuable in his present post to send him to sea.

After months of painstaking work getting his ship ready for sea, Bulloch learned in June that Mallory had given the *Alabama* to Raphael Semmes. This didn't come as a complete surprise. Shortly after leaving the CSS *Sumter* stranded at Gibraltar, Semmes had visited Bulloch in London. Bulloch told Semmes that although the *Enrica* was to be his own ship, he would willingly step aside if Semmes would accept command. Although he and most of his officers were available for reassignment, Semmes politely refused. Stopping at Nassau on his way back to the Confederacy, Semmes found orders waiting for him from Mallory asking him to return to England and take command of the *Enrica*. Bulloch smothered his disappointment graciously, and with characteristic energy continued to prepare the ship for sea.[13]

In the midst of the confusion over the command of the *Enrica*, Bulloch discovered that Dudley and his covey of spies had bribed several Laird employees to give false testimony. Even members of Bulloch's small staff had been offered attractive rewards for disclosing confidential information. Dudley laid his case before United States Minister Charles Francis Adams, who took it to the British Foreign Office. Under pressure, Lord John Russell dispatched customs officials to have a closer look at the ship. Finding no armament, the inspectors once again gave the *Enrica* a clean bill of health—but Bulloch knew time was running out.[14]

On Saturday, July 26, 1862, Bulloch received information from a reliable source that it would not be safe to leave the *Enrica* in Liverpool another 48 hours. He hurried to the Laird office and requested a thorough, all-day trial outside the harbor, and instructed Captain Butcher to ship a few more hands and be ready to sail with Monday's tide. None of the crew knew what was in store. Only Butcher knew the ship would not return to port.[15]

On Monday morning, July 28, the *Enrica* left the dock and anchored off Seacombe. In his convivial style, Bulloch invited a small party of distinguished ladies and gentlemen to enjoy the trial trip. The next morning, escorted by the steam tug *Hercules*, and with a few riggers and mechanics onboard to attend to any repairs, the *Enrica* headed for sea with pennants flying and a merry crowd parading the deck. The party uncorked bumpers of champagne and enjoyed an elegant luncheon, with Bulloch and his wife as the perfect host and hostess, followed by music and dancing.

Late in the afternoon, Bulloch apologetically asked his guests to return to shore on the *Hercules*. It seemed that it was necessary to keep the ship out all night to complete her trials. Leaving instructions with Captain Butcher to meet him the following day at Moelfra Bay off the coast of Wales, Bulloch and his merry party returned to the city. The *Enrica*, under the very noses of Dudley's spies, stole to sea to wait for Bulloch and more crew.[16]

As the guests stepped off the tugboat, Bulloch asked her captain to meet him the following morning at Woodside Landing on the Mersey, where he had arranged for a shipping master to recruit 30 or 40 seamen for the *Enrica*.

When Bulloch arrived at the landing at the appointed hour, he was stunned to see as many women as men. Until the articles of the cruise were properly signed and the first month's wages stuffed snugly inside their bodices, these seamen's "ladies" had no intention of allowing their men to leave. Bulloch protested, but he knew the methods used by crimps, who employed doxies to "befriend" unemployed seamen and collect their first month's wages when he found them ships, and ultimately had to concede.[17]

At 4 p.m. on July 30, amid scattered showers and lowering clouds, the tug arrived at the *Enrica*. The women insisted on boarding with the men, refusing to leave until they had been paid and fed. Anxious to be off—the USS *Tuscarora* had been reported off the coast—Bulloch hurried them aboard and ordered the ship's steward to prepare a supper, including enough grog to grease the wheels of the business at hand.

Captain Butcher then began the process of negotiating wages for a voyage to Havana. The seamen finally struck a deal acceptable to the ladies, who said their farewells and, with cash in hand, returned happily to shore to prey upon the next lonely sailor seeking feminine companionship. A few men refused to sign and returned to shore with the ladies.[18]

Shortly after midnight the weather worsened, blowing hard from the southwest with heavy rain. Nevertheless, at 2:30 a.m. Bulloch ordered Butcher to get up steam and head northward into the Irish Sea. George Bond, a pilot trusted and admired by Bulloch, carefully followed the Irish coast through the worst of the gale. By daylight, under a clearing sky and moderating wind, the ship reached the Calf of Man. Butcher loosed the sails and the *Enrica* stretched her wings, bowling along at 13½ knots.

At nightfall, Bulloch and Bond went ashore aboard a fishing boat hailed off the Giant's Causeway, leaving the cruiser and a set of instructions in the reliable hands of Captain Butcher.[19] Bulloch and Bond took rooms in the little Antrim Inn, where Bulloch recorded his reflections:

> During the evening it rained incessantly, and the wind skirled and snifted about the gables of the hotel in fitful squalls. Bond and I sat comfortably enough in the snug dining-room after dinner, and sipped our toddy, of the best Coleraine malt; but my heart was with the little ship buffeting her way around that rugged north coast of Ireland. I felt sure that Butcher would keep his weather-eye open, and once clear of Innistrahull, there would be plenty of sea room; but I could not wholly shake off an occasional sense of uneasiness.[20]

Bulloch's uneasiness had been justified, but for another reason. When he reached Liverpool on August 3, he learned that Dudley's perseverance had finally paid off, and the British government had ordered the *Enrica* seized just hours before she escaped. Only the illness of a key official had delayed the action long enough for the cruiser to escape.

Fortunately, Dudley's spies still knew nothing of the *Agrippina*, which had cleared the channel unnoticed for her appointed rendezvous at Terceira, the Azores, with the new Confederate cruiser. With the *Enrica* and her tender safely at sea and Semmes expected to arrive shortly from Nassau, Bulloch rechartered the *Bahama*, ostensibly for a voyage back to Nassau. Actually, he planned to use her to transport Semmes and his officers to Terceira, along with two 32-pounders and 30 more prospects for the raider's crew.[21]

Semmes arrived in Liverpool on August 8 with Lt. John McIntosh Kell and several other officers from the *Sumter*, and immediately began making final preparations for the trip to the Azores. Semmes, who vividly remembered his impoverished state at the close of the *Sumter*'s cruise, visited the offices of Fraser, Trenholm and Company, drawing funds and drafts to cover expenses—$100,000, an unprecedented amount.

On August 11, the night before the *Bahama* sailed for the Azores, Bulloch penned an uncharacteristic letter to Mallory. Tired of buying guns for others to shoot and ships for others to sail, he once again appealed for a fair chance to command a ship at sea. "If I had no ambition beyond that of a private agent to do the work assigned him properly, I should be content to labor in a private sphere, but I aspire to purely professional distinction, and I feel that to toil here as it were, in exile and then to turn over the result of my labors for the use of others is willingly to consign myself to oblivion."[22] Having relieved some of his personal frustrations, Bulloch, accompanied by Semmes and his officers, climbed aboard the *Bahama*, turning over command to Captain Tessier.

Semmes had retained 14 of his 21 officers from the *Sumter*, including First Lieutenant John McIntosh Kell, Second Officer Richard F. Armstrong, Third Officer James M. Wilson, Surgeon Francis L. Galt, Marine Lieutenant Becket K. Howell, Captain's Clerk W. Breedlove Smith, Chief Engineer Miles J. Freeman, and Third Assistant Engineer Matthew O'Brien. Both Kell and Freeman had been with Semmes in New Orleans when they converted the *Sumter* into a cruiser.[23]

The cadre from the *Sumter* was far too small to officer a warship the size of the *Alabama*, and Bulloch had gathered a competent staff from which Semmes was able to select the best. English-born John Low, who had returned from Nassau after delivering the *Florida*, enlisted as fourth officer. Another Englishman, Dr. David H. Llewellyn, signed as acting assistant surgeon. E. Anderson Maffitt had arrived in Liverpool in February, met Bulloch, and received the grade of midshipman. When the CSS *Nashville* fled back to the Confederacy in February, Charleston harbor pilot James Evans remained in England and offered his services. Bulloch also provided three more Englishmen, two steerage officers and a master's mate, George Townley Fullam, the *Alabama*'s boarding officer. Semmes used his Englishmen to great advantage, frequently boarding vessels under British colors. Many ships never realized they had been stopped by a Confederate cruiser.

Mallory himself assigned four Southerners, who by some stroke of good fortune happened to arrive in Nassau in time to join Semmes. These included Lieutenant Arthur Sinclair, fifth officer, and three midshipmen: Edwin A. Maffitt, the son of Commander John Newland Maffitt, Irvine S. Bulloch, the half-brother of James Dunwoody Bulloch, and William H. Sinclair, Arthur's younger brother.

For his staff, Semmes had some of the South's most distinguished men of the sea, with family naval traditions dating back to the War of 1812. These were bright young men who fought a different war, and believed deeply in the principles for which they were fighting. Their crew, on the other hand, was mainly English, Irish, and Scottish—few having been trained for service on a man-of-war. Under the officers of a new nation, these men developed into an effective fighting force. One traitor surfaced among the officers, however: Clarence R. Yonge, the assistant paymaster from Savannah. His name and misdeeds have been intentionally overlooked by many of the *Alabama*'s officers who later penned their memoirs.[24]

On August 20, seven days after leaving Liverpool, the *Bahama* steamed into the remote harbor of Terceira, joining the *Enrica* and the *Agrippina*. Captain Butcher had already lashed the ships together and begun transferring the heavy guns.

Semmes was entranced at the first sight of the ship he had been sent to command: "Her model was of the most perfect symmetry, and she sat upon the water with the lightness and grace of a swan. . . . Her sticks were of the best yellow pine, that would bend in a gale like a willow wand without breaking, and her rigging was of the best of Swedish iron wire. The scantling of the vessel was light compared with vessels of her class in the Federal Navy, but this was scarcely a disadvantage, as she was designed as a scourge of the enemy's commerce rather than for battle. . . . She was a perfect steamer and a perfect sailing-ship at the same time, neither of her two modes of locomotion being at all dependent upon the other . . . the *Sumter*, when her fuel was exhausted, was little better than a log on the water. . . ."[25]

A stiff wind forced the three ships to move to Angra Bay on the leeward side of the island, and the *Enrica*'s conversion to a warship continued in earnest for the next two days. Bulloch coordinated every detail, supervising the placement of the guns, gun carriages, and supplies that he had meticulously planned and laboriously acquired.

As his final act, Bulloch witnessed Semmes' commissioning ceremony, and watched proudly as the Confederate flag unfurled at the peak. Gone forever was the *Enrica*; in her stead stood the new and powerful CSS *Alabama*. His work completed, Bulloch bid Semmes farewell, and accompanied by Captain Butcher, returned to the *Bahama*. It was past midnight when they weighed anchor and headed for Liverpool. Bulloch never saw the ship again, but for the next two years he followed her career with pride, and a secret yearning.[26]

Confederate Naval Secretary Steven R. Mallory.

U.S. Naval Secretary Gideon Welles.

Captain Raphael Semmes of the CSS Sumter.

Lieutenant John McIntosh Kell, taken at New Orleans in 1861, the day before the Sumter *sailed.*

The officers of the Sumter. Sitting, left to right: Lieutenant W. Evans, Captain Raphael Semmes, Engineer M.T. Freeman; Standing: Francis Yalt, Lieutenant J.M. Kelly, Lieutenant R.T. Chapman, Lieutenant Becket K. Howell.

The Sumter firing at the brig Joseph Parks of Boston. Sketched by one of the Sumter's crew.

Captain Charles H. Poor of the USS Brooklyn.

Rear Admiral David Dixon Porter, circa 1863.

USS Powhatan.

USS Iroquois.

USS **Niagara,** *before her refit of 1862–63.*

Captain James S. Palmer (shown here as a Rear Admiral).

The Sumter captures prizes off Gibraltar, flying what appears to be the Argentine flag.

CSS Nashville.

Captain Charles Wilkes of the USS San Jacinto.

Confederate Commissioners Mason and Slidell being removed from the British Mail Steamer Trent by Captain Wilkes of the USS San Jacinto in Old Bahama Channel, November 8, 1861.

Confederate steamer Nashville *running the blockade at Beaufort, N.C., on February 28, 1862.*

The Nashville *at Southampton in late 1861. In the distance is the* USS Tuscarora.

James Dunwoody Bulloch.

CSS Florida.

Lieutenant John Newland Maffitt of the Florida.

The Florida burning the clipper ship Jacob Bell on December 13, 1863.

Lieutenant John M. Stribling of the Florida.

Lieutenant Charles W. Read of the Florida *and the* Tacony.

Lt. Read burning the Caleb Cushing off Portland, Maine.

The steamer Alexandra.

England's foreign minister, Lord John Russell.

U.S. Minister to Great Britain Charles Francis Adams.

U.S. Minister William L. Dayton.

Captain Charles M. Morris of the **Florida**.

Lieutenant Joseph N. Barney of the Florida.

Commander John Taylor Wood, commander of the CSS Tallahassee.

The CSS Tallahassee.

FRANK LESLIE'S ILLUSTRATED NEWS.PAPER

Entered according to the Act of Congress in the year 1863, by FRANK LESLIE, in the Clerk's Office of the District Court for the southern District of New York.

No. 380—Vol. XV.]   NEW YORK, JANUARY 10, 1863.   [PRICE 8 CENTS.

UNAVOIDABLE DELAY.

In consequence of difficulty in obtaining paper, and the intervention of the holidays, our paper has been delayed in its delivery to News Agents and Subscribers. Arrangements have been made which will prevent a recurrence of this difficulty—more annoying to us than it can be to our friends.

OUR SECOND PRIZE TALE.

WE shall, next week, publish *complete*, our Second Prize Tale,

OLD PROUTMAN'S BOY.

By a Gentleman of Pennsylvania—a tale of equal interest, but of different character and moral. It is called a Tale, but it is really an episode of real life, of absorbing interest, no more disguised in its personalities than the necessities of the case require.

CAPTAIN RAPHAEL SEMMES,
Of the Pirate ship Alabama.

RAPHAEL SEMMES, the notorious commander of the Sumter and the pirate Alabama, is also one of those officers now in rebellion against the flag who was educated at the Government expense, and developed his genius for battle under its auspices. He was born in Maryland, and must now be near 50 years old. He was educated at the Naval Academy, Annapolis, and became a midshipman in April, 1826. He was promoted to a lieutenancy in 1837, and lived the routine life of all naval officers until the period of the Mexican war, throughout which he distinguished himself both on sea and land.

Having served with the naval battery in March, 1847, at the siege of Vera Cruz, he was, at his own

CAPTAIN RAPHAEL SEMMES, OF THE PIRATE SHIP ALABAMA.

request, we believe, detailed on the staff for services where he might have a chance to distinguish himself. In the position of aid to the gallant Gen. Worth, he participated in the battle of Cherubusco, El Molino del Rey, Chepultepec, Cosme Gate and at the capture of the City of Mexico. He has detailed many of his experiences of the war in a clever book, suitably entitled "Services Afloat and Ashore." He is of an excitable, energetic and daring nature, was a strong Southern Rights man, intimate with the Southern conspirators, and on the breaking of the rebellion immediately entered their service. His career since has been one of uninterrupted energy, and his track may be followed in the light of the burning vessels he has captured. In person he is slim, quick in his movements, and of medium height.

THE CAPTURE OF THE CALIFORNIA
Steamer Ariel by the Rebel Pirate Ship Alabama.

WE are indebted to Mr. Thomas, first officer of the Ariel, for some very interesting sketches of the last and most audacious exploits of the pirate Alabama. The purser says:

"On the 7th of December, at 1.30 P. M., rounding Cape Maysi, the eastern point of Cuba, saw a vessel about four miles to the westward, under the high land of Cuba, bark-rigged and canvas. As there was nothing in her appearance denoting her to be a steamer, her smoke-pipe down, no suspicions were aroused, till in a short time we saw she had furled her sails, raised her smoke stack, and was rapidly nearing us under steam. American flag flying at her peak. Such was her speed in comparison to ours, that in about half an hour she had come up within half a mile of us. She fired a lee gun, hauled down the American flag and ran up the rebel flag, let fly her main topsail to the breeze, her black smoke-stack pouring out volumes of smoke, and the Ariel was pushed to her utmost speed.

. . . . . . she then came round on our port quarter, about 300 yards distant, fired two guns almost simultaneously, one shot passing

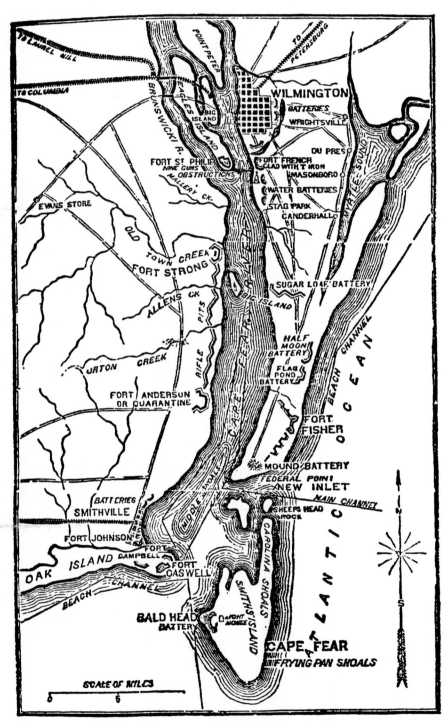

Approaches to Wilmington, North Carolina.

JOHN BULL. "Well, Friend Boney, that looks like a Good Blockade. I don't think there's any use trying to break it."

That looks like a good blockade. Contemporary political cartoon lampooning the U.S. blockade of Southern ports.

JOHN BULL'S OCCUPATION GONE.

JOHN BULL (*Coster-monger*). "My heyes!—Market shut up!—and I've got to trundle my combustibles and other wegetables back 'ome again!"

John Bull's occupation gone. Contemporary political cartoon lamenting loss of Southern markets after the fall of Fort Fisher.

CSS Chickamauga.

Lieutenant John Wilkinson of the CSS Chickamauga.

Rear Admiral Napolean Collins, as he appeared as commander of the South Atlantic Squadron, 1875.

The Wachusset cutting out the Florida at Bahia, Brazil.

The CSS Stonewall.

No. 290 in the graving yards.

The CSS Alabama.

Lieutenant Arthur Sinclair of the Alabama.

3rd Lieutenant Joseph D. Wilson.

Sailing Master Irvine S. Bulloch.

Chief Engineer Miles J. Freeman.

Master's Mate James Evans, Semmes' reliable scout.

Master's Mate George T. Fullam.

Surgeon and Acting Paymaster Francis L. Galt.

Acting Surgeon D. Herbert Llewellyn.

Lieutenant of Marines Beckett K. Howell.

Gunnery Officer Thomas C. Cuddy.

Commander's Secretary W. Breedlove Smith.

JOHN BULL AS PAINTED BY HIMSELF.

"England sells .... the component parts of Ships-of-War (the Pirate *Alabama*) to all comers.—*"London Times.*

John Bull's Variety.

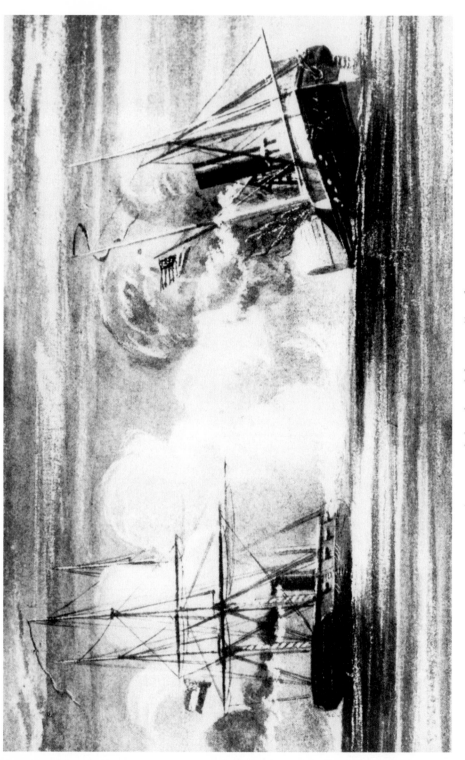

USS Hatteras being sunk by the Alabama off Galveston on January 11, 1865

JOHN BULL'S NEUTRALITY.—A DISTINCTION WITH A DIFFERENCE.

JOHN BULL (*solus*). "A few more Pirates afloat, and I'll *get all the carrying trade back into my hands.*"

John Bull's neutrality—a distinction with a difference.

CHART OF THE CRUISE OF THE "ALABAMA."

NOTE: of the 66 captures, given on this chart, 52 were burned; 10 were released on bond, namely, the *Emily Farnum, Tonawanda, Baron de Castine, Union, Ariel, Washington, Bethia Thayer, Punjaub, Morning Star,* and *Justina*; of the 4 not accounted for above, the *Hatteras* was sunk in action; the *Conrad* was named the *Tuscaloosa* and became a cruiser, or "tender, to the *Alabama*"; the *Sea Bride* was sold; the *Martha Wenzell,* captured in neutral waters, was released.

Chart of the cruise of the Alabama.

A U.S. merchantman sights the dreaded **Alabama.**

Captain Raphael Semmes, standing by the 110-pounder, and

*Lieutenant Arthur Sinclair, Jr. (left) and Lieutenant R. F. Armstrong
aboard the* **Alabama** *in Cape Town.*

LOOTING ABOARD A PRIZE

CHRISTMAS AT ARCAS KEYS

DIVERSION ON DECK
Life on the CSS Alabama.

USS Vanderbilt

USS Kearsarge

Captain John A. Winslow of the Kearsarge.

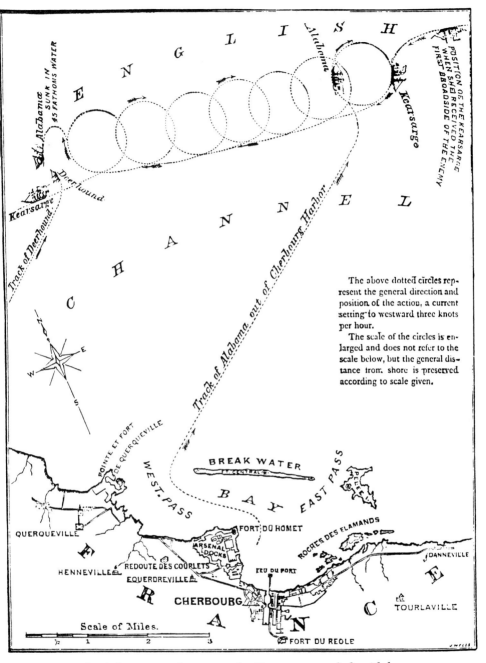

The above dotted circles represent the general direction and position of the action, a current setting to westward three knots per hour.

The scale of the circles is enlarged and does not refer to the scale below, but the general distance from shore is preserved according to scale given.

Track of the action between the Kearsarge *and the* Alabama.

Surrender of the Alabama to the Kearsarge.

The sinking of the Alabama.

The Kearsarge's deadly forward pivot gun.

Officers of the Kearsarge

The Alabama's *shell in the sternpost of the* Kearsarge.

Matthew Fontaine Maury.

Commander William Lewis Maury of the CSS Georgia.

CSS Georgia

James Iredell Waddell of the CSS Shenandoah.

The CSS Shenandoah.

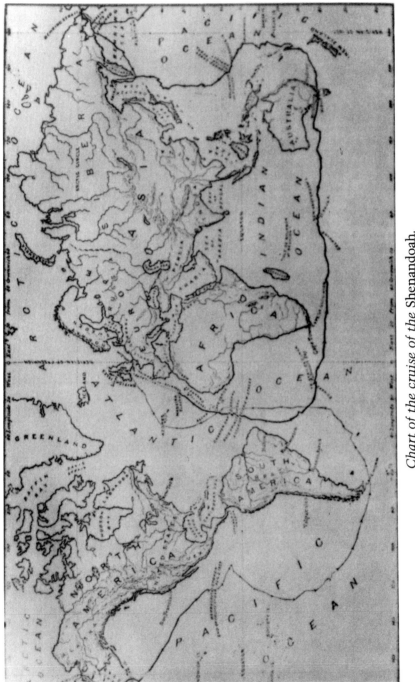

Chart of the cruise of the Shenandoah.

Visitors aboard the Shenandoah in Melbourne.

*The Shenandoah hauled out at the Williamstown Dockyard,
Melbourne, Australia, February 1865.*

The Shenandoah towing prisoners from three burning whaleships in the Bering Strait, June 25, 1865.

THE OLD *RIP* OF THE "SHENANDOAH."

CAPTAIN WADDELL (AS RIP VAN WINKLE). "Law! Mr. Pilot, you don't say so! The war in America over these Eight Months? Dear! dear! who'd ever a' thought it!"

The Old Rip of the Shenandoah.

THE DISPUTED ACCOUNT.

Britannia. "CLAIM FOR DAMAGES AGAINST *ME?* NONSENSE, COLUMBIA: DON'T BE MEAN OVER MONEY MATTERS."

The disputed account.

U.S. Secretary of State William H. Seward.

Senator Charles Sumner.

Secretary of State Hamilton Fish.

Minister to England John L. Motley.

"Lots of Prize Money"

DURING the Civil War, no commander of any warship garnered more fame—or more hatred—than Raphael Semmes. A fluent and prolific writer, his memoirs enthralled future generations, and preserved for history the remarkable cruise of the *Alabama* and her gallant commander.

With his aggressively pointed waxed mustaches, tightset mouth, taut face, and piercing clear blue eyes set below a high, broad forehead, Captain Semmes *looked* the part of a dashing sea raider. After many years of command, the 53-year-old Semmes had developed the forceful demeanor of a disciplinarian who expected to be obeyed.

Like many wartime heroes, Semmes was an anomaly. Before the war his career had been lackluster and unremarkable. Given a cause for which to fight, his energy and intellect brought him to the edge of genius. Self-trained in international law and seasoned aboard the *Sumter*, there was probably no other officer in the Confederacy better suited to command its most powerful cruiser.[1]

On his first day aboard, Semmes faced a critical moment: The Confederacy's newest cruiser had 24 officers but not a single enlisted man. He mustered together the crews of the *Bahama* and the *Enrica* and delivered a brief patriotic speech, to which his British audience remained impassive. Then he spoke of money, offering to pay the men in gold at a rate roughly double the usual wages, with "lots of prize money" to be distributed in shares at the close of the war. With cries of "Hear! Hear!" ringing out, Semmes said no more. Of the 90 men furnished by Bulloch, 83 enlisted aboard the *Alabama*.[2]

Gathered mostly from the wharves of Liverpool, the cruiser's new crew stepped up, signed their enlistment papers, and fell into line behind the paymaster. Semmes wrote that "the 'democratic' part of the proceedings closed as soon as the articles were signed . . . no other stump speech was ever made to the crew. When I wanted a man to do anything after this . . . I gave him a rather sharp order, and if the order was not obeyed in 'double-quick,' the delinquent found himself in limbo."[3]

In contrast with the crew, the *Alabama*'s officers were dedicated professionals. As he had on the *Sumter*, Semmes relied on the leadership and experience of executive officer John McIntosh Kell. A Georgian with 20 years in the U.S. Navy behind him, Kell was 39 years old, six feet two, and big boned. An admirer once wrote that "his mustaches could meet behind his head and his beard flowed down to his hips." A staunch disciplinarian when duty required, Kell's benevolent personality and strong character won the confidence and respect of both officers and crew.[4]

Second Lt. Richard F. Armstrong graduated from the Naval Academy just prior to the secession of his home state of Georgia. Ordered to duty with the *Sumter* at New Orleans, he served the entire cruise as midshipman and remained in command of the cruiser after she was blockaded at Gibraltar. A skilled gunner, he commanded the 100-pounder Blakely pivot gun and two of the 32-pounders. He was six feet tall, quick, sinewy, blue-eyed and, at 20 years of age, still a little brash. Semmes admired his energy, intelligence, and ability to lead.[5]

Another officer from the *Sumter* was Third Lt. Joseph D. Wilson, nicknamed "Fighting Joe" for his aggressiveness. Appointed to the Naval Academy in 1857, Wilson received his commission but resigned when his home state of Florida seceded. Wilson later distinguished himself in command of the after-gun division during the heavy fighting between the *Alabama* and the *Kearsarge*.[6]

In recognition of his valuable service to Bulloch, British-born John Low became the *Alabama*'s fourth lieutenant, and the only lieutenant who did not complete the cruise. In South Africa, Semmes gave Low command of the 348-ton prize bark *Conrad*, which was armed and recommissioned as the CSS *Tuscaloosa*. Semmes often used Low as a boarding officer, as his English accent helped pass off the *Alabama* as a British man-of-war.[7]

Fifth Lt. Arthur Sinclair, scion of an old Virginia naval family, had received his baptism behind the guns of the CSS *Virginia*. Young Sinclair commanded one of the *Alabama*'s gun divisions, and later became the cruiser's fourth lieutenant when Low took command of the *Tuscaloosa*. Sinclair's memoirs reveal a subtle understanding and compassion for the common sailor.

Like his brother James Dunwoody Bulloch, Irvine S. Bulloch of Georgia seemed destined from birth to follow the sea. He had served on the gunboat *Savannah* under Maffitt, and on the CSS *Nashville*, before being reassigned from the James River Squadron to the *Alabama*. Bulloch joined the cruiser at Terceira as sailing master, responsible for the ship's navigation directly under Kell, and later replaced Sinclair as fifth lieutenant. Bulloch didn't receive his official commission to lieutenant until November 6, 1865.[8]

Before Virginia seceded, Francis L. Galt had been an assistant surgeon in the United States Navy. As surgeon and acting paymaster on both the *Sumter* and the *Alabama*, he never lost a single sailor to disease. After the sinking of the *Alabama*, Galt returned to the James River Squadron, joined the exodus from Richmond, and finally surrendered with Lee's army at Appomattox. Adventurous by nature, he later joined an expedition to Peru in search of a freshwater route to the Atlantic,[9] before returning home in 1875 to establish a private practice in Virginia's Loudoun County.

While the Confederate Navy could boast a surplus of capable deck officers, trained engineering officers were scarce. When Semmes converted the steamship *Havana* into the CSS *Sumter*, he was so impressed with Chief Engineer Miles J. Freeman that he offered him a commission in the Confederate Navy. Semmes considered him indispensable. Without Freeman, the *Sumter*'s cruise would have ended sooner than it did. Born in Wales and educated in Scotland, the quiet, introspective Freeman kept the homeless *Alabama* repaired and at sea for two years under the most severe conditions imaginable. Indeed, much of her success can be attributed to Freeman and his unheralded engineering department.[10]

Freeman's first assistant engineer was William P. Brooks, who also had been on the *Havana* and the *Sumter* along with Second Assistant Engineer Eugene Matthew O'Brien, a native of Ireland who moved to New Orleans and joined the Confederate navy early in the war. O'Brien's sunny disposition helped preserve the engine room's fluctuating morale. Third Assistant Engineer Simeon W. Cummings was a Yankee from Connecticut who joined the Confederate Navy and enlisted on the *Sumter*. Estranged from his family for fighting on the side of the South, his life ended in a lonely grave along the windswept coast of South Africa, the victim of a freak hunting accident. Semmes replaced Cummings with John W. Pundt, a native of Charleston who had also served aboard the *Sumter*.[11]

The *Alabama* had four master's mates. James Evans, a Charleston bar pilot who had once guided blockade runners safely into port, was unmatched in his ability to correctly identify the nationality of passing vessels. Eventually, Semmes refused to chase a ship without first conferring with Evans. His shipmates considered him courageous to the point of recklessness.

George Townley Fullam, an Englishman from Hull who had signed on the *Enrica* for the trip to Terceira, became a converted Confederate in eight short days. In time, he became the chief boarding officer and guardian of most of the raider's 2,000 prisoners. A muscular lad of 21, full of fun and the instigator of many pranks, Fullam kept a journal of the cruise that was later published.

The other two master's mates, Baron Maximilian von Meulnier and Julius Schroeder, both well-trained seamen with exceptional language skills on leave from the Prussian Navy, had been shipwrecked near Cape Town during a worldwide cruise. When the *Alabama* reached Simon's Bay, the two young Germans boarded the vessel out of curiosity and were so captivated that they joined the Confederate Navy.[12]

The *Alabama*'s three midshipman were surrounded by naval tradition. William H. Sinclair, the cousin of the cruiser's fourth lieutenant, transferred to the *Tuscaloosa* as acting lieutenant under Low, and missed the *Alabama*'s final voyage. Eugene Anderson Maffitt, son of John Newland Maffitt, commanded the 32-pounders in Armstrong's gun division during the battle with the *Kearsarge*. The third midshipman, Edwin Maffitt Anderson, who commanded a 32-pounder in Wilson's division, was Eugene's cousin. Both had joined the Confederate Navy in November 1861, and received orders to join the *Alabama* simultaneously.[13]

Boatswain Benjamin P. Mecaskey, a Philadelphian by birth, was a workman in New Orleans rigging out the *Havana* as a warship when Semmes spotted him and signed him as boatswain for the *Sumter*. Years later, Arthur Sinclair remembered him as "a typical sailor; looked it all over. They have passed away, this type; but thirty years or more ago you could have picked out on board any American man-of-war his counterpart. Born, as the navy saying goes, 'with web feet and barnacles on his back.' Possessed of a strong and musical voice, his 'call' could be heard from deck to main-royal truck; and his word of command passed to the crew was electrifying."[14]

The *Alabama*'s career was marked by events that occurred on Sunday—her birth and death framed neatly by the Sabbath. On Sunday morning, August 24, 1862, riding quietly at anchor just beyond the marine league off Terceira, Semmes assembled his crew, the officers impressive in their uniforms of gray with gleaming gold braid. He first read his commission, then his instructions from Secretary Mallory: to take the cruiser to sea and destroy the commerce of the enemy. Down came the English flag and the small 290 banner; up went the Confederate colors, to cheers from the deck and a booming salute from the heavy guns.

Although now officially commissioned as a Confederate man-of-war, neither the vessel nor the men were ready for sea. Semmes wrote: "Below decks everything was dirt and disorder. Nobody had as yet been berthed or messed, nor had anyone been stationed at a gun or a rope. . . . I needed several days yet to put things 'to rights' and mould the crew into a little shape. I withdrew, therefore, under easy sail . . . and my first lieutenant went to work berthing, and messing, and quartering, and stationing his men."[15]

It had been Semmes's good fortune to precede every cruise with a stunning celestial display. The night following the *Alabama*'s commissioning Swift's Comet streaked across the sky, visiting the inner solar system for the first time since 1739. The superstitious crew viewed the glowing trail of ice as a heavenly omen of good fortune.

Comet or not, the next day Semmes began preparing his crew to accept his unquestioned authority. Keeping his own council, on rare occasions including Kell in his inner sanctum, Semmes projected an almost spiritual aloofness, never reversed a decision, and insisted on being obeyed rather than popular. His success built the crew's confidence, and in a short while they accepted his leadership without question.[16]

In 1862, whaling still flourished in America. With good luck, a single ship could bring home $50,000 worth of oil from a two-year cruise. The demands of war had pushed prices even higher. For generations the American whaling fleet had peacefully fished the fertile grounds off the Azores. That period of peace ended on September 5 when the *Alabama* captured her first prize.[17]

Sailing near the 39th parallel, with the mountains of Fayal and Pico on the eastern horizon, the lookout spotted the distant sail of a fleet brig. During her entire career, few vessels outsailed the *Alabama*, but this one did. The chase had its rewards, however: it led Semmes directly to the 454-ton *Ocmulgee* of Edgartown, Massachusetts. With sails half furled, she listed under the great weight of a sperm whale partially suspended from her cutting tackles, her crew busily stripping blankets of blubber for the trypots. Semmes dispatched Lt. Armstrong in the cutter to retrieve the captain and his papers.[18]

The *Ocmulgee*'s master and part owner, Abraham Osborn, impressed Semmes as "a genuine specimen of the Yankee whaling skipper; long and lean, and as elastic, apparently, as the whalebone he dealt in. Nothing could exceed the blank stare of astonishment that sat on his face as the change of flags took place on the *Alabama*. . . . He naturally concluded, he said, when he saw the United States colors at our peak, that we were one of the new gunboats sent out by Mr. Welles to protect the whale fishery."

Armstrong brought aboard 37 prisoners along with barrels of beef, pork, and other stores. Lt. Kell, the *Alabama's* chief appraiser, estimated the value of ship and cargo at $50,000. The forecastle statisticians, wondering where their prize money would come from if the whaler was burned, rated her oil alone at $100,000. Fearing that a fire at night might alert other whalers, Semmes delayed burning the oil-soaked vessel until morning—September 6, 1862.[19]

Arthur Sinclair described the procedure: "First, you cut up with your broadaxe the cabin and forecastle bunks, generally of white pine lumber. You will find the mattresses stuffed with straw, and in the cabin pantry part at least of a keg of butter and lard. Make a foundation of the splinters and straw, pour on top the lard and butter. One pile in cabin, the other in forecastle. Get your men in the boats, all but the incendiaries, and at the given word—"Fire!" shove off, and take it as the truth, that before you have reached your own ship, the blaze is licking the topsails of the doomed ship." [20]

The next day, Semmes held the first of many Sunday musters. Semmes wrote: "With clean, white decks, with the brass and iron work glittering like so many mirrors in the sun, and with the sails neatly trimmed and the Confederate States flag at our peak, we spread our awnings and read the Articles of War to the crew. A great change had taken place in the appearance of the men. . . . Their parti-colored garments had been cast aside, and they were all neatly arrayed in duck frocks and trousers, well-polished shoes and straw hats."

After muster, Kell paroled Osborn and the crew of the *Ocmulgee*, who packed their personal belongings—and enough bartering treasure to make their stay pleasant—into three whaleboats and rowed to the nearby island of Flores.[21]

Before the boats touched shore, the lookouts sighted another sail directly ahead, every stitch of canvas straining as she raced for the safety of the marine league. Semmes hoisted the English colors and filled away on the starboard tack in an attempt to intercept her. He fired the lee gun but the schooner refused to show her colors. Finally, after a third shot ripped between her fore and main masts a few feet above the heads of several passengers on deck, the American colors unfurled and she luffed up. Lt. Armstrong and a well-armed boarding party went to the prize and sent back Captain Samuel H. Doane and his crew.[22]

Doane, who owned part interest in the Boston schooner *Starlight*, was determined to protect his investment. Semmes noted that "the master was the cleverest specimen of a Yankee skipper I have met." After listening to a torrent of protests, he clapped Doane and his seven crewmen in irons in reprisal for the indignities suffered by the *Sumter*'s paymaster, Henry Myers, who had been trapped at Tangiers and imprisoned. To assure that the message got back to American officials, Semmes followed the same practice with several of his next captures. Unlike Myers, Doane was spared the indignity of a shaved head; rather than a long imprisonment in a damp cell, Doane's stint in chains lasted little more than 24 hours.[23]

There were several passengers on the *Starlight* bound for Flores, among them three alarmed ladies who were calmed and charmed by Lt. Armstrong. The following morning, Lt. Low took the passengers ashore in the cutter. When he reached the village of Santacruz, Low was welcomed by so many men, women, and children that he believed the entire population of the island had gathered to greet them. Later, Kell paroled Doane and his crew, and Low soon had them reunited with their former passengers.[24]

With several sails in sight, Semmes postponed burning the *Starlight* and captured a Portuguese whaling brig, an anomaly in an industry uniquely American. Suspecting a fraud, Semmes sent for the master. Finding both the captain and his papers perfectly legitimate, he released the ship with a brief apology. Years later, Semmes recorded that "this was the only foreign whaling ship I ever overhauled."[25]

Another whaler, lured by the stars and stripes, sailed up to the *Alabama*, and at sunset, a prize crew under Lt. Wilson boarded the 313-ton *Ocean Rover* of New Bedford. The captain and part owner, James M. Clark of Plymouth, had been homeward bound after a 40-month cruise with 1,100 barrels of oil when he decided to swing by the Azores to fill up a few empty casks. Like the captain of the *Ocmulgee*, Clark swallowed hard when he discovered that the approaching gunboat had not been sent here for his protection by Secretary Welles. Released by Semmes, Clark and his crew stuffed all six whaleboats full of supplies and rowed ashore under a starlit sky.[26]

The *Alabama* lay off the island of Flores and waited for morning to fire her two prizes. Shortly after midnight, the watch reported another sail about a mile away and bearing for the island. Semmes climbed back out of bed and ordered the chase. At dawn, Semmes raised the English ensign, hoping the vessel would show her colors. After receiving no response, Armstrong dropped a shot from the 32-pounder near enough to her stern "to give the captain a shower-bath." Up went the American colors and the ship rounded into the wind.

Armstrong boarded the prize and sent back Captain Charles E. Church of the 398-ton bark *Alert*, 16 days out of New London, bound for a whaling station in the South Indian Ocean, where she was to rendezvous with a schooner to hunt for sea elephants.[27] Kell and Low valued the prize at only $20,000, but had the satisfaction of transferring several bales of underclothing, some choice beef and pork, bread, boxes of soap, and a generous supply of "Virginia twist," tobacco being a scarce commodity on the cruiser.

As Armstrong plundered the *Alert*, Semmes burned the *Starlight* and the *Ocean Rover*. Paroled, released, and with their four boats packed to the gunwales with provisions and gear, Church and his crew rowed to Flores as flames consumed their vessel.[28]

The *Weathergauge*, a whaling schooner six weeks out of Provincetown, unsuspectingly approached—perhaps assuming the smoke came from the tryworks of successful whalers—and became the raider's fifth prize. The ship had little value except to Captain Samuel C. Small, who held part ownership. Two days later, Semmes torched the whaler and the prisoners rowed to shore, adding 15 more to the island's exploding population.[29]

After a day of inactivity, the *Alabama* captured the 119-ton hermaphrodite brig *Altamaha*. Five months out of New Bedford, her luck had been so bad that Captain Rufus Gray seemed unsurprised when it became worse. Before burning the ship, Kell and Low appraised her at a paltry $3,000, although her owners and others later filed claims totalling $48,000. It was not uncommon for the value of the *Alabama*'s prizes to increase meteorically between capture and trial.[30]

Late that evening, the watch roused Semmes and reported that a large ship had just passed to the windward. Hurrying on deck, he saw a fine whaler clearly outlined in the moonlight about three miles away. As the *Alabama* added sail, the stranger set her royals and flying jib, and headed to sea under a cloud of canvas. With conditions favoring the *Alabama*'s huge trysails, Semmes clawed up to windward, gaining rapidly. After a three-hour chase, the ship surrendered to Fullam, who took control of the prize until morning, while Semmes resumed his interrupted sleep.[31]

The 349-ton ship-rigged whaler *Benjamin Tucker*, eight months out of New Bedford, carried 340 barrels of oil. Her crusty skipper, William Childs, wrinkled and gnarled from years at sea, accepted the burning of his ship with the calmness of a man accustomed to being manipulated by fate. Kell manacled 30 prisoners in single irons and transferred nautical instruments and stores to the *Alabama*. He valued the ship and cargo at $18,000. The claims filed later by the owners totalled an astounding $179,835.[32]

As the morning mist evaporated on September 16, the lookout sighted another whaling schooner dead ahead and slowly approaching. After a brief chase, Low boarded the 121-ton *Courser*, six months out of Provincetown. Silas S. Young, one of the vessel's nine owners, so impressed Semmes that he would have commissioned him to the *Alabama* had Young not rooted himself so firmly to that "Universal Yankee Nation."

After adding the crew from the *Courser*, Semmes counted 68 prisoners swelling his decks and eight captured whaleboats in tow. Drawing nearer to Flores, he paroled the prisoners and released them, noting that "no doubt, the islanders, as they saw my well-known ship returning, with such a string of boats, congratulated themselves upon the prospect of other good bargains with the Yankees. The traffic must now have been considerable in this little island; such was the avalanche of boats, harpoons, cordage, whale's teeth, whalebones, beef, pork, tobacco, soap, and jack-knives that I have thrown on shore."[33]

Semmes let his inexperienced gun crews fire three rounds from each gun at the *Courser*, noting that only a few good line shots were made. At dark, he burned the prize and sailed westward.

On September 16 the ninth prize surrendered. Twenty days out of New Bedford, the 346-ton bark *Virginia*, bound for the distant whaling grounds of the Pacific, carried a handsome supply of stores and provisions—and a bundle of recent newspapers with inconclusive reports on the progress of the war. Captain Shadrach R. Tilton, who believed his *Virginia* a fast vessel, was astonished at the *Alabama*'s great speed under sail: "It was like a rabbit trying to run away from a greyhound." Late that afternoon, Semmes burned the vessel; the wreckage glowed late into the night.[34]

On Thursday, September 18, the wind changed, the sky darkened, and the ocean began to roll. Sailing under English colors, the *Alabama* chased a bark that did not break out the Stars and Stripes until fired upon. Now blowing half a gale, Semmes sent two of his best boats to the prize under the command of Lt. Wilson, stating that "I had a set of gallant and skillful young officers around me who would dare anything I told them to dare, and some capital seamen, and . . . by maneuvering the ship, I thought the thing could be managed." He instructed the boarding party to bring back nothing from the prize but the ship's chronometer, her flag, and the people on board—and to fire the ship before returning.

The 257-ton *Elisha Dunbar* became the only ship Semmes ever burned without first examining her papers. Her master, David R. Gifford, had sailed from New Bedford three weeks earlier on a four-year whaling voyage. On September 11, he had spoken the faster *Virginia* as it passed and exchanged words with Captain Tilton, never expecting to meet him again so soon.[35]

Semmes described the destruction of the *Dunbar*:

> This burning ship was a beautiful spectacle, the scene being wild and picturesque beyond description. The black clouds were mustering their forces in fearful array. Already the entire heavens had been overcast. The thunder began to roll and crash, and the lightning to leap from cloud to cloud in a thousand eccentric lines. The sea was a tumult of rage; the winds howled, and floods of rain descended. Amid this turmoil of the elements, the *Dunbar*, all in flames, and with disordered gear and unfurled canvas, lay rolling and tossing upon the sea. Now an ignited sail would fly away from a yard and scud off before the gale; and now the yard itself, released from the control of its braces, would swing about wildly as in the madness of despair, and then drop into the sea. Finally, the masts went by the board, and then the hull rocked to and fro for a while until it was filled with water and the fire nearly quenched, when it settled to the bottom of the great deep, a victim to the passions of man and the fury of the elements.[36]

In 11 days the *Alabama* had destroyed 10 vessels valued at $232,000. Bulloch had purchased the cruiser for $228,000. With the *Dunbar* as the last installment, the *Alabama* had repaid her initial cost to the Confederacy.

Confined to the deck and placed in irons, Captain Tilton of the *Virginia* later complained bitterly of his treatment while a prisoner, stating that he and his crew had been herded into the lee waist of the cruiser with only an old sail over them for protection and a few planks to keep them above the wet deck. Because Semmes kept the guns run out, the heavy sea came in the side ports and by morning the prisoners were drenched. Only one iron was loosened at the time food was served. Captain Gifford of the *Dunbar* related similar experiences, and Semmes later admitted that their comments were more or less correct.[37]

With the whaling season at the Azores nearing its end, Semmes set a course for the Banks of Newfoundland and the coast of the U. S. Like Southern cotton, American grain provided the gold to buy arms and munitions. With the bountiful Northern harvests just reaching the wharves of New York and Boston, Semmes expected to find a parade of Yankee ships deeply laden with cargoes for the bakeries of Great Britain.

It had been an exciting two weeks for the *Alabama*'s officers and crew. By now, every member of the ship's company had tabulated his share of the prize money and dreamt of a quiet life in some far-away countryside safe from the ravages of the sea. Never during their years at sea had this mixed British crew received better pay, better rations, better clothing, and the promise of such prize money. Morale soared.

Semmes considered the *Alabama* the best ship he ever commanded and probably the best ship on which he had ever sailed. Arthur Sinclair referred to the vessel as "both a perfect steamer and a perfect sailing vessel, each independent of the other." On this crest of euphoria, the *Alabama* sailed west to explore the sea lanes on Uncle Sam's doorstep.

New England Shudders

FOR THE next several days the *Alabama* struggled eastward under shortened sail against gale-force westerlies and heavy seas. With no other sails to be seen, the crew fell into the age-old shipboard routine: setting and taking in sail, caulking leaking decks, overhauling gear, looking forward to the evening meal and the customary issue of grog.

With a piece of canvas for a table cloth and a few tin dishes, Jack would sit on deck and gulp down his daily fare of salt pork or beef, hardtack, and beans, washed down with a mug of hot coffee. The men wasted little time eating, preferring to light their pipes and begin the evening's entertainment. To the skirl of harmonicas, violins, and tambourines, the men chose dancing partners—kerchiefs tied around the waists of the tittering and flirting "fairer sex"—and pranced wildly about the deck. Often, the officers stood aside and joined in the laughter, while Semmes looked on from the privacy of the bridge. The frolic closed with the singing of "Dixie," but the voices were not of the Confederacy, but of the waterfront of Great Britain.[1]

After encountering a wild northeaster as she entered the Gulf Stream, the weather slowly improved, and on October 3 the lookouts sighted three ships bowling along with the strong current toward Europe. Semmes captured two of them, but the third ship, being far to windward, escaped.[2]

The 1,119-ton ship *Emily Farnum*, her cargo of flour and grain carefully protected by certificates of neutral ownership, was released as a cartel with 68 paroled prisoners. Semmes chose not to bond the vessel, accepting the master's pledge to continue his voyage to Liverpool. Once the *Alabama* was out of sight, however, he raced back to Boston and alerted the authorities.[3]

The 839-ton ship *Brilliant*, carrying an identical cargo, was less fortunate. Although Captain George Hagar insisted it was neutral, he could produce no supporting documents. Semmes conducted his cabin-style admiralty proceedings and condemned the prize and its granary to the incendiaries.

Aware that unemployed English textile workers faced starvation at home, English-born Master's Mate Fullam recorded his remorse at the scene: "It seemed a fearful thing to burn such a cargo as the *Brilliant* had, when I thought how the operatives in the cotton districts would have danced with joy had they shared it amongst them. I never saw a cargo burn with such brilliancy, the flames completely enveloping the masts, hull and rigging in a few minutes, making a sight as grand as it was appalling."[4]

Three Englishmen from the *Brilliant*'s crew volunteered to join the Confederate Navy; Semmes sent the others to the *Farnum*. Assessor Kell estimated the *Brilliant*'s value at $164,000, the richest of all the *Alabama*'s many prizes. For once, Kell may have been overly liberal. Claims filed later by the owners amounted to $135,457.83, including personal losses.[5]

When the *Brilliant*'s captain, George Hagar, landed at Boston, he gave a lurid account of *Alabama* atrocities and hurried to New York, where he published an account of his capture in the *New York Journal of Commerce* demanding that the *Alabama* be destroyed. Hagar wrote: "The conduct of the captain of the pirate to the crew of the captured vessels was most inhuman. The unfortunate men were clustered together on deck, manacled, without room to lie down at night, or with only room for part of them, while the rest were compelled to stand; and in heavy weather they were continually washed by the sea—exposure and trials which only the stoutest and strongest men could endure. That is the way this pirate Semmes treats the sailors of our captured ships."[6]

New York insurance companies rallied behind Hagar's protest and pressured Secretary of State Seward to step up diplomatic efforts against the Confederate shipbuilding program in Great Britain. American Minister to England Charles Francis Adams renewed his attack upon the British Foreign Office.

Meanwhile, Secretary Welles received word of the whaling fleet's destruction off the Azores. Faced with differing descriptions from various sources, the Naval Office could not confirm whether one raider or many roamed the seas. Semmes took pains to disguise his ship's appearance: At times the *Alabama* had the look of a peaceful merchant sailing vessel laden with cargo; at other times she appeared to be a swift British man-of-war with two smokestacks, the second funnel being a black wind sail. His use of English boarding officers completed the deception, and many neutral ships never suspected they had not been boarded by a British warship. Between wild statements in the Northern press and a profusion of conflicting reports pouring into the Naval Office, Welles could not formulate a specific plan of action.

On October 7 two more grain ships fell victim. Although the captain and part owner of the 409-ton bark *Wave Crest*, John E. Harmon, claimed that his cargo was neutral, he was unable to produce supporting documents, and had to look on sadly as his vessel was plundered, used for target practice, and burned.[7]

While smoke from the *Wave Crest* still billowed skyward, Semmes pursued another sail off on the horizon. Correctly suspecting the cause of the smoke, Captain Samuel B. Johnson of the *Dunkirk* hauled off in the opposite direction, hoping to outsail the Confederate or, as it was late afternoon, hide in the approaching darkness. Semmes sat astride the hammock cloth on the weather quarter and watched the whole chase:

> As night threw her mantle over the scene, the moon, nearly at the full, rose with unusual splendor and lighted up the sea for the chase. . . . Although it lasted several hours, our anxiety as to the result was relieved . . . for we could see from the first that we had gained upon the fleeing ship, although her master practised every stratagem known to the skillful seaman. As soon as we approached sufficiently near to get a good view of her through our excellent nightglasses, which in the bright moonlight brought out all her features almost as distinctly as if we had been viewing them by the rays of the sun, we discovered that she was one of those light and graceful hermaphrodite brigs. . . . Her sails were beautifully cut, well hoisted, and the clews all spread . . . [and] looked not unlike so many silver wings in the weird moonlight, and with a little effort of the imagination, it would not have been difficult to think of her as some immense waterfowl, which had been scared from its roost and flown seaward for safety.[8]

At 9:30 p.m. Semmes fired one blank cartridge and the *Dunkirk* rounded into the wind. The 293-ton brig *Dunkirk*, eight days out of New York and bound for Lisbon, carried flour and several crates of tracts printed in Portuguese for distribution by the New York Bible Society and the American Tract Society of New York. Semmes referred to the Society as "that pious corporation . . . whose fine fat offices are filled with sleek, well-fed parsons whose business it is to prey upon the credulity of kind-hearted American women, and make a pretence of converting the heathen." The importation of religious tracts into Portugal being illegal, Semmes viewed burning the ship as a favor for a foreign government.[9]

Found serving aboard the *Dunkirk* was seaman George Forrest, who had deserted the *Sumter* at Cadiz. Semmes ordered him placed in double irons. A court martial convened the following morning convicted Forrest of desertion and ordered him discharged in disgrace from the Confederate Navy. In lieu of hanging, the court sentenced Forrest to serve without prize money or pay for the remainder of the *Alabama's* cruise. This decision proved unwise, as Forrest waited for an opportunity to get even with the officers.[10]

During the court martial, the *Alabama* chased and captured the 1,300-ton packet ship *Tonawanda* of Cope's Liverpool line, loaded with grain and 75 passengers, including 30 terrified women and children. With no room for so many prisoners, Semmes held the packet ship for four days, hoping to capture another ship capable of carrying the passengers to safety. When that failed, he freed the *Tonawanda* under an $80,000 bond, placing aboard all the prisoners from *Wave Crest*, *Dunkirk*, and *Manchester*, the latter a 1,062-ton grain ship captured and burned on October 11. The *Manchester's* owners and six insurors later claimed that British property had been destroyed when she was burned. If so, British merchants had failed to document it in the legally prescribed manner.[11]

Semmes enlisted two crewmen from the *Tonawanda*: William Halford, ordinary seaman, and David White, a 17-year old slave traveling with his master to Europe. On the premise that he was the property of the enemy, Semmes immediately emancipated White, who became a wardroom mess steward and a favorite among the officers. He often went ashore on liberty, never sought to desert, and became a fully paid member of the crew.[12]

Early on October 15 the lookout reported a sail bowling along under a stiff tail wind and heading directly toward the *Alabama*. Semmes was flying the St. Georges ensign and held his course, allowing the ship to come on. One shot from the bow gun, and the 365-ton bark *Lamplighter* surrendered. With the winds increasing to gale force, Semmes did not want to be troubled by the prize. The vessel carried a fine cargo of tobacco, however, and the incendiaries brought back several bundles along with the prisoners, barely making it back through the heavy seas as the gale continued to gain strength.[13]

From a stack of recent newspapers taken from the *Manchester*, Semmes learned that furious ship owners were demanding immediate protection, and that his ship had been targeted for destruction. He also learned exactly how the Union Navy planned to do this, writing that he was much obliged to the editors of the New York *Herald*, as: "I learned from them where all the enemy's gunboats were, and what they were doing. . . . Perhaps this was the only war in which the newspapers explained, beforehand, all the movements of armies, and fleets, to the enemy . . . which of course allowed me to take better care of the *Alabama*."[14]

As Semmes completed his raid along the coast of New England, Secretary Welles ordered his navy to search for the raider in the Azores. Commander T. Augustus Craven, who had been prevented by the British from chasing the CSS *Nashville*, and more recently had been watching the idle *Sumter* at Gibraltar, rushed the USS *Tuscarora* to the Azores, never suspecting that the elusive raider was far away and roaming off the Banks of Newfoundland.[15]

On October 6, while Semmes was burning two grain ships and about to burn two others the following day, Captain Charles W. Pickering reported to Secretary Welles that he had arrived at Fayal in the *Kearsarge* and reported that, "Ten whalers have been destroyed by the *Alabama* [290], commanded by Captain R. Semmes, and one other being missing, reported to have been sunk with all on board, though I can find no evidence to support this rumor."[16]

Up to now, the situation in Welles' Naval Office had been quiet and controlled. The blockade had tightened around the Confederacy, and more of the runners were becoming Union prizes. The Army of Northern Virginia, bloodied at Sharpsburg, had retreated south of the Potomac. Two Confederate cruisers had been bottled up in Gibraltar and Mobile, the only embarrassment being Maffitt's recent dash through Preble's squadron with the unarmed and under-manned *Florida*. But now another, much more menacing cruiser was reported on the loose, and Welles came under increasing pressure to do something. On October 16, the President of the Atlantic Mutual Insurance Company wrote Welles demanding "that vessels be sent in search of the rebel steamer *Alabama* forthwith."[17]

On October 18 Welles confided to his diary that "the ravages by the roving steamer 290, alias *Alabama*, are enormous. England should be held accountable for these outrages. The vessel was built in England and has never been in the ports of any other nation. British authorities were warned of her true character repeatedly before she left."

Operating on Hagar's reports from the *Brilliant*, Welles sent several gunboats to Nova Scotia—the raider's last reported position. As the Union Navy made preparations to steam northward, Semmes edged south, losing himself among the commerce off Boston and New York. In a few days, Welles issued a new series of orders, often vague, indecisive, and conflicting.[18] He had little confidence in his forces finding Semmes, or any other cruiser, and disliked weakening the blockade to chase stale reports.

At sea, the gale that had struck as the *Alabama* captured the *Lamplighter* built into a violent hurricane. On the morning of October 16, the barometer sank to 28.64. Semmes described it in his journal:

> The bad weather of the last four or five days culminated to-day in one of the severest gales of wind I have ever experienced. It did not last a great while, the whole being over in about four hours, but the wind blew furiously for about half of this time, forcing the ship down several strakes in the water, although she was only under the triangular storm staysail, the main yard having been carried away [and] the main topsail and fore staysail blown to ribbons. We lost also the lee quarter and stern boats, both stove by the force of the sea. A very heavy cross sea was raised, and the ship labored in and was pounded by it at a terrible rate. The gale was evidently a cyclone, though probably not of very great diameter, and the vortex of the gale passed over us. . . . During the violence of the gale the scud flew very low and with great rapidity. . . . The surface of the sea was one sheet of foam and spray (the latter blinding us) from the violence of the wind. In the afternoon sent down the two pieces of the broken main yard and stripped the main topsail yard of the fragments of its sail. I must capture another ship now directly to enable me to repair damages and replace my boats.[19]

For the next week, the *Alabama* tossed in an angry sea, as good prizes slipped by, saved by the rough weather. Late in the afternoon on October 23, the lookouts reported a sail approaching. With the rough weather, Semmes did not want to waste energy chasing a neutral, and called for Evans. After two minutes with the glasses he stated, "She is a Yankee, sir."

Semmes, maneuvering to within half a mile, fired a bow gun, and the 945-ton ship *Lafayette*, out of New York for Belfast with a large cargo of wheat, corn, and lard, rounded into the wind and shortened sail, skillfully holding her position like a duck bobbing on the rollers. Although captain and part-owner Alfred T. Small produced evidence showing that the grain was owned by two parties in Belfast, Semmes found several defects in the bills of lading, pronounced the documents a fraud, and ordered the ship burned.

Hereafter, Semmes seldom captured a vessel without documents— legitimate or forged—that declared the cargo to be neutral. Whether a ship was burned or released depended on whether he accepted the documents as genuine or false. Despite the questionable nature of the papers covering the *Lafayette*'s cargo, the United States filed protests with the British government, and the Northern press accused Semmes of committing flagrant acts of piracy against British property. This was the first of many accusations that followed Semmes as documents covering shipments in American bottoms became increasingly scrambled and puzzling.[20]

On October 26 the *Alabama* captured the 279-ton schooner *Crenshaw*, three days out New York, bound for Glasgow with grain. Again, the cargo ostensibly showed British ownership. Since no British subject had been specifically named, however, Semmes concluded that this was another clumsy attempt at falsification, and burned the vessel. From newspapers brought over from the schooner, he learned that Welles had dispatched several gunboats, including the huge *Vanderbilt*, toward the Newfoundland banks. He noted, "While they are running from New York I am running toward it."[21]

The weather turned cold, and Semmes ordered the prisoners, who were exposed on the main deck protected only by a flimsy tent, moved into the forward fire room. Three men came forward and enlisted, bringing the total to 11 men shipped from prizes. All but two were signed as ordinary seamen, one being a drummer and the other an able-bodied seaman.[22]

After another heavy gale, the lookouts sighted a small ship in rough seas late in the morning on October 27, and Semmes shaped a course to head her off. The stranger raised the Stars and Stripes in response to the cruiser's English blue, only to be greeted by a quick change to the Stars and Bars and a blank charge from the forward gun.

Captain Marshall M. Wells of the 284-ton bark *Lauretta* brought his papers aboard, announcing that his cargo of flour, staves, nails, and herring belonged to owners in Gibraltar and Messina, and in Funchal, Madeira. The only specific name Semmes could find on the documents, however, was a Mr. H. J. Burden, of 42 Beaver Street, New York City. He carefully filed the documents and ordered the ship burned.

The destruction of the *Lafayette* and the *Lauretta* made exciting copy for the readers of the *New York Commercial Advertiser*:[23]

THE *ALABAMA*
British and Italian Property Destroyed —
Portugal Also Involved.

The diminutive *Lauretta* attracted attention far out of proportion to her value. Claims filed later by the owners totaled $27,950, among the lowest on record of the many ships destroyed by the *Alabama*. Semmes later admitted that he had some doubts about the character of the *Lauretta*'s cargo, but felt justified when he read the account in the *Commercial Advertiser*, which stated that he had destroyed "the property of neutral merchants, domiciled in the enemy's country, and assisting him to conduct his trade." Since this was illegal, Semmes believed he would be exonerated once the British read the article.[24]

On October 29 the *Alabama* captured the brigantine *Baron de Castine*, bound for Cardenas, Cuba with a cargo of lumber. Although the cargo was undisputably Union, Semmes considered it not worth burning and took a $4,000 bond from her master in exchange for carrying his 44 prisoners to safety.

The *Castine* headed back to Boston, carrying a complete account of the *Alabama*'s activities since the day of her commissioning. This found its way into a widely read story in the November 15, 1862 edition of *Harper's Weekly*. Semmes also sent his respects to Mr. Low of the New York Chamber of Commerce, stating that by the time he received the message, the *Alabama* would be off that port. When the information finally reached Secretary Welles, Semmes had changed course to the southeast, once again leaving behind an empty sea for Union gunboats to search.[25]

Semmes had another reason for changing course—he was down to a four-day supply of coal, and the *Agrippina* awaited his arrival at Martinique. With banked fires, the *Alabama* spread her sail and sped south. On November 2 the lookouts sighted a whaler about four miles away, and after a one-hour chase, captured the 376-ton *Levi Starbuck*, five days out of New Bedford on a 30-month whaling voyage.

After 70 days at sea, subsisting only on salt pork, beans, and shipbread, the *Starbuck*'s stores of fresh vegetables were a welcome change for the *Alabama*'s crew. By nightfall, all the stores had been transferred, and 29 new prisoners came aboard to witness the whaler's burning.

The story of the *Levi Starbuck* later appeared in *Harper's Weekly*, along with a report that the USS *San Jacinto* had left in search of the raider.[26]

On November 5 the *Alabama* passed Bermuda and for the next two days sighted only neutral sails. Shortly after midnight on November 8, the midwatch reported a distant schooner standing south, about five miles to windward. After a four-hour pursuit with little progress, the lookouts reported a larger vessel to the northwest, and Semmes switched quarry, overhauling the 599-ton ship *Thomas B. Wales*, an East India trader bound for Boston from Calcutta with a large cargo of jute, linseed, and 1,704 bags of saltpeter consigned to Baring Brothers of Boston. Semmes condemned the vessel, certain that the saltpeter would be converted to Union gunpowder.[27]

Master Edgar Lincoln, who had sailed from Calcutta almost five months earlier and had heard nothing of the raider's presence, was accompanied by his wife and by former American consul at Mauritius, George H. Fairchild, Mrs. Fairchild, and three small daughters. Semmes moved the officers out of the wardroom to accommodate the two families. Although Mrs. Fairchild was heartbroken when she learned that her prized hand-carved ebony chairs would be burned with the ship, her husband never held a personal grudge against Semmes. Shortly after the war, when Semmes was captured and imprisoned for war crimes, Fairchild presented himself as a witness on Semmes' behalf and testified that prisoners on the *Alabama* received excellent treatment. This testimony and that of other prisoners led to the charges of inhuman treatment being dismissed.[28]

The capture of the *Thomas B. Wales* brought Semmes another bit of the good fortune that seemed to follow him: several of her spars were a close match for those damaged in the *Alabama's* brush with the hurricane. Eleven men signed enlistment papers. Although still 10 hands short of a full crew, for the first time the raider had enough men to serve all the guns.

Union Admiral David Dixon Porter knew Semmes throughout his career, respected him, disliked him, pursued him, and after the war finally wrote of him:

> Was there ever such a lucky man as the Captain of the *Alabama*? If he wanted a cargo of provisions it fell into his hands. If he required to visit a dock-yard to fit out his ship, a vessel came along filled with cordage, canvas and anchors. If he wanted lumber, a lumber vessel from Maine came right into his path; and if he needed to reinforce his crew, renegades from captured vessels would put their names to the shipping articles, after listening to the thrilling tales of the Norsemen, of burning ships and abundant prize-money.[29]

On November 17 the *Alabama* passed the coast of Dominica, close to the exact spot where the *Sumter* had eluded the USS *Iroquois* a year before. Now, many of the same officers were back in the faster and far more deadly *Alabama*. Taking the Dominica Channel around the northeast end of the island, Semmes lowered the propeller and called for steam, coming to anchor about mid-morning off the governing port city of Fort-de-France, Martinique—his first stop since leaving Terceira. Resting at anchor was the tender *Agrippina*, which had arrived eight days earlier with a full cargo of Cardiff coal.[30]

After an exchange of formalities with the governor and a visit from local health officers, Semmes landed his prisoners and sent the paymaster to obtain fresh provisions. What the men wanted was liberty and liquor, and they eventually succeeded in getting the latter from the bumboats surrounding the ship despite the officers' best efforts. Semmes later recalled that, "We had no marine guard on board the *Alabama*, and there was . . . no sentinel at the gangway in the daytime. We were necessarily obliged to rely upon the master-at-arms and the quartermasters for examining all boats that came alongside to see that no liquor was smuggled into the ship. These petty officers were old sailors like the rest, and I have rarely seen a sailor who could be relied upon, for any purpose of police, where his brother sailor was concerned."[31]

A little after sunset, Semmes was enjoying a quiet cup of tea in his cabin when the sound of angry voices and trampling feet broke out on deck. Kell came down to the cabin to report the ship in disorder and on the verge of mutiny. Semmes hurried to the deck and recognized the situation for what it was—a drunken disturbance and not a real cause for alarm. Kell had tried to restore order, only to be threatened and have a belaying pin hurled at his head.

Semmes ordered the ship to general quarters; after months of drill and discipline, even the hopelessly drunk fell in mechanically behind their guns. Thirty armed officers restored order and arrested all the drunks, among them the deserter Forrest.

The ringleaders were doused continuously with water until they gasped for breath; within two hours Kell removed the irons and the so-called mutiny ended. The dousing had loosened a few tongues, and several men fingered Forrest as the instigator who had brought the liquor aboard. He was arrested, put in double irons, and placed under guard. Wet and shivering, the troublemakers went below and fell asleep. It became a saying afterward among the sailors that, "Old Beeswax was h_ll upon watering a fellow's grog."[32]

Semmes' problems with alcohol did not end with his crew. Captain McQueen of the *Agrippina* had spent too many of his eight days at Martinique visiting the local bars, boasting of his connection with the now-famous raider. This time Union intelligence seemed to work: the USS *San Jacinto*, under Commander William Ronckendorff, arrived on November 19 and blockaded the harbor.

Although the Union warship had every advantage in size and armament, the *Alabama* had the advantage in speed. During a heavy rain on the evening of November 19, her men at their posts with every gun loaded, the *Alabama* escaped to sea. Semmes noted in his journal that "having received a pilot at 7:30 p.m., we got underway and ran out of the harbor, without seeing anything of the old wagon that was blockading us." Furious with McQueen, Semmes ordered him to the tiny Venezuelan island of Blanquilla.[33]

As the *Alabama* headed for her rendezvous with the *Agrippina*, Captain Ronckendorff attempted to explain the escape to Secretary Welles. The Maine brig *Hampton*, which had been discharging cargo nearby, had agreed to watch the raider and signal any movement. Shortly after the *Alabama* got underway, the *Hampton's* captain fired three rockets to the south, and Ronckendorff headed off in pursuit. Finding nothing, he returned to his post and kept the men at quarters. In the morning, the *Hampton's* captain stated that the *Alabama* had not escaped and was hiding in one of the many coves in the upper bay. After searching every inlet, Ronckendorff concluded that Semmes had escaped. He was a capable, conscientious officer who made no excuses. In his report to Welles, he stated in simple terms: "The enemy escaped, notwithstanding all our vigilance." Welles saw little honor in Semmes skirting his gunboats twice in the same place. He replied with a stinging reprimand that Ronckendorff never lived down.[34]

On the morning of November 21 the *Alabama* overtook the *Agrippina* and trudged along with her to an anchorage off the beach of Blanquilla, a neck of coral sand graced by a flock of scarlet flamingos. Nearby, greasy smoke stained the sky as the crew of the Yankee whaling schooner *Clara L. Sparks* rendered blubber on the beach.

Seeing the *Alabama* under American colors, the whaling captain came aboard and expressed his delight at having a powerful Northern gunboat close at hand, declaring that she was the very ship "to give the pirate Semmes fits." After a short time, Semmes quietly defused his ecstatic enthusiasm and told him the truth. Semmes described his reaction:

> He stood aghast for a moment. An awful vision seemed to confront him. His little schooner, and his oil, and the various little 'ventures which he had on board with which to trade with the natives along the coast . . . were all gone up the spout! And then he stood in the presence of the man whose ship he had characterized as a "pirate," and whom he had told to his face he was no better than a freebooter. But I played the magnanimous. I told the skipper not to be alarmed; that he was perfectly safe on board the *Alabama*, and that out of respect to Venezuela, within whose maritime jurisdiction we were, I should not even burn his ship.[35]

For five days the *Alabama* loaded coal while the crew took turns romping around the small island, fishing in the lagoon, and exploring the wonders of the coral bank. Semmes' court found the incorrigible George Forrest guilty of inciting a mutiny, and sent him ashore with his bag and hammock. Forrest joined the crew of the whaler; his mates chipped in $80 for his general welfare. Considering that the penalty for his crime was often death, Forrest suffered little.[36]

After removing half the *Agrippina*'s cargo of coal, Semmes directed McQueen to meet him next at desolate Arcas Island in the lower Gulf of Mexico. Here, too, the intemperate captain would find no bars to quell his thirst and loosen his tongue.

Semmes released the Yankee whaling schooner, telling the master to "make a free sheet of it, and not let me catch him on the high seas, as it might not be so well for him a second time." Moments later, the little schooner filled away and headed for the horizon. Semmes doubted that he stopped anywhere this side of Nantucket.[37]

On the evening of November 26 Semmes weighed anchor, hoisted the propeller, and set sail for the Windward Passage—a shipping highway that ran between Cuba and Haiti. He hoped to ambush a northbound treasure ship listed in the New York newspapers as leaving Aspinwall (now Colon) the first day of December. He figured he had just enough time to capture a few prizes along the way.

Since September 5 the *Alabama*, the only Confederate cruiser afloat, had destroyed 20 ships appraised by her officers at $1,184,311 — four times the cruiser's original cost. But the damage she inflicted was far more serious than that.

On October 8, 1862 the *New York Shipping and Commercial List* noted that, "Vessels under foreign flags command higher rates, in consequence of the reported seizure and destruction of American vessels by the Rebel Steamer 290." A week later the same publication noted, "Shipments making almost entire in foreign bottoms, American vessels being in disfavor."

Boston headlines announced: "Advances on Marine Insurance." New York papers stated that: "The damaging effect of the *Alabama*'s raid on our shipping upon the maritime interests of this port were as conspicuous to-day as yesterday. It was next to impossible for the owner of an American ship to procure freight unless he consented to make a bogus sale of his ship."

Historians point to this period as the beginning of the demise of the once-flourishing and prosperous American merchant marine.[38]

From Galveston to Bahia

A S ADMIRAL Porter wrote, "Was there ever such a lucky man as the Captain of the *Alabama*?" On November 30, off the coast of Santo Domingo, Semmes learned from a stack of Boston newspapers obtained from a Spanish schooner that Union Major General Nathaniel Banks intended to attack Galveston by sea. More important, he learned that Welles felt no need to send gunboats to guard the Union troop ships from the South's nonexistent navy. Faced with a rare opportunity to destroy the entire expedition, which could not cross the 12-foot bar at Galveston and would be vulnerable when offloading troops into small boats, Semmes began to shape a plan to intercept Bank's forces, without losing the chance of capturing a treasure ship along the way.

"If he wanted a cargo of provisions it fell into his hands," Porter wrote. Sure enough, along came the 136-ton Boston bark *Parker Cook*, and a sizable cargo of butter, cheese, beef, pork, dried fruit, and shipbread. Fullam's boarding party spent the rest of the day filling the cruiser's empty larder and at twilight, set the *Parker Cook* ablaze off Cape Rafael.[1]

For the next few days the *Alabama* cruised the Spanish Main, much like the pirate ships of old laying for a Spanish galleon laden with gold. Divided evenly among the officers and crew, the spoil from a California treasure ship might total $8,000 per man—more than $130,000 in today's dollars.[2]

On December 5, Semmes captured the 90-ton Baltimore schooner *Union*, bonded the vessel for $1,500, loaded the prisoners from the *Parker Cook* aboard, and continued searching for the California treasure ship. Finally, on December 7, the lookouts reported a steamer standing toward them. The stranger was headed *for* Aspinwall, and not toward it, but Semmes called all hands to quarters, ordered sail taken in, and asked the engine room for steam.[3]

Aboard the California packet *Ariel*, the first officer, R. C. Thomas, who later wrote of the event for *Frank Leslie's Illustrated Newspaper*, observed a bark under sail, four miles off and approaching fast. He was astonished when the bark suddenly sprouted a smoking funnel. As she closed, Thomas watched the American colors come down and the Stars and Bars go up. A puff of smoke signaled that a gun had been fired, and Thomas ordered full speed. Another shot hit the rigging, sending the panic-stricken passengers below, and Captain Albert J. Jones ordered the ship stopped.[4]

A passenger, Dr. George Willis Read, later wrote in his book, *A Pioneer of 1850*, that as soon as the *Ariel* hove to, a boarding party from the *Alabama* came alongside and bounded onto the deck. Captain Jones was taken aboard the *Alabama* and Lt. Low took charge of the prize crew. On learning that there were ladies aboard who were greatly distressed at being captured by ruthless pirates, Captain Semmes sent his handsomest young officers to their rescue. Dressed in their finest uniforms, Lt. Armstrong and Midshipman William H. Sinclair boarded the *Ariel* with the singular mission of charming the fairer sex and assuring them that the officers of the *Alabama* were gentlemen, and not the villains described in the Northern press. Arthur Sinclair described the results:

> It looked like a hopeless task trying to convince the passengers they would not have to walk the plank. Many of the ladies were in hysterics, fearing the worst. But it did not take our gallants long to secure the confidence of one of the ladies braver than the rest. This accomplished, one by one they came forward, and soon our lucky boarding-officers were enjoying the effect of the reaction. A perfect understanding must have been arrived at between the fair ones and our "rascally" lieutenant and middy, for the latter were soon minus every button from their uniforms, not "for conduct unbecoming an officer and a gentleman," but as mementos of the meeting.[5]

As Semmes suspected, "instead of being a homeward-bound steamer with a million of dollars in gold in her safe, I had captured an outward-bound steamer with five hundred women and children on board! This was an elephant I had not bargained for, and I was seriously embarrassed to know what to do with it."

While deciding, Semmes brought her captain and engineers aboard to prevent any possibility of escape, and disarmed and paroled a 140-man battalion of marines who were on their way to the Pacific. The total plunder from the prize was about $9,500 in specie, a 24-pounder rifled gun, 125 new rifles, 16 swords, and about 1,000 rounds of ammunition.

For several days Semmes kept the *Ariel* nearby, hoping to find a way to unload the prisoners and destroy the packet, unwilling to miss an opportunity to hurt her owner, Cornelius Vanderbilt—an outspoken enemy of the South—in the pocketbook.[6] Semmes considered taking her into Jamaica, but a passing ship informed him that Kingston was infested with yellow fever.

While chasing another ship passing nearby, the *Alabama*'s engine failed. The engine room reported they would need 24 hours to repair a broken valve casting. Now solely dependent on sails, Semmes saw little choice, and bonded the packet for $261,000.[7]

As the *Ariel* and the *Alabama* parted company on December 9, Kell claimed that some of the ladies "called for 'three cheers for Captain Semmes and the *Alabama*, which were heartily given with a waving of handkerchiefs and adieus.'" When the *Ariel* returned to New York and reported her close call, Cornelius Vanderbilt took no more chances and insisted that in the future his ships be escorted by at least one Union warship.[8]

Semmes sailed westward and eased the cruiser close to the quiet northern coast of Jamaica. For the next 48 hours, Chief Engineer Freeman worked his crew around the clock to hand-forge a new valve casting. By the evening of December 12, the engine was back in operation and running smoothly, but Semmes wanted to coal before heading up the Gulf in search of the Banks Expedition.

After bucking heavy winds for several days, the *Alabama* arrived off Arcas Island late on the evening of December 22, and was joined by the *Agrippina* the following morning. McQueen had been slowly making his way from Blanquilla for the past four weeks, but Semmes suspected the captain had stopped along the way for a little refreshment and unauthorized private trading.

For two weeks the crew coaled, recaulked, and careened ship to scrub the fouled copper sheathing. Christmas Day passed in idleness and ended with a hearty issue of grog. During the stay, the ship's company enjoyed many leisure hours ashore, catching fish, chasing turtles, sailing, swimming, and shooting. The bay in the center of the three islands comprising Las Arcas had a very narrow connection with the sea. As the tide fell, this formed a natural fish trap. The ship's resident daredevil, Coxswain Michael Mars, noticed a shark swimming in the shallows, dove into the water, and killed it with his knife.[9]

After filling the bunkers, Semmes sent the *Agrippina* back to Liverpool for another load of Cardiff coal and bided his time, watching the weather and calculating the precise moment of departure to intercept Banks' troopships as they headed toward Galveston. By the time the *Alabama* sailed on January 5, the crew suspected where Semmes was headed. They had read the same headlines, pondered the same possibilities, and were eager for action—but for different motives. Semmes sought to serve his beleaguered country; the crew sought the great personal fortunes that would come their way in the form of prize money.

At noon on Sunday, January 11, the *Alabama* stood 30 miles off Galveston. The lookout posted at the masthead had been instructed to watch for a large fleet anchored off the lighthouse. Semmes hoped to get a bearing on the transports' exact location and then lay out of sight until the moon rose at midnight. At length the lookout cried, "Land ho! Sail ho!", reporting five warships, but no transports. Instead, Union warships were throwing shells into Galveston. It appeared that Confederate forces had recaptured the city, thwarting Banks' expedition.[10]

After sighting an unknown ship standing offshore, one of the Union warships got up steam and headed out to investigate. Semmes lowered the propeller and ordered the boilers fired; the watch below came on deck and, without orders, prepared the guns for action. Still under topsails, the *Alabama* edged seaward as the gunboat continued to approach, almost timidly, as if her captain suspected something unnatural about the odd bark that seemed barely to move. As evening fell, Semmes slowly retreated, luring the Union vessel farther from her squadron until the intervening gap had increased to 20 miles. Semmes described the action that unfolded:

> Soon after dark . . . I clewed up and furled the topsails, beat to quarters, and doubled suddenly upon the stranger. He came on quite boldly, and when within hailing distance of us . . . enquired, "What ship is that?" To which we responded, "Her Majesty's steamer *Petrel*," and in turn enquired who he was. We could not make out his reply, although we repeated our enquiry several times. During this colloquy I endeavored to place myself in a raking position astern of him, which he . . . avoided by keeping his port broadside to me. From this maneuver I knew him . . . to be an enemy and, having approached within about 200 yards, I directed my first lieutenant to ask again what ship it was, being . . . loth to fire upon him without a reply, fearing that I might possibly make a mistake. This time we heard his reply very distinctly—that he was a United States something or other; the name [Hatteras] we could not make out. I then directed [Lt. Kell] . . . to tell him this was the Confederate States steamer *Alabama*, and to open fire upon him immediately, which we did from our starboard battery.[11]

In a minute or two the gunboat returned fire, and the ships ran side by side firing rapidly, at times only 40 yards apart. Master's Mate Fullam described the scene in his journal:

188 · · · · · · · · · · GRAY RAIDERS OF THE SEA

Twas a grand though fearful sight to see the guns belching forth, in the darkness of the night, sheets of living flame, the deadly missiles striking the enemy with a force that we could feel. Then, when the shells struck her side, and especially the percussion ones, her whole side was lit up . . . showing rents of five or six feet in length. One shot . . . struck our smokestack . . . wounding one man in the cheek, when the enemy eased his firing, and fired a lee gun, then a second, and a third, the order was then given to "Cease firing." A tremendous cheering commenced and it was not until everybody had cleared his throat to his own satisfaction that silence could be obtained. We then hailed him, and in reply, he stated that he had surrendered, was on fire and also that he was in a sinking condition. He then sent a boat on board and surrendered the U. S. Gunboat *Hatteras*, 9 guns, Lieut. Commr. Blake, 140 men.[12]

Semmes deployed every boat to rescue the crew of the stricken Union vessel, whose own boats had been smashed during the 13-minute engagement. Seventeen officers and 101 seamen were brought aboard; two crewmen had been killed, and five wounded. Semmes placed the Union crew in single irons, put the officers under guard in the wardroom, and graciously gave his cabin to Captain Blake. Within 45 minutes of her surrender, the *Hatteras* sank in 9½ fathoms of water. A search vessel found her next morning, her masts projecting just above water with the night pennant still flying.[13]

Prior to the war, the *Hatteras* had been a commercial passenger vessel on the Delaware River—a career which much better suited her. Purchased by the navy, fitted out at the Philadelphia Navy Yard, and commissioned in October 1861, the converted gunboat's exposed sidewheels and thin iron hull were no match for the *Alabama*'s heavy guns.

Initially her commander, Lt. Homer C. Blake, believed he was chasing a brig attempting to run the blockade, but when Semmes ordered steam, he realized he was chasing something bigger and cleared for action. Although Blake skillfully maneuvered his vessel, his ship was thoroughly outclassed, both in speed and armament. Later exonerated by a court, Blake went on to command the USS *Eutaw* and other ships, all more prestigious than the deficient *Hatteras*.[14] The *Alabama-Hatteras* duel was the only victory of a Confederate raider over a Union warship.[15]

The *Alabama* received only seven minor hits during the engagement. Fullam recorded the damage:

Only one man being hurt during the engagement, and he receiving only a slight flesh wound in the cheek. One shot struck under the counter, penetrating as far as a timber, then glancing off. A second struck the funnel, a third going through the side, across the berth deck and into the opposite side, another raising the deuce in the lamp room, and the others lodging in the coal bunkers . . . the enemy's fire being directed chiefly to our stern, the shots flying pretty thick over the quarter deck near to where our Captain was standing. As they came whizzing over him, he with usual coolness, would exclaim, "Give it to the rascals," "Aim low men," "Don't be all night sinking that fellow."

From conversation with her first Lieut. I learnt that, as soon as we gave our name and fired our first broadside, the whole after division on board her left the guns, apparently paralyzed—it was some time before they recovered themselves. The conduct of one of her officers was cowardly and disgraceful in the extreme. Some of our shells went completely through her before exploding; others burst inside, and set her on fire in three places. One went through her engines, completely disabling her, another exploding in her steam chest, scalding all within reach. Thus was fought 28 miles from Galveston . . . the first yard arm action between two steamers at sea. . . .[16]

At daylight the USS *Brooklyn* found the mast of the *Hatteras*, with pennant still flying, rising from the surface of the Gulf. There was no sign of the ship that had sunk her. Semmes had left in the night, his decks crowded with as many prisoners as he had crew. During a nine-day run to Jamaica, the *Alabama* chased a sail that turned out to be the *Agrippina*, homeward bound to England. Fearing that McQueen would jettison their mail bag, Semmes hauled down the English colors and hoisted the Stars and Bars, saluted, and kept on course, concealing the connection between the two ships from the Union prisoners on board.

On January 20, after a rough passage during which Semmes suffered from his old enemy, seasickness, the *Alabama* anchored at Port Royal. After a courtesy visit to local authorities he paroled his prisoners into the care of American consul John N. Camp, who reported them completely destitute of funds and clothing. Like Semmes, the prisoners had suffered much during the passage to Jamaica.[17]

Semmes left the ship in the care of Kell and spent four days resting in the mountains with a local friend. The citizens of Kingston, expressing support for the Southern cause, offered their homes to the weary Confederates. Sinclair noted that, "At no time during the cruise was our ship in such a state of confusion as during our stay in Kingston." During this social melee, Kell worked diligently to coal, repair, and re-provision the ship; the guests from the *Hatteras* had put a sizable dent in the larder.[18]

Shore leave, granted by watch, quickly deteriorated into a wild, drunken orgy. Semmes returned on January 24 to find the crew scattered all over the town and the officers searching for them. One of the officers sent to round-up the derelicts was Arthur Sinclair, who wrote:

One is reminded of the old problem of ferrying over the river the goose, the fox and the bag of corn; for no sooner is one lot delivered at the boat and another raid made up-town, than the prisoners break guard somehow and are up-town again. The writer, visiting a dance-hall after dark with a boat's crew in quest of the delinquents, was met at the threshold by a body of men from the English squadron backed by the lady participants in the ball, and good-naturedly but firmly informed that he could not come in. . . . One of the ladies remarked, "Say, middy, come some other time. The tickets are limited at this ball; and besides, the company is select!" "Tell old Beeswax," said another persuasive maiden, "your old piratical skipper, to go to sea, burn some more Yankee ships, and come back. We'll give up the boys then, and you shall have your turn."[19]

The officers gradually retrieved the crew from the bars and brothels of Kingston. Semmes recorded that, "The ship's cutters, as well as the shore-boats, were constantly coming alongside with small squads, all of them drunk. . . . Liquor was acting upon them like the laughing gas; some were singing jolly, good-humored songs, whilst others were giving the war-whoop and insisting on a fight. They were seized, ironed and passed below to the care of the master-at-arms as fast as they came aboard." Nine hands were never found and listed as deserters. Paymaster Yonge, who had been consorting with the prisoners before reaching shore, openly defected to the enemy, eventually returned to England, and went to work for Consul Dudley as a spy and informant. Many sailors deserted Confederate cruisers, but Yonge was the only officer to do so.[20]

Finally, on the evening of January 25, the *Alabama* steamed out of Kingston and headed for the coast of Haiti. The following day she captured the 255-ton bark *Golden Rule*, with a cargo of food and medicine for the Panama Railroad Company and the Pacific Mail Steamship Company. Also aboard were new spars and a full set of sails for the USS *Bainbridge*, idle at Aspinwall after losing her rig during a violent November storm. Semmes made sure she would be idled several more months waiting for another set to arrive. Some of the *Golden Rule*'s cargo had a neutral tinge, but without absolute proof, Semmes ordered the ship stripped and burned—the first merchant carrier destroyed since the *Parker Cook* on November 30, 1862.[21]

Two days later, off Santo Domingo, Semmes captured the 293-ton Boston brig *Chastelain*, in ballast from Guadaloupe to Cienfuegos. Before burning her, the prize crew removed the ship's chronometer and $700 in gold. With prisoners from two prizes now aboard, and a crew still ailing from their binge at Kingston, Semmes put into Santo Domingo, dropped off his prisoners, and on the morning of January 29 headed for the busy Mona Passage, still hoping for a treasure ship.[22]

On February 3 the *Alabama* captured the swift little 172-ton schooner *Palmetto*, 10 days out of New York. Captain Oren H. Leland testified that he did not know the owner of the cargo, although the written evidence pointed to him as charterer of the vessel as well as master. Since no documentation proved neutral ownership, Semmes removed the chronometer, cheese, and crackers, and burned the ship.[23]

During the balance of February, Semmes captured only two prizes, both falling on the 21st when the lookouts simultaneously sighted four scattered sails. Master's Mate Evans picked the two that looked most American, and the cruiser steamed off in pursuit. Sending an armed prize crew aboard the 1,121-ton clipper ship *Golden Eagle*, Semmes chased the other vessel, about 15 miles off. Under steam, the *Alabama* closed with the 360-ton New York bark *Olive Jane* in less than two hours. When he discovered the nature of her cargo—wine, brandy, and other delicacies from Bordeaux—Semmes ordered her burned. As he vividly remembered from the mutiny at Martinique and the uncontrollable frolic at Kingston, his crew could not be trusted around alcohol. He passed up some fancy meats as well, saving only the chronometer and the ship's flag.[24]

Semmes ordered the *Golden Eagle*, which was laden with guano from Howland's Island for Cork, Ireland, burned as well. Flames from the two ships, one on each side of the raider, cast a lurid spectacle across the darkened sea.[25]

The *Alabama* crossed the 30th parallel and entered the main highway of maritime traffic rounding the capes. At times as many as seven or eight vessels might be in sight, all neutrals. For a week the raider roved south, searching for American shipping. Finally, on February 27 Semmes captured the New York ship *Washington*, with guano bound from Callao to Cork. Peruvian agents in Antwerp owned the fertilizer, and Semmes settled for a $50,000 bond after forcing her master, William T. Frost, to take his prisoners. Two days later, the *Alabama* captured another guano ship, the 890-ton *Bethiah Thayer* of Rockland, Maine. With Peruvian papers identical to the *Washington*, Semmes issued another bond, this one for $40,000.[26]

At daylight on March 2 the lookout reported a large ship steering directly toward them, which Semmes captured without bothering to interrupt the morning watch's daily scrubbing of the decks. The *John A. Parks*, a ship of 1,047-tons from Hallowell, Maine, carried a large cargo of lumber for Montevideo. Although under American registry, the cargo papers left Semmes puzzled. After hearing testimony from Captain John S. Cooper, Semmes decided that the consulate seal was fraudulent and ordered the ship destroyed. While the vessel burned, a passing English bark agreed to take the *Park*'s captain and his family to London. From newspapers on the prize, Semmes learned for the first time that he now had a roving partner: the *Florida* had escaped from Mobile.[27]

Standing towards the equator on March 15, the *Alabama* captured the Boston ship *Punjaub*, carrying a properly certified English cargo of linseed and jute. Signing a ransom bond for $55,000, Captain Lewis F. Miller continued on his voyage to London from Calcutta after agreeing to take 20 prisoners from the *Parks*. The *Punjaub*'s owners, the Wales family, had suffered another loss at Semmes' hands when he burned the *Thomas B. Wales* on November 8, 1862. Later, Semmes recaptured the *Punjaub* on September 3, 1863, and again set her free because of her neutral cargo. After losing one vessel, the Wales family learned how to protect their ships.[28]

On March 23 the *Alabama* was 3 degrees above the equator and still tracking south when Semmes added two more names to the growing list of Yankee victims. Protected by her neutral cargo, bound from Calcutta to London, the *Morning Star* of Boston was bonded and released for $61,750. The 120-ton whaling schooner *Kingfisher*, out of Fairhaven, Massachusetts, was not so lucky. Semmes burned her at nightfall during a severe thunderstorm. Sinclair wrote:

> The little craft, though oil-soaked, blazed by fits and starts. In the lull of passing rain squalls, the flames would shoot mast-head high, seeming to play at hide-and-seek with the vivid lightning, anon shrinking beneath a drenching shower, leaving nature to keep up the pyrotechnic display—a weird like spectacle.[29]

On March 25 two more prizes surrendered, the 699-ton Boston ship *Charles Hill* and the Boston schooner *Nora*, both loaded with salt bound from Liverpool to Montevideo. During Semmes' Admiralty hearings after the war, both captains testified that their cargoes were British, but they could not produce unequivocal proof. Semmes had little patience with legal sloppiness and ordered both vessels destroyed. Captain Franklin Percival of the *Charles Hill* stated that some small stores and about 10 tons of coal were removed from his ship before it was burned. Among his papers was the following letter from the owners:

Boston, October 18, 1862

Dear Sir: I have received your several letters from Philadelphia. As a rebel privateer has burned several American ships, it may be well if you can have your bills of lading endorsed as English property, and have your cargo certified to by the English consul.[30]

Because of the questionable ownership of these cargoes, Seward wrote a position paper to Minister Charles Francis Adams on October 6, 1863, regarding the burning of the *Nora*, which became the foundation for the litigation between the United States and Great Britain known later as the *Alabama* Claims. The paper instructed Adams how to present the protest to Lord Russell, who had recently asked Adams to send him no more claims for damages caused by commerce raiders. Seward's paper reemphasized "that the British government is justly responsible for the damages which the peaceful, law-abiding citizens of the United States sustain by the depredations of the *Alabama*. I cannot, therefore, instruct you to refrain from presenting the claims which you have now in your hands of the character indicated."[31]

On March 29, 1863 the *Alabama* crossed the equator in thick, squally weather and headed south along the coast of Brazil, looking for the *Agrippina*. After boarding and passing a procession of neutrals, the lookouts reported seven sail on the morning of April 4. Master's Mate Evans picked out only one as American. A chase that began at 8:30 a.m. finally ended at 10 that night, with the capture of the 853-ton New York ship *Louisa Hatch*, 28 eight days out of Cardiff with 1,100 tons of smokeless coal.

Again, it seemed Semmes' famous luck was at work. The *Alabama*'s bunkers were nearly empty and the *Agrippina* had failed to arrive on schedule; here was a ship filled with the raider's ideal fuel. As events later proved, the hapless *Agrippina* and her hard-drinking captain never did arrive. McQueen made it a point to miss his scheduled rendezvous, sold his cargo of coal, pocketed the money, and eventually returned to England with some "cock-and-a-bull" story.

With the *Agrippina*'s whereabouts unknown, Semmes put Fullam on board the *Louisa Hatch*, instructing him to keep close, and sailed to the island of Fernando de Noronha, a Brazilian penal colony about 200 miles east of the mainland. On April 10 he announced his arrival to the governor and, in the swell of the open roadstead, proceeded to transfer 300 tons of coal from the *Hatch* by boat. Governor Sebastiao Jose Basilio Pyrrho, a social-minded sport who enjoyed visits from passing ships and was not particularly concerned about violations of his country's neutrality, allowed Semmes to do whatever he pleased. Nowhere else in Brazil could Semmes have delivered a prize and helped himself to its contents.[32]

On April 15 two whalers anchored about five miles from shore, and their masters rowed to the *Louisa Hatch* where Fullam, without his uniform coat, roamed the deck. Pretending to be a Yankee, he invited the whalers aboard, telling them that the unidentified warship nearby was a "Brazilian packet-steamer." To his surprise, they hurriedly retreated, beating the water to a froth as they rowed back to their vessels. Fullam then noticed that the *Alabama*'s coxswain had thrown a Confederate ensign over a spanker-boom to dry and a puff of wind had blown out the folds.[33]

Semmes, who had been watching the affair from the *Alabama*'s deck, immediately ordered steam and, with the Confederate flag flying, sped toward the two whalers, both of which surrendered after one shot. After burning the New Bedford bark *Lafayette*, Semmes towed the 132-ton whaling brig *Kate Cory* back to shore, intending to use her as a cartel to take the *Alabama*'s 110 prisoners. When a small Brazilian schooner came into port, however, he sent all his prisoners, along with a few barrels of flour and pork to keep them fed, to Pernambuco. He then took the *Louisa Hatch* and the *Kate Cory* back to sea and burned them, a twin red glow lighting up the sea that night.[34]

During the *Alabama*'s two week stay, the governor had grown increasingly concerned over Semmes' liberal interpretation of his country's laws, particularly after the arrival of the Brazilian schooner, which presumably would carry more than prisoners to Pernambuco. Semmes noted on April 16 that "The governor paid me a visit this morning and requested that I would write him on the subject of the captures yesterday, stating the fact (with which he was satisfied, or at least to which he made no objection) that they were captured beyond the league from the land, and requesting permission to land the prisoners, in order that our understanding should assume an official shape, which I did." But when the emperor learned of the situation, the letter apparently did not save the governor's career. A short time afterward, Maffitt stopped at the island and received a decidedly less cordial reception from his successor.[35]

On April 22 Semmes returned to sea, and two days later captured the 211-ton New Bedford bark *Nye*, homeward bound from the Pacific with 500 barrels of oil and a cargo of whalebone. Kell valued the ship and cargo at $31,127, but the New England owners ran their claims to an astounding $104,936. The oil-saturated ship made a spectacular bon-fire.[36]

Off the coast of Brazil on April 26 the *Alabama* captured the 699-ton ship *Dorcas Prince*, 44 days out of New York for Shanghai with a cargo of coal. Semmes had no room for the coal but removed the provisions and the 20-man crew, bringing the prisoner count to 44.[37]

Cruising near Bahia on May 3, Masters Mate Evans studied the constant flow of traffic and identified two American vessels. Chasing the nearest vessel, Semmes captured the 483-ton bark *Union Jack*, 36 days out of New York bound for Shanghai with a general cargo and six passengers. On board, Captain Charles P. Weaver had his wife, servant, and two children, a consul to China, and another gentleman. Both ladies were transferred to the cruiser by "whip," similar to a boatswain's chair, slung from the yardarm. The enraged Irish servant heatedly denounced Semmes to his face as a pirate and rebel. To cool her, he ordered her doused with water. The consul, Rev. Franklin Wright, who had edited a religious publication before joining the State Department, later filed claims for $10,015. Semmes commented, "I had no idea that a New England parson carried so much plunder about with him."[38]

The *Alabama* then captured the second ship, the 973-ton Boston clipper *Sea Lark*, bound for San Francisco with a general cargo so large and varied that Fullam's prize crew spent the entire day sorting through the plunder. Prisoners from the two vessels brought the total aboard the *Alabama* to 108, too many for the watch to guard. Anxious to discharge his prisoners, Semmes burned the prizes and headed for port, entering Bahia on May 11. Visiting health officials warned Semmes that three American gunboats stood off the coast, but he suspected it was ruse to encourage his departure. He had seen no evidence of Union warships.[39]

In less than nine months, the *Alabama* had captured and burned 38 prizes appraised at $2,544,618, 10 times the cruiser's original cost. Including bonded vessels, the tally exceeded $3,100,000.

When the *Alabama* began her cruise, she was alone, the only wolf among the sheep. Now she had company. The *Florida* had followed in her path, and found the sea lanes lightened of American commerce by her bigger sister. Maffitt had just commissioned and armed the *Clarence*, sending her back to New England for a wild raid up the coast. The *Georgia* had put to sea on April 9, 1863. Bulloch had ironclads under construction in England and France, and the trial of the *Alexandra* had not yet taken place. For now, at least, it seemed the Confederacy had the oceans to herself.

Secretary Welles continued to concentrate his navy's efforts on blockading Southern ports. His position on the loss of American commerce to the raiders in Europe and the Caribbean approached apathy. Only when raids were carried out on American coastal waters, or if the press hollered for his head or sent politicians to his door demanding action, did he stir himself to action. All this would change, but not for a while. With the absence of Union warships, the *Alabama*'s success would continue.

Cape Town Caper

SEMMES found many ships at anchor in the spacious harbor of Bahia, but not a Yankee trader among them. The only warship present was Portuguese. Despite rumors, a Union man-of-war had not been seen for months. The local newspaper carried a reprint of an earlier letter addressed to Semmes charging him with violations of Brazilian neutrality and demanding that he leave Fernando de Noronha within 24 hours. The letter originated in Pernambuco, where the *Alabama* left her last load of paroled prisoners. Finding Semmes in Bahia, the president of the province sent an aide-de-camp to demand answers to the allegation. Commenting that, "It reminded me very much of the 'stink-pots,' which the Chinese are in the habit of throwing at their enemies," Semmes responded with a letter that the president found "perfectly satisfactory." With formalities pleasantly concluded, and a five-day stay granted, the *Alabama* thrust another shipload of prisoners upon the generosity of Brazil and granted liberty to an ebullient crew.[1]

If the *Alabama*'s arrival at Bahia was not exactly welcomed in official circles, the citizenry at least found it an occasion to celebrate. A constant stream of visitors swarmed over the cruiser, and a magnificent ball was arranged for the captain and his adventurous young officers. Contrasting with this elegance, the *Alabama*'s crewmen characteristically debauched themselves in Bahia's waterfront bars and brothels.

Early on May 13 the watch reported that a strange steamer had arrived during the night and anchored a half mile away. Semmes ordered the Confederate colors raised; to his surprise, the stranger did the same. After exchanging signals, Semmes sent a boat, delighted to learn that the ship was the CSS *Georgia*, captained by an old navy chum, Lt. William L. Maury. Serving under Maury were Lt. Robert T. Chapman and Lt. William E. Evans, two of the *Sumter*'s officers who had remained behind in Europe when Semmes sailed for Nassau.

During the four-day reunion celebration while the *Georgia* loaded coal, a telegram from Pernambuco announced the *Florida*'s arrival.

"Now we can straighten up and put on airs," said Lt. Sinclair, "and boast of the Confederate Squadron of the South America Station."[2]

With two Confederate cruisers in his port and another at Pernambuco, the provincial president worried that he might incur the Emperor's disfavor. Heavy-handed lobbying from American Consul Thomas F. Wilson to prevent the *Alabama* from buying coal increased the president's worries. Upset by the consul's interference, Semmes paid the president a personal visit, which closed with an agreement that both the *Alabama* and the *Georgia* would leave the harbor after coaling. Semmes recorded one other complaint. "He said that my sailors had been behaving very badly on shore, and indeed I knew they had. I told him he would oblige me by seizing the rioters and putting them in prison." This would relieve the officers of much hard work in trying to find them later.[3]

Five days elapsed before the promised coal arrived. During that time, the president constantly pressed the Confederates to leave Bahia, but Semmes refused to budge without fuel. Finally, on the night of May 20, the long-awaited coal lighter pulled alongside the cruiser and filled her bunkers. Twenty-four hours later the *Alabama* sailed away, ending the president's worries — at least for a while. One year later, in a flagrant violation of international law, the USS *Wachusett* captured the *Florida* here under the nose of the Brazilian Navy.

The *Alabama* headed south, searching for vessels rounding Cape Horn. On May 25 she captured the 848-ton New York ship *S. Gildersleeve*, laden with English coal for Calcutta. A British concern allegedly owned the cargo, but Semmes found no proof and condemned the ship. The lookouts reported another ship close by, and a single blank charge from the pivot gun brought the Baltimore bark *Justina* to a halt. Because the *Justina* carried a small neutral cargo, Semmes bonded the vessel for $7,000 and forced her acting master, Charles Miller, to convey the prisoners from the *Gildersleeve* to Baltimore, forgoing a planned stop in the West Indies. Unlike some Union masters, Miller kept his word.[4]

Early on the morning of May 29, the lookout reported a distant sail glowing in the moonlight. After a six-hour chase, the cruiser fired a gun, which the stranger chose to ignore. Another two hours passed before a second shot brought her colors to the peak, and the 1,074-ton Maine ship *Jabez Snow* surrendered with a cargo of Cardiff coal and cordage bound for Montevideo. Among the passengers, Semmes found a woman listed on the ship's articles as a "chambermaid." He recognized the situation for what it was and wrote: "These shameless Yankee skippers make a common practice of converting their ships into brothels, and taking their mistresses to sea with them. For decency's sake, I was obliged to turn the junior lieutenant out of his state-room for her accommodation."[5]

The documentation for the *Jabez Snow's* cargo implied neutral ownership, but Semmes found the papers defective and ordered the ship burned. In a letter from the ship's owners, Semmes learned that he and the other cruisers seemed to be having the desired effect on Union commerce:

> November 25, 1862
> We hope you may arrive safely and in good season, but we think you will find business rather flat at Liverpool, as American ships . . . are under a cloud, owing to dangers from pirates . . . which our kind friends in England are so willing should slip out of their ports to prey on our commerce.[6]

On the morning of June 2, the *Alabama* passed a large ship heading the opposite way. Crowding on all sail, Semmes doubled back, and when six or seven miles distant, hoisted the Confederate colors and fired one blank, then another. Both were ignored. Finally, eight hours later, with the range closed to four miles, a shot from the pivot gun splashed close enough to convince the captain to clew up his sails and surrender. The master of the 480-ton bark *Amazonian* came aboard the *Alabama* without his papers, making Semmes' customary Admiralty hearing brief and decisive. After removing what small stores they could use, the *Alabama's* boarding party burned the ship. The following day, Semmes negotiated passage for his prisoners aboard the *Widna* of Hanover, in exchange for 10 days provisions and a $200 chronometer. They arrived safely at Rio de Janeiro a few days later.[7]

Before dawn on June 5, the *Alabama* captured the 1,237-ton medium clipper *Talisman*, New York to Shanghai with a cargo of coal. The prize crew removed four brass 12-pounders; Semmes intended to find a use for them later.[8]

In ugly, hazy weather on June 16, the *Alabama* overhauled two American vessels flying English colors. The bark *G. Azzopadi* had been built in Portland, Maine, as had the *Joseph Hale*, but now was British-owned and registered in Port Louis, Mauritius. After releasing her, Semmes captured the ship *Queen of Beauty*, an Australian packet carrying 300 passengers from London to Melbourne. As an American ship, she had sailed under the name *Challenger*. Semmes wrote, "These were both bona fide transfers, and were evidence of the straits to which Yankee commerce was being put. Many more ships disappeared from under the 'flaunting lie' by sale, rather than by capture, their owners not being able to employ them."[9]

On June 20, the eve of winter in these latitudes, the *Alabama* captured the 348-ton Philadelphia bark *Conrad*, a slim, racy bark with the cut of the early clippers. The evidence brought aboard by Captain William H. Salisbury indicated that the cargo, Argentinian wool and goatskins, was neutral property, but Semmes ruled that since the cargo was consigned for New York, it had to be American, and that the certificate had been forged. He brought aboard 21 men and one woman, and condemned the prize. Semmes had been looking for a fast sailer with a marketable cargo, and this time he spared the match.[10]

The following day, Semmes armed the *Conrad* with two of the brass 12-pounders from the *Talisman* and commissioned the new Confederate cruiser *Tuscaloosa*, under the command of Lt. John Low. Joining Low as officers were Acting Master William H. Sinclair, Joseph F. Minor, and Henry Marmelstein. Eleven crewmen also came aboard, and a quantity of small arms.

Late that evening, the vessels exchanged salutes, and the *Alabama*'s crew climbed into the rigging and gave the *Tuscaloosa* three hearty cheers as she sailed away in search of adventure. At this very moment, half a world away, John Newland Maffitt's offspring, the *Clarence* and *Tacony*, were creating havoc and hysteria along the New England coast. Low's fortunes would prove very different.

As the *Tuscaloosa* sailed out of sight, lookouts on the *Alabama* spotted a suspicious looking vessel in disarray. A boarding party reported that the crew of the English ship *Mary Kendall*, which was leaking badly from storm damage, were refusing to work unless her captain made for port. Semmes convinced her master to take his prisoners and head for Rio, a few days away, in return for a chronometer and a week's provisions. With extra hands to man the pumps, the *Mary Kendall* reached port safely.[11]

During three months of cruising the narrow shipping lanes off the Brazilian coast, Semmes had not sighted a single enemy gunboat, despite the fact that his presence had been observed and reported frequently. Semmes stated that he "was more than ever astonished at the culpable neglect or want of sagacity of the head of the Federal Navy Department. . . . If Mr. Welles had stationed a heavier and faster ship than the *Alabama*—and he had a number of both heavier and faster ships—at the crossing of the 30th parallel; another at or near the equator, a little to the eastward of Fernando de Noronha, and a third off Bahia, he must have driven me off. . . . But the old gentleman does not seem once to have thought of so simple a policy as stationing a ship anywhere." The *Florida* swept unmolested through the same area several days later.[12]

Both Maffitt and Semmes were masters at escape and evasion. They used every advantage in dodging danger, and capitalized on poor communications in planning their movements. Occasionally, however, conditions forced Semmes to disclose his plans. He told Low to deliver the *Tuscaloosa* to Saldanha Bay, north of the Cape of Good Hope, and headed there himself. This time, Semmes had left a trail. Commander Charles H. Baldwin of the huge USS *Vanderbilt* learned from two foreign ships off Bahia that Semmes had boarded them not far from Cape Town. Baldwin was still far behind, but he was headed in the right direction.[13]

Semmes was tired of the sea, fought a stubborn fever, and wanted to lay up for a while to rest. Directly across the Atlantic lay Cape Town, an unlikely place to find Union warships, but a good place to relax and give the crew a run. Unfortunately, weevils had destroyed the ship's entire supply of bread. Without bread, the crossing could not be made, so Semmes reluctantly headed for Rio de Janeiro, some 825 miles away, to obtain a fresh supply.

"Was there ever such a lucky man as the Captain of the *Alabama*? If he wanted a cargo of provisions it fell into his hands." On July 2, after an eight-hour chase, Semmes captured the 784-ton ship *Anna F. Schmidt*, the only American out of 11 ships sighted that day. Her hold contained not only a 30-day supply of bread neatly protected in airtight casks, but other needed items as well, including trousers, undergarments, boots, hats, patent medicines, and even the latest invention for killing bedbugs. With the larder filled and the crew newly attired, Semmes turned the ship about and headed for South Africa. At Sunday muster, the crew presented itself to the captain wearing shiny new shoes.[14]

With the flames from the *Anna F. Schmidt* still brightening the evening sky, the lookouts sighted a large, taut ship with the trim square yards of a Yankee clipper. When she sped by, taking no interest in the burning ship, Semmes called for all sail and full steam, and hurried after what he assumed to be an escaping clipper. At a range of three miles, he ordered a gun fired. To his surprise, the stranger fired back. California clippers often carried guns, however, and Semmes felt they were trying to masquerade as a warship.

As the chase wore on and the excitement built over the next four hours, the entire crew congregated on deck. Some thought that the *Alabama* had stirred up the fabled *Flying Dutchman*. About midnight,

Semmes overhauled a huge black vessel with five guns frowning from her ports. "What ship is that?" thundered Kell through his trumpet. "This is her Britannic Majesty's ship *Diomede*! What ship is that?" "This is the Confederate States steamer *Alabama*." "I suspected as much," said the officer, "when I saw you making sail, by the light of the burning ship." Semmes exchanged formalities and the two warships parted company. The sailors went back to their hammocks, disappointed to have missed a fight, a California clipper, or the *Flying Dutchman*.[15]

On July 6 the *Alabama* captured the 1,072-ton Boston ship *Express*, Callao to Antwerp. The cargo of guano from the Chincha Islands probably belonged to the Peruvian government, but the documents were not certified and contained no explicit proof of ownership, and she was condemned.[16]

After burning the *Express*, the *Alabama* did not sight another vessel in this unfrequented area of the South Atlantic until July 22, when Semmes stopped the English ship *Star of Erin* to secure passage for Captain William S. Frost and his wife, their maid, and Captain Twombly of the *Anna F. Schmidt*.

On July 26, Semmes hailed the English ship *Havelock*; her captain corroborated an earlier report that another steamer had been sighted bearing eastward. In the event that it might be a Union warship, Semmes decided to anchor well north of Cape Town, and entered sparsely populated Saldanha Bay on July 29. There, learning that the enemy had not been seen in the vicinity for several months, he noted that, "Mr. Welles was asleep, the coast was all clear, and I could renew my 'depredations' upon the enemy's commerce whenever I pleased."[17] Semmes was wrong. A few days later the *Vanderbilt* intercepted the *Havelock*, learned of the *Alabama*, and headed for Cape Town.

Saldanha Bay, on the west coast of Africa 60 miles north of Cape Town, offered an attractive and well-protected harbor. Aside from a few scattered farmhouses, the surrounding countryside was wild and picturesque and filled with game. The crew alternated painting, caulking, mending sails, and refitting, with periods of relaxing ashore and hunting and fishing. Paymaster Galt purchased fresh beef and mutton from the farms, and hunting parties went after the abundant local deer, antelope, pheasant, and quail. The crew welcomed the addition of fresh fish and game to their monotonous diet of salt pork and hard bread.

Curious visitors swarmed aboard, bringing along gifts for the dashing crew of the famous *Alabama*. The Dutch farmers had never seen such imposing guns; the ladies seemed more interested in the handsome young officers' imposing mustaches. The days passed pleasantly until some of the crew became unruly, and Semmes was forced to cancel shore leave. "One of these fellows drew a revolver on a master's mate," Semmes recorded. "The fact is, I have a precious set of rascals on board—faithless in the matter of abiding by their contracts, liars, thieves, and drunkards. There are some few good men who are exceptions to this rule, but I am ashamed to say of the sailor class of the present day that I believe my crew to be a fair representation of it."[18]

An unfortunate accident on August 3 marred the visit. As a party of young officers returned to the ship following a hunting expedition, Third Assistant Engineer Simeon W. Cummings accidently discharged his rifle when leaving the boat. Arthur Sinclair, an eye witness, wrote, "Cummings shot himself through the heart in an effort to pull the gun to himself by the muzzle. The hammer of the gun caught the thwart. Without an outcry or a groan, but with a look of despair and appeal never to be forgotten, he sank into the bottom of the boat, his body coming together as limp as a rag. It was so sudden and unexpected as to stun and appall . . . tears only relieved and restored our straying senses."

On August 4 a silent funeral procession carried Cummings ashore, Lt. Kell performed a simple service in the Episcopal Church, and Cummings was interred in the family burial ground of a sympathetic Dutch farmer with the honors due his grade. His tombstone remains the only monument in South Africa to a citizen of the Confederate States.[19]

The following morning the *Alabama* got underway, setting course for Cape Town. Semmes had been in one place too long, expecting the *Tuscaloosa* to join them for over a week, and was relieved when the watch sighted her approaching from the south. Low, who had been delayed by light winds and calms, reported stopping about four dozen vessels, but only one belonged to an American: the Portsmouth ship *Santee*, an East India trader carrying 1,500 tons of rice owned by a London firm. Because of the neutral cargo, Low was forced to let her go under $150,000 bond. Although disappointed in his results after six weeks of hard work, Low assured Semmes that the Confederate flag had been well displayed. Semmes directed Low to take his ship to Simon's Bay, east of Cape Town, to refit, reprovision, and await instructions.[20]

Five miles from Cape Town the lookout reported a sail approaching from the opposite direction and heading slowly for Table Bay in the light, variable winds. Calling for steam, Semmes rushed to cut her off before she reached the safety of the marine league. Flying the British colors, the *Alabama* overhauled the prize when she was still, according to Fullam's calculations, five miles from land. Later protests from the American consul that the capture had occurred in British territorial waters made this distance important. Fortunately, Semmes had taken several cross-bearings and had the captured vessel's exact position plotted precisely.

In one of Semmes' hurried Admiralty hearings, Captain Charles F. White, one of the many owners of the 447-ton Boston bark *Sea Bride,* learned that he had lost his ship and her cargo of East African trade goods to a Confederate raider. Semmes instructed Fullam and his prize crew to keep the prize to sea, outside the marine league, brought the prisoners on board, and steamed into Table Bay.[21]

The arrival of the *Alabama* at Cape Town had been expected. Several days earlier, Semmes had written Governor Philip E. Wodehouse that he had entered Saldanha Bay for repairs and requested permission to coal at Cape Town. News of the famous raider circulated rapidly and for several days Cape Tonians expectantly scanned the horizon. The August 6 issue of the *Cape Town Argus* recorded the event:

> The news that the *Alabama* was coming to Table Bay, and would probably arrive at four o'clock this afternoon, added to the excitement. About noon, a steamer from the north-west was made down by the signal-man on the hill. Could this be the *Alabama?* . . . . Just after one, it was made down 'Confederate steamer *Alabama* from the northwest, and Federal bark from the south-east.' Here was to be a capture by the celebrated Confederate craft, close to the entrance of Table Bay. The inhabitants rushed to get a sight. Crowds of people rushed up the Lion's Hill, and to the Kloof Road. All the cabs were chartered—every one of them; there was no cavilling about fares; the cabs were taken and no questions asked, but orders were given to drive as hard as possible. . . . As soon as our cab reached the crown of the hill, we set off at a break-neck pace, down the hill, on past the Roundhouse, till we came near Brighton, and as we reached the corner, there lay the *Alabama* within fifty yards of the unfortunate Yankee. . . . The *Alabama* fired a gun and brought her to. . . . Like a cat, watching and playing with a victimized mouse, Captain Semmes permitted his prize to draw off a few yards, and then he up steam again, and pounced upon her. She first sailed around the Yankee from stem to stern, and stern to stem again. The way that fine, saucy, rakish craft was handled was worth riding a hundred miles to see. She went around the bark like a toy, making a complete circle, and leaving an even margin of water between herself and her prize, of not more than twenty yards. . . . This done, she sent a boat with a prize crew, took possession in the name of the Confederate States, and sent the bark off to sea.[22]

A constant procession of visitors crowded the famous raider's deck to peer at her guns and meet her celebrated commander and his handsome young officers. Gifts flooded the deck. Bouquets of flowers and baskets of fresh fruit arrived daily. British officers stationed at Cape Town and city officials called frequently. A small group of Malays demonstrated their enthusiasm by writing a rollicking new song, "Daar Kom Die *Alabama*," which is still sung in South Africa.[23] The parade of guests showed genuine sympathy for the Confederate cause. These sentiments weren't universal, however, especially from the American community and some of the Dutch residents. And the wild celebrations of the *Alabama*'s predominantly English crew, who had found a number of old shipmates among the British squadron based at Cape Town, tested the tolerance of the more conservative townspeople.

The South African *Advertiser and Mail* printed their impression of Semmes: "He has nothing of the pirate about him—little even of the ordinary sea captain. He is rather below middle stature with a spare body frame. His face is care-worn and sunburnt, the features striking— a broad brow with iron-gray locks straggling over it, grey eyes, now mild and dreamy, then flashing with fire as he warms in conversation. . . . He was dressed in an old gray, stained uniform, the surtout, with battered shoulder straps and faded gold trimmings buttoned close up to the throat. In look, manners and dress he had more of the military than naval officer about him. He is 53 years old but looks somewhat older."[24]

By August 7, Semmes was embroiled in defending his capture of the *Sea Bride*. Protests from American Consul Walter Graham flooded the office of Governor Wodehouse: The *Alabama* had escaped England in defiance of British law; Semmes had taken his prize illegally, within the marine league.

Semmes, anticipating this problem, had prepared his position carefully, supported by depositions from competent Cape Town witnesses, including the collector of customs, the lighthouse keeper, and the signalman at the Lion's Rump telegraph station. Faced with this evidence, Cape Town officials rejected the consul's protests. Semmes now had legal possession of the *Sea Bride*; what to do with her was another question.

The solution appeared unexpectedly when a British merchant offered to buy the prize for $16,940, providing the transaction could be consummated at some secluded spot along the coast. Semmes knew the purchase was illegal, but hoped to skirt that problem by delivering the *Sea Bride* to her new owner at Luderitz Bay on the desolate coast of Angra Pequena, where none of the great powers claimed authority.[25]

Before heading north to Luderitz Bay, Semmes had to round the Cape of Good Hope and coal at Simon's Town. On the way to Simon's Bay, he stopped the Boston bark *Martha Wenzell*, bound from Akyab to

Falmouth with rice. After boarding, Semmes discovered that he was in neutral waters and immediately released the ship. The action was sharply criticized by British Rear Admiral Baldwin W. Walker, but he accepted Semmes' explanation that the capture inside the marine league was unintentional, and was rectified by the vessel's immediate release. The *Martha Wenzell* was the only ship Semmes ever admitted to capturing illegally, although his overall activities in South Africa raised many legal questions.[26]

When the *Alabama* anchored at Simon's Bay later that day, the *Tuscaloosa* and her master were ready to sail. Since Low's arrival, Consul Graham had been relentless in his efforts to force British authorities to return the vessel to her Yankee owners. Rear Admiral Walker, commander-in-chief of the British naval forces stationed at the Cape, did not know whether to seize the vessel or protect it. Governor Wodehouse, taking refuge in *Wheaton's Elements of International Law*, the accepted authority on the subject, wrote Walker that, "if the vessel received the two guns from the *Alabama* or another Confederate vessel of war, or if the person in command of her has a commission of war, or if she be commanded by an officer of the Confederate Navy—in any of these cases there will be a sufficient setting forth as a vessel of war to justify her being held to be a ship of war."

Since, thanks to Semmes' legal expertise, the *Tuscaloosa* met all three of Wodehouse's conditions, Graham's protests were rejected. That issue being settled, or so it seemed, Semmes instructed Low to head for Saldanha Bay, pick up the *Sea Bride*, and escort her to Angra Pequena for the prearranged sale.[27]

For the next week, Semmes and his officers enjoyed a round of parties, picnics, dances, and dinners with the officers of several British warships at Simon's Bay, including the HMS *Narcissus*, Read Admiral Walker's flagship, and the China station gunboat *Kwantung*, a side-wheel steamer built by the Lairds. Although much of Semmes' socializing can be characterized as soft diplomacy, he was not a young man and needed a reprieve from the pressures of the quarterdeck. The crew received shore liberty. Several apparently succumbed to the persuasive influence of consul Graham, and never returned.

On August 15 the *Alabama* hoisted sail and headed for her rendezvous with Low at Angra Pequena, but storms and dense fog delayed her arrival until August 28. By then, Low had sold the *Sea Bride* to Captain Thomas Elmstone, representing Robert Granger and Company of London and Cape Town, for £3,500. The *Tuscaloosa's* cargo of wool was consigned to the firm of De Pass, Spence & Company, to be conveyed to

England in a British vessel. Elmstone purchased the cargo, which had a commercial value of $75,000, for $16,940.

Semmes had hoped to take a prize or two during the voyage from Simon's Bay, but had seen only neutral vessels. Elmstone was disappointed as well; he had hoped for more bargains like these—despite the risk. If the *Sea Bride* entered Cape Town or any other civilized port, she could be seized and returned to her original owners. To protect his investment, Elmstone painted her black, changed her name to *Helen*, and gave her a Hamburg registry. The *Helen* traded between Madagascar and Mauritius in the Indian Ocean until wrecked some years later on the reefs off St. Mary's, Madagascar.[28]

Semmes had made no effort to dispose of prizes illegally since his unsuccessful attempts at Cienfuegos. In South Africa, the official attitude was no different. The local merchants, however, were happy to ignore the law with the prospects of fat profits in the offing, and offered to form a syndicate with Semmes. He would supply the prizes, they would assume the risk of ownership, and the Confederacy would pocket hard cash. Semmes listened, but ultimately declined. The venture was too risky and time consuming, and detracted from his primary objective of destroying enemy commerce. The *Sea Bride* remained the only prize he sold.[29]

While at Angra Pequena the *Alabama*'s freshwater condenser, which had produced all the ship's drinking water, succumbed to corrosion and failed. Only desert and rocks surrounded the harbor, and the men began to dehydrate. Semmes, again ill with fever, relied upon an occasional pitcher brought to him from the *Tuscaloosa*. Semmes good fortune could not desert him for long, however: Low discovered that Captain Elmstone's schooner had a surplus of water, and arranged to transfer 1,500 gallons—enough water for 20 days cruising—to the *Alabama*'s tanks.[30]

On August 31, Semmes headed back to sea, leaving orders with Low to take the *Tuscaloosa* back to the coast of Brazil, cruise there for a period of time, then rejoin the *Alabama* at the Cape when she returned from the East Indies.

When Semmes returned to Simon's Bay on September 16, he found things considerably less to his liking: two steamers had been there before him and bought up all the available coal. One, he was glad to note, was the CSS *Georgia*; the other, unfortunately, was the powerful USS *Vanderbilt*, which was now at sea hunting for him.[31]

Also, Consul Graham, who had uncovered the secret sale of the *Sea Bride*, was loudly protesting that the delivery had occurred at Ichaboe Island, a dependency of the Cape colony—and a direct and willful violation of British neutrality. Semmes admitted the sale, but insisted that ownership had been transferred not at Ichaboe Island but at Angra Pequena, an area not under the jurisdiction of any known power. Rear Admiral Walker accepted the explanation and so advised the Secretary of the British Admiralty, thereby settling the issue, at least for the moment.[32]

For nine days the *Alabama* lingered at Simon's Bay, waiting for coal to arrive from Cape Town. The officers enjoyed another round of elegant socializing, while the crew ran loose ashore. During the brief stay at Angra Pequena, both Confederate crews had become discontented and difficult to control. At Simon's Town, they behaved little better. On September 19 Semmes noted that, "Liberty men drunk and few returning." The following day he commented, "Liberty men returning in greater numbers to-day; the money is giving out and the drunk is wearing off." Two days later the situation showed little change: "The Yankee consul, with usual unscrupulousness, is trying to persuade them to desert, and the drunken and faithless rascals will, many of them no doubt, sell themselves to him. With one or two exceptions the whole crew have broken their liberty—petty officers and all."

Semmes was ready to sail on September 23, but 20 men—including Michael Mahoney, the Irish fiddler whose lively music lifted the men's spirits—still had not returned. Semmes offered a reward for their recovery, but the Simon's Town police found only six. Semmes reluctantly resorted to the crimps, and purchased 11 hungry and nearly shirtless vagabonds, to whom he assigned the status of "passengers" until they could be legally enlisted at sea. These derelicts were a poor replacement for the well-trained and competent sailors who had deserted. Arthur Sinclair described the difficulties: "Their places we could only fill by stealth, the shipping-offices not being open to us, and the neutrality laws not permitting us to ship them openly. We got men enough all the same; but getting them on board had to be done secretly; and then it was not wise to remain in port until the consul could lodge information (doubtless his spies kept him well enough informed of all our movements in spite of our precautions) with the authorities."[33]

Upon learning from the British Navy that the *Vanderbilt* had returned to Cape Town, Semmes hurried to sea on the night of September 24, bounding over the seas before a fierce easterly gale "like a staghound unleashed" into the Indian Ocean.

The *Vanderbilt*, commanded by Captain Charles H. Baldwin, was a huge sidewheeler whose 11-inch guns could throw twice as much metal as the *Alabama*'s. Baldwin learned at Cape Town that the *Ala-*

bama had spent several days there and at Simon's Bay. He also learned that the *Georgia* had been seen, and that a third Confederate vessel, the bark *Tuscaloosa*, had been commissioned and reported cruising off the western coast.

Baldwin searched a small stretch of coastline for the Confederate vessels for nearly a month, to no avail. He never realized how close he came to actually confronting Semmes. On one thick, dark night, Semmes' glasses revealed a vessel, unquestionably a warship and a big one, so close that he could hear the splash of her giant paddle wheels. When Baldwin finally realized that he had missed the *Alabama*, he suspected that Semmes had headed for the Indian Ocean. While the *Vanderbilt* tracked north along the eastern side of South Africa, the *Alabama* sailed eastward across the South Indian Ocean toward Java, Sumatra and Singapore.[34]

September 27 was Semmes' birthday. Faced with mountainous seas, a falling barometer, and eroding health, he confided to his journal: "Today is the fifty-fourth anniversary of the birth of the unworthy writer. How time flies as we advance towards old age! May God in His mercy protect and preserve us and restore us, before another anniversary shall roll around. . . . How strange seems the drama of human life when we look back upon it; how transient, how unsatisfying!"

Three weeks later, halfway across the Indian Ocean and still buffeted by gales, neither Semmes' mood nor his health had improved. After taking the ship's position, he lamented: "Well, there is one comfort, I can not get any farther away from home. Every day's run from this point, whether east or west, must carry me nearer to it, so that whether I look east, or whether I look west, I am looking equally towards home. When will the Almighty, in His providence, permit me to return to it? The merciful veil that hides from us the future keeps this secret alive." He had not seen his home for 28 months.[35]

Since leaving Bahia, the toll of ships destroyed had grown to 46, with an appraised value of $3,506,218. All fell victim in the first year at sea. Over the next nine months, Semmes would capture and burn only nine more. Although many New England-built vessels still roamed the seas, their owners were no longer American; the great sell-off had reached its height. For Semmes, the rotting evidence of the Confederate raider's impact on the American carrying trade awaited his arrival at Singapore.

An Aging Greyhound

ON OCTOBER 21, 1863, 4,410 miles out of Cape Town, the *Alabama* crossed the Tropic of Capricorn, leaving behind the violent winter storms of the lower latitudes. It had been a lonely, dismal voyage, and the ship, slowed by a foul bottom and curling copper bottom-sheathing, was no longer the fleet-footed greyhound of a year ago. Until the *Alabama* could reach a port and be overhauled, Semmes would have to adopt new tactics.

Near the Strait of Sunda at dusk on October 26, Semmes learned from the master of an English ship that the USS *Wyoming* and a three-masted schooner serving as her tender patrolled the Strait, anchoring off the island of Krakatoa each evening. Although the *Alabama* was both faster and heavier armed than the Union screw steamer, Semmes worried that they might meet under circumstances that would nullify his advantages. Feeling he would have ample time to maneuver, he moved three 32-pounders to the opposite side of the deck, placing seven guns at broadside.[1]

To get more information from the neutral shipping thronging the straits, Semmes passed his ship off as the USS *Mohican* en route to relieve the *Wyoming*. He was able to verify the Union warship's location, and also learned that an American clipper ship, the *Winged Racer*, had passed through the Strait a few days earlier. The lookouts kept a careful watch on the horizon for signs of the returning clipper—or for smoke from the *Wyoming*. Fullam recorded the mood of the crew: "Everybody calculating the chances of a brush with the enemy, all apparently certain we should whip her."[2]

On November 6, while cruising off Java Head, Master's Mate Evans finally identified an American ship. She flew no colors, but confident of Evans' ability to pick out the one Yankee from among dozens of different sails, Semmes pursued and captured the 598-ton bark *Amanda*, bound for Queenstown from Manila. Although her cargo of sugar and hemp ostensibly belonged to British merchants, Semmes found the documents flawed and doomed the vessel.

The *Alabama* had not burned a ship in four months. Earlier, Lt. Sinclair had grumbled, "We want to burn something. We are like the fire-laddies after a long and tedious interregnum, spoiling for a fire." As night fell over the Asian seas, he finally got his wish.[3]

After months of salted food, Semmes wanted fresh provisions, and thought to buy some from the natives. After failing to obtain supplies on the north side of the Strait, the cruiser entered a narrow channel under steam, maneuvering carefully through the difficult passage past near-naked natives gaping at the warship steaming close by their thatched huts. Several sails dotted the horizon, but the lookouts had only one objective—to find the *Wyoming*, before the *Wyoming* found them. Semmes' famous luck still held, however: the *Wyoming* had gone to Batavia for coal.

As the *Alabama* entered the Java Sea on November 10, Semmes' luck was still with him. Dead ahead a stately clipper ship emerged from a squall. After a short chase through bursts of blinding rain, the 1,768-ton New York-bound *Winged Racer* surrendered after one blank shot. "If he wanted a cargo of provisions it fell into his hands." Fullam discovered a windfall of supplies aboard the prize: sugar, coffee, Manila tobacco—all the fresh provisions needed to fill the *Alabama's* empty larder.

Captain George Cumming presented his papers to Semmes and, after hearing that his ship was condemned, asked permission to keep his boats and row with his family and crew to shore. Semmes agreed, and packed Captain Isaiah Larabee and the crew of the *Amanda* into another boat. Both boats left on a calm sea and arrived safely at Batavia the following day.[4]

At midnight, stores were still being transferred from the clipper, and Malay bum-boatmen surrounded the ships to ply their ancient trade of peddling fruits, vegetables, and livestock to ships passing through the Strait. During the height of the transactions, the clipper ship burst into flames. Semmes recorded the scene: "The boatmen had no suspicion that the *Alabama* had captured the *Winged Racer*, and was about to destroy her. They were lying on their oars, or holding onto lines from the two ships, with the most perfect innocence. Presently a flame leaped up on board the *Winged Racer*, and in a few minutes enveloped her. Terror at once took possession of the Malay boatmen, and such a cutting of lines, and shouting, and vigorous pulling were perhaps never before witnessed in the Strait of Sunda."[5]

The *Winged Racer*, built by Robert E. Jackson at East Boston in 1852, had seen many owners over her 11-year life. In the early San Francisco trade, this proud clipper had once raced and handily beat the *Ja-*

cob Bell, burned earlier in the year by Maffitt. Just before the war, she had been reduced to ferrying Chinese coolies to the guano mines of the Chincas Islands. She had not been a lucky ship, having run aground several times and been damaged by ice and storms, with enormous repair bills. Kell estimated the vessel's value at $150,000, but her owners filed claims for $385,867.91. To owners such as these, Semmes provided countless bargains.[6]

On November 11, the *Alabama* stood outside the shallow Gaspar Strait, which Semmes did not want to enter during darkness. While raising the propeller to put the cruiser under shortened sail, the lookout reported an American clipper bearing away. With steam down, Semmes called for full sail and started in pursuit as the engine room poured coal into the fireboxes. Seeing that the clipper had the wind and was moving rapidly away, Semmes kept the *Alabama* slightly off her course, hoping to delay suspicion until he had steam up.[7]

Like the *Winged Racer*, the 1,098-ton *Contest*, built 10 years earlier in the New York yards of Jacob A. Westervelt, had been a famous clipper. Now, bound for New York from Yokohama and Hong Kong with a rich cargo of tea, silk, and China trade goods, she found herself in a race for her life.

James D. Babcock, the *Contest's* first mate, described the action later in a report that Commander McDougal of the *Wyoming* forwarded to Secretary Welles:

On the morning of 11th Nov., about 70 miles east of Batavia, at 10 a.m. saw a steamer abeam, bearing right down upon us; about 20 minutes after, she hoisted the American ensign. We ran up our colors and kept on our course. In about 20 minutes more, she fired a blank shot, we still keeping on our course. About 11:45, being then about three miles off, she hauled down the ensign, ran up the Confederate flag and gave us a shot. We crammed on every sail we could carry, 14 knot breeze blowing, and dropped her until she got about a point on our quarter. She crammed on everything, full steam and all hands aft to trim her. Finding us gaining, she headed up and gave us a 100 pound shot which fell about one-half mile astern. About 12:30 the wind died away to a six knot breeze when she rapidly overhauled us. From about one-fourth mile astern she fired a shot which passed between fore and mainmast, doing no harm but we thought it time to lay to. An armed boat came off and declared us a prize of the Confederate steamer *Alabama* and our captain was ordered to report himself on board thereof with his papers. I, with my crew, was ordered to break out the stores and provisions. We were anchored in 17 fathoms. The ship was plundered of every thing valuable and we were sent aboard the privateer. . . . They fired our ship about 9:30 P.M., and then hoisting the propeller, sailed N. E.[8]

Babcock and the rest of the crew arrived safely at Batavia aboard the British ship *Avalanche* about 10 days later. In the same report, Babcock noted his observations of the *Alabama*'s deteriorating condition:

Manned by 23 officers and 130 men; crew much dissatisfied, no prize money, no liberty, and see no prospect of getting any. Discipline very slack, steamer dirty, rigging slovenly. Semmes sometime punishes, but is afraid to push too hard. Men excited, officers do not report to captain, crew do things for which would be shot on board American man-of-war; for instance, saw one of crew strike a master's mate; crew insolent to petty officers; was told by at least two-thirds of them that [they] will desert on first opportunity. Crew all scum of Liverpool, French, Dutch, etc. *Alabama* is very weak; in any heavy sea her upper works leak badly; she has a list to port that she may fight her starboard guns. Fires kept banked; can get full steam in twenty minutes. . . . While on board saw drill only once, and that at pivot guns, very badly done; men all ill disposed and were forced to it; lots of cursing.[9]

After the capture, Semmes had been much more charitable, complimenting Captain Frederick G. Lucas and his first mate on their superb seamanship. Semmes' only regret in burning the ship was his inability to convert her into another cruiser. He had neither the armament nor the men to spare for such an enterprise.[10]

During the latter part of November, many ships were boarded, but all were neutrals. Semmes seemed to have run low on luck. Sinclair, who often shared boarding duty, observed:

Luck has departed—no prize. . . . Our captain begins to show the wear and tear of weary months of watching, thinking, and anxiety. It is true, we of the watch and boarding-party must be on hand always, and stand up to the calls at all times and all hours. We get the weather with no back-out, answer the notice of the quartermaster at dead of night that a sail is to be boarded, frequently board a vessel in wet clothes, and remain in charge of her until time had made them dry and warm again; yet we are young, and full of warm blood, and pull through all right.[11]

For several days the *Alabama* threaded through the treacherous currents and coral reefs of the South China Sea, at times buffeted by sudden gales; at other times becalmed for many days in intense heat. The crew took frequent soundings, and Semmes spent sleepless nights pacing the quarterdeck as his ship crossed the most dangerous stretch of water in the world.

After running along the coast of Cochin China (Viet Nam), the *Alabama* entered one of the bays of Pulo Condore, a group of 12 mountainous islands 45 miles off the coast along the sea route between Saigon and Singapore, and dropped anchor in 18 fathoms on December 2, 1863. Cochin China had just become a French possession, and a dilapidated junk armed with one small carronade and commanded by a French naval officer represented the sole symbol of French authority. With only this tiny force to protect French neutrality, Semmes kedged the *Alabama* into a position where her broadside faced the harbor's entrance, just in case the *Wyoming* made a surprise appearance.

Twenty-two-year-old Governor Bizot, the sole civil authority on Pulo Condore, enthusiastically welcomed Semmes to his headquarters in the sleepy Malay village, and granted the famous raider permission to repair and refit. While Kell set his mechanics to work repairing the ship, the off-watches enjoyed an uncharacteristically relaxing form of shore leave. With no rum, dance halls, bordellos, or Union consuls to lure them away, the men spent a restful two weeks hunting, fishing, shooting huge vampire bats, and heckling a colony of apes.

If the *Alabama* was to recover her lost speed, it was essential that her coppered bottom be cleaned and repaired—normally a drydock job. But Kell developed an ingenious device that solved the problem—a hydraulic caisson that fitted snugly to the ship's side, while a suction hose pumped out the water. Constructed by William Robinson, the ship's carpenter, this crude but efficient diving bell enabled the men to move about below the waterline and stay dry. With work completed on December 14, Semmes prepared for sea and set course for Singapore, where he hoped to purchase coal before starting the long trip back to Cape Town to rendezvous with the *Tuscaloosa*.[12]

Passing vessels had spotted the raider at Pulo Condore and spread the alarm, and the lookouts failed to sight a single American ship during the six-day voyage to Singapore. The only moment of excitement occurred on December 21 when a steamer appeared unexpectedly out of a rain squall. Believing that battle with the *Wyoming* was imminent, Semmes called the men to quarters, but the warship passed within point-blank range, flying British colors. Semmes showed the French flag and, relieved, ordered the men to stand down.

On December 21 the *Alabama* entered the crowded harbor of Singapore, one of the principal seaports of the Orient and an important stopping place for ships engaged in the China trade. Attesting to the fear created by the *Alabama*'s presence in Asia, Semmes counted 22

American vessels lying idle and rotting in the harbor, and read reports of other Yankee ships bottled-up at Bangkok, Canton, Shanghai, Japan, and the Philippines.

The Yankee captains were not happy about their self-imposed inactivity. Five Confederate officers who checked into a local hotel were at first greeted with hospitality by a group of American captains. Later, insults were exchanged over drinks in the hotel's billiard parlor, and a furious fistfight developed. The Confederates sped back to the ship in a taxi, pursued by local authorities, to whom Semmes refused to surrender his officers. The entire affair ended with much amusement aboard the *Alabama*.[13]

Semmes learned that the *Wyoming* had been out searching for him during the past month, and had passed by Pulo Condore while he was there. Like the *Alabama*, the *Wyoming* was not in top shape. She had just returned from a battle with the Japanese in the Strait of Shimonoseki, and had sustained 11 casualties during a mission of reprisal for the Japanese attack on the American steamer *Pembroke*. Like the *Alabama*, the *Wyoming* had trouble with her boilers, could not produce fresh water, and badly needed a shipyard overhaul. Despite his difficulties, Commander David McDougal roved all over the China Sea looking for the *Alabama*. What could have resulted in a dramatic Civil War naval battle in the Far East ended in another futile chase.[14]

After Semmes exchanged amenities with the Governor and received permission to coal, Mr. Beaver of the firm of Cumming, Beaver and Company came aboard the cruiser and offered to supply all the ship's needs. Semmes spent an evening on shore as Beaver's guest, and was astounded by the elegance and enormity of the British merchant's estate — much in the tradition of Southern plantations. With a touch of regret, and no doubt homesickness, Semmes returned to his ship the following evening and found her ready to sail, and found still more problems with the crew.[15]

While coaling, some of the crew had slipped ashore and become drunk and disorderly. Most were arrested by the ship's officers and returned in irons, but 10 deserted, two having been convicted earlier of desertion by court martial. Kell secured four replacements before the *Alabama* left Singapore, but they were not officially shipped until the cruiser got to sea.

As Semmes sailed up the Malacca Strait on Christmas Eve, 1863, he knew that his business in the Far East had ended. Although there were Confederate sympathizers in Singapore, his reception had been much less cordial than at Cape Town.[16] He had seen little active shipping in the area, the American China fleet was rotting at anchor, his own vessel needed a thorough overhaul, and coal was scarce—even in major seaports.

Later in the day, he was surprised when the lookouts reported an American-built ship under English colors approaching from the opposite direction. A blank charge stopped the vessel, but the master, Samuel B. Pike, refused to come on board the cruiser, claiming his rights as a neutral British citizen. Fullam boarded the vessel, returned, and reported that the 799-ton ship *Martaban* appeared to be British, but he suspected that her papers were counterfeit. Semmes ordered his gig and boarded the prize himself, noting that every detail of the ship reflected New England craftsmanship, and the paint over her new name looked wet.

Semmes found the insolent Captain Pike to be what he felt was the epitome of a typical Yankee mariner. He noted the anxious faces of the mates as he entered the cabin. Even the food being prepared in the galley was distinctly American—potatoes and codfish. Pike could produce no bill of sale or provide any proof of neutral ownership for the cargo of rice shipped in Moulmein by a Mr. Cohen. Under any circumstance, the cargo follows the fate of the ship, and Semmes ordered the *Martaban* burned. In a rage, Pike demanded recognition of the British colors. Undeterred, Semmes removed the flag and the chronometer, and sent the incendiaries to do their work.[17]

Semmes, who believed that the cargo was actually British property, commented that if the owner had simply left the vessel under American registry and properly documented the cargo, he would have been forced to release the vessel under bond. After burning the ship, Semmes put Captain Pike under oath and asked if the transfer had been bona fide. Now with nothing to hide, Pike admitted that in his alarm over rumors of the *Alabama*'s presence, he had transferred ownership with a sham sale, and that the ship was really the *Texan Star*. This satisfied Semmes. Although the Far East press sharply criticized the destruction of the *Martaban*, when the case finally reached litigation before the *Alabama* Claims Commission, Semmes' ruling was officially upheld.[18]

Christmas Day passed with little ceremony. Semmes anchored off the village of Malacca and set the prisoners free. The previous year, Christmas had been spent on the other side of the world at Arcas Island in the Gulf of Mexico. Then, after capturing 28 prizes, spirits had soared, with high hopes of great personal fortunes in prize money for everyone. Now, one year later, hard reality confronted a disconsolate and homesick crew. In the evening, the ship's company drank to the health of sweethearts and wives. The newspapers at Singapore had painted a grim picture of life at home, and the ship's company prayed for the preservation of the war-ravaged South.[19]

Early the next morning the *Alabama* got underway, capturing the 708-ton ship *Sonora* and the 1,050-ton clipper *Highlander* of Boston. Both vessels were in ballast and headed for Akyab, Burma, for rice. Fourteen seamen from the *Contest*, which Semmes had burnt on November 11, had signed on the *Sonora* in Singapore, and now found themselves Confederate prisoners for the second time in as many months. The *Sonora* was the first ship to risk sailing from Singapore since late October. Hearing that Semmes intended to burn his ship, Captain Lawrence W. Brown complained to Lt. Sinclair that the *Wyoming* should have been on station in the Straits of Malacca instead of wandering off after coal.[20]

Captain Jabez H. Snow of the *Highlander* accepted his misfortune philosophically. With his ship's papers snugly under his arm, he clambered aboard the *Alabama* and offered Semmes his hand: "Well, Captain Semmes, I have been expecting every day for the last three years to fall in with you, and here I am at last!" Semmes replied, "I am glad you found me after so long a search." Snow then responded, "The fact is, I have had constant visions of the *Alabama* by night and by day; she has been chasing me in my sleep, and riding me like a night-mare, and now that it is all over, I feel quite relieved."[21]

After leaving the Malacca Strait, another vessel from New England's shipyards approached from the opposite direction showing the colors of the free city of Bremen. Multilingual Master's Mate Baron Max von Meulnier boarded the vessel to verify ownership, and found that the *Ottone* had been sold to a Bremen merchant by her American owner the previous May. Finding the master and the crew all Dutchmen, Semmes released the vessel—recording it as another instance of Yankee shipping abandoning the seas to the competition.[22]

On New Year's Day, the *Alabama* began the long westward crossing of the Bay of Bengal and for the next 14 days sailed toward Ceylon, off the southern tip of India. Along the way, Semmes stopped a small English bark to gather information, telling the master that he was the USS *Dacotah*, in search of the *Alabama*. The master said, "It won't do; the *Alabama* is a bigger ship than you, and they say she is iron plated besides," adding that the raider was last reported at Simon's Bay. Semmes was now reasonably satisfied that no Union warship was stationed near India; every steamer rounding South Africa coaled at Simon's Bay.[23]

Confederate officers boarding neutral ships frequently were told extraordinary stories about the fabled Confederate cruiser's adventures. In the Far East, a rumor circulated that Semmes released a company of fighting black giants from the hold whenever the ship was threatened. A group of Moslem passengers aboard an English ship asked if it was true that the black giants were fed live Yankees. The boarding officer replied, "We had made the experiment, but the Yankee skippers were so lean and tough that the giants refused to eat them."[24]

After doubling Ceylon on the afternoon of January 14, 1864, the *Alabama* burned the 1,097-ton ship *Emma Jane* of Bath, Maine, in ballast to Burma. She had sailed on January 6 from Bombay, unable to obtain a cargo with the *Alabama* reported nearby. After loading fresh provisions at Anjengo, Semmes headed for the eastern coast of Africa. For many of the men, it was a moment of joy: They knew they were going home. For the exhausted Semmes, it was a moment of relief. He could do no more.[25]

On January 30, the *Alabama* crossed the equator for the third time, and 10 days later came to anchor at the Comoro Islands, where she remained for a week. Even at this remote island by the entrance to the Mozambique Channel the natives had heard the lore of the *Alabama*, and gathered to visit the famous raider. With no liquor and no women, the crew was uncharacteristically well behaved, and returned to the beach each evening to be rowed back to the ship. The *Alabama* sailed on February 15 with her entire crew, a large supply of fruits and vegetables, and six live bullocks for the larder.

A strong southwest current carried the cruiser through the Mozambique Channel and into the southern Indian Ocean toward Cape Town. The monotony of the voyage was broken on February 28 by a thrilling rescue at sea. Seaman Henry Goodson had been on the sick list for several weeks, and the surgeon felt that fresh air would aid his recovery. As Goodson rested on the deck over the topgallant forecastle, he lost his balance. Someone shouted "Man overboard!" The ship's daredevil, Michael Mars, grabbed a grating and rushed to the lee gangway. Kell warned Mars not to attempt a rescue in such rough water, but Mars said, "Keep cool, Mr. Kell, I will save the poor fellow," and dove off the deck after him. Goodson was feeble and unable to keep himself afloat, but Mars managed to reach him and secure him to the grating while the *Alabama* rounded up and lowered a boat. When the boat returned, a wild cheer rose from the men as Mars climbed to the deck. Semmes mustered the crew and praised Mars, urging others to follow his example in times of danger.[26]

On March 11 the *Alabama* reached the Cape of Good Hope. Semmes hoped to take a prize before entering harbor, but after nine days of cruising, he concluded that American shipping had vanished from the seas, and anchored the raider off Cape Town. Friends welcomed them back with warmth and hospitality, and Semmes collected payment in gold sovereigns for the sale of the *Tuscaloosa*'s cargo of wool, but an unexpected problem had developed during his absence: The *Tuscaloosa* had been seized by order of the British government. Instead of resting and relaxing at Cape Town, Semmes would have to fight another legal battle.

When the British permitted the *Tuscaloosa* to enter Simon's Bay on August 8, 1863 as a commissioned Confederate warship, her legitimacy was legally established. When she returned 19 weeks later, in January 1864, the British changed their minds and notified Lt. Low that his vessel would be detained and possibly returned to her former owners. Low and his men remained on the ship, along with a 28-man detachment of British marines to prevent their escaping. Despite vigorous protests from Low that the commissioning of the *Tuscaloosa* as a warship had been previously established, Governor Wodehouse explained that he was following orders from the home government, and could not release his ship. Not knowing when, if ever, to expect the *Alabama*, Low paid off the crew and returned to England on January 20 with Lt. Sinclair.[27]

Furious with the seizure, Semmes presented Admiral Walker with a lengthy paper supporting his position that "one nation cannot inquire into the antecedents of the ships of war of another nation," which read like an extract from *Wheaton's Elements of International Law*.[28]

Although the case eventually involved even the House of Commons, in the end, Semmes won his last lengthy legal battle, and the *Tuscaloosa* was ordered restored to Lt. Low, or any other designee of the Confederate government. By then, however, Confederate representation in South Africa had ended. For many months the *Tuscaloosa* lay at Simon's Bay awaiting the arrival of a duly qualified Confederate naval officer. When the war ended, the ship reverted to the United States, and on November 29, 1865, was sold at auction.[29]

As the *Alabama* steamed out of Cape Town on March 25, past boats filled with cheering spectators, the Yankee steamer *Quang Tung*, a fast new China trade packet, entered the safety of the harbor. Semmes regretted missing an opportunity to capture such a prize, and the two crews stared in silence as the vessels passed. When clear of the entrance, Semmes ordered the fires banked and the sails hoisted. His ship needed extensive repairs to the hull and machinery, which meant finding a safe drydock somewhere. But with Great Britain's tightened neutrality policies, it seemed unlikely the *Alabama* would ever be released if she entered an English port. He had heard that the French were building ironclads for Bulloch; Cherbourg was a well-equipped port, not easily blockaded. He would go there.[30]

Once at sea Semmes scanned a bundle of newspapers gathered from his friends at Cape Town. He had heard little of the war's progress during his six-month absence, and the news seemed all bad: Huge Union armies occupied parts of the South; the blockade had strangled the Confederacy's life blood; only two major ports remained open. Semmes wrote, "From the whole review of the 'situation,' I was very apprehensive that the cruises of the *Alabama* were drawing to a close."

There was precious little encouragement to be found in the newspapers, with the possible exception of a speech made by Mr. Milner Gibson, President of the British Board of Trade, on January 20, 1864. Among other things, it said:

> There is the fear among the American merchant shipping of attacks by certain armed vessels that are careering all over the ocean, and that are burning and destroying all United States merchant ships that they find upon the high seas. The fear, therefore, of destruction by these cruisers, had caused a large transfer of American carrying to British ships. Now the decrease in American shipping is very great in the trade between England and the United States. It is something like 46 or 47 per cent. I mention these facts to show you that it is right that the attention of this great commercial nation should be seriously turned to those laws which govern the action of belligerents upon the high seas—(Hear! Hear!)—for if some two or three armed steamers, which a country with no pretensions to a navy, can easily send upon the ocean, armed with one or two guns, can almost clear the seas of the merchant shipping of a particular nation, what might happen to this country, with her extensive commerce over the seas, if she went to war with some nation that availed herself of the use of similar . . . vessels. (Hear! Hear!).[31]

He was gratified to learn from a British authority that he had been able to accomplish the mission given him by Secretary Mallory. But the speech clearly lobbied for stricter British policies against commerce raiding, reinforcing Semmes' decision to seek sanctuary in France rather than England.

The *Alabama* sailed northwest, into the sea lanes of vessels homeward bound from the Pacific. Semmes had not taken a prize since January 14, 1864. On April 23 his luck changed. After a long stern chase lasting throughout the night, the now much slower *Alabama* captured the 976-ton ship *Rockingham*, of Portsmouth. After removing a few supplies, Kell used the prize to exercise the starboard gun battery. Although Lt. Sinclair wrote that the marksmanship was excellent, Kell noted that some of the shells failed to explode.[32]

Four days later, just south of the equator, the *Alabama* captured her last prize. The 717-ton New York bark *Tycoon* sailed right up to them, and Semmes barely had to alter course to make the capture. After bringing the crew and a large quantity of stores aboard, Semmes burned the vessel and sailed on. John H. Little, the *Tycoon's* third mate and carpenter, later testified that he was a prisoner aboard the *Alabama* for 45 days, 44 of which were spent in irons "without shelter or clothing." After being released at Cherbourg, Little went to London and signed on the *Adriatic*, bound for New York. On August 12, the *Tallahassee* captured the *Adriatic*, and Little again became a prisoner of the Confederate States.[33]

For the next six weeks, the *Alabama* continued slowly north, rounding her old hunting grounds off the Azores. Ships of every nation dotted the sea, but none flew the American flag. As they neared Europe, the crew worked cheerfully and enthusiastically. After all, they were going home. But the homes of Semmes and his faithful officers lay in a war-ravaged country; their futures uncertain. After three long years at sea, Semmes, proud and competitive, found defeat hard to accept.

Late at night on May 24, the *Alabama* chased what turned out to be a Nova Scotia schooner on her way to Rio. When a blank cartridge failed to stop them, the gun crew fired a shell. Like the one fired at the *Rockingham*, this, too, failed to explode.

The weather worsened and for several days the cruiser battled stiff headwinds. As she lifted over the swells, the officers noticed that more of the copper sheathing had peeled from the hull. The leaking, waveswept decks sent streams of water into the hold. By month's end the weather moderated, but Semmes had fallen ill. Arriving off Cherbourg on June 10, Kell made a few hurried modifications to the ship's rigging to conceal their identity. The next day at noon, the *Alabama* steamed into Cherbourg and dropped anchor.[34]

On Sunday, June 12, Semmes visited the port admiral and requested the use of the government's facilities to repair his ship. Among other things, the vessel needed to go into drydock for new copper sheathing. He was told that only the Emperor, who was away on vacation at Biarritz and not expected back for several days, could grant such permission. Semmes returned to the comfort of his cabin to await events, which developed quickly.

The following day, a letter arrived warning that the USS *Kearsarge* had just left Flushing, the Netherlands, for Cherbourg. On June 14, she appeared off the eastern entrance of the harbor but did not enter. Semmes sent an order to shore for 100 tons of coal and took the precaution of preparing his ship for battle.[35]

On Wednesday, June 15, the French admiral informed Semmes that he considered his request for coal as a sign that the application for repairs was being withdrawn. Semmes agreed, and the coaling began. He then sent a note to Flag Officer Barron, commander of the Confederate Navy in Europe, informing him that he intended to fight the *Kearsarge*. He sent a similar note to the United States consul, ostensibly offering a challenge.

Semmes wrote, "My crew seem to be in the right spirit, a quiet spirit of determination pervading both officers and men." Ill and frustrated but still combative, he began to prepare for a fight he believed he could win. He would fight on Sunday—his lucky day.[36]

The *Kearsarge* and the *Alabama*

For more than two years the USS *Kearsarge* had patrolled the English Channel, the Bay of Biscay, and the Mediterranean Sea. Her mission was to destroy Confederate raiders operating in Europe and protect American commerce. But the *Nashville* escaped from England before she arrived, both the *Georgia* and the *Florida* had evaded her, and American shipping was being captured and burned with impunity. Only the *Sumter* failed to escape, but this was caused more by Semmes' inability to purchase coal at Gibraltar than by the *Kearsarge*'s imposing presence. Although she would soon become one of the most famous warships in the history of the United States Navy, before June 11, 1864, when the *Alabama* steamed into Cherbourg, the *Kearsarge*'s career had been lackluster.

Launched from the Portsmouth Navy Yard in New Hampshire on September 11, 1861 and commissioned January 24, 1862, the 1,031-ton sloop-of-war *Kearsarge* left the United States on February 5 for foreign duty under the command of Captain Charles W. Pickering. Late in 1862, Secretary Welles recalled Pickering to join the North Atlantic Blockade Squadron and sent Captain John Ancrum Winslow to the Azores to take command.

Winslow arrived at Fayal to find that Pickering had put the ship in drydock at Cadiz, Spain; he would have to wait three and one half months for repairs to be completed—ample time for him to brood over being given a command he thought beneath his rank. To Winslow, the *Kearsarge* was a third-rate man-of-war, normally skippered by a commander or a lieutenant commander. Most full-fledged captains with his seniority expected a squadron of armed blockaders, one of the new double-turreted monitors, or a noble old steam frigate like the *Hartford* or the *Minnesota*. But Winslow had complained too often and too loudly about being passed over for squadron command, and had few friends in Washington.

Winslow's deteriorating health caused him more concern than his deteriorating career. Already ill when he arrived in the Azores, his health steadily worsened; inflamed lungs, persistent chills, and chronic malaria combined with an infected eye to keep him bedridden. By the time his new command arrived, he had nearly lost the sight in his diseased eye. Only personal fortitude and a deep sense of duty gave Winslow the strength to take command of the *Kearsarge*, and he expected no rewards.[1]

As a young midshipman, Winslow, a native of Wilmington, North Carolina, had been a contemporary of Semmes. During the Mexican War, the two became fast friends while serving together on the USS *Cumberland*. Both received their first commands at about the same time: Winslow was given a small captured Mexican vessel renamed the *Morris*; Semmes received command of the brig *Somers*. Both commands ended in disaster: Winslow lost the *Morris* on a reef outside Tampico; Semmes got caught with all sails standing in a violent norther, the ship capsized, and he barely escaped with his life. Their brief roles as "captains" abruptly terminated, both were reassigned to the USS *Raritan*, where they shared the same stateroom and often joked about their common misfortune. Eighteen years later they were both captains again—but in different navies.

For more than a year Winslow had searched for the elusive *Alabama*, following every rumor received from the network of Union agents operating throughout coastal Europe. Finally, while lying in the Scheldt, off Flushing, the Netherlands, Winslow received a telegram from United States Minister to France William L. Dayton in Paris: the *Alabama* had just dropped anchor at Cherbourg. Winslow ordered the crew recalled, assembled them on deck, and said, "Men, I congratulate you in saying that the *Alabama* has arrived at Cherbourg, and the *Kearsarge*, having a good name in France and England, is to have her cruising ground off that port."

Winslow reached the Cherbourg breakwater on the morning of June 14. Poised inside the harbor lay the dreaded *Alabama*; he had cornered the enemy at last, but that was the easy part. Given Semmes' well-known genius for escape, Winslow was unsure about his next move. To his surprise, his old friend supplied the solution.[2]

When the *Kearsarge* appeared off Cherbourg, Semmes had few alternatives: The Confederacy faced disaster on all fronts, and the *Alabama* was irreplaceable. She desperately needed an overhaul, the men and officers were exhausted, and the powder showed signs of decay. Even if he could escape past Winslow, whom he knew to be a man of singular determination, where and how far could he go? He was no longer welcome in England or Spain. And if he stayed at Cherbourg much longer, other Union warships would surely arrive to bottle him up for the remainder of the war.

Although Kell sensed that he had made up his mind already, Semmes sought his opinion on the likely outcome of a battle between the two vessels. The *Kearsarge* was larger and had been built to fight. The *Alabama* had been built for speed; with her longer-range guns, she could stand off at a distance and pound the *Kearsarge*. However, the curls of copper sheathing sprung loose from her hull negated the two-knot advantage. Close in, the *Kearsarge's* two 11-inch Dahlgrens would be devastating; she could throw 430 pounds of projectiles compared with the *Alabama's* 360 pounds.

Kell reminded Semmes that every third shell had failed to explode during target practice on the *Rockingham*, but Semmes said nothing, apparently choosing to ignore the warning. Both agreed that they could count upon the willingness and bravery of their young officers to carry the fight; the men, although mostly English, were equally eager to match their skill against the Yankees. On paper the vessels were closely matched. In reality, the *Alabama* was in poor condition to fight a freshly refitted warship manned by skilled, practiced gunners.[3]

For the next few days the *Alabama* prepared for battle. Semmes, who hoped to cripple the *Kearsarge* with his long guns and then sweep her decks with a crushing attack from his boarders, had the men training daily with pikes and cutlasses. Gunner Cuddy overhauled his guns and drilled his crews. Boatswain Mecaskey detailed men to take down the light spars, stopper the standing rigging, and dispose of top hamper. By the end of the week, Kell reported the *Alabama* and her crew ready for battle. On Saturday, June 18, Semmes advised the port admiral that he intended to meet the *Kearsarge* the next day—a Sunday. The crew called it his Lucky Day.[4]

In his journal, Semmes wrote: "My crew seem to be in the right spirit, a quiet spirit of determination pervading both officers and men. The combat will no doubt be contested and obstinate, but the two ships are so equally matched that I do not feel at liberty to decline it. God defend the right, and have mercy upon the souls of those who fall, as many of us must."[5]

Semmes took the precaution of transferring 4,700 British gold sovereigns, more gold than the *Alabama* carried at the beginning of her cruise, to Confederate agent Bonfils, along with the payroll records, the ransom bonds of vessels captured and released, and the chronometers from the prizes less fortunate. Semmes kept the flags, which numbered nearly 100, along with other trophies, including the sword that had belonged to Captain Blake of the *Hatteras*, which adorned the wall of the wardroom. Semmes' meticulously written journal remained with him on the ship, and there is no record that he ever left a farewell letter to his family or urged his men and officers to make a will. He radiated confidence, reportedly saying that he would "prove to the world that his ship was not a privateer, intended only for attack upon merchant vessels, but a true man-of-war. . . ."[6]

Not since the War of 1812 had one ship of the United States challenged another in a classic sea battle. News that such an event was about to transpire off Cherbourg swept across Europe, and people from all over the continent streamed into town hoping to witness the battle.[7]

Landlocked Confederate naval officers flocked to Cherbourg from Paris to join Semmes, and prisoners released when the *Alabama* reached Cherbourg attempted to join the *Kearsarge*, but French officials interceded. Neither ship would be allowed to increase either manpower or armament. They would fight as they stood.

Even Lt. William Sinclair, recently returned to Europe from the *Tuscaloosa*, was not allowed to rejoin the ship. But Sinclair delivered another warning to Semmes: He had learned from a French officer who had visited her that the *Kearsarge* wore chain armor. Semmes would later insist that he knew nothing of the *Kearsarge*'s armor beforehand, otherwise he would not have engaged her. Kell confirmed Semmes' position. Yet the chain armor had not been a closely guarded secret: the *Kearsarge* had worn 120 fathoms of chain, hidden by one-inch planking, around her vital midriff for more than a year.[8]

Sunday was a beautiful day. A soft westerly breeze danced across the water, and the sun shone down on the festive crowds that had been gathering on the heights above Cherbourg since early morning. Residents hung from upper-story windows; artists with their easels, among them Edouard Manet, dotted the heights, hoping to capture the scene on canvas. Many sightseers waved miniature Confederate flags, adding their sentiments and a splash of color to the throng. Never had such an important naval battle been fought within sight of so many nonparticipating spectators. Fifteen thousand people had assembled to witness a once-in-a-lifetime event. They would not leave disappointed.[9]

The men of the *Alabama* enjoyed a hearty, leisurely breakfast, and at 9:45, escorted by the French ironclad frigate *Couronne*, weighed anchor and headed straight for the western entrance. Following along at a safe distance was a large fleet of spectators, including the yacht *Deerhound*, owned by John Lancaster, a wealthy Englishman who was vacationing with his wife, daughter, niece, nurse, and three sons. Earlier the family had voted to decide whether to go to church or see the fight.

Nine-year old Catherine cast the deciding ballot. Raphael Semmes and 41 of his officers and men would soon owe their lives to this little girl.[10]

During the 45 minutes it took to run the seven miles out to the *Kearsarge*, Semmes called the crew aft and delivered a brief address — the first time he had spoken formally to the men since the commissioning ceremony:

> Officers and Seamen of the *Alabama*! You have, at length, another opportunity of meeting the enemy — the first that has been presented to you since you sank the *Hatteras*! In the meantime, you have been all over the world, and it is not too much to say that you have destroyed, and driven for protection under neutral flags, one half of the enemy's commerce which, at the beginning of the war, covered every sea. This is an achievement of which you may well be proud; and a grateful country will not be unmindful of it. The name of your ship has become a household word wherever civilization extends. Shall that name be tarnished by defeat? The thing is impossible! Remember that you are in the English Channel, the theatre of so much of the naval glory of our race, and that the eyes of all Europe are at this moment upon you. The flag that floats over you is that of a young Republic, who bids defiance to her enemies, whenever and wherever found. Show the world that you know how to uphold it! Go to your quarters.[11]

Off the coast waited Winslow and the *Kearsarge*. John M. Ellicott, in his book on Winslow, described the scene:

> ... inspection over, the quarterdeck was equipped for church, and services began, conducted by the captain. ... the quartermaster continued to gaze ... and levelled his glass over the rail towards Cherbourg. Almost immediately he cried out: "She's coming!" Winslow closed his service without ceremony, went quietly to the rail and took the glass. There indeed, was the *Alabama*, steaming rapidly toward him, accompanied by a French ironclad.
>
> After more than a year of tempestuous cruising and blockade, of super-irritating diplomatic wrangle, of physical wear and tear, and of bitter disappointment, a reward for his indomitable perseverance was at last in sight, greater than he had ever anticipated. The greatest of Confederate commerce destroyers had been brought to bay, and forced to an open fight. ... She had been sought in vain by twenty-five United States warships, and her pursuit had cost over seven millions of dollars. Besides this, there was a personality in the coming encounter: her captain had been Winslow's shipmate, messmate and roommate during a previous war, and his daring, skill and bravery then had well-nigh made him a hero in the eyes of the more modest man. Can

it be doubted that, when Winslow focused his glass upon the oncoming *Alabama*, he realized that the supreme moment of his life was at hand? Returning his glass to the quartermaster, he quietly directed his executive to beat to quarters.[12]

When the *Alabama* rounded the breakwater, Semmes observed the *Kearsarge* steaming slowly away. With his crew cheering, he took his battle station on the horseblock. The vessels closed to within a mile, and the *Kearsarge* turned and presented her starboard guns. The *Alabama* fired first, followed rapidly by two more wild shots. The *Kearsarge* then wheeled and came on at full speed. At first it appeared that Winslow intended to ram, but at 900 yards he unleashed his full starboard broadside, which fell short, bringing cheers from the Confederate crew. The *Alabama*'s first full broadside whistled ineffectively through the *Kearsarge*'s rigging.[13]

Winslow tried to maneuver into position to rake—cross his opponent's unprotected stern at right angles and unleash his full broadside through the length of the ship. Semmes, finding the *Kearsarge* much faster than he had expected, barely escaped by sheering off. The ships jockeyed for position, exchanging broadsides at distances ranging between 800 and 1,300 yards and making seven complete clockwise circles as a three-knot current carried them westward. Semmes could not get out of range of Winslow's heavy guns, nor could he get close enough to board—a tactic he felt would carry the day. Although he had fewer men, his crew was toughened by 22 months at sea and embittered by slurs from the American press, which referred to them as the scum of England. Winslow, unwilling to be boarded, used his speed to maintain the ideal range for his 11-inch smoothbore guns. The battle would be decided by superior gunnery—or a lucky shot.

About 15 minutes after the engagement started, Semmes got his lucky shot. Up to now, the *Alabama* had been firing twice as fast as the enemy, but the fire had been wild. After shouting at the gunners to aim lower and make their shots count, Semmes watched as a shell penetrated the *Kearsarge*'s hull and lodged in her sternpost. A few anxious seconds passed, then he realized that it had failed to explode. Semmes wrote: "If the cap had performed its duty and exploded the shell, I should have been called upon to save Captain Winslow's crew from drowning, instead of his being called upon to save mine. On so slight an incident—the defect of a percussion cap—did the battle hinge. The enemy were very proud of this shell. It was the only trophy they ever got of the *Alabama*."[14]

After 18 minutes of frantic firing, the *Alabama*'s gunners began to find the range. A Blakeley shell crashed through the *Kearsarge's* bulwark and exploded on the quarterdeck, wounding three of the crew at the 11-inch after gun. Two more shots plowed through open gun ports but did no damage. A shell exploded in the hammock nettings, setting the ship on fire. A shell from a 32-pounder struck the forward 11-inch gun, almost toppling both gun and carriage, but like the 100-pounder lodged in the sternpost, it failed to explode.

Through his glasses, Semmes observed that the excellent gunnery of his lieutenants, Armstrong and Wilson, seemed to have little effect on the *Kearsarge*. From the horseblock he shouted, "Mr. Kell, our shell strike the enemy's side, doing little damage, and fall off in the water; try solid shot." Kell alternated with shot and shell, scoring many direct hits, but the unseen chain mail continued to shield the *Kearsarge* from damage. Aboard the *Alabama* it was a very different scene.

The superbly trained gunners on the *Kearsarge* wasted hardly a shot. Huge shells from the 11-inch smoothbores crashed into the raider's hull, sending a hail of deadly splinters in every direction. Shells ripped enormous holes in her side, blew out her bulwarks, and disabled the rudder, leaving her an easy target. Above the roar of the guns came the screams of the wounded. As the crew ran out the 8-inch gun, an 11-inch shell plowed through the gunport and exploded, killed or wounding 19 men and covering the deck with a mass of human fragments. Only Michael Mars, the compressor man, was miraculously spared. Seizing a shovel, he scooped up gobs of flesh and bone and tossed them overboard.

A shot carried away the *Alabama's* gaff and her colors came down, sending up a cheer on the *Kearsarge*, but Kell raised a new ensign at the mizzen masthead. More 11-inch shells tore into her decks, killing one man and wounding several others, and a third shell struck the 8-inch gun carriage. This one failed to explode, and it spun around on the deck until a seaman grabbed it and heaved it overboard. Another shell tore through the hull at the waterline and smashed into the engine room.

A cheer went up on the *Alabama* when a shell from the 100-pounder plunged through the *Kearsarge's* engine room skylight. For a brief moment it seemed they had made a direct hit on the *Kearsarge's* boilers, but this shell, too, failed to explode. Semmes continued to fight, but all hopes of victory had faded.

Firemen still at their stations gasped for breath as fires raged in the *Alabama's* engine room. Water poured into the hull through the shell hole at the waterline, and the ship began to list. The *Kearsarge* continued to pump 11-inch shells into the sinking ship. A shell fragment gashed Semmes' right arm, sending blood dribbling to the deck. The quartermaster wrapped the wound and put the captain's arm in a sling. Semmes saw that the men were still steady, but too many guns had become disabled. Without the ability to fight, he faced a massacre. As the two ships completed their seventh circuit, Semmes shouted, "Mr. Kell, as soon as our head points to the French coast . . . shift your guns to port and make all sail for the coast."

As the *Alabama* headed for the safety of the marine league, Winslow, who had anticipated the move, moved into position to rake. For some reason, perhaps friendship or pity, he held his fire. To increase speed, Kell sent seaman John Roberts aloft to loose the jib. As he returned to the deck, a gun boomed from the *Kearsarge* and a shell fragment ripped into his groin, slitting it open like a fresh-sliced melon. Arthur Sinclair remembered it as, "the most remarkable case of desperate wounding and after-tenacity of life" he had ever witnessed. In this pitiful state, Roberts clung to the jibboom and worked his way along a footrope to the topgallant deck, climbed to the spar deck, and hesitated. Shrieking and beating his head with his arms, he died where he stood, his entrails spewing out in a red mass.

The *Kearsarge* moved into position between the *Alabama* and the coast, blocking Semmes' only hope of escape. Engineer Freeman emerged from the smoke-filled engine room and reported that the engines were flooding. Semmes sent him back with an order for more steam, and Kell followed to assess the damage. He was shocked by what he found: All the partitions had been ripped to splinters; water poured into the hull through huge holes; a shell struck the table where Dr. Llewellyn was operating, carrying his patient away from under his bloody hands. This would be the last time Kell saw Dr. Llewellyn alive.

Kell went back on deck and told Semmes that the ship could float, "perhaps ten minutes." Staggering and groggy from his wound, Semmes replied, "Then, sir, cease firing, shorten sail, and haul down the colors. It will never do in this nineteenth century for us to go down and the decks covered with our gallant wounded." Kell promptly executed the order; inexplicably, the *Kearsarge* fired five more shots after the colors were plainly struck. Winslow later admitted to Secretary Welles that he had ordered it, assuming Semmes was planning a ruse of some kind. Kell ordered the men back to their guns to return fire, but the situation was hopeless. A white flag raised at the stern finally brought the battle to an end.

With the ship sinking, Semmes sent Fullam in the dinghy to ask the *Kearsarge* to save the wounded. All the other boats had been damaged, but when Kell saw no help coming, he loaded as many wounded as possible into the least damaged of his quarterboats and sent them with Fullam, Surgeon Galt, and Lt. Wilson to the Union warship. Still no rescue boats came, and the ship began to settle. Semmes told Kell to give the order to abandon ship, and for all hands to save themselves. Clutching for anything that floated—an oar, a grating, or a spar—the men plunged into the cold waters of the English Channel. Heads bobbed up and down among the wreckage as the men pulled and kicked to get away from the vortex, which they knew would suck them under with the ship when she went down. Still the *Kearsarge* stood off, seemingly moving farther away rather than closing.[15]

Semmes and Kell were the last to leave, accompanied by Semmes' faithful steward Bartelli, Sailmaker Alcott, and the indomitable Michael Mars. Mars asked Semmes if there was any duty he could perform for him before leaving the ship. Until that moment, Semmes had forgotten his diary and the ship's papers. Together Mars and Bartelli waded into the captain's cabin and secured them, carefully wrapping them between two slats. Mars carried one and Quartermaster Freemantle carried the other.

Semmes and Kell removed their swords and cast them overboard: these trophies would not hang in a Union wardroom. Feet first from the taffrail they splashed into the sea, exerting every muscle to get clear of the sinking ship. Semmes had a life preserver but with his useless right arm, quickly became exhausted.[16] Kell, clutching a grating, barely reached him in time. Holding onto Semmes, Kell looked in vain for a lifeboat. He later wrote: "On the wild waste of waters there came no boats, at first, from the *Kearsarge* to our rescue. Had victory struck them dumb, or helpless—or had it frozen the milk of human kindness in their veins?"[17]

One hour and 27 minutes after the battle opened, the career of the *Alabama* came to a spectacular conclusion. Lt. Sinclair was in the water and watched as the ship sank in 40 fathoms: "The *Alabama's* final plunge was a remarkable freak, and witnessed by O'Brien and self about one hundred yards off. She shot up out of the water bow first, and descended on the same line, carrying away with her plunge two of her masts, and making a whirlpool of considerable size and strength."[18]

During the contest the English yacht *Deerhound*, brought here by nine-year old Catherine Lancaster's desire to watch a sea battle, stood off at a safe distance to windward. At 12:30 p.m., observing that no help was coming from the *Kearsarge*, owner John Lancaster steamed up to the Union ship, where carpenters were frantically trying to repair their shot-ridden boats. Winslow shouted down from the rail, "For God's sake, do what you can to save them!"[19]

Ten minutes later the *Deerhound's* boats began sifting through the floating debris, picking up survivors. The yacht's chief steward, William Roberts, recognized the exhausted Semmes, having met him two years earlier at Gibraltar. Semmes, half conscious when lifted aboard, was laid in the stern sheets "as if dead," still bleeding from his wound. Later, Lancaster picked up Kell, who was relieved to find Semmes still alive. A boat from the *Kearsarge* passed and an officer in blue asked the men of the *Deerhound* if they had seen Semmes. Kell quickly answered, "Captain Semmes is drowned." The Union boat passed and resumed its belated search for survivors.[20]

The *Deerhound's* two small boats picked up 42 men, including 12 officers. The *Kearsarge* recovered 70, but only five officers, including the wounded men delivered by Fullam. Ordered by Winslow to return to the raider and gather more survivors, Fullam took them instead to the *Deerhound*. Arthur Sinclair and a sailor were both rescued by a boat from the *Kearsarge*, but managed to slip over the side and swim to one of the *Deerhound's* boats. Two French pilot boats pulled in 15 more survivors; one took the men to the *Kearsarge*, but the other landed them in Cherbourg.

Miserable and exhausted, Semmes was led below and wrapped in blankets. John Lancaster, unsure of the correct procedures under international law, asked Semmes, "I think every man is saved, where shall I land you?" Without the least hesitation, Semmes replied, "I am under English colors; the sooner you land me on English soil the better." Lancaster agreed and told Captain Evan P. Jones to head for Southampton. Winslow's officers, sure that Semmes was aboard, urged him to fire a shell to halt the *Deerhound*. He declined, stating, "It was impossible, the yacht was simply coming round."[21]

The only criticism Winslow would receive over his conduct of the battle concerned his handling of the prisoners. He paroled and released most of the men, retaining only four officers and a number of wounded. Both Welles and Charles Francis Adams criticized Winslow for paroling *any* of them, however, and were especially incensed that Semmes and the principal officers had escaped.

Winslow defended his decision to release prisoners by stating that his decks were so crowded with wounded that he had difficulty repairing battle damage. Other Confederate naval activity was reported in the area, and he was unaware that other Union warships had been ordered to Cherbourg. As for Semmes, historians have conjectured that Winslow privately hoped his old friend would escape. Certainly Semmes could not be blamed for trying; Winslow can be blamed, however, for allowing it to happen.[22]

Realizing that Winslow had become a national hero—escaped prisoners or not—Welles sent his congratulations, adding that President Lincoln intended Winslow to receive a vote of thanks and promotion to commodore.[23]

In the final assessment, the battle had been lopsided. The Confederates fired 370 times to the Union's 173, but the *Kearsarge's* gunnery had been deadly accurate. The *Alabama* listed nine men killed in action and another 12 lost by drowning, including Dr. Llewellyn. Of the 21 men lost, 13 had served since the beginning of the cruise and of them, at least 11 were foreigners. Another 21 men were wounded, including Armstrong, Anderson, and Semmes.[24]

By contrast, the *Kearsarge* had received only minor damage. One gun carriage had been dislodged and some of the top hamper splintered, but the chain armor, which had received several hits, did its job. Only three men were wounded; one later died.

Naval observers who watched the fight from the Cherbourg heights noted the difference in the appearance of the gunpowder used by the two ships, without noting its full significance. In a report to Bulloch, these experts stated that the shells of the *Kearsarge* "emitted a quick, bright flash and the smoke went quickly away in a fine, blue vapor, while those of the *Alabama* exhaled a dull flame and a mass of sluggish gray." Kell had warned Semmes about the defective ammunition, and on that hinged the outcome of the battle.[25]

When the *Deerhound* steamed into Southampton with 42 Confederates aboard, including Captain Semmes, relations between Great Britain and the United States sank to a low ebb. Union officials insisted that, once the *Alabama* raised the white flag, Winslow was entitled to all the prisoners. During a series of interviews, John Lancaster claimed that the men he had rescued had not been taken prisoner by any Union force, and when he saved their lives by taking them aboard his yacht, they were then technically on English soil and free. Semmes argued on his behalf that a white flag was an "offer" to surrender and that the victor must take physical possession of the defeated. He cited several legal precedents that the Confederates had every right to escape and that the *Deerhound* had acted clearly out of humanity.

Responding to angry demands from Minister Adams that John Lancaster be censured, Lord Russell stated that Lancaster instead deserved praise for his actions, and denied that the British government had any obligation to deliver the Confederates to the United States as escaped prisoners. Aside from the gratitude of those he saved, Lancaster received a letter of appreciation from President Davis and a Joint Resolution of Thanks from the Confederate Congress.[26]

On July 8, 1864 Welles wrote Winslow that the *Alabama's* value was being assessed for the purpose of distributing prize money to the crew. The ship's company received the news enthusiastically, but eight months later, David H. Sumner, an acting master at the time of the battle, wrote President Lincoln complaining of the government's lack of action in awarding prize money. He cited instances where both governments had promoted the officers involved—Semmes to rear admiral, Kell to commander, Winslow to commodore—but the men who fought the battle and exposed their lives for their country received no reward.

There is no record of Sumner's request ever being addressed, but Winslow continued to be celebrated. He arrived in Boston on November 7, 1864 to a jubilee given in his honor. The Boston Board of Trade organized a large banquet at the Old Revere House. The New York Chamber of Commerce awarded him a gift of $25,000 for destroying the hated *Alabama*. As for the men, they were left only with their memories and stories for their grandchildren.[27]

Within a week after landing at Southampton, Semmes completed arrangements to pay off the men, setting aside funds at Liverpool to compensate the survivors as they presented themselves. Semmes and Kell stayed with the Reverend Francis W. Tremlett while the captain's wound healed, and received laudatory letters daily from naval and civil officials all over Great Britain. A group of friends in the Royal Navy replaced the sword Semmes had cast into the Channel. When he returned to the Confederacy, he prudently left the sword with Reverend Tremlett. It now resides in the Museum of the City of Mobile.[28]

When his strength returned, Semmes spent six weeks travelling through Europe with the Tremletts and other friends. Kell returned home to his wife, Blanche. During his absence, two of his children had died, his once fine Georgia farm had become scrub land, and his family had been reduced to poverty.[29]

In early October, Welles' agents reported that Semmes had sailed for the Confederacy. Welles intended to capture the man who had caused him so much trouble; when he tried to run the blockade, he would be taken. In this, too, Welles would be thwarted. Instead of running the blockade where he was expected, at Wilmington or Charleston, Semmes landed at Matamoros, Mexico, took a skiff across the Rio Grande to Brownsville, Texas, and made his way across the war-torn South to Richmond.

On February 10, 1865, Mallory promoted Semmes to rear admiral and placed him in command of the James River Squadron. When the Confederate government evacuated Richmond, Semmes blew up his ironclads and, with his naval brigade, followed the retreating army. He joined President Davis and Secretary Mallory at Danville, Virginia, receiving a commission as brigadier general while retaining the rank of rear admiral. On May 1, 1865, Semmes finally surrendered to Union General William Hartsuff at the Britannia Hotel, in Greensboro, North Carolina, and signed in his presence the guarantee of nonmolestation. He insisted that his parole signify that he was a brigadier general as well as a rear admiral. This point eventually proved important. When Semmes was later arrested on charges of violating the laws of war, the signed guarantee showed that he had made no attempt to conceal his true identity at the time he surrendered.[30]

His return to civilian life did not mark the end of his problems. A vindictive Welles still sought his arrest, and on the morning of December 15, 1865, 22 armed regulars appeared at his home at Mobile and removed him by order of the Naval Secretary. The whimsical charge stated that he had violated the "usages of war" by escaping after surrender to the *Kearsarge* and later engaging in more fighting. At this time, there was no charge of piracy, privateering, inhuman treatment of prisoners, treason or other serious allegations—these came later, when Secretary Welles tried to bring Semmes to trial.

For four months Semmes reflected in prison while Welles pleaded with President Andrew Johnson to sign an executive order to try the one-time Confederate raider. Johnson hesitated, and for good reason. Judge Advocate General John A. Bolles admitted that Semmes could not be tried for his ordinary naval activities, and after further investigation, concluded that the litigation against Semmes should be dropped and he be released. Once again, Welles was frustrated. No Confederate naval officer had caused him more personal and professional embarassment than Raphael Semmes, nor had anyone caused more damage to the Union. Welles continued to consider Semmes a pirate, but the issue died when President Johnson finally proclaimed the war at an end on April 3, 1866. Semmes received a pardon and freedom without a trial.[31]

Public interest in the Confederate cruisers did not die out with the end of the Civil War. The *Alabama* and her sisters—ships built and crewed mostly in Great Britain—had inflicted millions of dollars in damage on the U.S. merchant fleet; both the public and the government felt Great Britain should pay. These demands later evolved into the lengthy litigation known as the *Alabama* Claims. Of the $15,500,000 in gold awarded to the United States at the Geneva Arbitration in 1872, the *Alabama* alone had accounted for $6,750,000, nearly half the total award.

The United States won handsomely at arbitration, but Great Britain really didn't lose: New principles of international law regarding blockades and commerce raiding were established that could benefit England's large navy in later wars on the high seas. More important, for a relatively modest sum Britannia had regained her commercial dominance of the seas and eliminated her primary competitor—the United States of America.

The *Georgia* and the *Rappahannock*

ONE OF the most interesting and frequently overlooked Confederate naval officers is the famed oceanographer, Commander Matthew Fontaine Maury. Although his scientific accomplishments, which transformed the trackless oceans of the world into a network of efficient shipping lanes, are well known to everyone who has studied navigation, little has been written about Maury's mission to Europe for the Confederacy. Even the Official Records of the Union and Confederate Navies in the War of the Rebellion published only 14 of his letters. In 30 volumes containing thousands of documents, Maury is mentioned only 34 times. His contemporaries—Anderson, Bulloch, Kell, Semmes, and Sinclair—barely mention him in their memoirs.

Much of this can be attributed to Maury's prickly personality and his constant criticism of Confederate naval policies. Even in the Old Navy he was considered an eccentric scientist and an outspoken maverick holding unpopular views. Yet in Europe, Maury was a popular and highly respected individual. Through his influence, he succeeded in becoming the only other Confederate official besides Bulloch to get a cruiser to sea, and he managed to do this undetected at a time when Bulloch's ironclad program had been brought nearly to a standstill by Union agents.[1]

Born in Virginia and raised in Tennessee, Maury entered the United States Navy as a midshipman in 1825 at the age of 19. Despite a lack of formal education, he devoted his energies to the study of navigation, and had become particularly fascinated by the winds and currents during a circumnavigation aboard the USS *Vincennes*. Confined to shore duty by a crippling injury, Maury became superintendent of the navy's Depot of Charts and Instruments in July 1842, and two years later took on the additional superintendency of the new Naval Observatory, which was located in the same office in Washington, D.C.

Maury's rise from obscurity began in this dusty depository of charts, records, and logs of naval voyages dating back to the 18th century. To a mind like Maury's, these forgotten papers had much to say. After much study and analysis, Maury concluded that there were patterns of winds and currents whose seasonal behavior throughout the world could be predicted with reasonable accuracy. Using this data, ships could plan voyages to take advantage of favorable winds and currents and to avoid areas particularly prone to storms at certain times of the year.

After publishing a few widely read articles on the subject, Maury produced his guide, *A New Theoretical and Practical Treatise on Navigation*, which attracted worldwide attention, especially from the seagoing nations of Europe. Maury then developed forms for all navy captains to complete that provided him with a continuous supply of information about currents, wind direction and velocity, storms, temperatures and barometric pressures. In addition, 5,000 copies of his abstract logs were filled out by merchantmen. This research led to his publication, in 1847, of the *Wind and Current Chart of the North Atlantic*. The following year he published *Explanations and Sailing Directions to Accompany the Wind and Current Charts*. By 1855, no vessel went to sea without these references.

Two years earlier, after pushing for scientific cooperation among all nations, Maury had succeeded in forming the International Maritime Meteorological Conference in Brussels, where high-ranking naval and government engineers gathered to hear Lt. Maury of the United States deliver the opening address. Impressed by his presentation, they collectively agreed to adopt Maury's forms and began contributing to the expanding knowledge of the sea. At Brussels, Maury gained enormous respect and developed lifelong friendships, one of which later played an important part in acquiring a Confederate cruiser.

While the European scientific and naval communities paid tribute to the value of his visionary work, Maury found only jealousy from his contemporaries at home.[2] American naval scientists considered him unfit because he lacked a higher education, and they successfully suppressed his work for several years. Maury never forgave this slight, and his outspoken criticism succeeded in alienating such future influential figures as Jefferson Davis, Stephen Mallory, Judah P. Benjamin, and many senior Confederate naval officers. Despite Maury's international acclaim, Senator Mallory and the United States Navy wanted to retire Maury on half pay.

At the outbreak of the Civil War, Maury regretfully turned his back on his career, resigned his post with the Naval Observatory, and accepted an appointment to Virginia Governor John Letcher's advisory council. Maury participated in high-level decisions, developed strategies for Virginia's military forces, and established a laboratory to perfect underwater mines. When his old enemies—Davis, Benjamin, and Mallory—moved to Richmond, the governor's advisory council held its last meeting, and Maury received no further assignments. "I begin to feel very useless," he wrote. "Davis, it appears to me, is grasping for patronage. Don't think he likes Lee. Lee told me yesterday that he did not know where he was—nor do I."[3] Maury was appointed a commander in the Confederate Navy, and spent the next 14 months in relative obscurity, dividing his time between trying to construct a small fleet of wooden gunboats and perfecting the electric mine.

Always impatient and outspoken, Maury meddled in affairs of state and blamed Mallory for delays in funding. His opinions often collided with policy. Mallory ridiculed Maury's mines until they started sinking ships. Using a pen name, Ben Bow, Maury wrote scurrilous articles about the secretary's mismanagement of the Navy Office. To get him out the country, Mallory eventually shipped him off to Cuba, but Maury exercised enough political leverage to force him to rescind the order.

During the summer of 1862, the Confederate Congress established by joint resolution a select committee to "investigate the administration of the Navy Department under its present head." No other officer in the Confederate Navy had been more openly critical of Mallory's leadership than Maury. Through fear or coincidence, within 24 hours following the joint resolution Maury received orders "banishing" him to Europe on secret service. On October 9, 1862, Maury and his 13-year-old son, Matthew, sailed for England. Without Maury to testify against him, Mallory weathered the investigation.[4]

Whether by accident or design, Secretary Mallory could not have sent a more distinguished or famous representative from the Confederate States to England than Matthew Fontaine Maury. Mallory's exact orders to Maury do not exist, although he informed Bulloch that "Commander Maury goes to England on special service, and you will please advance to him his current expenses and pay."[5] Years later, Bulloch speculated that, "The Confederate Government very probably had a political purpose in sending Commander Maury to Europe." He believed that Maury's principal mission involved the investigation of submarine devices, torpedoes, magnetic exploders, insulated wire, and electricity, although he admitted that Maury had been given "general authority to buy and dispatch a vessel to cruise against the commerce of the United States."[6]

When Maury arrived at Liverpool on November 23, he limped directly from the ship to the offices of Fraser, Trenholm and Company, where he met Bulloch for the first time, and doubtless outlined the purpose of his mission and arranged for operating funds. Maury and his son moved to London a few days later and rented inexpensive third-floor rooms on Sackville Street. Almost immediately, naval officers, scientists, and old friends from the Brussels Conference days converged on his apartment, among them Captain Marin H. Jansen of the Royal Netherlands Navy.

Jansen, who was in England on official business, had maintained a warm, almost affectionate, correspondence with Maury since 1853. When he learned that his friend was in London, he rushed to see him, and offered to use his influence to help Maury in any way he could.

On November 7, 1862, Mallory sent a letter to Maury pertaining to the building and purchasing of vessels in England. When that letter arrived is uncertain, but Maury discussed the matter with Jansen, and on December 20 sent him a confidential letter:

> Let me be frank and friendly and to the point, with the condition if you don't like this proposition, that you will commit this to the flames and to oblivion.
>
> You are visiting for your own information the building yards. . . . Will you not visit all of them? And in your mind note every vessel that they have in progress—from the frames to completion—Her size and draft and fitness for armaments. She should be not over 15 ft. draft—good under canvas, fast under steam—with the ability to keep the sea for a year—using steam only when necessary. . . .
>
> Also note any gunboats or ironclads that you may come across. In short make a note of all that comes under your observation upon a subject which you know is a hobby with me. As soon as you find one which you think would interest me particularly and fulfill certain conditions, please drop me a line.[7]

While Maury used all his influence to convince his British admirers to lobby the government for intervention, Jansen secretly scanned the shipyards of England and Scotland on his friend's behalf. By early 1863 Maury received a list of several potentially suitable ships; all he needed to proceed were funds and Mallory's formal authorization. Both arrived with Lt. William Lewis Maury, a distant cousin, around February 1, 1863.

Matthew Fontaine Maury was anxious to get started, but he discovered that his $1,500,000 in cotton certificates could not be executed without Confederate Commissioner James M. Mason's signature. Mason, worried that the appearance on the market of such a huge amount could jeopardize the $15,000,000 Erlanger loan being negotiated in France by John Slidell, finally agreed to endorse them with the understanding that Maury would not put them on the market for 60 days. Maury deposited the signed certificates in a commercial bank and used them as collateral to borrow the funds he needed. Six weeks later he had a cruiser ready for sea—a remarkable achievement when you consider the months of difficulty Bulloch endured with the *Florida* and the *Alabama*.[8]

Maury's lack of difficulty can be attributed in part to his high public profile, which appeared to disassociate him from the clandestine shipbuilding efforts then under increasing surveillance by Union and British agents. And Maury was ably assisted by his friends and relatives. His cousin, Thomas Bold of Liverpool—who was already supplying arms to the Confederacy as a ship chandler and employee of Fraser, Trenholm and Company—arranged Maury's loan and in his own name personally purchased the merchant vessel *Japan*, then under construction at Dumbarton, Scotland.[9]

Maury himself never went near the site, instead sending his cousin William Lewis Maury to pose as someone on a quiet holiday who received an occasional visitor at his lodgings in a nearby village. Lewis Maury never went to the ship—his eventual command. His mysterious visitor, Marin Jansen, tended to all the details. Jansen, who admitted to playing "a dangerous part" in the affair, had the vessel ready to sail by the end of March. Maury wrote: "A thousand thanks to my good friend for going ahead with such vision. I am charmed with the prospects of your being ready so early. I shall give the passengers notice."[10]

The "passengers" were Confederate naval officers, most of whom had been selected by Bulloch and Lt. John R. Hamilton to serve aboard the *Alexandra*. Now that she had been seized by the British government, Maury exercised his rank and the principle of immediate need and took command of Hamilton's officers. Maury wrote: "They [the British] have seized Hamilton's vessel. They can do nothing with her at present. But if they let her go, he can do nothing with her for want of officers. I had to take those that had been sent to him, and sent them out with Lewis Maury."[11]

Of the nine officers selected to serve under Lewis Maury, Lieutenants Robert T. Chapman and William E. Evans had been in Europe since arriving from the CSS *Sumter*. Mallory had forwarded the others from the Confederacy at Bulloch's request. Always quick to find fault with Mallory, Matthew Fontaine Maury complained that the naval secretary had failed to send enough qualified Southern officers, and he was forced to sign on 11 Englishmen to fill the roster.[12]

On April 1, 1863 the *Japan* sailed out of Scotland's Clyde River as an ordinary merchant vessel, inspected, cleared, and approved by British customs officials. Like Bulloch, Maury purchased arms, munitions, and supplies in London to be shipped aboard a merchant vessel to a prearranged rendezvous with the cruiser. The *Alar*, a small vessel regularly engaged in trade with the Channel Islands, attracted no unusual attention, although a customs official observed 20 men and 10 mechanics heavily laden with baggage were embarking as passengers. He noted that "a man, rather lame, superintended them." The description fit Matthew Fontaine Maury. If so, it is the only instance where Maury personally involved himself in the project or risked being identified.[13]

After five nights of hard work off Brest, William Lewis Maury commissioned the CSS *Georgia*. From the original crew of the *Japan*, he shipped all but 10 men, who refused to sail under Confederate colors. When the men returned to Liverpool to demand their pay from Jones and Company, they also informed the authorities. Consequently, two of Thomas Bold's partners were prosecuted for engaging Englishmen to serve aboard a Confederate cruiser—a violation of Her Majesty's neutrality—and each paid fines of £50.

Although this created a small scandal, neither Thomas Bold nor Matthew Fontaine Maury were implicated in the conspiracy, and the *Georgia* was on her way to the South Atlantic before Minister Charles Francis Adams was able to present a case for her detention to Lord Russell.[14]

Few records exist that describe the *Georgia*. The United States consul at Glasgow referred to her as a "screw-steamer—about 500 tons register, built by Denny Brothers, Dumbarton . . . short thick funnel—got a number of compartments forward on both sides from eight to ten feet square and stronger than a jail—strong doors to them with hinges about three inches thick and brass padlocked . . . a strong magazine forward in the bow. Her battery consisted of two 100-pounders, two 24-pounders and one 32-pounder, all Whitworth guns."[15]

Unlike Bulloch's wooden-hulled, high-rigged steamers, she followed the contemporary commercial practice of a thin iron hull, steam propulsion, a screw propeller, and only auxiliary sails.

Restricted to coaling at a neutral port every 90 days, and having few ports available for that purpose, Lewis Maury spent most of his time with fires banked, virtually immobilized, hoping to capture a prize laden with coal. Only the *Constitution*, captured on June 25, 1863, provided that opportunity, but it took more than two weeks to transfer the coal aboard in buckets.[16]

On October 28, 1863 Lt. Maury entered Cherbourg, and shortly thereafter traveled to Paris to meet with Flag Officer Samuel Barron. After seven relatively unsuccessful months at sea, Maury was dissatisfied with the *Georgia*: "The propelling power of the sails is so small that she can not cruise advantageously and capture enemy's vessels under them. She has to chase always under steam, which necessarily causes great consumption of fuel, and to cruise actively it is necessary for her to coal frequently." He requested that he be relieved of command. On January 19, 1864, Barron placed Lt. Evans in temporary charge of the cruiser.[17]

In the abstract log of the *Georgia*, Maury reported that he bonded five prizes valued at $240,000 and burned four prizes valued at $191,270, although he left no record of the valuation placed upon the *Bold Hunter*, his last prize. Northern shippers claimed damages of $406,000 at the Geneva Tribunal of 1872, but all claims were denied. The Tribunal decreed that Great Britain had not failed in its neutral obligations in the *Georgia* case.

Using either Maury's valuation or that presented by Northern claimants, the cruise of the *Georgia* provided no strategic advantage to the Confederacy beyond posing for a short time the threat of a third commerce raider operating with the *Florida* and the *Alabama*. The *Georgia* accomplished even less than the little *Sumter*, both in actual damage to the North's carrying trade and indirect damage to shippers' insurance rates.

Matthew Fontaine Maury's exemplary effort to provide the Confederacy with another raider had produced a costly white elephant. Maury had gotten a ship, but by not conferring with Bulloch, he had blundered on the fundamentals.[18]

His efforts to acquire cruisers for the Confederacy did not end with the *Georgia*, however. Mallory was so pleased at the speed with which Maury had gotten a raider to sea that he instructed him to purchase more "anti-mercantile cruisers." This time Maury sent Lieutenant William F. Carter "to visit the shipyards on the Thames, examine the vessels there for sale, and report such as may be suitable for our purposes."[19] After a superficial evaluation of several available steamers, Carter recommended that Maury purchase the former HMS *Victor*, a retired screw gunboat used by the British as a dispatch vessel.

The *Victor* carried six guns, all 24-pounders mounted from the twin funnels forward. Her trim lines and 350-horsepower engines made her fast under steam, but her three square-rigged masts crossed only single topsails; she was not designed for sailing. She did have a condenser for making fresh water—an absolute necessity for a cruiser, but the British Admiralty had acquired the vessel for use in coastal waters, not for long cruises. Her 150-ton coal capacity barely covered four days of steady cruising, and she could only carry 20 days' provisions for her 125-man crew.[20]

Although Maury never inspected the vessel personally, he sent others to survey the ship. One report stated that, "This is a fine ship and we will do well to get her." Maury did not discover until later that the year before Captain Sherard Osborne, acting for the Chinese government, had rejected the vessel because "she was rotten."

When the British firm of Gordon Coleman and Company, agent for Thomas Bold, offered to purchase the ship from the Admiralty for £9,375, Lord Russell stated that, "There can be no objection to the sale of the rotten hull of the *Victor*. . . ." Of course, neither Russell nor the Royal Navy realized that they were selling a British gunboat to the Confederate Navy. Not even Bulloch had been that creative.[21] Maury so completely disguised the underlying ownership that the Royal Navy willingly provided equipment and manpower for some of the more difficult changes in the ship's overhaul and conversion at Gordon Coleman and Company in Sheerness.

Finding the *Victor* proved far easier than funding its purchase and repair. Erlanger bonds, the Confederate hope for solvency in Europe, began their plunge on the London stock exchange at the same time Maury needed money for his project. Although Erlanger bonds were backed by cotton certificates, Union victories at Gettysburg and Vicksburg made Confederate cotton look like poor collateral to British investors. Nevertheless, Maury dug into his personal cache and handed 100 cotton certificates to Thomas Bold, who managed to convert them into enough currency to purchase the *Victor*. By November 24 repairs had been completed and paid for without ever implicating Maury or his cotton certificates.[22]

Although Maury's covert activities escaped the notice of British officials, they did not escape Freeman H. Morse, United States consul at London. After he expressed his concern to the British Admiralty, customs officials inspected the vessel on November 23, but gave the ship clearance. Surprised by the inspection and fearing that someone had informed the authorities, Maury ordered the ship to sea the next day. With much work still incomplete, the *Victor* suddenly left harbor at midnight with about 15 astonished British workmen still aboard.[23]

Somewhere in the middle of the English Channel, Lt. William P. A.

Campbell boarded the *Victor* and commissioned her the CSS *Rappa-hannock*. Finding her boilers unreliable and work still underway, Campbell entered Calais on November 27 and sent Maury a telegram reporting the vessel as "unseaworthy." Shocked by Campbell's message, Maury dispatched Lt. William F. Carter to Calais to determine what could be done. He then turned the *Rappahannock* over to Flag Officer Barron, who had intended to put the vessel to sea as a fully armed commerce destroyer as soon as a crew could be assembled. At this point, Maury's responsibility for the ship ended.[24]

Lt. Campbell applied to French authorities for repair facilities to make the ship seaworthy, a request normally granted any belligerent whose vessel had been damaged at sea. When Union consuls learned that the *Rappahannock* had left Sheerness in the same condition as she had arrived at Calais, United States Minister to France William L. Dayton lodged a protest with French Foreign Minister Drouyn de Lhuys, an able protector of France's neutrality.

Moreover, Campbell had only 35 men aboard when he entered port—nearly half of whom were employees of the British Navy. If he expected to put to sea, he would need a crew. The officers assigned by Maury did not join the ship until she arrived at Calais, an open violation of French neutrality, duly reported by Union consuls. Consequently, Campbell could neither recruit a crew nor complete repairs. The crippled *Rappahannock* soon involved both the *Georgia* at Cherbourg and the *Florida* at Brest in her diplomatic troubles.[25]

Flag Officer Barron decided to transfer the guns from the deficient *Georgia* to the *Rappahannock*, and on January 28, 1864 he instructed Lt. Campbell that, "When the *Rappahannock* is ready for sea, you will sail directly for the place of rendezvous agreed upon by the commander of the *Georgia* and yourself; and after receiving on board the armament, munitions, etc., you will proceed to cruise against the enemy's commerce. . . ."

Barron had planned to send the *Florida* to meet the other two ships off the northwest coast of Africa, but this proved difficult because the French government was pressing each vessel to depart. Ordered to leave within 24 hours, the *Florida* and the *Georgia* sailed on February 9 and 16 respectively, but the *Rappahannock* remained in port, unable to go anywhere.[26]

Minister Dayton had learned that the cruiser intended to receive arms from a tender leaving England, and on February 2 informed de Lhuys that if the *Rappahannock* sailed, the United States would file claims against the French government for every ship she destroyed. Already convinced that the cruiser had not entered Calais in distress and irritated that it was still there, de Lhuys ordered port officials not to let the ship sail without orders from the Minister of Marine. De Lhuys' detention order arrived on February 15, one day before the *Georgia* was forced out of Cherbourg.[27]

In Calais, Lt. Campbell continued to have problems with his crew. Plagued by desertions, he made an impossible demand, advising Barron that he would not sail unless one-third of the crew were natives of the South. Because he had neither the coal nor the personnel to depart Campbell missed a five-day window in early February when he could have left Calais without interference from the French government. Confederate Commissioner John Slidell reprimanded him for the delay and Mallory suggested that he be replaced. Barron agreed, and on March 21 Lt. Charles M. Fauntleroy relieved him of command.[28]

Fauntleroy had arrived on the day before, inspected the vessel, and on March 22 sent a report to Barron describing the ship as unseaworthy. He wrote that the detention of the ship by the French was "especially fortunate," as he did not believe that the *Rappahannock* could go anywhere.[29]

For nearly a month Fauntleroy continued to correspond with Barron, listing the vessel's many defects. He complained that: "There is no longer any secret, to my mind, for the English in disposing of the vessel. It is fully explained by the vast amount of space occupied by her machinery, to the detriment of her storage, both for provisions, coals, and crew. The magazine is almost the largest apartment in the ship, and there is very little space for either crew or provisions. . . . The interior arrangements . . . are altogether experimental, and it is quite obvious why she was deemed to be a failure as a cruiser." Moreover, Fauntleroy's crew now was down to only 12 deckhands, and he appealed to both Bulloch and Barron for more men.

Barron neither visited the vessel nor made any effort to verify Fauntleroy's reports, despite the warning that "if a board of officers were ordered now to report or had looked into the vessel earlier she would never have been in our hands today."[30]

Barron, determined to have the ship armed and sent to sea, closed his eyes to the *Rappahannock*'s deficiencies. After the *Georgia* returned from a futile North African cruise, he sent Lt. Evans to Calais to arrange a transfer of armament. The detention order prevented this, but the two commanders did meet to review the *Georgia*'s armament. Fauntleroy reported to Barron "that from Evans I had learned for the first time the exact character of the *Georgia*'s battery . . . it appears certain that he has but one gun that will be of use to this vessel, and it is a most important and serious question to decide whether, even with the other two 30-pounders, the battery would be such as could be usefully employed on board so large a vessel as this. . . . Now, my dear sir, from all this it must appear to you as it does to me, namely, if the ship is fit to go to sea as a man-of-war, she should have a battery in a greater degree suitable for her than the *Georgia*'s will be."[31]

Barron was not to be dissuaded, however, and with diplomatic help from John Slidell, pressed Drouyn de Lhuys and the French government to release the vessel. Slidell appealed directly to Napoleon III, forcing de Lhuys into a compromise that worried Bulloch, who feared that irritating the wrong French officials would sabotage his ironclad program. Bulloch had learned enough about the *Rappahannock* to recommend that it be sold, adding that the French government "would be well satisfied to end the matter in this way."

Fauntleroy, supported by Bulloch, protested Slidell and Barron's insistence that he retain the ship. Finally Barron's temper flared. On May 16 he wrote, "Rest assured that I alone, as the senior naval officer abroad, am responsible for the course pursued towards the French Government with reference to the *Rappahannock*, which you command." Fauntleroy returned to the problems at hand and glumly awaited further developments.[32]

The *Rappahannock* suffered as much from a weakness of Confederate leadership in France as she did from her weakened timbers. Barron, who had made commitments to both Slidell and Mallory to arm another commerce raider, refused to admit that he had spoken too soon and seemed intent upon accomplishing the impossible, regardless of the *Rappahannock*'s readily apparent unsuitability and the advice of Fauntleroy and Bulloch.

Slidell knew little or nothing of the ship's condition, but enjoyed upstaging the French foreign minister by taking the issue directly to Napoleon III, not realizing that Drouyn de Lhuys was strong enough politically to temporize and delay the emperor's directives. Despite Barron and Slidell's best efforts, the cruiser remained detained, a condition that Fauntleroy privately preferred to sailing. As time passed and the Confederates in France lost popularity, Fauntleroy and his gunless, deteriorating vessel lingered on in Calais, immobile and frustrated.

Changing tides and open sea gates left the *Rappahannock*, moored in the crowded inner harbor, high and dry for 12 hours each day. Constant grounding and exposure to the air strained the hull and opened seams. On April 27, a dockside accident with the French merchant vessel *Nil* precipitated a minor court action in which the Tribunal of Commerce at Calais found the *Rappahannock*'s executive officer at fault and awarded damages to the *Nil*'s owners. Every new difficulty escalated into a diplomatic issue that reached Paris.[33]

On June 9 John Slidell again appealed to Drouyn de Lhuys for the vessel's release, but was ignored. Ten days later, he wrote the Duke de Persigny, who had been a strong supporter of the South, asking for his help in again appealing to Napoleon III. While Slidell waited for a favorable development in Paris, Fauntleroy watched his crew melt away, wooed by Union agents.[34]

The final insult came on July 8, when Fauntleroy found a bill of sale posted on the mainmast of his ship. No one had bothered to pay the judgment from the *Nil* case, and the Minister of Marine had authorized a sheriff's sale.

Barron authorized the funds, but advised Fauntleroy to hire a local lawyer and make the payment under protest. Calais authorities took the money, but rejected the protest. A few days later, Fauntleroy wrote Barron that he had heard a rumor that the *Rappahannock* "was to be towed around to Brest by a French man-of-war, after placing on board a crew of Frenchmen."

Barron finally conceded defeat, and on August 2 ordered Fauntleroy to "pay off and discharge your officers and crew . . . and lay up the ship." With a sigh of relief, Fauntleroy sent Barron his last official report on October 19, 1864, advising him that "the port officially notified me today that on Monday next the water would be let out of the basin . . . for several months." There the *Rappahannock* remained until July 1865, when she was sold by the United States and taken to Liverpool.[35]

Frustrated in his attempts to rendezvous with the *Rappahannock*, and with the USS *Kearsarge* patrolling off the French coast, Lt. Evans brought the *Georgia* to Liverpool on May 2, 1864 and turned her over to Bulloch. One month later, Bulloch sold the *Georgia* for £15,000 to British merchants.

Although Matthew Fontaine Maury had shrewdly acquired both the *Georgia* and the *Rappahannock* in the face of difficult obstacles, neither vessel performed a useful service for the Confederacy. In fact, the presence of Maury's acquisitions in France increased Union surveillance, instigated a flurry of high-level diplomatic activity, and alienated the French government at a time when Bulloch was attempting to build an ironclad fleet to break the blockade. By excluding Bulloch from his plans and failing to take advantage of his experience in selecting ships, Maury actually disrupted one of the Confederate navy's better strategies.

Mallory had sent Maury to Great Britain specifically to buy ships and convert them to cruisers, allowing Bulloch to devote full time to his ironclads. Unfortunately, he failed to instruct him to coordinate his activities with Bulloch. Always sensitive, critical, and independent, Maury doubtless would have balked at that order anyway, because Bulloch was his junior. And under no circumstances did Mallory want Bulloch reporting to Maury. Mallory had clashed with Maury many times over the years, and knew his personality. The fact that he made no effort to facilitate cooperation between Bulloch and Maury suggests that he did not appreciate Bulloch's difficulties.

Maury was a renowned scientist, not a man who understood the requirements of a commerce raider. He never examined the two vessels he purchased, but left the selection up to friends and relatives. Had he been properly briefed by Mallory, who usually avoided him, Maury would have known the delicacy and importance of Bulloch's mission. Maury and his friends and relatives could have become a great asset to Bulloch and the cause of the Confederate navy. Unfortunately, his efforts were counterproductive—and much of the blame can be laid at the door of Naval Secretary Mallory and his dislike for a brilliant but difficult subordinate.

The *Sea King*

THE NEWS that the *Kearsarge* had sunk the *Alabama* brought jubilation to the North, but despair to the South. Confederate Naval Secretary Mallory wrote Bulloch that "the loss of the *Alabama* was announced in the Federal papers with all the manifestations of universal joy which usually usher the news of great national victories, showing that the calculating enemy fully understood and appreciated the importance of her destruction."[1]

The only Confederate cruiser still representing a threat to Union commerce was the *Florida*. Bulloch had sold the ineffectual *Georgia* on June 1, 1864, and the unseaworthy *Rappahannock* remained at Calais, detained by the French Minister of Marine. In August, Commander John Taylor Wood made a dash up the New England seaboard in the converted blockade runner *Tallahassee*, but the vessel's total dependency upon coal proved too great a liability. With the *Alabama* at the bottom of the English Channel, Mallory still felt the need to keep pressure on the American shipping trade; only Bulloch could fill this void.

Over the past three years, Bulloch had observed a striking change in British public sentiment toward Confederate commerce raiding. Early in the war, the destruction of Northern shipping had been applauded by the press and cheered by maritime interests. But as horror stories of the wanton destruction of personal property crept into the news, public enthusiasm gradually cooled, and Her Majesty's government began wondering privately how much of the blame for this damage could be laid at their door.

Bulloch's memoirs reveal his own growing distaste for commerce raiding. Moreover, he believed that the strategy had been counterproductive.[2] After three years, commerce raiding still had not accomplished its principal objectives: the Union had not sued for peace to halt the destruction of its maritime fleet and Welles had not materially weakened the blockade to send ships in pursuit, although he kept a dozen ships at sea. Instead, building and arming the Confederate cruis-

ers had focused so much attention on Bulloch's activities in Europe
that it was hampering his ability to provide the Confederacy with an
ironclad navy.

Bulloch believed that only the ironclads could save the South, and
he had focused all his energy on this single objective. No other force
could dismantle the blockade and attack the prosperous port cities of
the Northeast. More commerce raiders could not save the South; they
could only further inflame the growing wave of anti-Confederate sentiment in Europe, and most probably bring the ironclad-building program to a close. Yet Mallory wanted another commerce raider, a ship
capable of demonstrating to European powers that the South could still
take the offensive. When Bulloch received Mallory's order to replace the
Alabama on July 16, 1864, he accepted the assignment with reluctance. The result was a ship that ultimately would strike fear into the
hearts of Union whalers around the world: the CSS *Shenandoah*.

Although Bulloch had spent the past year concentrating on ironclads, his agents had continued to scour Great Britain's shipyards and
docksides for sound, seaworthy vessels. The previous summer, while at
the Clyde River to look at a blockade runner, Bulloch and Lt. Robert R.
Carter noticed the *Sea King*, "a fine, composite, full-rigged ship, with
something more than auxiliary steam-power, and all the necessary arrangements for disconnecting and lifting her screw."[3] Brand new and
fresh from her trials, the *Sea King* had many of the qualities Bulloch
demanded in his cruisers. Unfortunately, she was about to embark on a
10-month maiden voyage to Bombay, and was not for sale.

Shortly after the *Sea King* sailed for the Far East, Lt. Carter returned to Richmond and joined Mallory's staff. When word came of the
Alabama's sinking, Mallory met with Carter and Commander John M.
Brooke to discuss alternatives. Brooke suggested that a raid be directed
at the Pacific whaling fleet. Carter, remembering his earlier impres-
sions of the *Sea King*, suggested that Bulloch search for a similar ship.
Mallory sent Carter back to Liverpool with a packet of instructions for
Bulloch, including an August 16 letter asking him to look for "two such
ships . . . to operate against whalemen." Carter did not reach England
until late September. By then, Bulloch had already bought the *Sea
King*.[4]

Because of constant travel commitments, Bulloch had employed
Richard Wright, Charles K. Prioleau's father-in-law, to find a suitable
replacement for the *Alabama*. By early September, Wright reported
that the *Sea King* had returned to Glasgow and was available. Bulloch
wired Wright to purchase the ship in his own name immediately. He

then placed his old friend Captain Corbett, a British master and former blockade runner, in charge of the vessel, with instructions to sail to London, purchase a cargo of coal, and remain there in readiness.[5]

Following his formula of past success, Bulloch hurriedly dispatched agents to locate a tender while he concentrated on gathering a staff of officers, buying arms and munitions, and securing a crew. Officers were easily found. British and French interruptions of Bulloch's ironclad program had left a large pool of qualified naval officers at loose ends. Bulloch requested Lt. William H. Murdaugh as commander. Flag Officer Barron explained that Murdaugh had been removed from his jurisdiction by the Bureau of Ordnance, and instead sent Lt. James Iredell Waddell.[6]

Born in Pittsboro, North Carolina on July 13, 1824, Waddell had been appointed a midshipman in the United States Navy by Naval Secretary George E. Badger on September 10, 1841. A duel with another midshipman left him with a permanent limp, but he remained with the navy and was promoted to lieutenant in 1855. Waddell was stationed with the East India Squadron at the outbreak of the Civil War. After losing hope that the Union and the Confederacy would reconcile their differences, he abruptly resigned his commission on November 20, 1861 while returning from the Orient. Unwilling to defer his resignation until arriving back in the United States, he walked off the USS John Adams at St. Helena, with little money in his pocket, and booked passage home.

This move revealed much about Waddell's personality. He pondered long over a decision, but once deciding what course to take, he stubbornly held to it. He also seemed unable to evaluate the consequences. Other officers who had resigned from the Union navy had been paid, but because of Waddell's precipitous action, Secretary Welles informed him that his name had been "stricken from the rolls." He tried unsuccessfully to collect his back pay for three months, including a direct appeal to President Lincoln, but he would not give Welles his word of honor not to take part in the war, and thus received nothing. Although Bulloch supported Waddell's appointment as commander of the Sea King, his confidence was based not upon Waddell's personality, but his experience, patriotism, and professed willingness to destroy unarmed merchant vessels.[7]

Joining Waddell as executive officer was Lt. William C. Whittle. Whittle graduated from the Naval Academy in 1858, resigned his commission in 1861, and at the age of 20, served with distinction under Pegram on the Nashville. Regarded as an able and intelligent officer, Whittle exercised a great deal of influence over Waddell. This is a further indication of Waddell's indecisiveness, an ironic deficiency for a stubborn man holding strong convictions. Although commanders such as Semmes and Maffitt would not have tolerated Whittle's interference, with Waddell it provided a balance.

As Bulloch assembled officers for the *Sea King*, he sent them to Waddell, who quietly maintained an apartment with his wife on Clegg Street in Liverpool. Scattered in rooms throughout the city, the young officers avoided contact and notice, waiting to be called. A number of trustworthy men from the *Alabama*'s crew returned to Liverpool and agreed to join the cruise. Waddell hoped that such men as George Harwood, boatswain; Andrew Bachman, boatswain's mate; John O'Shea, carpenter; Henry Alcott, sailmaker; John Guy and William Crawford, gunner's mates, could help recruit men from the *Laurel* and the *Sea King* for service on the raider. If they failed to enlist 50 or 60 men, the ship would be seriously understaffed.

Meanwhile, Bulloch purchased the *Laurel*, a fast little iron screw steamer in packet service between Ireland and Liverpool, and placed her in the hands of Henry Lafone, a Liverpool shipping agent. As her commander he selected Confederate Navy Lt. John F. Ramsey, who had served several years in the British merchant service and held a Board of Trade master's certificate. Ramsey began loading arms, munitions, and provisions aboard the *Laurel*, ostensibly still a British merchant ship advertising for a voyage to Havana.[8]

On October 5, 1864 both vessels were ready for sea. The following day, Bulloch ordered Whittle to proceed to London and take a room at Woods Hotel, giving the name of Mr. W. C. Brown. At exactly 11 the following morning, an unnamed Confederate agent [Richard Wright] would meet him in the dining room with additional instructions. He would then meet Captain Corbett, book passage on the *Sea King*, and sail to the rendezvous point at the Bay of Funchal, Madeira. Bulloch emphasized the importance of not communicating or exchanging signals with any passing ship during the voyage:

> The object in your going out in the *Sea King* is to acquaint yourself with her sailing and other qualities, and to observe the crew. You can also inspect the internal arrangements, and discuss with Captain Corbett the necessary alterations; and you can learn the stowage of the provisions and other stores and pick out the position for magazine and shell-room. Perhaps the construction of these might be actually begun under ... Captain Corbett. You will bear in mind that until she is regularly transferred, Captain Corbett is the legal commander of the *Sea King* ... [and] you will express all your wishes in the form of requests. When you reach Madeira and the *Laurel* joins company,

you will report to Lieutenant Commanding Waddell, and thereafter act under his instructions.[9]

At 3 a.m., Whittle checked out of Wood's Hotel and walked to the waterfront. For a few minutes he waited in the shadows of a nearby warehouse and surveyed the dock, then, like any seaman returning from a binge, wobbled over to his ship and crawled unnoticed over the side. Within an hour the *Sea King* headed downriver, passing two Union warships patrolling outside the mouth of the Thames.

Richard Wright, Bulloch's intermediary in the purchase of the *Sea King*, had already given Corbett a bill of sale for the vessel, authorizing him to sell it at any time within the next six months for £45,000. Wright sailed with the *Sea King* and remained aboard until she reached the English Channel port of Deal, where he debarked and returned to Liverpool.

On the morning of October 8, after receiving the welcome news that the *Sea King* had sailed without difficulty, Bulloch sent a message to Lt. Ramsey directing him to sail that evening in the steamship *Laurel*, and "carry Lieutenant Commanding James I. Waddell, his staff of officers, and the other passengers [Confederate officers] of whom you have been advised, to Funchal. . . . The *Sea King*, Captain Corbett, has sailed from London this morning, and her commander has been instructed to time his passage so as not to arrive off Funchal until the 17th. . . . In communicating afterwards with the *Sea King* you will be governed by the directions of Lieutenant Commanding Waddell, and you will render him all the assistance in your power in transferring the supplies."[10]

By prearrangement, Ramsey sent a messenger scurrying from boardinghouse to hotel notifying Confederate officers and crew to report to the *Laurel*. Individually and without drawing attention, the men gradually converged at Prince's Landing Stage, where a tug waited to take them to the steamer. Their personal luggage, uniforms, and side arms had already been packed aboard. By midnight, all the passengers—strangers to one another traveling under assumed names, with receipts for £32 paid for passage to Havana, Cuba—had retired to their cabins. With a full load of coal and a heavy cargo of Confederate arms, Ramsey got up steam, and at 4 a.m. on October 9 the *Laurel* swung into the Mersey and headed for sea.[11]

In his cabin, Lt. James Waddell sat down to read a lengthy letter from Bulloch, which began: "You are about to proceed upon a cruise in the far-distant Pacific, into the seas and among the islands frequented by the great American whaling fleet, a source of abundant wealth to our enemies and a nursery for their seamen. It is hoped that you may be able to greatly damage and disperse that fleet, even if you do not succeed in utterly destroying it. Considering the extent of ocean to be sailed over, the necessarily incomplete equipment of your ship at the beginning of the cruise, and your approaching isolation from the aid and comfort of your countrymen, a letter or specific instructions would be wholly superfluous. . . ."

After this portentous preamble, Bulloch added another 3,500 words of advice covering every subject from navigation and coaling points to international law and seaman's pay. Bulloch also provided a box of ransom bonds and charts, which included a set of Whale Charts published by Commander Matthew Fontaine Maury in his *Physical Geography of the Sea*—a book found in the cabins of most American whalers.

Far less specific instructions came from Flag Officer Barron in Paris: a brief note with much of the character of a pep talk.[12]

Hardworking Thomas Dudley, whose agents had been watching the *Laurel*, wrote Minister Adams on October 7 that he suspected the ship was to become a Confederate privateer. Adams was out of town, but Benjamin Moran, the legation's secretary, notified Commodore Thomas T. Craven of the USS *Niagara* to intercept the vessel if she left harbor. In turn, Craven notified Captain Henry Walke of the USS *Sacramento*. Unfortunately for both Craven and Walke, the *Laurel* had sailed before either message arrived.

On the morning the *Sea King* sailed, Craven was across the English Channel at the Dutch port of Flushing. As he prepared to go ashore, the officer of the deck reported that a large steamer, bark-rigged and flying the Spanish colors, was moving down the Scheldt estuary. Moreover, the acting master had overheard a remark in a Dutch tavern that the Spanish steamer *Cicerone* carried a turret and plating intended for a Confederate ironclad. The United States navy had developed a healthy fear of ironclads, and Craven decided to stop the Spanish vessel. For the next eight hours the slow *Niagara* pursued the *Cicerone*, but failed to come within hailing distance until she reached the safety of English waters. Craven continued to follow her throughout the day and into the night. Sometime after dark, he passed within a few miles of another black ship flying the Union Jack, but Craven, intent upon the *Cicerone*, paid no attention to the departing *Sea King*.[13]

When the *Niagara* finally stopped the *Cicerone* the following morning, Craven immediately sent search parties aboard. After three days of prying apart crates, the Union crew returned empty-handed. Disappointed, Craven went ashore at Dover on October 12 to wire Adams for instructions. There he received Moran's message, only partly erroneous, that: "Captain Semmes sailed in her [the *Laurel*] on Sunday with eight officers and about 100 men. Forty of them were of the crew of the No. 290, or *Alabama*. She cleared for Matamoras, via Havana and Nassau, which means that she will go anywhere. She took on board in cases six sixty-eight pounders, with the requisite gun carriages, and also small arms. It is doubtless Semmes's purpose to meet and arm some other vessel, as the *Laurel* is not large enough for all the guns. . . . Mr. Dudley, the consul at Liverpool, will take the responsibility of her capture anywhere at sea. . . ." [14] Unfortunately for Craven, the sluggish old *Niagara* had no hope of overtaking the speedy little *Laurel*.

Once again, Bulloch evaded Dudley's network of spies and saw both vessels safely away before the United States could intervene. Adams was not surprised to learn that the Confederacy had purchased the *Sea King*. In a letter to Secretary of State Seward, he stated, "She is the same vessel that I saw at Glasgow on the occasion of one of my visits to that town last year. I regarded her then as a most likely steamer for the purposes of a privateer and so reported to you at that time. If I mistake not, she will prove herself a dangerous and destructive craft to our commerce." [15]

While Bulloch closed his file on the *Sea King*, Waddell's troubles were just beginning. He was a man who found decisions hard to make and, once made, even more difficult to change. Ahead lay uncharted seas, ice floes, and desolate lands far from communication with the world. He would be operating independently, relying only on his own resources and skill as a commander and navigator. Although he was determined to do his duty, in the back of his mind, he wondered if he could.

A Rough Start

As the *Laurel* headed for the Madeira Islands off northwest Africa, Waddell kept to his cabin and studied Bulloch's charts. He had sailed the Pacific, and knew that many sections of the world's oceans remained unsurveyed and hazardous. For sheer danger, however, nothing surpassed the shallow Arctic Ocean and its unpredictable ice-fields. Waddell had been a good navigator, but he expected this long, difficult voyage to test all his technical skills.

The responsibilities of commanding a Confederate cruiser would test much more than his technical skills, however. Waddell had complete confidence in his seamanship and his ability to handle a disciplined crew, but in the back of his mind lurked many doubts about operating on his own, far from the support of his country or the counsel of higher authority. Yet Semmes and Maffitt had earned glory under similar conditions; this would be the opportunity to prove himself their equal. By the time the *Laurel* reached Funchal on October 16, Waddell had steeled himself to this difficult mission and was prepared to take over his new command. Unfortunately, the *Sea King* was not there.

After anchoring, Waddell posted a lookout, advised both officers and crew that there would be no shore liberty, and went ashore to cash a draft of £5,000 for the raider's sailing fund. When questioned by Portuguese officials why no one came ashore, Waddell replied that the passengers were emigrants from Poland bound for the West Indies who had no interest in visiting the island.

After the *Laurel* finished coaling, a customs official asked why she had not yet departed. Captain Ramsey explained that the *Laurel* required repairs, and when asked for proof, presented some broken cogs he had brought along for just such a purpose. The official took the parts ashore to have new ones made at a government workshop, and told Ramsey they would be ready the following day. Having bought another day, Waddell paced the deck, listening for the call of the lookout to announce the arrival of the *Sea King*.[1]

On the moonlit evening of October 18, the lookout quietly slipped down from aloft and reported a dark, ship-rigged vessel showing signal lights steaming across the entrance to Funchal. Waddell peered into the darkness as the vessel disappeared to the south. A short time later the vessel returned, and the entire crew turned out to watch her pass to the north, still displaying signal lights. Both Waddell and Ramsey felt certain this was the *Sea King*, but no one rested comfortably knowing that the stranger just as easily could be an enemy cruiser. At any rate, nothing could be done until morning. The *Laurel*'s papers were ashore in the customshouse and could only be recovered between sunrise and sunset.[2]

At dawn, Ramsey sent a boat ashore to retrieve the ship's papers and ordered the engine room to get up steam. Shortly afterward, the mysterious steamer dipped back into the harbor flying the Union Jack—this time distinctly showing the prearranged recognition pennant of the *Laurel*—went about, and headed back to sea. From the *Laurel*'s deck, Waddell could distinctly see lettered in white on her black stern: *Sea King—London*. At 9 a.m., customs officials returned the *Laurel*'s papers, but by then, even the Portuguese fruit peddlers had guessed her business and shocked Waddell by shouting: "Otro *Alabama*! Otro *Alabama*!" Another *Alabama*! With the secret out, Waddell had no time to waste. Now everyone in port knew the *Sea King* was another Confederate cruiser.[3]

Ramsey headed at full speed for a sandy trio of islands a few miles south of Madeira known as Las Desertas. Waddell and the *Laurel* soon overtook the *Sea King*, and signaled for Ramsey to follow. Both vessels dropped anchor in the sheltered cove of Porto Santo, a narrow, scrub-covered island inhabited only by a few curious fishermen. After lashing the vessels together, First Lt. Whittle scrambled aboard the *Laurel* and reported to Waddell.

Whittle wasted no time in dropping his role as George Brown and assuming his new duties. Work parties soon had tackles rigged aloft and began swinging heavy crates marked "machinery" across to the *Sea King*. If the Englishmen in the work parties wondered about their contents, their doubts were dispelled when one of the crates swung too low and splintered against the bulwark. An inquisitive member of the crew, thrusting his hand into the broken crate and feeling the smooth, cylindrical surface of the big gun, exclaimed: "Machinery! Yes, the same kind of machinery the *Alabama* carried! I know a 68-pounder when I lay my hand on it."[4]

Everyone worked, officers and men, with lookouts posted aloft to report the approach of any vessels. Portuguese fishermen who sailed alongside to visit found themselves impressed into service. By 9 that night, 10 tons of guns were aboard the *Sea King*, and Waddell finally consented to half an hour's rest and supper.

After a brief respite the men returned to work, transferring gunpowder, shot, shell, and provisions. Cabin boys kept the men well supplied with grog, the fuel they needed to keep them working. A box slipped loose and crashed to the deck, scattering 24-pound shot like oversized marbles. By 2 a.m. the men began to collapse. When the boatswain called a layoff, they dropped where they stood and instantly fell asleep. Three hours later they were shaken awake, the cabin boys poured more grog into tired bodies, and the officers hustled them back to work. By late morning, the *Sea King*'s decks were heaped with equipment, guns, provisions, and clothing, all in total disarray. The last object extracted from the *Laurel*'s hold was a heavy safe. As four men strained to push it aft into the captain's quarters, the jingling of gold and silver coins could be heard.[5]

For Waddell, a critical moment had arrived. He had a ship, he had officers, but as yet he had no crew. Whittle ordered the men of the *Sea King* aft for an announcement from the captain. Outside the cabin stood Waddell, now dressed in the full uniform of a Confederate naval officer. Captain Corbett stood at his side, dressed in the black suit of a merchant captain, and announced that he had sold the *Sea King* to the Confederacy; her new mission was to destroy the commerce of the United States. After offering the men a bonus of two month's wages for enlisting in the Confederate Navy, Corbett turned the discussion over to the new captain.

Waddell read his commission, offered good pay, promised prize money, and asked the men who wished to join to step forward. Much to his surprise, both he and Corbett were accused of duplicity. One man openly assailed Corbett for violating the Queen's Foreign Enlistment Act. Waddell tried to calm the men with money. Although his letter of instruction had predicted that he would be able to recruit about 50 men from the hand-picked crews of the *Sea King* and the *Laurel*, only two men stepped forward, a cabin boy and a fireman.[6]

Waddell ordered a bucket of sovereigns brought on deck. As he ran his hands through the coins, he raised Corbett's offer of a two-month bonus — £8 — to £12, then £15, and finally £17 for a six-month enlistment. Ordinary seamen's pay rose to £5, then £6, and finally £7. Two more volunteers stepped forward, an engineer and another cabin boy. Disgusted, Corbett retired to the *Laurel*; of the 55 men comprising the *Sea King*'s original crew, 51 went with him.

In a final effort to recruit a few more men, Whittle asked John Elli-

son, an argumentative British quartermaster who had disrupted the negotiations, why he would not enlist. Ellison pointed to the Naval
Reserve insignia on his cap and replied, "Sir, I never earned a shilling in
my life in America, and I do not wish to fight her battles. England is
my country, and I am not ashamed to own it. Under no circumstances
could I go. . . . If I were to desert from this [British Naval Reserve] you
could not place any confidence in me."[7]

Ellison not only discouraged the men of the *Sea King* from enlisting, but his arguments also influenced the crew of the *Laurel*. When
Waddell called a separate meeting to clink the coins and coax the men
of the *Laurel* to sign-up, only five men joined, leaving Waddell with a
total of 19 crewmen, including the 10 men who had come as passengers. Counting his 23 officers, Waddell had but 43 men to man a warship that needed a crew of 150 to sail and fight her effectively.[8]

This was the first test of Waddell's leadership. Twenty-three years
in the navy had not prepared him for moments like this; somebody else
had always made the tough decisions. Unlike Semmes or Maffitt, who
were confident, self-reliant, and kept their own counsel, Waddell
turned to others for advice—to men who could give advice cheaply and
not have to bear the burden of failure should they be wrong. Corbett
and Ramsey thought he would be foolish to go to sea, and suggested
that he sail south to the Canary Islands and try to recruit more men.
Waddell wavered, fearing that his presence there would alert Union
agents and attract enemy warships. Young Whittle suggested that he
call his officers together and learn from them "what they can and will
do."[9] Waddell must have found the word "will," coming from his executive officer, a bit perplexing.

Waddell assembled his officers, explained the current difficulties,
and laid out the options, suggesting that the safest course would be to
sail to the Canaries. But Waddell's officers were young and eager for
glory. Charles Lining, the ship's surgeon and the oldest, had just passed
his 31st birthday. Whittle, at 24, was older than the other lieutenants,
John Grimball, Sidney Smith Lee, Jr. (nephew to General Robert E. Lee),
Fred Chew, and Dabney Scales. Matthew O'Brien, chief engineer, was
26. Midshipmen John Mason and Orris Browne were both 20. Acting
Master Irvine S. Bulloch and Acting Paymaster William Breedlove
Smith had sailed with Semmes and provided experience, but were both
in their twenties. This was not a group to take a conservative course.
They felt they could recruit sufficient seamen from captured prizes and
unanimously recommended that Waddell take to the ocean. He quietly
concurred and, with lingering doubt, issued the necessary orders.[10]

Wasting no time on ceremony, Waddell read the articles commissioning the CSS *Shenandoah* while the men worked to clear the deck for sea. As Ramsey cut loose the *Laurel* and eased away, a lookout reported a bark approaching with the cut of a man-of-war. Alarmed and unprepared to meet any threat, Waddell sent Ramsey to investigate. The *Laurel* made a full sweep around the vessel, which had hoisted British colors, before reporting back that the stranger was a harmless merchantman.

Before departing, the *Laurel* lowered a boat and delivered three more inductees who had changed their minds. Waddell sent back dispatches and the ships separated—the *Laurel* bound for Tenerife, and the *Shenandoah* to sea and the unknown. The Confederate colors unfurled over the new cruiser, impressing one member of the crew as "a sort of a white flag with a blue cross up in the corner and a lot of stars—a right pretty flag."[11]

As the cheers from both vessels gradually faded, the *Shenandoah* found herself afloat in a sea of uncertainty. Although officially commissioned as a Confederate man-of-war on October 20, 1864, the *Shenandoah* was still technically a merchantman, unable to attack or defend herself. Years later, Waddell recalled the first difficult days:

> We were now fairly afloat in a vessel of 1,100 tons, English measurement, constructed for peaceful pursuits but metamorphosed into an armed cruiser. The deck had to be cleared of the stores pitched on it pell mell before the battery could be mounted on the carriages and gunports must be cut, fighting belts driven, gun tackles fitted, before that battery could be used in our defense. All this service which is ordinarily done at a navy yard before a vessel is commissioned devolved upon us, out in mid ocean, without even a hope of successful defense or a friendly port to take shelter in, if attacked in the interim.
>
> The carpenter of the vessel could find no one who was capable of assisting him in his department. He therefore unassisted, was to make the necessary alterations, the work would progress slowly.
>
> Besides the work already mentioned, the bulwarks were discovered to be too weak for resistance to a shotted gun, and therefore some plan must be devised for strengthening them, which being decided upon and arranged, the next work of importance was the selection of a place in the vessel's hold where a powder magazine could be built.
>
> The hold as well as the berth deck was filled with coal and not being able to move the coal from the forehold which was selected as the place for the magazine, the powder was placed under tarpaulins in my starboard cabin, while I occupied the port one. Was it not a warm companion?
>
> If we had fallen in with the enemy's cruiser at this time we might,

in attempting to escape, have received a missile which, taking effect in the stern of the vessel, would have exploded or otherwise put an end to all our hopes, by blowing up the magazine. There was, however, no other place at that time so safe for powder as the cabin where we had twenty-four officers. . . .[12]

While mounting the guns, Whittle discovered that no gun tackles had been shipped; without tackles, the guns could not be fired because the recoil would pitch them through the far side of the ship. The gun bolts had also disappeared, but were later found buried in a beef barrel. The muzzles of the big guns soon frowned from freshly fashioned ports, apparently ready for action, but only a pair of tiny 12-pounders could be fired safely. And with the exception of a single shell, the 12-pounders carried only blank charges. Now Waddell not only needed to capture a prize with men who would sign on as crew, but he also needed to find one with heavy tackles.

Anxious to put distance between himself and Madeira, Waddell headed south, running under both steam and sail during the day as the crew worked frantically to convert a merchantman to a man-of-war far from any shipyard, and altering course slightly at night under easy canvas to minimize work aloft and allow the crew time to rest. Waddell himself took regular turns at the wheel, brooding over the condition of his ship. Officers slept uncomplainingly on deck, with iron tanks filled with bread for furniture and wooden buckets for wash basins. His personal quarters, partially occupied by gunpowder, consisted of "one broken arm chair, one covered with velvet, no berth or bureau, no place to put clothing, no washstand, pitcher or basin; as cheerless a spot as the sun ever shone on." On October 25 Waddell noted that "the powder was removed to a small apartment under the cabin . . . below the surface of the ocean . . . but still in a very insecure place."[13]

Waddell, feeling the burden of his first command, remained silent, and some of the officers began to doubt his competency. Dr. Lining, the ship's surgeon, confided in his diary: "Now it was that the officers came out in their true colors and some that should have been the last to be disheartened flunked, and were only kept up to their work, or rather duty, by the influence of some of the younger officers."[14]

After a week of constant labor, Waddell gave the crew a brief reprieve and ordered that no work would be done on Sunday. As the men relaxed for their first extended rest, however, the wind died, and the captain ordered steam, sending five angry stokers into the engine room. The following day, the *Shenandoah* struck her first squall, weathering it well, but the decks leaked badly, soaking—and angering—the men trying to sleep on the berth deck. The following day the engine broke down. Although it needed only minor repairs, the men wondered, "Would the machinery hold up?" By the end of the first week at sea, the entire ship's company was exhausted and showing signs of discontent. Although the *Shenandoah* looked formidable with her big guns mounted, she was in no condition to fight.[15]

When the lookouts sighted a square-rigged vessel on October 28, Waddell ordered the chase, assuming by the cut of the rig that the bark was American. Although his instructions from Bulloch had specifically stated that he was to "make no prizes until Captain Corbett has had time to reach England and cancel the register. . . ."[16] Waddell needed men and supplies and could not afford to wait another three weeks to get them. After a three-hour chase, the *Shenandoah* overhauled the vessel, and a boarding party led by Irvine Bulloch, veteran of the *Alabama*, rowed expectantly toward their first prize.

Disappointment struck when Bulloch read the name painted on her stern: *Mogul—London*. The British master greeted Bulloch at the rail and invited him into his cabin to examine the ship's registry. The *Mogul* had indeed been built in the United States, for the Far East trade, but had been legitimately sold to an English company the previous year. Bulloch returned to the *Shenandoah* with the bad news. Although Semmes had stopped and released many such vessels, this was Waddell's first experience, and he released the *Mogul* with regret tinged with doubt: "The *Mogul* of London . . . may have been sold in good faith. So far as her papers were concerned, the sale was in form, but that is not infallible proof."[17]

Two days later Waddell captured his first fair prize, the brand-new 574-ton bark *Alina* of Searsport, Maine, bound for Buenos Aires with a cargo of railroad iron. After studying the *Alina*'s papers, Waddell advised her captain that his ship would be destroyed. The captain, who had thought the sinking of the *Alabama* in June had meant that Confederate raiders had been swept from the sea, had most of his life's savings invested in the *Alina*. As he headed back to collect his personal property, he glumly confided to Master's Mate Hunt, "I've a daughter at home that craft yonder was named for, and it goes against me cursedly to see her destroyed. . . . I hope I shall have an opportunity of returning your polite attentions before this muss is over. . . ."[18]

The prize crew found the *Alina* well equipped, including tackles for the guns and a large supply of cotton canvas for sails. Besides canned meat and other provisions, the crew liberated missing amenities such as crockery, knives, forks, basins, pitchers, and books. Waddell even acquired a spring-bottomed mattress and some cabin furniture.

Waddell ordered the *Alina* scuttled, and ship's carpenter John O'Shea and five men went aboard to carry it out. O'Shea found little pleasure in destroying such beautiful workmanship. With sails still set, the *Alina* moved slowly in a light breeze, settling gradually, until her bow shot up and she slid back stern first, her masts snapping as she sank beneath the waves.

Of the *Alina*'s three officers and 12 sailors, seven joined the *Shenandoah*: three Frenchmen, three Germans, and one Malay, none of whom owed allegiance to the United States. On hearing of the new recruits, Surgeon Lining wrote: "Seven men! What a deal of work that will take off the officer's hands."[19]

For the next week, Waddell continued south, eventually entering the 1,800-mile gap between equatorial Africa and South America. Semmes had taken many prizes here, but Waddell saw nothing but foreign flags and a series of furious squalls. Forced continually aloft to set and take in sails, many of the tired crew applied for the sick list.

The weather—and the monotony—broke on November 5, with the capture of the tiny 150-ton schooner *Charter Oak* of Boston, bound for San Francisco with a mixed cargo of fruits and vegetables. When Waddell informed her captain, Sam Gilman, that his ship would be burned, Gilman giggled and said, "Well, if you're going to burn her, for God's sake bring the preserved fruit aboard." Besides two mates and four Portuguese seamen, Gilman had his wife, her widowed sister, and her sister's four-year old son aboard.

To Waddell, all ladies were pretty, and in their presence he conducted himself in a courtly and chivalrous manner. His young officers disagreed with their captain's assessment, however. To them, the two ladies of the *Charter Oak* were at best "plain." Speaking for himself, Waddell wrote, "We all felt a compassion for these poor women, and we had no idea of retaliating upon them for the injuries which General Hunter, Sheridan, Sherman, and their kind had inflicted on our unhappy countrywomen." When Waddell discovered that Gilman carried $200 in gold in the ship's strongbox, he secretly returned it to Mrs. Gilman on her promise not to give a cent to her husband.[20]

Waddell, still needing crew, looked over the Portuguese sailors, but they turned out to be deserters from the Union army. Waddell decided that they would probably jump ship at the first opportunity and had them put in irons.

On November 7, six degrees north of the equator, the *Shenandoah* captured the sluggish old 299-ton Boston bark *De Godfrey*, heavily laden with pork, beef, and lumber for Valparaiso, Chile. Waddell wanted all the meat brought on board, but the prize crew reported 40,000 feet of lumber stowed on top that would take a day to remove. Waddell would not wait, settled for 44 barrels of meat, and ordered the ship burned. Her captain, Sam Hallett, joined Whittle, Mrs. Gilman, and her sister at the rail to watch his ship go up in flames. Hallett lamented: "That was a vessel which had done her duty well for forty years. She faced old Boreas in every part of the world . . . and after such a career to be destroyed by man on a calm night, on this tropic sea—too bad, too bad."[21]

The cruiser was now crowded with prisoners, some of whom were becoming unruly. On November 9, Waddell shipped them aboard the Danish brig *Anna Jane* in exchange for the *Alina*'s chronometer and some provisions. Waddell commented dryly, "Captain Staples accompanies his instrument." Captain Gilman and the two ladies, who were quite at home on the cruiser, convinced Waddell that they should remain aboard until suitable passage to California could be arranged. The younger officers disapproved of releasing any prisoners, arguing that Union agents would learn their destination and discover their weaknesses as soon as the Danish vessel reached port. They also saw no reason to retain the Gilmans, who seemed intent on remaining permanent guests. Lining suspected that any ship headed for California was likely to be a Yankee and therefore a fair prize.[22]

The following day, the *Shenandoah* overhauled the most curious vessel captured by any Confederate cruiser, the 134-ton New York hermaphrodite brig *Susan*, which the lookout first reported as a steamer. After studying the vessel through a glass, Waddell noticed that the so-called steamer had a single paddle wheel rotating off one side, but he saw no smoke, no funnel, and no apparent explanation for the paddle wheel.

The boarding party returned with the news that the *Susan* was probably the worst ship afloat. She leaked so badly that the crew could not pump her out as fast as she filled. The captain, a German named Frederich Hansen, explained that the paddling device had been rigged to pump out the ship automatically as she moved with the wind. At the time of her capture, the *Susan* was 46 days out of Cardiff with coal for the Rio Grande, and her crew doubted that she would make it. Three men and a dog joined the crew of the *Shenandoah*, but Waddell turned down the master's application for the position of acting master's mate.

For some reason, Waddell mistook Hansen for a Jew and allowed his religious and racial prejudices to override the importance of adequately manning his ship.[23]

Waddell missed another chance to fill out his crew on Friday, November 11. A chase that began in the afternoon ended past midnight with the capture the 1,100-ton clipper ship *Kate Prince*, Portsmouth to Bahia with Cardiff coal. Lt. Sidney Lee boarded the vessel and sent the master, Captain Libbey, back to the *Shenandoah* with the ship's papers. Mrs. Libbey took Lee aside, declared herself a Southern woman, and said she "would enjoy nothing better than sailing aboard the Confederate raider." Her husband's 21-man crew, Southern sympathizers all, would join the *Shenandoah* as well.

But Waddell had ruled that the *Prince's* cargo was neutral, and ordered her released under a $40,000 bond. Lee, with several junior officers, appealed to Waddell to enlist the entire crew, including Mrs. Libbey, but this time the captain said no and meant it. Two women on board had been enough of a problem without adding a third. And it would not do to upset the British by violating their neutrality. Instead, Waddell seized the opportunity to liberate his remaining prisoners, including the Gilmans—an action they protested vehemently. To them it was a breach of faith. At length, Waddell finally persuaded the Gilmans to accept their freedom.[24]

In his journal, Surgeon Lining noted that, although he was pleased to see the end of the Gilmans, a great opportunity to enlist a competent crew had been lost. "This, I think, was a great mistake. A ship worth so much money and ransomed for the sake of a cargo not worth over seventeen thousand dollars at the most. Better to have burned her and let our government settle about the cargo afterwards."[25]

Twelve hours later the *Shenandoah* stopped the bark *Adelaide*, a vessel obviously crafted in New England shipyards but flying the colors of Argentina. Suspecting a ruse, Waddell sent for the vessel's master, Captain Williams, who could produce no bill of sale. After further questioning, Williams admitted that he was bound to Rio from New York with a cargo of flour belonging to Phipps & Company of New York. Mr. Pendergrast of Baltimore, whom Williams described as "a good Southerner," owned the vessel, but he had transferred her registry to Argentina in order to save his property from the hated Yankees. Under oath, Williams' statements were inconsistent, and Waddell felt the captain had perjured himself in an attempt to mask the ship and cargo's true ownership.[26]

As the prize crew removed hams, preserved fruits, and other delicacies, Bulloch discovered a bundle of letters. As Waddell shuffled through them, he discovered that Pendergrast owned not only the bark, but also the cargo. Moreover, Pendergrast was a Southern shipping merchant who had somehow managed to maintain his business through the port of Baltimore without attracting attention. This was a completely unexpected turn of events, and Waddell ordered that everything removed from the *Adelaide* be returned. By then, furniture had been smashed, the cabin knocked to pieces, and kerosene sloshed all over the hold and deck. The incendiaries were about to strike the match when Waddell changed his mind.

Waddell wrote an apology to Mr. Pendergrast. To allay suspicions in New York about why the bark was released and to protect Pendergrast, Waddell bonded the cargo for $24,000, falsely declaring that he found the ship to be under neutral colors. Captain Williams returned to his vessel and promptly sped away, delighted that he had escaped the torch, but unwilling to give Waddell another opportunity to change his mind.[27]

On November 13, slightly north of the equator, the *Shenandoah* burned the 140-ton Boston schooner *Lizzie M. Stacy*, bound for the Sandwich Islands (Hawaii) with a mixed cargo of pine, salt, and iron. Captain *Archer* of the schooner left a graphic description of the event:

He [Waddell] asked me if there was any jewelry, gold, silver or other valuables on my vessel. I told him none that I was aware of. . . . He sent a coxswain to tell Mr. Grimball to burn our vessel. I asked him if he was not going to let me go on board again, and he said they had no room for any baggage on their vessel. He said, however, that I might go on board and get a suit of clothes if I wished. I went, and found that they had been over our vessel and taken about everything there was of any value. They had been through my stateroom and taken everything out. I should think there were as many as twenty or thirty men went onboard from the Cruiser, tearing everything to pieces and taking whatever they wanted. I took a suit of clothes from the vessel and that was all I could get.[28]

Shortly after the schooner broke into flames, a breeze sprang up. With all her sail still set, the flaming vessel lurched toward them. Whittle sprang to the deck and issued a few crisp orders to brace back the yards, heeling the ship to starboard, and the blazing schooner passed harmlessly by. Waddell had toyed with the idea of transferring a 32-pounder aboard and using the prize as a tender, but he was too short-handed. Three men signed on from the *Lizzie*, but the crew still numbered only 41 men.[29]

Waddell headed south along the coast of Brazil, taking no more prizes for three weeks. Meanwhile, the secret of the *Sea King*'s conversion to the CSS *Shenandoah* made headlines in Great Britain and the United States. The *Alabama* was gone; the *Wachusett* had illegally captured the *Florida* on October 7, but now Secretary Welles found himself confronted with another Confederate commerce raider.

The first evidence came on October 21 when the *Laurel* arrived at Tenerife with the sailors who had refused to join the *Shenandoah*. Captain Ramsey allowed no one ashore until the his ship had been coaled and readied for sea. He then approached port authorities and requested permission to land 43 passengers, who he identified as the officers and crew of the *Sea King*, which had been wrecked off the Desertas Islands. Hearing of the ship's loss, British Consul Henry Grattan waited for Captain Corbett to appear with the *Sea King*'s papers. After several days, Grattan finally sent for Corbett, who brought the ship's register and explained that the *Sea King* had not been lost, but sold.

Still annoyed with Corbett for deceiving him, Quartermaster John Ellison also visited Grattan and testified that Corbett had attempted to deliberately trick the *Sea King*'s crew to supply hands for a Confederate cruiser. On October 30, the day the *Shenandoah* captured her first prize, Grattan arrested Corbett for violating Britain's Foreign Enlistment Act. He forwarded all testimony to Foreign Secretary Lord Russell, writing that Corbett would arrive in England on the British mail ship *Calabar*.[30]

When Corbett reached England, he learned that the Law Officers of the Crown had studied the charges against him and decided that he had not violated the Foreign Enlistment Act. Ruling on a technicality, they stated that, "The criminal act must have been committed within some part of her Majesty's dominions, a word which as here used does not—in our opinion—include a British ship at sea. . . ." Corbett was absolved of the charges and released.[31]

Some of the *Sea King*'s crewmen, annoyed that they had been forced to settle for three month's pay from what was to have been a two-year voyage, furnished the U.S. consul with damaging depositions. Crown Officers reviewed the statements from John Wilson, seaman, and John Hercus, carpenter, and again arrested Corbett. Released on bond, his trial was finally held several weeks after the *Shenandoah*'s voyage ended, and he was again acquitted.[32]

Although the United States Navy now knew that another Confederate cruiser was loose, her whereabouts were unknown until Captain Libbey of the bonded *Kate Prince* landed at Bahia and told them where he had been captured. The USS *Onward*, a sailing vessel commanded by Acting Master William H. Clark, was the only vessel on station at Brazil and no match for the *Shenandoah*. Through Clark, Libbey provided Welles with an accurate description of the cruiser and the shorthanded conditions aboard, but he could shed no light on the raider's next destination. Before Libbey returned to sea, he wrote Clark on December 28 requesting that he "convoy the ship off the land to such a distance as might . . . be necessary to prevent capture . . . as it is understood in Bahia that the Confederate steamer *Shenandoah* is off the coast. . . ."[33] At this time Libbey had no real cause for fear. The *Shenandoah* was deep in the South Indian Ocean, stretching all canvas for Australia.

To the Other Side of the World

ON NOVEMBER 15, 1864 the *Shenandoah*, no longer an innocent merchantman but a ship-of-war, crossed the equator, booming along
under sail down the southern coast of Brazil. Two rifled 32-pound
Whitworths stood at the forward ports. The two 12-pounders remained
aft. Four smoothbore 68-pounders rested amidships on heavily reinforced decking. Any pair of guns could be fired simultaneously, but
Gunner John Guy warned that a full broadside might shake the ship
apart.

The ship's dinginess and disorder was gone; stores and munitions
had been stowed. Belowdecks, space amidships had been cleared and
furnished with tables and chests for the crew. The captain's staterooms,
which Waddell had once described as "the most cheerless and offensive
spot I ever occupied," had been transformed with carpets, plush furniture, and a fine library, all gleaned from prizes, into luxurious apart-
ments. Eight cabins, built originally for affluent passengers, became
officers' quarters. These opened into a central saloon that served as the
wardroom, which grew in splendor—its library held 600 volumes—
with the capture of each prize.

Life aboard had settled into a routine. A typical meal consisted of
hard-tack, or unleavened biscuit, salt beef, commonly called salt horse,
and duff, a mixture of flour, lard, and yeast boiled until hard and served
with molasses. The officers ate the same food as the crew, although the
cooks made sure they got the choicest pieces. Standard sea fare improved when delicacies were taken from prizes, or when Dr. Lining decided that the antiscorbutic properties of fresh meat were needed to
prevent scurvy. Then livestock, penned in the topgallant forecastle,
were slaughtered and divided among the entire ship's company. Following the age-old custom of the sea, the captain ate alone in his own quarters.

A generation of age and experience separated Waddell from his
young officers. Like most youngsters, they quarrelled among themselves, formed intense likes and dislikes, and enjoyed passing judgment

on their commander. Although no one openly challenged Waddell's authority, they often questioned his decisions. Keeping the *Shenandoah* under short canvas at night in perfect sailing weather was interpreted as timidity, not just a concern for the safety of a seriously undermanned ship with an untested crew. The captain had unquestioned responsibility for the protection of the ship, but he often underestimated the experience and intellectual capacity of his 20-year-olds.

After three weeks with no sign of enemy vessels, Waddell headed east, intending to pass close by the isolated island of Tristan da Cunha, a popular whaling site deep in the South Atlantic. As the cruiser approached, the lookout reported a vessel showing American colors hove to under topsails; greasy black smoke from the trypots revealed that she had recently taken a whale. Lt. Grimball led a boarding party to the old 274-ton whaling bark *Edward*, four months out of New Bedford, and took possession. Captain Charles P. Worth accepted his sudden change of fortune with a measure of good humor. He greeted the *Shenandoah's* assembled officers with, "Good afternoon, gentlemen. You have a fine ship here for a cruiser." When Lt. Mason asked the *Edward's* age, Worth said, "She was laid on the stocks before you or I were born."[1]

The *Edward* contained a huge supply of stores and a crew of 25. Waddell did not want the tough and angry seamen, but he did want the provisions. He wrote:

> The outfit of the *Edward* was of excellent quality, and we lay by her two days, replenishing the *Shenandoah* with what we were in want of. We removed from her 100 barrels of beef and as many of pork, besides several thousand pounds of ship biscuit, the best we had ever eaten, put up in large whiskey seasoned hogsheads capable of holding 300 gallons of oil . . . etc. Two of her boats were new and they were removed to the *Shenandoah* in place of her old and worthless ones. She was burned, and I visited a settlement on the northwest side of Tristan da Cunha and arranged with the chief man, (a Yankee) of the island who was called governor, to receive the crew of the *Edward*, most of whom were Sandwich Islanders. . . .[2]

On December 7 the *Shenandoah* headed east toward Cape Town. That night a strange, faint grating sound coming from the drive shaft beneath his cabin kept Waddell awake. In the morning, he put the vessel under sail and ordered the propeller hauled up and inspected. Chief Engineer O'Brien discovered a crack along the brass band that fit over the coupling on the propeller shaft. Only temporary repairs could be carried out at sea, and putting into Cape Town for repairs meant running the risk of being trapped by a Union warship. Waddell decided to remain under canvas and head for Melbourne, 6,000 miles away.

As Waddell sailed east, Commander C. R. P. Rodgers of the USS *Iroquois*, just completing boiler repairs in Montevideo, read with interest an account in a Brazilian newspaper of the *Shenandoah*'s activities off Bahia. Guessing that Waddell was headed for Cape Town, Rodgers steamed off after him. At Tristan da Cunha he learned that the *Shenandoah* had been there three weeks before. After taking on the refugees from the *Edward*, he steamed toward Cape Town, arriving there on January 9, 1865, only to learn that the *Shenandoah* had not been seen. One rumor held that the raider had been lost near the Canary Islands. To Rodgers this sounded unlikely, and he advised Welles that he would sail to the East Indies and search near Batavia.[3]

As Rodgers headed northeast toward Sumatra, Waddell, halfway to Australia, sailed steadily eastward through the Roaring Forties. Snow and hail, driven by a series of squalls, buffeted the ship. Huge seas swept the decks, exhausting the crew and, on one occasion, filling the wardroom with sea water and sending the specially prepared Christmas goose to the deck. Waddell edged northward, seeking fairer skies.

On December 29 the weather improved, and after a spirited chase Waddell captured the 705-ton Bangor bark *Delphine*, in ballast for Akyab and a cargo of rice. When told that his ship was a prize of the Confederate States and would be burned, Captain William G. Nichols pleaded that his wife was on board and ill, and that, "It may cause the death of my wife to remove her." Always sensitive to the frailties of women, Waddell sent Dr. Lining to examine Mrs. Nichols. Lining returned, reporting that "She is a woman of some culture, in perfect health and very decided."[4]

A tall, shapely, and temperamental woman of 26 years, half her husband's age, Lillias Nichols was the owner's daughter and accustomed to having her own way—and she meant to retain her possessions. Two whaleboats were required to transfer her and her son, her maid, her baggage, a library, and a caged canary to the *Shenandoah*. As she came on board she glared at Whittle, passed a haughty look over the cruiser's storm-littered decks, commented sharply, "If I had been in command, you would never have taken the *Delphine*," then demanded that Waddell, whom she called the "pirate chief," put her ashore instantly. Waddell offered to put her ashore on the nearest land, the isolated, uninhabited island of St. Paul. The formidable Mrs. Nichols replied with an indignant "Oh no; never!" and retired to her new and unwanted quarters—the captain's own—and slammed the door in his face.[5]

Taking only livestock, Waddell burned the *Delphine* and continued east. Six hands elected to join the cruiser's crew, bringing her strength to 47 men.

On January 2 the cruiser stopped off St. Paul Island, and Waddell sent a party ashore. Mrs. Nichols, holding back tears, anticipated an order to debark at any moment, but Cornelius Hunt assured her that the captain would not deposit her and her baggage on the desolate island. The shore party discovered a small French fishing village and returned with a supply of fresh and salted fish, some chickens and a penguin. When Waddell sailed the following day, Mrs. Nichols finally relaxed.

During the remainder of the voyage to Australia, Mrs. Nichols flirted with the Southern officers and, to his growing annoyance, ignored her husband, who tried to interrupt every conversation she held with the dashing young officers. Dr. Lining, an astute observer of human behavior, commented: "The fool and ass, a man obliged to suspect his wife and to have to keep his eyes on her to prevent her doing wrong! I shall now go on talking to her to plague him, if nothing else."[6]

On January 17, 100 miles off the southwestern coast of Australia, the *Shenandoah* overhauled the *Nimrod*, a New England-built clipper. Like so many U.S. merchantmen, the *Nimrod* had been sold to an English firm the previous year, and was released.

During unfavorable weather on the final leg of the journey to Melbourne, the watch reported another sail. Waddell studied it through his glass and proclaimed it the *Nimrod* again. His officers disagreed and recommended pursuit, but Waddell, satisfied with his identification, held to the decision. Lillias Nichols, who now spent much of her time in the officers' wardroom, overheard the discussion. She, too, had been on deck, seen the ship, and recognized it at once as the *David Brown*, another of her father's vessels. A few days later she mentioned it to the officers, one of whom wrote, "We caught the January mail, but we did not catch the *David Brown.*"[7]

On January 25 the *Shenandoah* stood off Port Philip, Melbourne, and signaled for a pilot from a nearby boat. Pilot Edward Johnson, who had been waiting for an overdue mail steamer, did not expect to find himself aboard a Confederate cruiser, and asked Waddell why he had come to Hobson's Bay, adding that his orders prevented him from bringing a belligerent into harbor without an acceptable reason. After Waddell described the problem with the shaft coupling, Johnson guided the vessel to the heads, where a health official came aboard. Just before returning to shore to telegraph Melbourne that a Confederate warship was coming into port, he confided to Dr. Lining that, "You have a great many friends here, and some enemies."[8] Boats of every description streamed into Hobson's Bay to watch and wave as the raider crossed to her designated berth. A few others looked on, intent on providing a very different kind of welcome.

That evening Lt. Grimball went ashore with a message for Governor Sir Charles Henry Darling asking for the use of the port, and Breedlove Smith, the paymaster, prepared to release the prisoners. On finding that everyone except Mrs. Nichols had signed paroles—a promise not to bear arms or do anything detrimental to the Confederate cause—he prevailed on her to sign one now, adding that the parole was only a formality, and that she would not be released until she signed. Protesting that she was not a prisoner of war, she grudgingly signed the paper and declared that the moment she reached shore she would go directly to the American consul, parole or not. When she asked indignantly if her little son Phinny must sign, too, Smith replied: "No, madam. We are much more afraid of you than we are of him."[9]

The following morning Lillias Nichols, accompanied by young Phinny and still ignoring her husband, hailed a passing launch and left the *Shenandoah*, collecting all her possessions save a copy of *Uncle Tom's Cabin*, which Whittle had tossed overboard. As she shoved clear, her final words carried to the officers at the rail: "I wish that steamer may be burned."[10]

When word reached Waddell that the governor's executive council had approved his request to stay in port, buy provisions, and repair the propeller shaft, he pronounced the ship open to visitors,[11] and young, isolated Melbourne, with 50,000 inhabitants eager for diversion, turned out en masse to view the first highly publicized "Rebel Pirate" to touch Australian shores. Melbourne society feted the *Shenandoah*'s officers with a succession of great dinners and balls. Meanwhile a small faction of Northern interests quietly gathered their resources to bring about the raider's destruction.

When U.S. Consul William Blanchard arrived at his office on the morning of January 26, he found eight refugees from the *Delphine* waiting for him. Through careful questioning, Blanchard gathered enough information to send an accurate report of the cruiser's activities to Minister Charles Francis Adams in London and to the U. S. consul at Hong Kong. Later that afternoon, Blanchard, who had thus far not enjoyed his tour of duty in mostly pro-Southern Victoria, protested to Governor Darling that the raider could not be landed on the grounds that she was the *Sea King*, that she had not touched at any British port since leaving England, and was, consequently, not a warship but a pirate.[12]

Four days later the governor advised Blanchard that the law officers of the Crown had "come to the decision that, whatever may be the previous history of the *Shenandoah*, the Government of this colony is bound to treat her as a ship of war belonging to a belligerent power."[13] Undetered, the ill-tempered Blanchard, anticipating the Governor's response, had already decided to take another tack. He sent word that he would protect any *Shenandoah* crewmember who had shipped from captured American vessels. Almost immediately, eight men deserted, followed by six more later.[14]

Morale aboard the *Shenandoah* was deteriorating rapidly. After hearing a rumor that Blanchard was offering £100 to any man who jumped ship, Waddell cut off all shore liberty. Now even more men looked for an opportunity to desert. Denied help in recovering deserters by the local police department,[15] Waddell's only alternative seemed to be recruiting replacements for his rapidly thinning crew from the Melbourne waterfront.

At the same time, Waddell began to receive anonymous threatening letters; a Southern sympathizer warned of a plot from Northern agents involving a torpedo; a local carpenter installing a bureau in Waddell's cabin said that he had overheard some Americans discussing the feasibility of smuggling themselves on board and capturing the cruiser when she returned to sea. Waddell snapped back, "If it is attempted they will fail, and I will hang every mother's son of them."[16] Several times an elderly lady came to the ship with her grandchild, a 12-year-old boy whom she claimed had been born in Mobile. She said she could no longer support him, and asked that he be enlisted in the service of the Confederate States. Waddell suspected a plant and turned the old woman away.[17] Then he appealed to Thomas Lyttleton, superintendent of police, for protection. Seven days passed before Lyttleton replied that he had "instructed the Williamstown water police to give particular attention to the vessel."[18]

As repairs dragged on, Blanchard became convinced that Waddell was attempting to enlist new crew in contravention of the Foreign Enlistment Act. Deserters reported that several new recruits were already on board, identifying one of them as "Charley the cook." On Friday, February 10, Blanchard forwarded affidavits to Governor Darling demanding action. For the entire weekend the Australian authorities dodged the damning evidence, hoping the raider would finish her repairs and leave, but on Monday she was still there, and the governor's officials could no longer procrastinate.

Later in the day Superintendent Lyttleton and Inspector Beam of the Victoria police came on board in Waddell's absence and presented Lt. Grimball with a magistrate's warrant to search for a person said to be a British subject, namely, "Charley the cook."[19] Although a large police force and about 50 militia surrounded the vessel, Grimball refused to allow a search and suggested that Lyttleton refer the matter to the captain when he returned. The following day Lyttleton tried again. Waddell wrote, "I refused the search, and stated that I had neither enlisted nor shipped any person for service in the Confederate cause since my arrival."[20]

Lyttleton returned empty-handed and reported to the governor, who at once summoned the executive council into emergency session. Frustrated by Waddell's refusal to honor the search warrant, the Council drafted a message threatening to suspend repairs and detain the vessel until such time as the warrant was satisfied. Forewarned by a Southern sympathizer, and certain that the police would not try to board the vessel, Waddell convinced the slip managers to keep the workmen on board until the repairs were finished. At 4 p.m. the police took over the slip, cleared the yard, and prevented any Australians from going on board. A short time later a government messenger delivered the official letter to Waddell, stating that he had been instructed to wait for an answer.[21]

Waddell delayed his reply until 10 p.m. After fully assessing how long it would take to complete repairs, he advised Commissioner of Trade and Customs James G. Francis that he would be ready to sail on February 19. In a second letter to Francis he explained that, "the execution of the warrant was not refused, as no such person as the one (Charley the cook) therein specified was on board; but permission to search the ship was refused." Waddell stated that two Confederate officers had made a thorough search of the ship and found "no person on board except those who had entered this port as part of the complement of men."[22]

While Waddell was writing his letters to Francis, Constable Alexander Minto of the Williamstown water police noticed a boat at the cruiser's gangway, approached in his police boat, and observed four men descending rapidly from the *Shenandoah*. He chased them to the patent slip, captured two at the nearby railway station, and found the other two hiding in a water closet. Police Chief Lyttleton jailed all four on suspicion of violating the Foreign Enlistment Act. One of them, James Davidson, fit the description of "Charley the cook."[23]

In another emergency meeting of the executive council the following morning, the governor reviewed the new evidence, carefully sidestepping the issue of whether Waddell, an officer and a gentlemen, could also be a liar. During the session, a messenger arrived with a letter from Waddell, who had been told by the manager of the patent slip that the *Shenandoah* had been seized. Waddell wanted to know if the seizure had been authorized by the governor.[24]

News of the seizure circulated through the streets of Melbourne. As the Crown law officers discussed the case, furious citizens called for a town meeting at the Criterion Hotel at 3 p.m. to protest the seizure.

Governor Darling wanted a compromise and the Crown lawyers gave him one. Shortly before the town meeting was scheduled to convene, Thomas H. Fellows of the Crown Court publicly posted the following statement: "I am of the opinion that the government have not the power which they claim. A ship of war commissioned by a foreign government is exempt from the jurisdiction of the courts of other countries."[25]

Anxious to be rid of the *Shenandoah*, the governor authorized Francis to give Waddell a scolding and demand that the raider leave no later than February 19. Francis accused Waddell of sending "Charley the cook" and three other men to shore moments before releasing his statement denying any violation of the Foreign Enlistment Act. Waddell objected to the tone of Francis' letter, but admitted that four strangers had been discovered on board after a third search. Since nobody knew who they were, the stowaways had been sent to shore.[26]

On February 17, after loading 250 tons of coal, the *Shenandoah* raised steam and prepared for sea. Smoke curling from the cruiser's funnel telegraphed a signal to shore, and that night nearly 40 men gathered around a patch of bushes near the Sandridge Pier. Although the night was cloudy with poor visibility, Constable Minto, who was without his police boat, observed three boats draw up to shore, load men, and pull toward the *Shenandoah*. He could not tell whether these men were illegal recruits or regulars returning to the ship, but he thought he saw a man wearing an officer's uniform giving directions.

At the same time, Consul Blanchard sat at his desk writing a letter to the governor about Confederate recruiting activities when a Union sympathizer burst in saying that a number of men were waiting at the Sandridge Pier to join the *Shenandoah*. Excited over the opportunity of catching Waddell in the act, Blanchard dashed to the Crown Law Office with his new witness, Andrew Forbes. The office had closed for the day, however, and a Crown attorney who had returned to pick up some papers refused to help, suggesting that Blanchard see a magistrate—or take up the matter with the attorney general or minister of justice.

Blanchard raced to the police, who claimed the matter was beyond their jurisdiction, but suggested that the county magistrate could execute a warrant. Still determined, Blanchard hurried to Parliament and located George Higinbotham, the attorney general. He, too, refused to help, but suggested that he see a Mr. Sturt, a county magistrate who lived a mile away. Sturt listened to Forbes' testimony but refused to issue an affidavit or even take testimony, and told Blanchard to file the charge with the waterfront police at Williamstown, across the bay.

In a violent temper, Blanchard returned to his office, wrote down Forbes' testimony, sent it by messenger to the attorney general, grabbed Forbes, and started for Williamstown, intending to coerce the waterfront police into action. Halfway there, Forbes decided that appearing in Williamstown in company with the American consul would jeopardize his personal safety, and refused to go on. Having no case without his witness, Blanchard stormed back to his office.

Unexpectedly, George W. Robbins, a master stevedore, rushed into the consulate and informed Blanchard that he had seen boatloads of men and baggage leaving Sandridge and crossing to the *Shenandoah*. He claimed he knew some of the men by name. Discouraged and exhausted, Blanchard told Robbins to take the information to the Williamstown police.

Robbins ran back to his boat and started rowing toward Williamstown. As he neared the *Shenandoah*, he observed a boat heading in his direction, manned by a waterfront pair who had been transferring men from shore to the cruiser. Robbins recognized them as Jack Riley and Robert Muir, two shady characters, who soon overhauled Robbins and threatened to harm him if he talked. Robbins hit one on the head with an oar and smashed the other's fingers, and reached shore ahead of his pursuers. At 4 a.m., as Robbins told his story to the Williamstown police, the *Shenandoah* weighed anchor and steamed across Hobson's Bay toward the open sea.[27]

Once well at sea, strange faces emerged from hiding places below. Cornelius Hunt described the scene in his memoirs:

> A surprise awaited us upon getting fairly outside. Our ship's company had received a mysterious addition of forty-five men, who now made their appearance from every conceivable place where a human being could conceal himself from vigilant eyes. Fourteen of the number crept out of the bowsprit . . . where they had come very near ending their existence by suffocation, twenty more turned out of some water tanks which were dry; another detachment was unearthed from the lower hold, and at last the whole number of stowaways were mustered forward, and word was passed to the Captain to learn his pleasure concerning them. . . . Captain Waddell soon made his appearance, not in

the best humor . . . and demanded of our new recruits to what country they belonged and for what purpose they were there. The old sea-dogs chuckled, rolled over their tobacco, hitched up their trousers, and with one accord, protested that they were natives of the Southern Confederacy, and had come on board . . . for the purpose of joining us.[28]

In his memoirs Waddell wrote that: "The *Shenandoah's* people were not the custodians of British law and least of all of a British law which ran counter to their own immediate interests as the British Foreign Enlistment Act did. The British are the proper custodians of British law; with them alone it rests to take care that no breach of neutrality does take place in the event of an armed vessel of a belligerent power entering their ports and harbors."[29]

Although this was an oversimplification of a belligerent's responsibility toward a friendly neutral power, like other Confederate naval commanders, Waddell's standards of honor and compliance necessarily varied according to need.

After the *Shenandoah* sailed, Victoria newspapers printed Robbins' story and announced that Waddell had shipped from 40 to 80 British subjects. Muir and Riley confessed, and drew brief jail terms for assaulting Robbins. James "Charley the cook" Davidson and his three accomplices went to trial in mid-March, drawing a packed courtroom of mostly Southern sympathizers. It quickly became evident that as far as the prosecution was concerned, the *Shenandoah* was on trial, not "Charley the cook."

Early in the trial, Defense Attorney Aspinall confounded the prosecutor by asking him to prove that the Confederate States and the United States were at war. Without proof of war, there could be no violation of the Foreign Enlistment Act. Stunned, the prosecutor subpoenaed Consul Blanchard to testify that the Confederate States were in fact a government. Blanchard flew into a rage, claimed that the summons was an outright insult, and reminded Governor Darling that the authorities had allowed the ship into port *because* she was a belligerent, and now expected him to provide the proof. Darling apologetically replied that it was all a mistake.

After several days of confused testimony, buttressed by a rowdy courtroom who favored acquittal, James "Charley" Davidson and his three companions faced the judge and received their sentences. Since all four of the men had already been in jail 30 days, Davidson and one of his cohorts received 10-day sentences. One man was released because he was American, and the other because he was 17.

Australia considered the case closed, although Waddell and his band of officers were branded as liars. No protest of the insult came from the Confederate government, however. By the time news of the trial reached Richmond, the Confederate Government had ceased to exist.[30]

Arctic Nightmare

A S THE *Shenandoah* sailed into the South Pacific, not a single Union cruiser lay ahead to stop her. The sailing sloop *Jamestown* was laid up at Shanghai for repairs. The *Wyoming*, once stationed at Batavia, had been ordered home. The *Iroquois* struggled under short canvas across the Indian Ocean toward Singapore.

When news of the *Shenandoah*'s appearance at Melbourne reached Washington in late March, Welles sent the *Wyoming* after her. Based on the usual rumors and false reports, Welles believed the South Pacific or the coast of Chile would become the raider's new cruising grounds. Instead, Waddell cruised north for the Okhotsk Sea off eastern Siberia and the great American whaling fleet.

A month passed without capturing a prize. Bad weather forced Waddell to bypass the northern coast of New Zealand, a popular hunting ground for whalers. The officers, still doubting their commander's competency, felt he had let a little headwind cause them to miss a grand opportunity.

A short distance south of the Equator the *Shenandoah* raised tiny Drummond Island, a watering stop for northbound whalers. A canoe manned by three naked natives covered with tattoos came alongside, and Waddell learned through a Malay crewman who spoke the language that no whalers had stopped at the island for several months. Disappointed, he raised steam after trading for some fruit and continued north.[1] A few days later he learned from the Hawaiian schooner *Pelin*, a neutral tortoise shell trader plying the Caroline Islands, that five whalers had been seen at Ponape. The cruiser raced for the island before the northeast trades, hoping to catch up with the Yankees before they started north.

On the morning of April 1, Totolom, Ponape's jungle-covered peak, rose above the fog. As the mist cleared the lookout reported four sail in the harbor and a small boat coming out from shore. The boatman looked like a native with his brown, tattooed body, but he introduced himself in English as Thomas Hardrocke, an escaped convict from Australia who had married a native girl and settled on the island. Hardrocke agreed to lead the raider safely into harbor for $30 worth of whiskey and tobacco. To ensure his pilot's fealty, Waddell strapped on his pistol and jumped into the canoe with him, threatening to kill him if any damage befell the *Shenandoah*. Four vessels raised their colors—three American and one Hawaiian—as the raider eased into the anchorage. Waddell announced his arrival by firing a 12-pounder and dispatching four armed prize crews. At the sound of the gun the curious natives lining the shore fled into the jungle.[2]

John Grimball returned with the papers of the *Edward Carey* of San Francisco, followed by Smith Lee with the *Hector* of New Bedford, Fred Chew, the *Pearl* of New London, and Dabney Scales, the *Harvest* of Oahu. Only the *Harvest* proved a problem. Although a bill of sale showed a legal transfer to Hawaiian owners, she carried American flags in her hold, had an American registry, a Yankee master, and listed the same mates who had sailed on previous voyages. The *Shenandoah*'s officers initially accepted the transfer as legitimate, but on the basis of some technical irregularities, Waddell declared the vessel a fair prize and condemned all four ships.[3]

Later in the afternoon a small boat bearing the masters of the whalers came through the channel from shore. At the sight of the bounty crews stripping provisions and equipment from their ships, the captains guessed what had happened and pulled for shore. Waddell sent a boat after them, and within an hour had them in irons.

Among the most valuable plunder taken from the prizes were several whaling charts, which showed every track the whalers took and where they had been most successful in taking whales. Waddell noted: "The charts were all important. . . . With such charts in my possession I not only held the key to the navigation of all the Pacific Islands, the Okhotsk and Bering seas, and the Arctic Ocean, but the most probable localities for finding the great Arctic whaling fleet of New England without a tiresome search."[4]

On April 2 Waddell sent Master's Mate Hunt and Hardrocke, the escaped convict, to shore to open discussions with the native king for the disposal of the prizes. Hunt found the village filthy and filled with "ferocious-looking" villains who glared at him as a prospect for their next barbecue. Hunt described the king as "a miserable little savage, scarcely more than five feet high, naked with the exception of a tappa made of grass worn about his waist, and smeared from head to foot with coconut oil." According to Hardrocke, the king had recently poisoned his wife in order to remarry. When Waddell later met the king's new mate, he declared that "the queen was downright ugly, the first really ugly woman I have ever seen."[5]

Hoping to convince him that the whalers were desperate enemies who deserved to be destroyed, Waddell invited the king and his retinue to visit the *Shenandoah*. After a shower of gifts, including 70 old muskets, the king began to warm to his new Southern benefactors. Told that his tribe could remove anything they wanted from the prizes before they were burned, the king agreed to retain the prisoners in exchange for the plunder, so long as Waddell agreed not to fire the big guns again and scare his people. With negotiations ended, the king handed Waddell a basket of coconuts and two dead hens wrapped in coconut leaves. Waddell responded by giving the king a silk scarf. Not to be outdone, the king presented Waddell with the royal princess. With help from Hardrocke's interpretive skill, Waddell diplomatically skirted the issue without arousing the proud father's displeasure.

For the next week, while the whalers were gradually stripped of valuables, first by the prize crews and then by the natives, the officers and crew enjoyed a romp on shore. As the native men would trade anything for tobacco—including their wives and daughters—the crew in particular enjoyed this interlude.

Meanwhile, at Appomattox Courthouse, Virginia, a saddened Robert E. Lee surrendered to Ulysses S. Grant. The bad news would travel slowly.

Before leaving Ponape, Waddell landed all the *Shenandoah*'s prisoners, except for seven men who elected to join the cruiser's crew. In his memoirs, Waddell wrote: "The morning of the 13th of April saw all prisoners clear of the *Shenandoah* and at noon her anchors were tripped and she stood to sea, leaving to the tender care of the king and his tribe one hundred and thirty disappointed whalers who had been in the habit of ill treating and cheating the natives and had introduced diseases . . . before unknown to them and for which the poor creatures knew no care."[6]

On April 3 incendiaries set the bark *Pearl* afire, and torched the others as the natives finished relieving them of valuables. Smoke curled skyward from the sheltered lagoon of Ponape for more than a week.

For six weeks the *Shenandoah* worked north through periods of sweltering heat punctuated by vicious typhoons. Across the 45th parallel the weather changed to thick fog banks and sudden snow squalls. Surgeon Lining called for woolens and suggested that the men stay below until needed on deck. On May 21 the weather cleared; in the distance rose the snow-covered peaks of the Kuriles, a string of volcanic islands between the northern tip of Japan and Siberia's Kamchatka peninsula.

As the raider entered the Okhotsk Sea, the patches of floating ice dotting the waves thickened gradually into solid fields, and Waddell doubled the lookouts. Unlike the typical whaler, the *Shenandoah* had not been built to withstand ice. All night passing floes scraped against the thin-hulled cruiser. Anxious to be out of the ice, Waddell studied the whaling charts for clues to the location of the missing whalers, and decided to head for Shantaski Island, northwest of Sakhalim, where Yankee ships sometimes congregated.

On May 27, while moving along the edge of an ice field in a light fog, the lookout reported a sail on the opposite side. For several hours the two ships cruised parallel, separated by five miles of ice. When a channel opened, Waddell raised the Russian ensign and initiated his first pursuit since leaving Ponape. At 500 yards the gunners fired a blank charge, but the whaler sailed on, unconscious of a threat until Whittle shouted, "Heave to on the starboard tack, damn quick!"

Captain Ebenezer Nye of the *Abigail* had been expecting a Russian supply vessel, but not a Confederate raider. Thomas S. Manning, one of the *Abigail's* mates, turned to his captain and complained, "You are more fortunate in picking up Confederate cruisers than whales. I will never go with you again, for if there is a cruiser out you will find her."[7] Manning claimed that Nye had lost a ship to the *Alabama*, but this later proved to be one of many lies that Manning told. Manning, who was from Baltimore, professed Confederate sympathies, and knew the whaling grounds, signed aboard the *Shenandoah* as acting master's mate. Fourteen of the 35 men captured on the *Abigail* eventually joined the Confederate Navy.[8]

Although the *Abigail* carried little oil or whalebone, she was well supplied with barrels of whiskey, brandy, rum, pure alcohol, and cases of wines and cordials that Nye had hoped to trade for furs with the northern natives. Unfortunately, the *Shenandoah's* prize crew found them instead. When they failed to return, Waddell sent a second crew, and in a short time they also succumbed. Finally, Whittle went over with an armed party and ordered the drunks topside. When they refused he sent men below to get them, but they elected to stay below, too. Whittle then called for the marines, who arrived with good intentions, but soon joined the party as well.

Meanwhile the lookouts had reported another sail, and Waddell ordered his officers to get over to the *Abigail* immediately and bring back all the men. After they boarded, the officers paused for a little refreshment and got drunk themselves—but in a more gentlemanly fashion. Finally, a few clear minds managed to get everyone back on board—along with quantities of liberated alcohol—but before the drunken crew could get the ship underway, the whaler had vanished in a squall.[9]

Seamen dropped to the deck to sleep it off; Waddell locked the drunken officers in the wardroom. Enraged at the behavior of his officers and the loss of a prize, he issued this order to Whittle:

> Sir: Private appropriation of prize property is prohibited. All articles sent from prizes to the ship must be sent to you, to be transferred to the paymaster's department. You will be pleased to call the attention of the officers to this order, and require rigid adherence to it. Any violation of it, coming under your observation, must be brought to my knowledge.[10]

But Waddell's tenuous grip on discipline was loosening further. The men ignored the order, kept their personal stock, and on Sunday, half the crew got drunk again and stayed that way for four days. During this period Waddell suspended Scales, sent his clerk, J. C. Blacker, into the steerage and disrated the boatswain's mate, before eventually restoring order.

Although the crew sobered up, they continued to complain, especially the officers, who sought every opportunity to criticize the captain and find fault in his every action, even one based apparently on friendship. On the evening of June 3, three days after the drunkenness stopped, Waddell, who usually dined alone, entered the officer's mess in full uniform carrying several bottles of champagne. It was Jefferson Davis's 57th birthday and an occasion to celebrate; many toasts were drunk to the success of a government that no longer existed and a president imprisoned in Fortress Monroe. Coming on the heels of the harsh punishment for unauthorized drinking, the irony of the affair in the officer's mess did not go unnoticed.

The ice continued to thicken, and still no whalers were sighted. Finally, on June 6 Waddell turned the vessel south and headed for the Bering Sea. As the ship passed Jonas Island, the watch counted 10 whalers tucked safely behind an impenetrable field of ice.

After leaving the Amphrite Strait, the *Shenandoah* sped north before a blustery wind. But as the warm Japanese current mixed with the frigid waters of the shallow Bering Sea, the weather changed suddenly to thick black fog, so dense that light barely penetrated. On June 21 the sky cleared to reveal what looked like a nearby sail as well as the coast of Siberia five miles to port. The short chase ended when the sail proved to be a rock, but pieces of butchered blubber drifting on the current foretold better hunting ahead.[11]

By the summer of 1865, the once huge North Pacific whaling fleet had been reduced to 85 ships by the introduction of kerosene—a cost-effective competitor for whale oil. By June 22 the *Shenandoah* had already reduced that count by six. Ten whalers had escaped at Jonas Island, protected by the ice. Eleven more ships were moving northward through the Pacific and had not yet reached the whaling grounds. This left 58 vessels in the Bering Sea or in the Arctic, hunting whales.[12]

At 9 a.m. on June 22, the lookouts reported two ships, and Waddell prepared his best prize crews for the difficult feat of capturing both vessels simultaneously. The preparations proved unnecessary. The 495-ton *William Thompson* had a whale lashed to her side, and Waddell dropped off Orris Browne with a prize crew as he passed. The master of the 364-ton *Euphrates*, believing that the steamer flying Russian colors was friendly, made no effort to escape and concentrated on the business of whaling, until the *Shenandoah* fired a blast from her signal gun. Smith Lee boarded the *Euphrates*, removed the prisoners and navigation instruments, and set her afire.[13]

When Waddell returned to the *William Thompson*, Francis Smith, the ship's master, insisted that the war had ended. Since he had no proof, Waddell suspected that Smith was simply trying to protect his ship. By 3 the next morning, the *William Thompson*, largest of the New Bedford whalers, had been plundered of her stores and torched. Waddell moved on, unsure of his country's status.[14]

The following day the lookouts had eight vessels in sight at one time.[15] Still flying the Russian flag, the *Shenandoah* ran close to the nearest vessel, the 410-ton *Milo* of New Bedford, and dropped off a prize crew. Her captain, Richard Baker, came aboard and remarked that he had heard the *Shenandoah* had been in Australia, but did not expect to see her "up here," especially since the war had ended. Again, Waddell asked for proof. Baker, who had the information secondhand from other captains who had read it in the San Francisco newspapers, had none. Waddell hesitated, and decided to bond the *Milo* for $46,000—a good opportunity to rid himself of the numerous prisoners he expected to crowd his decks before the day was out.[16]

The unusual activity did not go unnoticed aboard two nearby whalers; when the breeze suddenly freshened, they added sail and moved off in opposite directions. Waddell brought the *Milo's* crew aboard to prevent their escaping and went in pursuit. The first vessel headed into the ice, hoping to find safety among the floes. A 32-pound shot from the

Whitworth barely missed the figurehead, but failed to stop her. A second shot ripped through the main topsail and finally ended the chase. Moses Tucker, master of the 426-ton *Sophia Thornton*, came about and worked back to the *Shenandoah's* prize boat. Waddell stuffed Tucker and his mates into the forward coal bunker and steamed after the other ship.

Captain Thomas Williams of the 428-ton *Jireh Swift* almost reached the safety of the Siberian coast before the wind changed. By the time Smith Lee reached the *Swift*, Williams and his crew had their trunks packed, prepared for the inevitable. Thirty minutes after her capture, the ship burst into flame.

With four more sail still in sight, Waddell chased the closest two, but found them to be foreign. Two other vessels had seen the smoke and snugged into ice floes, temporarily out of danger. The captains of the three prizes all held differing opinions about the end of the war. Captain Williams told Waddell that "He did not believe the war was over, but believed the South would yield eventually."[17] This helped mollify Waddell's misgivings, at least for a while.

Waddell returned to the *Milo* and sent all the prisoners to the *Sophia Thornton* with instructions to remove whatever they needed for the voyage to California, set fire to the vessel, and return to the *Milo*. To prevent the prisoners from sailing away, Waddell had his carpenters cut down all the *Thornton's* spars. As he went after two other vessels, smoke rising from the *Thornton* confirmed that his orders had been followed.[18]

Ebenezer Nye, the *Abigail's* unpredictable master, had his own ideas, however. Although he was under parole and could have been executed if recaptured, he decided to eschew the comfortable voyage to California in the *Milo* and spread the alarm. He and his first mate sailed north 187 miles in an open whaleboat to Cape Bering, where he was picked up by the *Mercury*, and was able to warn five other whalers that the raider was coming.[19]

As the *Sophia Thornton* burned in the distance, the busy *Shenandoah*, under U.S. colors, overhauled the 159-ton *Susan Abigail*, fresh from San Francisco with a stack of California newspapers. Her captain, seeing the Stars and Stripes, climbed on board the *Shenandoah* expecting to enjoy a social call. When Waddell gave him a very different greeting, he was shocked. To the *Susan Abigail's* captain, there was no doubt that the war was over. Both he and his mate had heard the guns of the Presidio thunder in final victory as they left San Francisco. While still inside the Golden Gate they had read of Lincoln's assassination and lowered their flag to half mast.

But Waddell read a different story in the newspapers. One said that, "the Southern Government had been removed to Danville, and that the greater part of the Army of Virginia had joined General Johnston in North Carolina where an indecisive battle had been fought with General Sherman . . . at Danville a proclamation was issued by President Davis, announcing that the war would be carried on with renewed vigor, and exhorting the people of the South to bear up heroically under their calamities."[20]

Certainly Waddell recognized that without a war and without a country, any further depredations against Union vessels would be considered piracy. But when he and his officers left the South, the Confederacy's military had been dominant. They had never heard the details of the crushing defeats that followed, despite what they occasionally read in the enemy's press. Without absolute evidence, it's no wonder that Waddell could not accept the idea that his country had been defeated. Although he was clearly worried, he ordered the *Susan Abigail* burned. As his president ordered, he would carry on the war with renewed vigor.

By June 24 the *Shenandoah* had sailed so far north that "night and day were mere arbitrary terms."[21] The Bering Strait, just above St. Lawrence Island, seemed a solid field of ice, but still Waddell pushed cautiously forward, looking for open channels through the ice. The following day he captured and burned the 419-ton *General Williams* of New London, referring to her querulous and sniveling master as "a dirty old dog."[22]

Under the midnight sun on June 26, the *Shenandoah* collected five more prizes. At 1:30 a.m., a prize crew boarded the 389-ton bark *William C. Nye*, six months out of San Francisco and already laden with 240 barrels of oil. The moment Captain Cootey and his crew climbed aboard the raider, Waddell hurried to the next vessel, the 384-ton *Catherine*. Within 30 minutes the prize crew removed the prisoners and lit the match. Before the first flames leapt skyward, the *Shenandoah* steamed after her third prize.

Smith Lee boarded the 340-ton *Nimrod* and recognized a familiar face. The master, James Clark, had been captain of the *Ocean Rover* when she was captured by the *Alabama*. Clark and Lee had known each other well, and Clark was horrified to see Lee coming over the rail once again. Not waiting to exchange pleasantries, Lee hustled the enraged captain and prisoners over to the cruiser and fired the prize.

With nearly 200 prisoners crammed aboard the shorthanded *Shenandoah* and two more prizes in sight, Waddell confined the masters and mates to the coal hold and loaded their shivering crews into 12 whale boats. With the prison boats under tow, the *Shenandoah* steamed toward her next conquest. According to Hunt, "It was a singular scene upon which we now looked. . . . Behind us were three blazing ships, wildly drifting amid gigantic fragments of ice; close astern were the twelve whaleboats with their living freight; and ahead of us were five other vessels now evidently aware of their danger but seeing no avenue of escape. It was a tortuous way we now had to pursue, winding about among the ice floes, like the trail of a serpent. Six knots an hour was the highest speed we dared to attempt, so intricate was the navigation. . . ."[23]

Waddell passed the next vessel by, as the prisoners warned him smallpox was aboard, and headed for the General Pike. The Pike had lost her master, and First Mate Hebron Crowell, who had taken charge, asked Waddell to bond his ship as a special favor, arguing that "if you ransom the vessel her owners will think me well to do in getting her out of this scrape, and it will give me a claim on them for the command."[24] Waddell needed a cartel, liked Crowell's candid appeal, and bonded the vessel for $30,000. Unfortuantely, Crowell repaid the favor with a blistering account in the Pike's log: "Waddell, the pirate chief . . . said he should put about 160 men on board of me, but instead of that the brute, as he is, put 222 men on board, making with my own crew 252 men all told, crowded into this small ship. . . . As I was leaving the pirate ship to return to my ship he said that if I did not have provisions enough on board to reach San Francisco I must cook Kanakas (Hawaiians) as I had plenty of them."[25]

Before releasing the Pike, Waddell took two more prizes, the 315-ton Isabella and the 360-ton Gipsey. Three Yankee captains pleaded with Waddell to bond their vessels; the war was over. Waddell refused to listen, commenting that he could not believe what he read in Northern newspapers.[26] By midnight both ships were burned and all personnel transferred to the General Pike, ending a hectic and exhausting 24 hours for the officers and crew of the Shenandoah. But the destruction had not ended.

The raider steamed north through thickening ice fields. At 6:30 a.m. on June 28, the lookout sighted Diomede Island to the northeast and soon afterward reported a bark. The 327-ton New Bedford whaler Waverly, trapped in a dead calm, became an easy prize, and a magnificent pyre. Waddell continued north into the Bering Strait, flying the colors of the United States and still believing that the Confederate banner was backed by a legitimate government.

Shortly after noon Captain A. T. Potter of the whaler Brunswick, leaking badly from an earlier collision with an iceberg, looked for another vessel to take his cargo of oil before his ship sank. There were 10 whaleships in the area, and negotiations were underway aboard the nearby *Congress* to see who would help. The other captains, anxious to fill their own casks, refused to take the oil. Potter saw two more whalers headed for the group; perhaps they would take his cargo. Fog rolled in as the *Hillman* and the *Martha* drew near; when it lifted, Potter saw a black steamer cruising slowly among the whale ships. Thinking his prayers had been answered, he shoved off in a whale boat to ask for assistance. After explaining his problems to a deck officer on the steamer, he received a courteous but brief reply: "We are very busy now, but in a little while we will attend to you."[27] Potter returned to the *Brunswick* with new hope, not realizing that the steamer was busily preparing five prize crews for a coordinated raid.

While still in Ponape, Waddell had heard that S. L. Gray, master of the whaler *James Maury*, had died, and that Mrs. Gray and her three small children were still aboard. She was carrying her husband's body home in a cask of whiskey for a proper Christian burial, and was continuing the voyage, transferring command to First Mate Cunningham. Waddell had been inquiring for the *Maury*, and Potter obligingly pointed her out. Waddell sent Lt. Chew to take her, with instructions to assure Mrs. Gray that she and her ship would be spared. After Cunningham signed a $37,000 ransom bond, Waddell sent a message back to Mrs. Gray, informing her that "she and the children were under the protection of the *Shenandoah* and no harm would come to her or the vessel, that the men of the South did not make war upon women and children."[28]

Meanwhile, Lt. Whittle and his boarding party faced a very different situation with the whaling bark *Favorite*. Captain Young, a gray-haired old giant, stood beside a harpoon gun with a revolver in one hand and a cutlass in the other; the crew crouched behind the bulwark with their muskets leveled. When Whittle ordered them to lay down their weapons, Young threatened to open fire with his bomb gun. Unwilling to risk an unnecessary fight, Whittle returned to confer with Waddell. In a few minutes, the towering *Shenandoah* steamed alongside the *Favorite* and ran out four guns. Waddell sent the boarding party back to the whaler, advising Young that at the first shot he would open fire. Young, who had now substituted a whiskey bottle for the cutlass, hollered that he had been under fire before and that it didn't bother him, but the crew, unreinforced by spirits, threw down their weapons. Whittle grabbed Young, still ranting and raving, and discovered that he had forgotten to cap his pistol. Master's Mate Hunt wrote: "It was evident that he had been seeking spirituous consolation; indeed to be plain about it, he was at least three sheets to the wind, but by general consent he was voted to be the bravest and most resolute man we captured during the cruise."[29]

The *Shenandoah* moved slowly through the fleet, taking off stores and prisoners and leaving burning whaleships in her wake: The 399-ton *Isaac Howland*; the 350-ton Baltimore-built *Covington*; the *Hillman* and the *Martha*, commanded by the brothers Macomber; the 40-year-old *Nassau*. Master Daniel Wood, who had wrecked the *Fabius* off the coast of California four years before and the *Polar Star* in the Okhotsk Sea five months later, now watched as his third command, the *Congress*, burst into flames. Captain Young's *Favorite* followed last. The *Brunswick* tipped on her side and remained partially afloat, supported by the buoyancy of her oil casks. By 10 p.m., smoke from eight charred hulls spiraled skyward in the Arctic twilight, a sad climax to a busy day.[30] Waddell packed the cartels *James Maury* and the old bark *Nile*, which had had 11 masters during its jinxed two-year voyage, with 336 prisoners and a stock of provisions.

Shortly after midnight on June 29 the *Shenandoah* passed through the Bering Strait, with Siberia in sight to port and Alaska to starboard, and entered the Arctic Ocean, following a tip. Thomas Manning had learned from several Yankee whalers that 60 vessels had passed through the Bering Strait 10 days earlier, headed north. Although Waddell doubted it, he could not ignore the opportunity.

By midday the *Shenandoah* reached the edge of an impenetrable ice field. After cruising the rim for several hours without finding an opening and bringing up hard against two ice floes, Waddell turned back, noting, "In consequence of her great length, the immensity of the icebergs and floes, and the danger of being shut in the Arctic Ocean for several months, I was induced to turn her head southward, and she reached East Cape just in time to slip by the Diomedes when a vast field of floe ice was closing the strait."[31] There were also three cartels headed for San Francisco that would report his position. He noted that: "The time had arrived to take the steamer out of these constricted waters into more open seas. . . ." For once, Waddell's officers unanimously seconded his decision.

Since leaving Melbourne on February 18, the *Shenandoah* had captured 29 vessels—three bonded for $124,600, four at Ponape appraised at $117,759, and 21 burned between May 27 and June 28 appraised at $843,028. With the exception of the four whalers destroyed at Ponape, all had been captured after the fall of the Confederacy. Word of this destruction finally reached the United States on July 20, when the *Milo* limped into San Francisco. Captain David McDougal reported the news to Secretary Welles, but the message inexplicably failed to reach his desk until August 18, long after the raider had gone.[32]

Waddell left the Arctic whaling grounds and headed for California, toying with a plan to attack the shipping at San Francisco. But first he must somehow find out whether or not the war had really ended. He could not trust the word of whalers on long voyages, out of contact and willing to believe any rumor. Long before he got there he found his worst fears realized: it was no rumor.

Cruiser Without A Country

A s THE *Shenandoah* headed south, Waddell pondered his next strategy. He could cruise off the coast of Baja California and pounce on
steamers carrying rich cargoes between Panama and San Francisco. Or
he could launch a daring raid on San Francisco itself.[1] From captured
newspapers, Waddell read that an old shipmate, Captain David Mc-
Dougal, commanded the navy yard at Mare Island. "McDougal was fond
of his ease. I did not feel that he would be in our way, any officer of the
Shenandoah was more than a match for Mc in activity and will. There
was no other vessel of war there, as I concluded from San Francisco
newspaper reports, and to enter that port after night and collide with
the iron ram (USS *Saginaw*) was easy enough, and with our force
thrown upon the ironclad's deck and in possession of her hatches, no
life need to have been lost. Mc could have been with the officers secured, and e'er daylight came, both batteries could have been sprung on
the city and my demands enforced."[2]

At San Francisco, the story of the *Shenandoah*'s exploits began to
emerge. California newsmen repeated an item from the June 24 *Hono-
lulu Advertiser* that the Hawaiian schooner *Pfiel* had been stopped by
the raider, and that she was hunting whalers. On July 20, Charles
James, San Francisco's customs collector, wrote the Secretary of the
Treasury that the *Milo*, 28 days from the Arctic, had just arrived with
"the crews of 10 whalers."[3]

Following an earlier dispatch to Welles that failed to reach him for
nearly four weeks, on July 23 McDougal wrote:

> Great apprehensions felt by mercantile community of San Francisco
> in consequence of depredations of *Shenandoah*. Merchant ship own-
> ers and underwriters have addressed memorial requesting me to tele-
> graph department for authority to charter, arm and man steamer
> *Colorado* of Pacific Mail Company to pursue that vessel.[4]

With no word from Washington, McDougal dallied at Mare Island,
unsure what to do. He had no warship to chase the *Shenandoah*, and no

idea where to begin looking; nevertheless, the public fumed over the navy's inaction. Just as the uproar over the arrival of the *Milo* subsided, the *General Pike* limped into port with another load of prisoners. The following day, headlines in the *Alta California* accused the government of apathy and called for private initiatives, suggesting that vessels "be fitted out with an armament equal to the task of taking the *Shenandoah*."⁵

By the time Welles received McDougal's wayward correspondence on August 18, Waddell's focus had shifted from aggression to survival. He had decided to bypass San Francisco and concentrate on the treasure ships, but he first wanted to shed any doubt that the war had ended. "Prudence indicated communication with a vessel recently from San Francisco before attempting the ransom enterprise."⁶

On August 2, Irvine Bulloch boarded the British bark *Barracouta*, 13 days out of San Francisco, and returned with a stack of recent newspapers that told the story: Lee and Johnston surrendered, all the armies in the field gone, Jefferson Davis imprisoned in irons, and the navies of the world searching the seas for the *Shenandoah*—a ship without a country, and in the eyes of the world, a true pirate: They had destroyed 21 vessels and bonded four others after hostilities had ended.

Cornelius Hunt wrote: "It was as though every man had just learned of the death of a near and dear relative." Dr. Lining lamented: "This is doomed to be one of the blackest of all the black days of my life, for from today I must look forward to begin life over again, starting where I cannot tell, how I cannot say—but I have learned for a certainty that I have no country."⁷ Dabney Scales wrote in the ship's log:

> Having received . . . the sad intelligence of the overthrow of the Confederate Government, all attempts to destroy the shipping or property of the United States will cease from this date, in accordance with which the first lieutenant, William C. Whittle, Jr., received the order from the commander to strike below the battery and disarm the ship and crew.⁸

Waddell, without true authority and haunted by doubt, sought the views of his officers. One suggested that the *Shenandoah* be blown up, and the ship's company allowed to seek refuge in a foreign land. Another claimed that the raider now belonged to the enemy and should be surrendered at the nearest American port. Others suggested that Waddell go to a British or French port and surrender the ship as public property; the men belonged to no government, and should be free to leave without fear of arrest. Some feared that the mongrel crew would mutiny once they realized that no nation backed the captain's authority.

The crewmen who rowed Bulloch to the *Barracouta* had seen the head-lines and knew that their ship had been labeled a pirate—a crime that Whittle described as "not against one nation but against all. A pirate is an enemy to mankind, and as such amenable to trial and punishment under the laws of nations, by the courts of the country into whose hands he may fall."⁹ Already the men were stirring.

On August 3, Waddell headed for Sydney, hoping to find safety and sympathy among the friendly Australians. But the debate over their fate continued, and before the sun set that evening, Waddell changed course: Liverpool was home to most of the men; it was nonsense to turn them penniless upon a strange continent. Despite pressure from other officers to seek refuge in Sydney, Cape Town, New Zealand, or any nearby British port, Waddell set course for Cape Horn, knowing that once rounded, he would have several days before the crew realized that they were not headed for South Africa, but Great Britain.

The crew petitioned Waddell for a commitment, and at 1 p.m. he addressed them briefly, complimenting them for their fidelity, confirm-ing the war's end, and stating that he would take the vessel into the "nearest English port." Both officers and men cheered and voted him their trust. After several weeks, however, the men began to wonder what the captain meant when he promised them the "nearest English port." Few suspected that he meant Liverpool. In his notes Waddell wrote: "I first thought that a port in the South Atlantic would answer all my purposes . . . but upon reflection I saw the propriety of avoiding those ports and determined to run the ship for a European port, which involved a distance of 17,000 miles—a long gauntlet to run and escape. . . . I considered it due the honor of all concerned that to avoid everything like a show of dread under the severe trial imposed upon me was my duty as a man and an officer in whose hands was placed the honor of my country's flag and the welfare of 132 men."¹⁰

The *Shenandoah*, again an innocent merchantman with every war-like vestige stowed below, sailed south, avoiding the popular sea lanes, her lookouts no longer scanning the horizon for ships to chase, but to avoid. Hunt observed that "the hilarity which had so long been observ-able through the ship was now gone, and there were only anxious faces to be seen in the cabin, wardroom and forecastle. . . ."

Sailing fast before strong westerlies, the *Shenandoah* found herself being overhauled by a vessel cut much like a man-of-war. Waddell added sail, but still the stranger came on. She proved to be an English mer-chantman, a close counterpart to the *Shenandoah*, built by the same firm on the Clyde. Hunt wrote: "It was the first time we had fallen in with a vessel that could outsail us, and had we been in equally good trim with the Englishman, I do not think either would have had an opportunity of claiming a victory."[11] Nonetheless, the fact that they had been outsailed bothered them: speed was their sole protection.

Even before rounding Cape Horn, the seeds of discontent, bred of uncertainty and months of close confinement, began to grow. Officers and crew argued among themselves and with each other. Fights broke out. Even Waddell lost patience: Although he later countermanded the orders when he realized the burden it placed on the other officers, he relieved Scales for oversleeping, Hunt and Browne for protesting his orders, and Lee for smoking on deck while on watch.

After rounding the Cape, stiff gales pushed the *Shenandoah* deep into the South Atlantic, once again among towering icebergs. With barely enough coal remaining to ballast the ship and run the boilers to produce fresh water, the ship rolled and pitched until the officers and crew grew indifferent to their misery and longed for land—any land. Waddell edged northeastward, on an apparent course for Cape Town. When the weather settled, the entire ship's company developed an intense interest in the science of navigation.

On September 26, everyone knew that the ship had reached a point where another day's run would reveal Waddell's destination: If he turned east, it was South Africa; if he continued north, it was Europe. The crew split into two camps—one strongly favoring Cape Town and the other England.

On the morning of the 28th, six officers handed Waddell a signed petition recommending that the vessel be taken to Cape Town. The petition closed with a pledge of support should the captain choose to land elsewhere: "We leave all that with perfect confidence in your judgment." A second petition, drawn up by James Blacker, the captain's clerk, and signed by 10 junior officers, took a more challenging tone. It questioned the captain's judgment, listing several reasons why he should land at South Africa and not attempt to reach England, including the risk of being taken by a warship and tried as pirates. Waddell fumed at Blacker that, "I will be captain, sir, or die on this deck."

With the exception of Lt. Chew, who had consistently annoyed the captain throughout the cruise, none of the senior officers had signed either petition. Four junior officers had refused to sign as well.[12]

With control of the vessel at stake, Waddell summoned a council of the senior officers—Whittle, Grimball, Scales, Lee, and Chew. After showing them the petitions, he explained that his original intention had been to go to Cape Town, but after further evaluation, he thought it best to go to Europe. After he explained his reasoning, he left the decision to his lieutenants. Whittle, who favored Cape Town, declined to vote; as executive officer, he was duty-bound to support the captain. The others voted three to one in favor of Liverpool.

On September 29, Waddell received a third letter, signed by five officers and 71 petty officers and crewmen, that revealed a strong difference of opinion with the junior officers and supported his decision to take the vessel either to England or France.

> Sir: We, the undersigned, take the liberty of writing this petition in consequence of a certain paper purporting to be the petition of the crew having been laid formerly before you. Sir, in complete denial of this paper and its object, and of petitioning you on such a subject whatsoever, and to show our complete reliance and trust in whatever it should please you to do under any circumstances is the earnest and sincere feeling which has caused us to lay this before you.[13]

Surgeon Lining, who had excluded his name from any of the petitions but remained an interested party, wrote: "I consider this the smartest thing the Captain has ever done on board this ship. He knew before he called them (the senior officers) into the cabin the opinion of every officer, because this thing had been openly and loudly and angrily discussed, time and time again, in the wardroom, where every word could be heard in the cabin. He knew that he would have a majority on his side. He left out of the Council, Bulloch, who had always heretofore been called in—not to mention other officers who were present at important consultations. . . . In this way, certain that it would be decided as he wished, he threw all the responsibility on the shoulders of the Council, and said goodly, 'Gentlemen, I will be guided by you.' "[14] Although Lining might accuse Waddell of "rigging the jury," the verdict satisfied the crew, most of whom preferred to take their chances back home compared with the uncertainty of landing at Cape Town, or in some deserted bay, as the junior officers had suggested.

The crisis over the petitions passed, and the ship's company steeled themselves to the last leg of their voyage home. Although Waddell now knew he had the crew's endorsement, there remained dissension within the wardroom. When the *Shenandoah* crossed the path of her outbound voyage, Waddell sent in a bottle of champagne, congratulating the officers for being aboard the only Confederate warship to circle the globe. Three of the Cape Town advocates refused the gesture and walked out.[15] For the rest of the voyage, the wardroom suffered from constant bickering, bouts of drunkenness, accusations of theft, gun-pointing threats, and challenges of duels to be fought once ashore. Waddell tried to maintain discipline, but he felt that he no longer had the power to punish without running the risk of creating a larger, more unmanageable problem.[16]

Near dusk on October 25, two weeks after crossing the equator, the lookouts reported a steamer under short sail. The ship appeared to be positioning herself to cross the *Shenandoah*'s track. Waddell didn't want to arouse suspicion by changing course while he could still be seen, and ordered the sails trimmed and the propeller lowered to slow the ship. As the sun set, the lookouts confirmed that the stranger was a man-of-war. After dark, with the vessel only three miles off, Waddell put the cruiser under a full head of steam, using smokeless Cardiff coal, and stood due east for 15 miles before again heading north. By morning, the mysterious stranger had disappeared from sight.[17]

Waddell kept the *Shenandoah* under sail during the day but changed to steam at night as they neared the southern coast of Europe—the cheering smells of land fragrant on the offshore breeze. Since leaving the Aleutians, 122 days and more than 23,000 miles had passed without sighting land. On the morning of November 5, as a thick fog lifted, the green shores of Ireland shone off the port beam. Late that evening, the *Shenandoah* hailed a pilot boat off St. George's Channel.[18]

To the age-old question, "What ship is this?" Whittle casually answered, "The late Confederate steamer *Shenandoah*." "The hell you say," said the pilot. "I was reading but a few days ago of her being in the Arctic Ocean."

The voyage of the *Shenandoah* had come to an end. Waddell wrote: "On the morning of the 6th of November, 1865, the *Shenandoah* steamed up the Mersey in a thick fog under the Confederate flag, and the pilot, by my order, anchored near H.B.M. ship of the line *Donegal*, commanded by Captain Paynter, R.N."[19]

Waddell wrote a lengthy letter to Lord Russell, surrendering his ship to the British government, explaining the long delay in learning of the war's end, and asking that the vessel be turned over to the United States.[20] For Russell, the *Shenandoah*'s reappearance could not have come at a worse time.

In the summer of 1863, after the Southern losses at Gettysburg and Vicksburg, Lord Russell had begun to reverse Her Majesty's informal policy of providing naval aid to the Confederacy. The British now wanted to forget the past and establish a new international law that would prevent neutrals from building navies for nations at war. With her greatest maritime competitor no longer a threat, this would favor Great Britain in future wars.

But United States Minister to England Charles Francis Adams was unwilling to forget the past, and had been pressing the British Government for reparations for damages caused by the *Alabama* and other English-built raiders. The British Foreign Office had just disclaimed any responsibility in the matter when the *Shenandoah* anchored beside the *Donegal* like a long-lost child returning to its mother.

The British press and public were no more happy than their government. The London *Times* wrote that, "The reappearance of the *Shenandoah* in British waters at the present juncture is an untoward and unwelcome event." She should have been "excluded from the Mersey and left to rove the seas till she should fall into the hands of her pursuers."[21]

The *Pall Mall Gazette* reported, "Small thanks are due to the commander of the *Shenandoah* for the preference which he has given to Liverpool for the purpose of bringing his cruiser to an end. It is some satisfaction to know that he is under the charge of an English officer, but it is most unsatisfactory to remember that we shall now have to say what is to be done with him. . . ."[22]

Rallying to Waddell's side, the Tory *Herald* wrote that: "Even if, for the sake of vengeance on the destroyers of his country, Captain Waddell had gone on burning their ships after he knew that they had accomplished their work, his crime would have been essentially a political one; and Englishmen will never consent to give up political offenders."[23]

While the public debated the fate of the raider and her officers, the Royal Navy lashed a gunboat alongside, and Captain Paynter of the *Donegal* issued orders that no one was to leave the ship. After Waddell arranged for the men to receive part of their pay, many of them slipped over the side and never returned. The desertions were observed by British officers, one of whom told Waddell, "I don't care if the lads do take a run on shore at night . . . you won't leave the vessel, I know, so it don't matter about the lads going on a bit of a lark."[24]

Two days after Waddell's letter reached Lord Russell, Crown Law officers issued a ruling that the United States declared "smacked more of convenience than conscience." Sidestepping the issue of British responsibility for damage to American shipping, the counselors ruled that the *Shenandoah* should be turned over to the United States, and that the crew, except for British subjects who had violated the Foreign Enlistment Act, would be released.[25]

The decision was telegraphed to Captain Paynter, who came out to the *Shenandoah* to announce that everyone except British subjects would be released. Word of the decision had preceded Paynter's official announcement, however. When Waddell assembled the ship's company, the men fell into line with knowing smiles. When asked for a list of

British subjects aboard, Waddell replied that he had paid no attention to nationalities, but was certain that most were Americans. As Whittle called the roll, each man stepped forward, and a British officer asked his nationality. One after another claimed homes in Virginia, South Carolina, Georgia or other Southern states. Not one sailor confessed to British citizenship. Paynter shrugged and released the entire crew. Waddell wrote, "On the 10th of November, 10 officers, 14 acting appointments, and 109 men who constituted the ship's company, were unconditionally released. My tumblers, decanters, and bedding, with a few trophies from the islands, were presented to the Lieutenant-commander [Paynter] as a souvenir of our acquaintance."[26]

Waddell then made his last speech to the men, telling them he was proud that the last gun in defense of the old Confederacy had been fired from the deck of the *Shenandoah*; she had never abandoned a chase, and was "second to no other cruiser, not excepting the celebrated *Alabama*." The men gave him three rousing cheers, gathered their belongings, and with Waddell and his officers, clambered aboard the ferry *Bee* for a final voyage.

Waiting at Prince George Landing were reporters from the Liverpool *Mercury*, who attempted to capture the crew's sentiment as they paraded off the landing and into the city. Most of the men expressed pride in their service aboard the cruiser. One sailor was quoted as saying, "I am sorry to leave the ship, especially as the Confederate flag is not at the gaff, where it has been so long."[27]

The next day, Waddell received a large sum of money from the Confederate Naval Fund set aside by Bulloch. After paying off the officers, quartermaster Lewis Wiggins went to the Sailor's Home and paid off the men with the remains of Bulloch's emergency fund. They received one shilling in three—less than they had earned, but more than many had expected.

In reviewing the *Shenandoah*'s cruise—which covered 58,000 miles over a span of 13 months, included the destruction of 32 vessels, and was marred by but two deaths, both from natural causes in the final days of the cruise—Waddell proudly wrote: "I claim for her officers and men a triumph over their enemies and over every obstacle, and for myself I claim having done my duty."[28]

Waddell, with his wife Ann, remained in England until 1870, when he returned to Annapolis. Later he became a captain for the largely British-owned Pacific Mail Line, which operated between San Francisco, Japan, and Australia. After losing a steamer on an unmarked rock off the coast of Mexico, he returned to Maryland and commanded the state patrol boats policing the Chesapeake oyster beds. One dark night he surprised a fleet of Virginia oyster raiders and ordered them to strike their flag. They responded with laughter. Waddell opened with his howitzers, drove three boats ashore, sank one, and captured three others. When he died on March 15, 1886, the Maryland State Legislature adjourned in his honor.[29]

The *Shenandoah*'s career ended with considerably less aplomb. Thomas Dudley, the American consul at Liverpool, took possession and hired an experienced captain, Thomas F. Freeman, to sail her to New York. Freeman and a crew of 55 sailed for the United States on November 21, 1865, but returned to Liverpool on December 6, "short of coal and loss of sails," after an encounter with a fierce winter storm.[30] Convinced that the ship was unseaworthy, Freeman refused to take her back to sea again. For several weeks, Dudley tried unsuccessfully to hire another captain and crew. He petitioned the United States Navy to send officers to command her, but they refused to supervise a civilian crew. The American Legation, who had fought so hard to gain possession of the cruiser, now found itself in possession of a white elephant.

For several months the black-hulled ship with the ragged sails lay listless at Liverpool. Eventually, the Sultan of Zanzibar purchased her for his personal yacht. The vessel later reappeared in the tea trade, the business for which she was originally built. In 1879, a storm in the Indian Ocean hurled her upon a coral reef and ripped open her hull, taking the lives of all but five of the crew.[31]

The *Shenandoah*'s short career as a Confederate commerce raider added more fuel—$1,361,983 to be precise—to the diplomatic fire ignited by the depredations of the *Alabama* and the *Florida*. But there was a difference: Most of the *Shenandoah*'s destructive work had been carried out after the official end of the war. Despite steadfast denials of responsibility from the British government, American shipping companies, insurance companies, cargo consignors, ship owners, masters, seamen, passengers, and American newpapers—all screamed for reparations.

The final chapter in the narrative of the Confederate cruisers during the American Civil War did not end with the surrender of the *Shenandoah* on November 6, 1865. A diplomatic war, popularly known as the *Alabama* Claims, continued between Great Britain and the United States for seven more years. The battle was fought on a different stage, away from the sea, the moonlit chases, the roar of guns, and the scattered bonfires that lit up the oceans and nearly annihilated the American shipping industry.

The *Alabama* Claims

A FTER THE fall of Gettysburg and Vicksburg in the summer of 1863, a feeling of doom spread through the chambers of the British Foreign Office. It appeared that British capital and British officials had "backed the wrong horse." U.S. Minister Charles Francis Adams, his files bulging with damning evidence of British complicity in allowing the building and escape of the *Alabama* and *Florida*, demanded reparations for the destruction they had wrought. British Foreign Secretary Lord John Russell denied that his government was in any way responsible for the "acts of parties who fit out a seeming merchant ship, send her to a port or to waters far from the jurisdiction of British Courts, and there commission, equip, and man her as a vessel of war." Nevertheless, in an eleventh-hour attempt to mend fences with the apparently victorious Union, Lord Russell stiffened his heretofore liberal interpretation of the Foreign Enlistment Act, prevented the departure of the cruiser *Alexandra*, and ended the Confederacy's ironclad building program in Britain.

Although tensions between Great Britain and the U.S. eased for a while, they worsened dramatically in the autumn of 1864, when yet another British-built Confederate cruiser, the *Shenandoah*, slipped to sea. Adams renewed his attacks on the Foreign Office. The British government faced two choices, neither attractive: admit they had been derelict in their neutral responsibilities and offer to settle claims, or deny any wrongdoing and face the eternal enmity of a growing nation whose friendship they needed.

On August 30, 1865, Russell addressed a letter to Adams reopening the subject of settling the claims through arbitration, which Adams had suggested two years earlier. While still denying any liability, Russell stated that Her Majesty's Government was ready to consent to the appointment of a commission to review "all claims arising during the late civil war," providing the two powers could agree on what the claims actually were.[1]

Secretary of State William E. Seward studied Russell's proposal and shrewdly concluded that the British had no intention of considering reparations or compensation for damages caused by the *Alabama*. And if this were so, there would be no basis for recovering damage done by either the *Florida* or the *Shenandoah*. He asked Adams to clarify the ambiguities with Russell before any further steps were taken to form a commission.[2]

On October 14, 1865, Russell agreed to allow all claims, "upon which the two powers could agree that they are fair subjects of investigation to be referred to the commission."[3] But Adams, still expecting duplicity, petitioned Russell to commit to the precise nature of the claims allowable.[4]

Meanwhile, Russell left his post as British Foreign Secretary and was replaced by Lord Stanley. And Seward, suspecting that Russell's suggested joint commission was a ploy to entrap the United States into an agreement that would benefit only the British, wanted no part of it. Consequently, on November 21 Adams advised Lord Clarendon, Secretary of State for Foreign Affairs, that "the creating of a joint Commission is respectfully declined."[5] Thus ended the first diplomatic attempt at claims settlement.

In Parliament, many members felt uneasy over Lord Russell's refusal to identify "the precise nature of the claims" the British government would consent to discuss. In the August 20, 1866 London *Times*, one MP, who had just returned from a trip to the United States, strongly "deplored" the rejection by Lord Russell of all attempts to settle the difficulties by arbitration, and described the strong anti-British sentiment in America "on account of the fitting out of the Confederate cruisers in English ports."[6]

If the British government needed another nudge to get them to the bargaining table, they got it when the double-turreted monitor USS *Miantonomoh* crossed the Atlantic and visited several strategic English ports. Experts in the Royal Navy freely admitted that there was no ship in England that could compete with her. The July 17, 1866 issue of the London *Times* described the visit and its impact: "There was not one of them [British warships] that the foreigner could not have sent to the bottom in five minutes, had his errand not been peaceful . . . not one of these big ships . . . could have avenged the loss of its companion, or saved itself from immediately sharing its fate. In fact, the wolf was in the fold, and the whole flock was at its mercy."[7]

In late 1866 Britain's Foreign Secretary Stanley favored an amicable settlement of American claims and instructed Sir Frederick Bruce, British Minister at Washington, to propose a limited form of arbitration. Bruce delivered the communication to Secretary of State Seward on January 7, 1867, agreeing to arbitration but listing several conditions, including a provision that the United States would not demand concessions that would bring discredit upon the Queen's officials or any members of the British Executive or Legislature. Further, Stanley did not want to defend Seward's accusation that the British government prematurely awarded belligerent status to the Confederacy. Seward wrote Adams that the United States would not object to arbitration if the British government desired it, but would decline arbitration with the limitations imposed by Lord Stanley.[8]

Throughout 1867 and well into 1868, learned counsels on both sides of the Atlantic discussed different methods of getting their respective countries into arbitration and the festering issue of claims settled. New faces entered into the discussions. The able Charles Francis Adams resigned in December 1867, but remained in the post until replaced by Reverdy Johnson, of Maryland, in May 1868. A few months later Lord Clarendon replaced Lord Stanley as Britain's Foreign Secretary.

Finally, on January 14, 1869, after many months of negotiation, the Johnson–Clarendon convention providing for the settlement of the *Alabama* claims was signed. Four commissioners would be appointed—two from each power—to whom all claims would be submitted in Washington. If the commissioners failed to reach agreement on any claim, they were to choose an umpire; if they could not agree on the choice of an umpire, each side would select its own umpire, and from these two designees an umpire would be chosen to settle each issue in dispute. As complicated as this process seemed, it represented a first step toward the settlement of claims.[9] But there were still hurdles to clear.

Charles Sumner, the feisty and powerful senator from Massachusetts and chairman of the Committee on Foreign Affairs, strongly opposed the convention. In an executive session on April 13, 1869, he argued that its sole purpose was to settle the claims for damage caused by the cruisers, which he estimated at $15,000,000, while ignoring the broader claim of "the prolongation of the war and the expense of the blockade, all of which may be directly traced to England."[10] Sumner felt that Great Britain owed the United States half the cost of the entire war, approximately $2.5 billion. But he did not want a cash settlement. Instead, he wanted Great Britain to relinquish Canada, Newfoundland, Bermuda, and the British West Indies.[11] Spurred by Sumner's fiery speech, the Senate rejected the treaty with only one dissenting vote.

On April 19, 1869, Hamilton Fish, the new Secretary of State, advised Reverdy Johnson of the Senate's rejection, but wrote that President Ulysses S. Grant remained hopeful that the two countries might yet find a satisfactory means of resolving their differences. Lord Clarendon accepted the news with some disappointment, stressing that Her Majesty's government desired that all difficulties between the two nations be settled honorably, and that relations be both friendly and amicable.[12]

With changes taking place in the Grant administration, Fish recalled Reverdy Johnson and sent John Lothrop Motley to London as the new Minister to England. He instructed Motley to state that the rejection of the Johnson–Clarendon convention was not an unfriendly act and to propose a suspension of further discussion until public sentiment, inflamed by Sumner's speech, had subsided. He also directed Motley to make it clear that the United States would "not base its claims for damages against England on the latter's recognition of the Confederate States as a belligerent."[13] This statement contradicted Sumner's demand for indirect compensation and eased Britain's worries over the Senate's appetite for Canada.

For the next 20 months, special envoys and diplomats from both nations held secret discussions in an attempt to pave the way for a settlement. Almost on cue, on December 5, 1870 President Grant delivered a message to Congress asking that the two governments reach an understanding. The basis for an agreement had been formulated before the president's message, and by February 27, 1871 a Joint High Commission had been established to meet at Washington and settle all outstanding differences between the two nations.[14]

Britain was anxious to restore friendly relations with the United States, and for good reason: Europe was in turmoil. The victorious armies of a new Germany encircled Paris. The United States Navy was now one of the world's largest, with the most formidable ships afloat, manned by experienced, battle-hardened personnel. Any alliance between Germany and the United States for the purpose of reprisal, settlement of claims, or the occupation of Canada would be disastrous for Great Britain and her colonies. In a remarkably short time the negotiators reached an agreement.

The Joint High Commission, five men from each nation, signed the Treaty of Washington on May 8, 1871.[15] The first 11 of its 43 articles pertained to the *Alabama* claims. The next six referred to the claims of United States citizens against Great Britain and claims of British subjects against the United States arising from acts committed against persons or their property during the course of the Civil War.[16] The remaining 26 articles pertained to fishing rights, lumber rights, and other issues with no bearing on reparations.

The Treaty of Washington did not reconcile the *Alabama* claims, but it did outline the process for settling them. A Tribunal of Arbitration, composed of five arbitrators selected by the heads of state from Great Britain, Italy, Brazil, Switzerland, and the United States, would convene at Geneva, Switzerland, as soon as its membership could be named.[17] To no one's surprise, President Grant appointed Charles Francis Adams to represent the United States. Queen Victoria could have countered by selecting Lord Russell, but in the interest of resolving old issues amicably, chose instead Sir Alexander Cockburn, Lord Chief Justice of England. The King of Italy appointed Count Frederic Sclopis, a distinguished judge and lawyer. The president of the Swiss Confederation named Monsieur Jacques Staempfli, who had served three terms as president of Switzerland. Finally, the Emperor of Brazil selected Marcos Antonio d'Araujo, Baron d'Itayuba, the Brazilian minister to Paris.[18]

On December 15, 1871, in the Salle des Conferences at the Hotel de Ville in Geneva, the court met, organized, and named Count Sclopis as president. The principles by which the arbitrators were to be guided were reviewed, after which the two litigants, Adams and Cockburn, presented their cases. The tribunal then directed Adams and Cockburn to prepare their counter cases for presentation on or before April 15, 1872. The following day, the court met briefly and adjourned until June 15.[19]

Response was mixed in Great Britain to the possibility of settling Anglo-American differences. While some members of Parliament expressed relief that longstanding issues could now be settled, Lord Russell attacked several points of the treaty, claiming that it would prevent neutral traders from selling arms and munitions of war in the ordinary course of commerce. When the contents of the American case became public, the British press condemned it as being "unfriendly," focusing their criticism on the "indirect claims" put forward by the United States.

The claims presented by the United States Commissioners were classified as:

1. The claims for direct losses growing out of the destruction of vessels and their cargoes by the insurgent cruisers.
2. The national expenditures in pursuit of those cruisers.
3. The loss in the transfer of the American commercial marine to the British flag.
4. The enhanced payments of insurance.
5. The prolongation of the war and the addition of a large sum to the cost of the war and the suppression of the rebellion.[20]

When the Treaty of Washington was signed, the United States commissioners believed that indirect claims were admissible, but the English commissioners distinctly understood that indirect claims would not be referred to the court of Arbitration. Sensing a growing anger among her subjects, the Queen appeared before Parliament on February 6, 1872 and declared that she had "caused a friendly communication to be made to the Government of the United States." This helped bring the two governments back together without incurring a clash that would upset or end further efforts at arbitration.[21]

When the tribunal reconvened on June 15, 1872, Lord Tenterden, instead of delivering a pointed argument for Great Britain, requested that the court adjourn for eight months. Count Sclopis asked counsels representing Britain and the United States to meet and try to reach a common understanding on the issue of indirect claims so that arbitration could proceed. Over the next four days, Charles Francis Adams, J. C. Bancroft Davis, Lord Tenterden, and Sir Roundell Palmer argued the matter until they reached an agreement.

On June 19 Count Sclopis summarized the discussions: "On behalf of all the members of the court that, without expressing any opinion on the point of difference as to the meaning of the treaty, the court thought, individually and collectively, that the 'indirect claims' did not constitute, upon the principles of International Law applicable to such cases, good grounds for an award of damages between nations, and, upon such principles, the tribunal, even if there were no disagreement between the two litigant governments . . . would exclude them altogether in making their award."[22]

This ended the dispute. A few days later, Davis informed the court that since they did not have jurisdiction over 'indirect claims,' his Government had empowered him to say that it would not press those claims further. Two days later, Tentenden withdrew his request for adjournment, and the tribunal finally began the process of hearing arguments germane to specific claims.[23]

Under the new limited agenda, Davis presented the claims for the depredations of the *Sumter, Alabama, Florida, Georgia, Tallahassee, Shenandoah, Nashville, Chickamauga*, and the four tenders commissioned by Maffitt, Semmes, and Read. The British contested all of the claims. After weeks of debate, the court narrowed the scope to claims for damages caused by the *Alabama, Florida, Shenandoah*, and by the tenders *Tuscaloosa, Clarence, Tacony* and *Archer*, ruling that such auxiliary vessels "must necessarily follow the lot of their principles."[24]

Depredations of the *Shenandoah* prior to her arrival at Australia were excluded from the case. By a vote of three to two, the court ruled that Great Britain had failed to enforce her neutrality after the vessel entered Hobson's Bay and was therefore responsible for the acts of the *Shenandoah* after her departure from Melbourne on February 18, 1865.

After resolving the scope of the case, the court quickly reached a decision. On September 14, 1872, the day set for the announcement of the long-awaited settlement, bells rang throughout the streets of Geneva to celebrate an end to a controversy that had led two great powers to the brink of war.

The other members of the tribunal were already exchanging congratulations when Sir Alexander Cockburn arrived at the meeting, 45 minutes late. Without greeting his fellow arbitrators, Cockburn handed Count Sclopis a dissent nearly 300 pages long—a bitter and confused tirade nearly four times longer than that of his colleagues—and hastily departed. Even the London press condemned it, criticizing their champion for a public display of bad sportsmanship. Caleb Cushing, one of the four American lawyers who had argued the case, exclaimed that the Lord Chief Justice of England had "gone clean daft."[25] Nonetheless, the tribunal, by a vote of four to one, awarded the United States the flat sum of $15,500,000.

The Treaty of Washington established new rules of international law governing the acts of neutrals in their relationships with warring nations. The most important of these changes were:

> A neutral Government is bound—First, to use due diligence to prevent the fitting out, arming, or equipping, within its jurisdiction, of any vessel which it has reasonable ground to believe is intended to cruise or to carry on war against a power with which it is at peace; and also to use like diligence to prevent the departure from its jurisdiction of any vessel intended to cruise or carry on war as above, such vessel having been specially adapted, in whole or in part, within such jurisdiction to warlike use.
>
> Secondly, not to permit or suffer either belligerent to make use of its ports or waters as the base of naval operations against the other, or for the purpose of the renewal or augmentation of military supplies or arms, or the recruitment of men.
>
> Thirdly, to exercise due diligence in its own ports and waters, and, as to all persons within its jurisdiction, to prevent any violation of the foregoing obligations and duties.[26]

The new treaty protected the United States and Great Britain from each other's unneutral acts in future wars, but Sir Travers Twiss, England's preeminent maritime lawyer, expressed the opinion that his government had purchased a valuable precedent at a bargain price. American lawyers had pressed for indirect damages and lost, and Twiss believed that the "due diligence" clause in the new treaty gave England, in the event of a future war, much of the same latitude it had enjoyed in the Civil War. If a cruiser did, by chance, get to sea, England's liability would be limited to direct damages.

Other nations argued these principles until 1907, when they finally became incorporated in a broader body of international law at the Hague Conference. They were not enacted by Congress as the municipal law of the United States until 1917.[27]

A court was created in the United States to hear evidence in support of claims for direct losses from the raiders incurred by shippers, owners, and others. Eventually this court distributed $9,416,120.25, leaving an undistributed balance of $6,083,879.75, plus accumulated interest. Although some in Congress favored giving the remainder back to England, a second claims court was created to pay claims for losses caused by the other cruisers, those outside the scope defined by the Geneva Tribunal. Thereafter, any balance remaining would be prorated as refunds for premiums paid for war-risk insurance. Eventually, every cent awarded by the Geneva Tribunal was distributed, although 25 years elapsed between the time the damage occurred and the books were finally closed.

Although the payments of indemnity helped individual cases in some small way, they failed to revive the moribund American carrying trade. The United States won the Civil War but Great Britain won undisputed dominance of maritime commerce — for a very small sum, and without a shot fired. Her Majesty's victory was won by her civilian shipyards, aided by James Dunwoody Bulloch.

The victory lasted nearly 80 years.

Captures by the
Confederate Cruisers

CSS *Sumter* (1861–1862)

Captures made by Raphael Semmes:

DATE	VESSEL	TYPE	DISPOSITION
3 July 61	*Golden Rocket*	Ship	Burned
4 July 61	*Cuba*	Brig	Recaptured
4 July 61	*Machias*	Brig	Released
5 July 61	*Ben Dunning*	Brig	Released
5 July 61	*Albert Adams*	Brig	Released
6 July 61	*Naiad*	Brig	Released
6 July 61	*Louisa Kilham*	Bark	Released
6 July 61	*West Wind*	Bark	Released
25 July 61	*Abby Bradford*	Schooner	Recaptured
27 July 61	*Joseph Maxwell*	Bark	Released
25 Sept 61	*Joseph Park*	Brig	Burned
27 October 61	*D. Trowbridge*	Schooner	Burned
25 November 61	*Montmorenci*	Ship	Bonded
26 November 61	*Arcade*	Schooner	Burned
3 December 61	*Vigilant*	Ship	Burned
8 December 61	*Eben Dodge*	Bark	Burned
18 January 62	*Neapolitan*	Bark	Burned
18 January 62	*Investigator*	Bark	Released

CSS *Nashville* (1861–1862)

Captures made by Robert B. Pegram:

19 November 61	*Harvey Birch*	Clipper Ship	Burned
26 February 62	*R. Gilfillan*	Schooner	Burned

CSS *Florida* (1862–1864)

Captures made by John Newland Maffitt:

19 January 63	*Estelle*	Brig	Burned
22 January 63	*Windward*	Brig	Burned
22 January 63	*Corris Ann*	Brig	Burned

Date	Vessel	Type	Disposition
12 February 63	Jacob Bell	Clipper Ship	Burned
6 March 63	Star of Peace	Clipper Ship	Burned
12 March 63	Aldabaran	Schooner	Burned
28 March 63	Lapwing	Bark (tender)	Burned
30 March 63	M. J. Colcord	Bark	Burned
17 April 63	Commonwealth	Ship	Burned
20 April 63	Kate Dyer	Ship (Lapwing)	Bonded
23 April 63	Henrietta	Bark	Burned
25 April 63	Oneida	Ship	Burned
6 May 63	Clarence	Brig (raider)	Burned
14 May 63	Crown Point	Ship	Burned
6 June 63	Southern Cross	Clipper Ship	Burned
14 June 63	Red Gauntlet	Clipper Ship	Burned
16 June 63	B. F. Hoxie	Ship	Burned
17 June 63	V. H. Hill	Schooner	Bonded
7 July 63	Sunrise	Ship	Bonded
8 July 63	W. B. Nash	Brig	Burned
8 July 63	Rienzi	Schooner	Burned
6 August 63	F. B. Cutting	Ship	Bonded
6 August 63	Southern Rights	Ship	Bonded
21 August 63	Anglo Saxon	Clipper Ship	Burned

Captures made by Charles M. Morris:

29 March 64	Avon	Ship	Burned
18 May 64	George Latimer	Schooner	Burned
17 June 64	W. C. Clarke	Brig	Burned
1 July 64	Harriet Stevens	Bark	Burned
8 July 64	Golconda	Bark	Burned
9 July 64	M. Y. Davis	Schooner	Burned
9 July 64	Greenland	Bark	Burned
10 July 64	General Barry	Bark	Burned
10 July 64	Zelinda	Bark	Burned
10 July 64	Howard	Schooner	Bonded
10 July 64	Electric Spark	Steamer	Scuttled
22 August 64	Southern Rights	Ship	Bonded
26 September 64	Mandamis	Bark	Burned

Clarence and Tacony (1863)
Captures made by Charles Read:

6 June 63	Whistling Wind	Bark	Burned
9 June 63	Mary Alvina	Bark	Burned
12 June 63	Tacony	Bark (Raider)	Burned
12 June 63	M. A. Shindler	Schooner	Burned
12 June 63	Kate Stewart	Schooner	Bonded

Date	Vessel	Type	Disposition
12 June 63	*Arabella*	Brig	Bonded
15 June 63	*Umpire*	Brig	Burned
20 June 63	*Isaac Webb*	Ship	Bonded
20 June 63	*Micawber*	Schooner*	Burned
21 June 63	*Byzantium*	Ship	Burned
21 June 63	*Goodspeed*	Bark	Burned
22 June 63	*Marengo*	Schooner*	Burned
22 June 63	*Elizabeth Ann*	Schooner*	Burned
22 June 63	*Rufus Choate*	Schooner*	Burned
22 June 63	*Ripple*	Schooner*	Burned
22 June 63	*Florence*	Schooner*	Bonded
23 June 63	*Ada*	Schooner*	Burned
23 June 63	*Wanderer*	Schooner*	Burned
24 June 63	*Shatemuc*	Ship	Bonded
24 June 63	*Archer*	Schooner*	Recaptured
26 June 63	*Caleb Cushing*	Revenue Cutter	Burned

CSS *Tallahassee* (1864)

Captures made by John Taylor Wood:

11 August 64	*S. A. Boyce*	Schooner	Scuttled
11 August 64	*James Funk*	Pilot Boat	Burned
11 August 64	*Carrie Estelle*	Brig	Burned
11 August 64	*Bay State*	Bark	Burned
11 August 64	*A. Richards*	Brig	Burned
11 August 64	*Carrol*	Schooner	Bonded
11 August 64	*Wm. Bell* (24)	Pilot Boat	Burned
12 August 64	*Atlantic*	Schooner	Burned
12 August 64	*Adriatic*	Ship	Burned
12 August 64	*Suliote*	Bark	Bonded
12 August 64	*Spokane*	Schooner	Burned
12 August 64	*Billow*	Brig	Scuttled
12 August 64	*R. E. Packer*	Schooner	Bonded
13 August 64	*Glenavon*	Bark	Scuttled
13 August 64	*L. Du Pont*	Schooner	Burned
14 August 64	*J. Littlefield*	Ship	Scuttled
15 August 64	*Mary A. Howes*	Schooner	Scuttled
15 August 64	*Howard*	Schooner	Scuttled
15 August 64	*Floral Wreath*	Schooner	Scuttled
15 August 64	*Sarah B. Harris*	Schooner	Bonded
15 August 64	*Restless*	Schooner*	Scuttled
15 August 64	*Etta Caroline*	Schooner*	Scuttled
16 August 64	*P. C. Alexander*	Bark	Burned

*Fishing Schooner

DATE	VESSEL	TYPE	DISPOSITION
16 August 64	*Leopard*	Schooner	Burned
16 August 64	*Pearl*	Schooner*	Burned
16 August 64	*Sarah Louise*	Schooner	Burned
16 August 64	*Magnolia*	Schooner*	Burned
17 August 64	*North America*	Schooner*	Scuttled
17 August 64	*Neva*	Brig	Bonded
17 August 64	*Josiah Achom*	Schooner	Burned
17 August 64	*Diadem*	Schooner	Released
17 August 64	*D. Ellis*	Schooner	Released
20 August 64	*Roan*	Brig	Burned

CSS *Olustee*: formerly the *Tallahassee* (1864)

Captures made by William H. Ward:

1 November 64	*Empress Theresa*	Bark	Burned
3 November 64	*A. J. Bird*	Schooner	Burned
3 November 64	*Arcole*	Ship	Burned
3 November 64	*E. F. Lewis*	Schooner	Burned
3 November 64	*T. D. Wagner*	Brig	Burned
3 November 64	*Vapor*	Schooner	Burned

CSS *Chickamauga* (1864)

Captures made by John Wilkinson:

30 October 64	*Mark L. Potter*	Bark	Burned
31 October 64	*Emily L. Hall*	Bark	Burned
31 October 64	*Shooting Star*	Ship	Burned
31 October 64	*Albion Lincoln*	Bark	Bonded
1 November 64	*Goodspeed*	Schooner	Scuttled
1 November 64	*Otter Rock*	Schooner	Scuttled
2 November 64	*Speedwell*	Bark	Bonded

CSS *Georgia* (1863)

Captures made by William Lewis Maury:

25 April 63	*Dictator*	Ship	Burned
8 June 63	*George Griswold*	Ship	Bonded
13 June 63	*Good Hope*	Bark	Bonded
14 June 63	*J. W. Seaver*	Bark	Bonded
25 June 63	*Constitution*	Ship	Burned
28 June 63	*City of Bath*	Ship	Bonded
16 July 63	*Prince of Wales*	Ship	Bonded
30 August 63	*John Watts*	Ship	Bonded
9 October 63	*Bold Hunter*	Ship	Burned

*Fishing Schooner

Date	Vessel	Type	Disposition
CSS *Alabama* (1862–1864)			
Captures made by Raphael Semmes:			
5 September 62	Ocmulgee	Ship	Burned
7 September 62	Starlight	Schooner	Burned
8 September 62	Ocean Rover	Bark	Burned
9 September 62	Alert	Ship	Burned
9 September 62	Weather Gage	Schooner	Burned
13 September 62	Altamaha	Brig	Burned
14 September 62	B. Tucker	Ship	Burned
16 September 62	Courser	Schooner	Burned
17 September 62	Virginia	Ship	Burned
18 September 62	Elisha Dunbar	Bark	Burned
3 October 62	Brilliant	Ship	Burned
3 October 62	Emily Farnum	Ship	Bonded
7 October 62	Wave Crest	Bark	Burned
7 October 62	Dunkirk	Brig	Burned
9 October 62	Tonawanda	Ship	Bonded
11 October 62	Manchester	Ship	Burned
15 October 62	Lamplighter	Bark	Burned
23 October 62	Lafayette	Ship	Burned
26 October 62	Crenshaw	Schooner	Burned
28 October 62	Lauretta	Bark	Burned
29 October 62	B. de Castine	Brig	Bonded
2 November 62	Levi Starbuck	Ship	Burned
8 November 62	T.B. Wales	Ship	Burned
30 November 62	Parker Cook	Bark	Burned
5 December 62	Union	Schooner	Bonded
7 December 62	Ariel	Steamer	Bonded
11 January 63	USS Hatteras	Gunboat	Sunk
26 January 63	Golden Rule	Bark	Burned
27 January 63	Chastelaine	Brig	Burned
3 February 63	Palmetto	Schooner	Burned
21 February 63	Olive Jane	Bark	Burned
21 February 63	Golden Eagle	Ship	Burned
27 February 63	Washington	Ship	Bonded
1 March 63	Bethiah Thayer	Ship	Bonded
2 March 63	John A. Parks	Ship	Burned
15 March 63	Punjab	Ship	Bonded
23 March 63	Morning Star	Ship	Bonded
23 March 63	Kingfisher	Schooner	Burned
25 March 63	Nora	Ship	Burned
25 March 63	Charles Hill	Ship	Burned
4 April 63	Louisa Hatch	Ship	Burned

Date	Vessel	Type	Disposition
15 April 63	*Lafayette*	Bark	Burned
15 April 63	*Kate Cory*	Brig	Burned
24 April 63	*Nye*	Bark	Burned
26 April 63	*Dorcas Prince*	Ship	Burned
3 May 63	*Sea Lark*	Ship	Burned
3 May 63	*Union Jack*	Bark	Burned
25 May 63	*Gildersleeve*	Ship	Burned
25 May 63	*Justina*	Bark	Bonded
29 May 63	*Jabez Snow*	Ship	Burned
2 June 63	*Amazonian*	Bark	Burned
5 June 63	*Talisman*	Ship	Burned
20 June 63	*Conrad*	Bark	*
2 July 63	*A. F. Schmidt*	Ship	Burned
6 July 63	*Express*	Ship	Burned
5 August 63	*Sea Bride*	Bark	Sold
9 August 63	*Martha Wenzell*	Bark	Released
6 November 63	*Amanda*	Bark	Burned
10 November 63	*Winged Racer*	Ship	Burned
11 November 63	*Contest*	Ship	Burned
24 December 63	*Texan Star*	Bark	Burned
26 December 63	*Sonora*	Ship	Burned
26 December 63	*Highlander*	Ship	Burned
14 January 64	*Emma Jane*	Ship	Burned
23 April 64	*Rockingham*	Ship	Burned
27 April 64	*Tycoon*	Bark	Burned

By estimates provided by the *Alabama*'s officers, the value of vessels burned was $4, 613,914 and the value of the vessels bonded was $562,250.

CSS *Shenandoah* (1864–1865)

Captures made by James I. Waddell:

Date	Vessel	Type	Disposition
30 October 64	*Alina*	Bark	Scuttled
6 November 64	*Charter Oak*	Schooner	Burned
8 November 64	*D. Godfrey*	Bark	Burned
10 November 64	*Susan*	Brig	Scuttled
12 November 64	*Kate Prince*	Ship	Bonded
12 November 64	*Adelaide*	Ship	Bonded
13 November 64	*Lizzie M. Stacey*	Schooner	Burned
4 December 64	*Edward*	Bark	Burned
29 December 64	*Delphine*	Bark	Burned

*Fitted as a tender and commissioned the CSS *Tuscaloosa*

DATE	VESSEL	TYPE	DISPOSITION
1 April 65	Edward Cary	Ship	Burned
1 April 65	Hector	Ship	Burned
1 April 65	Pearl	Ship	Burned
1 April 65	Black Harvest	Bark	Burned
27 May 65	Abigail	Bark	Burned
22 June 65	William Thompson	Ship	Burned
22 June 65	Euphrates	Ship	Burned
22 June 65	Milo	Ship	Bonded
22 June 65	Sophia Thornton	Ship	Burned
22 June 65	Jireh Swift	Bark	Burned
23 June 65	Susan Abigail	Brig	Burned
25 June 65	General Williams	Ship	Burned
26 June 65	Nimrod	Bark	Burned
26 June 65	William C. Nye	Bark	Burned
26 June 65	Catherine	Bark	Burned
26 June 65	General Pike	Bark	Bonded
26 June 65	Gipsey	Bark	Burned
26 June 65	Isabella	Bark	Burned
28 June 65	Waverly	Bark	Burned
28 June 65	Hillman	Ship	Burned
28 June 65	James Maury	Ship	Bonded
28 June 65	Nassau	Ship	Burned
28 June 65	Brunswick	Ship	Burned
28 June 65	Isaac Howland	Ship	Burned
28 June 65	Martha	Bark	Burned
28 June 65	Congress	Bark	Burned
28 June 65	Nile	Bark	Bonded
28 June 65	Favorite	Bark	Burned
28 June 65	Covington	Bark	Burned

In accounts provided by the officers of the *Shenandoah* the estimates of the value of the vessels and cargoes destroyed is $1,172,223. The value of the vessels bonded totalled another $118,600, which does not include the *General Pike*, for which no value was recorded.

Notes

1. SETTING THE STAGE

1. For further study of Stephen R. Mallory's involvement in Confederate naval policy, see Joseph T. Durkin, *Stephen R. Mallory: Confederate Naval Chief* (Chapel Hill, N.C.: University of North Carolina Press, 1954), hereinafter, Durkin, *Mallory*.

2. J. Thomas Scharf, *History of the Confederate States Navy: From Its Organization to the Surrender of Its Last Vessel* (New York: Rogers and Sherwood, 1887), 30, hereinafter, Scharf. An excellent early work on the Confederate States Navy. It is not well indexed, however, and contains little information on the activities of the cruisers.

3. Ibid., 31

4. John Niven, *Gideon Welles, Lincoln's Secretary of the Navy* (New York: Oxford University Press, 1973), 359–360, hereinafter, Niven; F. M. Bennett, *The Steam Navy of the United States* (Pittsburg: Warren and Company, 1896), 214–228; Charles O. Paullin, *The Navy Department During the Civil War* Vol. II, (U. S. Naval Institute Proceedings, Vol. 39, No. 1, Mar. 1913), 168–170; Scharf, 32. Confederate bullion quickly vanished, and foreign purchases were later secured by cotton certificates.

5. Durkin, *Mallory*, 199–200; *The Richmond Examiner*, March 20, 1862. The *Merrimack* was renamed CSS *Virginia* when recommissioned by the Confederacy.

6. United States Department of the Navy, *Official Records of the Union and Confederate Navies in the War of the Rebellion*, 30 volumes, and index (Washington, D.C.: Government Printing Office, 1894–1927), hereinafter, ORN; statistical data, ORN Series II, 1: 27–246; James Russell Soley, *The Blockade and the Cruisers* (New York: Charles Scribner's Sons, 1890), 53–54, hereinafter, Soley; *Compilation of Laws and Decisions of the Courts Relating to the War Claims* (Washington, D.C.: Government Printing Office, 1912), No. 1112, 195–235.

7. Frank Lawrence Owsley, *King Cotton Diplomacy*, 2nd ed. (Chicago: University of Chicago Press, 1959), 260–262, hereinafter cited as Owsley, *King Cotton*; Robert U. Johnson and Clarence Buell, editors, *Battles and Leaders of the Civil War*, four volumes, (New York: The Century Company, 1884–1887), 1:149, hereinafter, B&L.

8. United States War Department, *War of the Rebellion: A Compilation of the Official Records of the Union and Confederate Armies*, 128 volumes, and index (Washington, D.C.: Government Printing Office, 1880–1901), hereinafter, ORA; Davis to Semmes, 21 February, 1861; ORA IV, 1:106–107; Mallory to Bulloch, 9 May 1861, ORN II, 2:64–65.

9. Semmes to Walker, 28 February 1861, ORA IV, 1:118–119; Raphael Semmes, *Memoirs of Service Afloat During the War Between the States* (Baltimore: Kelly, Piet and Co., 1869), 86, hereinafter, Semmes, SA. Semmes' memoirs offer interesting insight into the cruises of the *Sumter* and the *Alabama* and provide enjoyable reading. While accurate, there are many omissions.

10. Semmes, SA, 88.

11. Scharf, 33.

12. Ibid., 89–90, 263, 658, 670.

13. Mallory to Semmes, 18 April 1861, ORN I, 1:613.

14. Semmes to Mallory, 22 April 1861 and 14 June 1861, ORN I 1:614, 615; Semmes, SA, 94–106; Charles G. Summersell, *The Cruise of the CSS* Sumter (Tuscaloosa, Ala.: Confederate Publishing Company, 1965, 23–30, hereinafter, Summersell, *Sumter*. Summersell's *Sumter* is the most accurate and comprehensive of all the works on the subject.

15. Mallory to Bulloch, 6 May 1861,

ORN II, 2: 64–65; James D. Bulloch, *The Se-cret Service of the Confederate States in Europe or How the Confederate Cruisers Were Equipped* (New York: Putnam's, 1883), two volumes, 47–48, hereinafter, Bulloch, *Secret Service.*

16. Bulloch, *Secret Service*, 1: 33–38. Benjamin would later serve as Secretary of War and ultimately Secretary of State under Jefferson Davis. An extremely capable administrator, Benjamin fled to England at the end of the war and became wealthy by applying his legal and business skills.

17. Ibid., 41. In addition to Bulloch's memoirs on European shipbuilding, several fine scholarly works on the subject of Confederate financing abroad have been published by Frank Owsley, Warren F. Spencer, Frank J. Merli, and Richard Lester, to name a few.

18. Mallory to Lt. James H. North, 17 May 1861, ORN II, 2:70–72

2. THE *SUMTER* GOES TO SEA

1. Mallory to Semmes, April 18, 1861, *ORN* I, 1:613; Semmes, SA, 89–94; Durkin, *Mallory*, 130.

2. Summersell, *Sumter* , 16; Semmes, SA, 93; Semmes to Mallory, 22 April 1861, ORN I, 1: 614.

3. Ibid.; Summersell, *Sumter*, 17; Semmes, SA, 95.

4. Ibid., 98;James M. Merrill, "Confederate Shipbuilding at New Orleans," *Journal of Southern History*, XXVII, 1, 87–93; Summersell, *Sumter*, 22. Of 1,362 vessels registered or enrolled in New Orleans between 1851 and 1861, only 179 are listed as built in Louisiana.

5. Norman C. Delaney, *John McIntosh Kell of the Raider* Alabama (Tuscaloosa: University of Alabama Press, 1973), 73, hereinafter, Delaney; Semmes, SA, 123–125. Aside from Kell's own memoirs, Delaney leaves the best record of Semmes' executive officer. Much of Semmes' success was due to Kell, yet Semmes refers to him sparingly in *Service Afloat.*

6. Ibid., 124; Summersell, *Sumter*, 18.

7. Ibid., 27; Semmes, SA, 125.

8. Semmes to Mallory, 14 June 1861, ORN I, 1:615.

9. Semmes to Mallory, 23 May 1861, Ibid., 1:614.

10. Journal of the *Sumter*, Ibid., 692; Semmes, SA, 104.

11. Ibid., 108; John McIntosh Kell, *Recollections of Naval Life, Including the Cruises of the Confederate Steamers* Sumter *and* Ala-bama (Washington, D.C.: Neale Publishing, 1900), 146–147, hereinafter, Kell, *Recollections*; Journal of the *Sumter*, ORN I, 1:692.

12. Semmes to chief pilot, 22 June 1861, ORN I, 1:616; Semmes, SA, 109.

13. Semmes to Farrand, 24 June 1861, and Semmes to Fry, 25 June 1861, ORN I, 1:617–618; Journal of the *Sumter*, ORN I, 1:693; Kell, *Recollections*, 147–148; Summersell, *Sumter*, 46.

14. Semmes to Mallory, 30 June 1861, ORN I, 1:618; Semmes, SA, 112.

15. Ibid., 113; Journal of the Sumter, ORN I, 1: 694.

16. Ibid.; Kell, *Recollections*, 148; Semmes, SA, 114–115.

17. Ibid., 116; Robert W. Nesser, *Statistical and Chronological History of the United States Navy 1775–1907* (New York: MacMillan, 1909), two volumes, 2:320–322, hereinafter, Nesser; Kell, *Recollections*, 148–149; Summersell, *Sumter*, 46–48.

18. Journal of the *Sumter*, ORN I, 1:694; Semmes, SA, 117.

19. Ibid., 117–118.

20. Poor to Mervine, 30 June 1861, ORN I, 1:34; Colyer Meriwether, *Raphael Semmes* (Philadelphia: George W. Jacobs, 1913), 118–122, hereinafter, Meriwether; David D. Porter, *The Naval History of the Civil War* (New York: Sherman Publishing, 1886), 605–606, hereinafter, Porter, *Naval History*; Harpur A. Gosnell, ed., *Rebel Raider: Being the Account of Raphael Semmes Cruise of the CSS* Sumter (Chapel Hill: The University of North Carolina Press, 1948), 29, hereinafter, Gosnell.

21. Semmes, SA, 127–128; Kell, *Recollections*, 149; Journal of the *Sumter*, ORN I, 1:695.

22. Porter, *Naval History*, 606–607. Porter advanced the opinion that the burning of the *Golden Rocket* was an illegal act because belligerent status had not yet been awarded to the Confederacy. Unlike Seward and Lincoln, Porter accepted the *Sumter* as a legal vessel of war after belligerency was granted. Lincoln and Seward, however, persisted on referring to the raider as a pirate or a privateer. Kell, *Recollections*, 149; Semmes, SA, 129.

23. Summersell, *Sumter*, 56. Semmes is credited with being the first ex-officer of the United States Navy to fire on a Union merchant vessel. Summersell cites William Bailey's protest in the House of Representatives, 37 Congress, Second Session, Executive Document 104, 176–177.

24. Summersell, *Sumter*, 56–60; Semmes

to Hudgins, 7 July 1861, and the journal of the *Sumter*, ORN I, 1:621, 695; Semmes, SA, 133–134.

25. Journal of the *Sumter*, ORN I, 1:695; Summersell, *Sumter*, 61; Porter, *Naval History*, 608.

26. Ibid., 607–608; journal of the *Sumter*, ORN I, 1:695–696; Kell, *Recollections*, 150; Semmes, SA, 137–138.

27. Ibid., 138.

28. Ibid., 139–141; Semmes to Don Jose de la Pozuela, 6 July 1861, ORN I, 1:619–620; Meriwether, 123–147. The British proclamation of June 1, 1861 was explicit in forbidding prizes from entering its ports. Summersell, *Sumter*, 64–65.

29. Ibid., 67; Mountague Bernard, *A Historical Account of the Neutrality of Great Britain During the Civil War* (London: Longmans, Green, Reader and Dyer, 1870), 135–150, hereinafter, Bernard.

30. Summersell, *Sumter*, 68–69.

31. Semmes to Don Mariano Diaz, 6 July 1861, and Semmes to Hudgins, 7 July 1861, ORN I, 1:620–621.

3. A SCARCITY OF GAME

1. Semmes, SA, 150.

2. Summersell, *Sumter*, 71. Semmes never mentioned his seasickness in his memoirs. See also Journal of the *Sumter*, ORN I, 1:696–697.

3. Semmes to Governor Crol, 7 July 1861, Semmes to Mallory, 9 November 1861, Jesurun to Edgar, 18 July 1861, Journal of the *Sumter*, all in ORN I, 1:47–48, 621–622, 631, 696–697. Semmes, SA, 151–153. In their official correspondence, Union consuls typically referred to all Confederate cruisers as pirates. This strong language was used in the hope that the Confederates would be refused the use of neutral ports and ultimately banished from the sea. Meriwether, 135–137; Summersell, *Sumter*, 73; Porter, *Naval History*, 610–611.

4. Ibid., 611; Semmes, SA, 154. A show of force was standard naval procedure when a major power disputed with a minor one. Semmes target practice was a euphemism. In 1861, the Confederate Navy was in no position to attempt to intimidate the Netherlands, although the immediate result appeared to have succeeded.

5. Ibid., 158–162. Summersell, *Sumter*, 76, 79–80; Journal of the *Sumter*, ORN I, 1:697–698.

6. Semmes to governor of Puerto Cabello, 26 July 1861, Semmes to Mallory, 9 November 1861, and journal of the *Sumter*, ORN I: 623–624, 632–633, 698–699, also Semmes to Quartermaster Ruhl, 26 July 1861, ORN I, 1:624; Porter, *Naval History*, 612.

7. Ibid.; Porter to Secretary Welles, August 13 and 16, 1861, ORN I, 1: 65, 68–69; Semmes SA, 161–162.

8. Ibid., 167.

9. Ibid., 168–178; Porter to Secretary Welles, Semmes to Midshipman Hicks, Semmes to Mallory, ORN I, 1:104, 625, 632; journal of the *Sumter*, ORN I, 1:699; Summersell, *Sumpter*, 85–88.

10. Ibid., 89, 93–97; journal of the *Sumter*, ORN I, 1:699–700; Semmes, SA, 185; Meriwether, 137–140; Welles to Breese, 12 July 1861, Breese to Palmer, 12 July 1861, Welles to Scott, 19 July 1861, and Latham to Welles, 16 July 1861, ORN I, 1:39, 40–41, 44, 48; Summersell, *Sumter*, 93–97. See Porter's correspondence covering the chase of the *Sumter* in ORN I, 1:68, 78, 91, 103–104; other correspondence in ORN I, 1: 69–95, 122–123, 628–643; Porter, *Naval History*, 612–615. Kell, *Recollections*, 152. In the end, Porter had the last word. He published his *Naval History of the Civil War* after the death of Semmes.

11. Semmes, SA, 194–197; Semmes to Mallory, 9 November 1861, and journal of the *Sumter*, ORN I, I:633, 702–703.

12. Ibid., 703–704.

13. Commander Scott to Welles, 25 September 1861, ORN I, 96–97, 634, 704–705. In ORN I, 1:93, Porter advises the governor of Maranhao, Brazil, that Semmes had been ordered by the governor of Surinam to depart within 24 hours and that Semmes had refused. Brazilian pilots were told never to bring into port another ship bearing the Confederate flag. Summersell, *Sumter*, 105.

14. Ibid., 107; Scott to Welles, 7 August 1861, Porter to Welles, 19 August and 23, 24 September 1861, and journal of the *Sumter*, ORN I, 1:56, 68–69, 90–92, 705–706.

15. Summersell, *Sumter*, 104–105; Kell, *Recollections*, 156–157; Semmes, SA, 206.

16. Ibid., 208; journal of the *Sumter*, ORN I, 1:708.

17. Ibid., 708–709; Semmes, SA, 212; Summersell, *Sumter*, 108–110.

18. Ibid., 115; Porter, *Naval History*, 616; Porter to Welles, 23 and 24 September 1861, ORN I, 1:91–95; Semmes, SA, 217–219; journal of the *Sumter*, 710.

19. Ibid., 711–712; Summersell, *Sumter*, 116–117.

20. Semmes, SA, 220–221; Kell, *Recollections*, 158; Semmes to Evans, ORN I, 1:627–628; and journal of the *Sumter*, 711–713, 744.

21. Ibid.; Semmes, SA, 223.

22. Summersell, *Sumter*, 118–119; Porter, *Naval History*, 617.

23. Ibid.; journal of the *Sumter*, ORN I, 1:715–716; Semmes, SA, 226–231; Kell, *Recollections*, 158–160.

24. Ibid., 160–162; Semmes to Cande, 12 November 1861, Semmes to Mallory, 16 January 1862, Cande to Semmes, 12 November 1861, and journal of the *Sumter*, ORN I, 1:644–649, 720; Semmes, SA, 232–237.

25. Ibid., 253; for Plamer's correspondence, see ORN I, 1:208–215. Semmes' report on his stay in Martinique appears in his correspondence to Mallory dated 16 January 1862 in ORN I, 1:644–647.

26. Palmer to Welles, 17 November 1861, log of the *Iroquois*, Semmes to Mallory, 10 January 1862, and journal of the *Sumter*, ORN I, 1:208–209, 213–216, 645, 718–721; Gideon Welles, *Diary of Gideon Welles* (Boston and New York: Houghton, Mifflin, Co., 1911), three volumes, I:299, hereinafter, Welles, *Diary*; Porter, *Naval History*, 617; Semmes, SA, 254.

27. Ibid., 255–260; Palmer to Welles, 23 November 1861, Semmes to Mallory, 16 January 1862, and journal of the *Sumter*, ORN I, 1:212–213, 645, 721–723; Summersell, *Sumter*, 132–136; Kell, *Recollections*, 163–164.

4. A HARBINGER OF DISASTER

1. Journal of the *Sumter*, ORN I, 1:723–725. Semmes, SA, 261–262. Semmes quotes the signal lights on the American schooner as blue in the journal but red in his memoirs.

2. Ibid., 262; Palmer to Welles, 23, 25, and 28 November 1861, Annandale to Palmer, 3 December 1861, log of *Iroquois*, log of *Sumter*, and Semmes to Mallory, 16 January 1862, ORN I, 1:212–217, 645, 724, 727; Soley, 175; Summersell, *Sumter*, 136–138 lists Union warships in pursuit of Sumter as *Iroquois, Powhatan, Ino, Niagara, Richmond, Keystone State , San Jacinto,* and *Dacotah*; Porter, *Naval History.*

3. Ibid.; Gosnell, 146.

4. Summersell, *Sumter*, 138–139; ransom bond for Montmorenci, ORN I, 1:653–654. Note: The *Montmorenci* was the largest vessel captured by the *Sumter* and compared in size to the largest vessels captured by other

Confederate cruisers; journal of the *Sumter*, ORN I, 1:724.

5. Ibid., 724–725. Summersell, *Sumter*, p. 140.

6. Journal of the *Sumter* and Semmes to Mallory, 16 January 1862, ORN I, 1:646, 727; Kell, *Recollections*, 165; Semmes, SA, 275.

7. Ibid., 278–279; Semmes to Mallory and journal of the *Sumter*, ORN I, 1:646, 728; Summersell, *Sumter*, 144; Kell, *Recollections*, 165–166.

8. Ibid., 166; Semmes, SA, 280–281. During the winter of 1861–1862, storms of unusual violence and frequency ravaged the North Atlantic. Summersell, *Sumter*, 144.

9. Department of the Navy, *Civil War Naval Chronology: 1861–1865* (Washington D.C.: Government Printing Office, 1871) I:37, hereinafter cited as *Naval Chronology*; Semmes, SA, 284–285; journal of the *Sumter*, ORN I, 1:732.

10. Ibid., 732–734; Semmes, SA, 284–296; Kell, *Recollections*, 166–167; Summersell, *Sumter*, 145–147.

11. Ibid., 147–148; Semmes, SA, 298; London *Times*, January 7, 8, and 13, 1862; journal of the *Sumter*, and Semmes' correspondence in ORN I, 1:638–647, 652–653, 734–735.

12. Ibid., 735–737; Semmes, SA, 301–302; Owsley, *King Cotton*, 79–86.

13. Semmes to Yancey, 7 January 1862, ORN I, 1:639. Summersell, *Sumter*, 149–150.

14. Ibid., 152–154; journal of the *Sumter*, ORN I, 1:737–738; Semmes, SA, 307–308, 327–328; Gosnell, 169.

15. Summersell, *Sumter*, 154.

16. Semmes to Mason, 24 January 1862, ORN I, 1:659–660; Semmes, SA, 313–319.

17. Ibid., 316. Semmes' correspondence in ORN I, 1:660–666 covers the scope and difficulties confronting the *Sumter* in Gibraltar.

18. Semmes, SA, 320–321.

19. Ibid., 321; Summersell, *Sumter*, 158–161. See Semmes' correspondence in ORN I, 1:325–332, 680–681.

20. Semmes, SA, 322–325; journal of the *Sumter*, ORN I, 1:739–740. Freemantle wrote an autobiography covering his tour in America entitled *Three Months in the Southern States* (London, 1863).

21. Journal of the *Sumter*, ORN I, 1:740–741; Semmes, SA, 327–328.

22. Ibid., 330–332. The concern over the purchase of coal covered several days of futile negotiations. See journal of the *Sumter*, ORN I, 1: 740–743.

23. Summersell, *Sumter*, 163–166;

Semmes, SA, 332–341. Kell, *Recollections*, 175. Semmes' correspondence covers the entire adventure of Myers and Tunstall in ORN I, 1: 663–674. Tunstall was an American who had been appointed consul to Cadiz by President Pierce in 1856. Lincoln removed him in 1861 for his pro–Confederate leanings.

24. Semmes, SA, 344. For Semmes' correspondence, see ORN I, 1:674–682.

25. There is some dispute among historians whether Great Britain was simply trying to apply her written but untested laws of neutrality or whether she was taking advantage of the war to establish future precedents that improved her position as the world's dominant maritime power. The court case involving the little *Alexandra* upheld the obsolete Foreign Enlistment Act. This forced the government to change her policy on neutrality without amending the Act. See Chapter 11 for the case of the *Alexandra*.

26. Mason to Benjamin, 30 October 1862, and Mallory to Mason, 22 February 1863, ORN I, 1:688–689; Moore to Benjamin, 13 February 1863, and Benjamin to Moore, 16 February 1863, ORN II, 2:698–700; Kell, *Recollections* 177; Summersell, *Sumter*, 169–171.

27. Ibid., 171–172; George W. Dalzell, *The Flight from the Flag* (Chapel Hill: University of North Carolina Press, 1940), 62–63; Bulloch, *Secret Service*, 1:234. For correspondence concerning the sale of the Sumter, see ORN I, 2:74, 77–78, ORN I, 5:752, ORN I, 1:420, 432–433, 595–601, and ORN I, 9:127–129.

28. Dudley to Dabney, 5 April 1863, ORN I, 2:144–145; Dalzell, 62–63; Gosnell, 194; Summersell, *Sumter*, 173–176.

29. Semmes, SA, 345; Kell, *Recollections*, 176.

5. THE CSS NASHVILLE

1. Statistical Data, ORN II, 1:261; H. Jerry Morris, "Nashville," *Civil War Times Illustrated*, Vol. 24, 11, 38–45, hereinafter cited as Morris, Nashville.

2. Stevens to Memminger, and Stevens to Mallory, 4 May 1861, ORN II, 1:334–335. Dalzell, 64.

3. Pegram to Mallory, 10 March 1862, ORN I, 1:745.

4. William M. Robinson, *The Confederate Privateers* (New Haven: Yale University Press, 1928), 251–252, hereinafter, Robinson. The selection of the Gordon by Mason and Slidell was a good tactical move, as the vessel

had been used by Pegram for reconnaissance and was often observed off Charleston by the Union blockaders. Her presence outside the harbor created little alarm. The Gordon had her name changed to *Theodora* and was eventually purchased by the Confederates as a blockade runner. With her name again changed to the *Nassau*, she was commanded by John Newland Maffitt before he took command of the CSS *Florida*.

5. Morris, Nashville, 40.

6. Pegram to Mallory, 10 March 1862, ORN I, 1:745–746.

7. Wilkes to Welles, 15 November 1861, ORN I, 1:129–131. For a thorough account of the Trent Affair, see Norman D. Ferris, *The Trent Affair* (Knoxville: University of Tennessee Press, 1977)

8. Pegram to Mallory, 10 March 1862, ORN I, 1:746.

9. Ibid.

10. Dalzell, 65. The prisoners were placed in the Sailor's Home by the American consul and were repatriated the following week, returning to New York on a steamer of the North German Lloyd Line.

11. Welles to Wilkes, 30 November 1861, ORN I, 1:148.

12. Dalzell, 66.

13. Pegram to Mallory, 10 March 1862, ORN I, 1:746.

14. Pegram to Mallory, and Pegram to North, 10 March 1862, ORN I, 1:746 and ORN II, 2:118.

15. Welles to Craven, 6 December 1861, ORN II, 2:230–231.

16. Craven to Welles, 9 January 1862 and 13 January 1862, ibid., 275, 277–278.

17. See correspondence between Craven and Patey, and Pegram and Patey, January 1862, ibid., 279, 294, 295, 749, 750.

18. Patey to Craven, 3 February 1862, ibid., 300.

19. Craven to Welles, 23 January 1862, ibid., 293.

20. Pegram to Duke of Somerset, 27 January 1862, ibid. 750–751.

21. Craven to Welles, 3 February 1862, ORN I, 1:299–300.

22. Ibid.

23. Dalzell, 69.

24. Pegram to Mallory, 10 March 1862, ORN I, 1:747.

25. Ibid.; Morris, Nashville, 42–43.

26. Armstrong to Goldsborough and Welles, 28 February 1862, 18 March 1862, and Pegram to Mallory, 10 March, 1862, ORN I, 1:332, 333–334, 748.

27. Welles to Marston, 6 March 1862, ibid., 333.

28. Dalzell, 70.

29. Warren F. Spencer, *The Confederate Navy in Europe* (Tuscaloosa: University of Alabama Press, 1983), 28, hereinafter, Spencer; Ferris, 213; Caleb Huse, *Supplies for the Confederate Army, How They Were Obtained in Europe and How Paid For. Personal Reminiscences and Unpublished History* (Boston: Press of T.R. Marvin and Son, 1904), 32–33.

30. Spencer, 28–31, 216; Ferris, 37–41, 49.

31. Dalzell, 71.

6. WHAT'S NEW IN PALERMO?

1. Spencer, 17–18; Bulloch, *Secret Service,* 1:67. When Bulloch arrived in Europe, he was the sole representative of the Confederate Navy. As time passed, other arrived who began exercising a multitude of duties both within and without the scope of purely naval interests. Eventually, Commodore Samuel Barron reached France and became the officer in charge of all Confederate naval activities. Of this influx of naval personnel, only Bulloch consistently took charge and made things happen. The only possible exception was Commander Matthew Fontaine Maury, who held the status of international celebrity and liberally used his friends and relatives to support his efforts in behalf of the South. See Chapter 23.

2. Ibid., 46–54.

3. Frank L. Owsley, Jr., *The CSS* Florida: *Her Building and Operations* (Philadelphia: University of Pennsylvania Press, 1965), 20, hereinafter, Owsley, *Florida.* Owsley's short work on the *Florida* is well researched and accurate.

4. Dudley to Seward, Jan. 24, 1862, United States Consular Despatches, Liverpool, Vol. XX, State Department, Record Group 59, National Archives, Washington, D.C.: cited by Owsley, *Florida,* 21.

5. Owsley, *Florida,* 22.

6. Bulloch, *Secret Service,* 1:157–159; Bulloch to Low, 21 March 1862, ORN I, 1:755–756.

7. William Stanley Hoole, *Four Years in the Confederate Navy* (Athens, Ga.: University Press, 1964), 1–4. Low would later serve on the *Alabama* and captain the CSS *Tuscaloosa,* a captured merchantman converted by Semmes into a sailing commerce destroyer.

8. Bulloch to Low, 21 March 1862, and Low to Bulloch, 1 May 1862, ORN I, · 1:756–757, 757–758.

9. While the *Florida* was under construction, Bulloch returned briefly to the Confederacy, bringing a cargo of arms on the blockade runner *Fingal.* During this time, considerable confusion arose over the command of the *Florida.* Bulloch, North, and Semmes were all under consideration, but when Mallory promised Bulloch command of the *Alabama,* he eliminated himself as a candidate to captain the Florida. In the interim, Semmes was delayed and North never received the official notice from Mallory that he had been selected. Unaware of the award, North declined further consideration and withdrew, believing that he would command the *Alabama.* North suspected double–dealing on command decisions and complained. Bulloch returned to Liverpool in time to prevent North from inadvertent disclosure of the whole scheme. Spencer clarifies this command confusion. See 39–47.

10. Hoole, 31.

11. Ibid.

12. Ibid., 32; journal of Maffitt, ORN I, 1:763. There were several journals covering the cruises of the *Florida.* The journal in the above volume covers the period between May 4, 1862 and December 31, 1862.

13. Owsley, *Florida,* 25.

14. Ibid., 26–27.

15. Welles to Winslow, 4 July 1862, and Welles to Gansevoort, 11 July 1862, ORN I, 1:397–398, 399–400. Hoole, 33. Semmes' presence in Nassau was coincidental. He soon returned to England to receive command of the *Alabama.*

16. Journal of Maffitt, ORN I, 1:764. Owsley, *Florida,* 27–28.

17. Ibid., 29; Maffitt to Mallory, 1 August 1862, ORN I, 1:759. Hoole, 34–35.

18. Journal of Maffitt, ORN I, 1:764. Owsley, *Florida,* 29–30.

19. It is likely that one or more of the crew was already infected with yellow fever at the time the *Oreto* left Nassau for Green Cay.

20. Journal of Maffit, ORN I, 1:764.

21. Ibid.

7. "I HAVEN'T TIME TO DIE"

1. Journal of Maffitt, Maffitt to Bulloch, 20 August 1862, ORN I, 1:760, 765.

2. Ibid., 765; Edward Boykin, *Sea Devil of the Confederacy: The Story of the* Florida *and Her Captain, John Newland Maffitt* (New York: Funk & Wagnalls Co., 1959),113–115, herinafter cited as Boykin, *Florida.* Boykin's work is historically accurate, but he takes lib-

erties in building the story through the use of questionable dialogue.

3. Journal of Maffitt, ORN I, 1:765–766.

4. Ibid.

5. Ibid., 766.

6. Boykin, *Florida*, 117.

7. Journal of Maffitt, ORN I, 1:766–767. Emma M. Maffitt, *The Life and Services of John Newland Maffitt* (New York: Neale,1906), 135–138, 383, 411, hereinafter, *Life of Maffitt*. Maffitt's memoirs were written by his wife and published after his death. ORN II, 2:165 lists Oneida with two 9–inch guns, but both Preble and Maffitt state they were 22–inch guns. Preble to Farragut, 8 October 1862, and Maffitt's journal, ORN I, 1:435, 766–767.

8. Preble to Farragut, 10 September 1862, ORN I, 1:436–440.

9. Boykin, *Florida*, 120–123. Owsley, *Florida*, 38– 39.

10. Ibid., 38–39; journal of Maffitt, ORN I, 1:766–767; Boykin, Florida, 124.

11. Owsley, *Florida*, 38–39

12. Journal of Maffitt, ORN I, 1:766–767; Boykin, *Florida*, 125. Owsley, *Florida* 39.

13. Preble to Farragut, 4 September, 6 September, and 10 October 1862, ORN I, 1:432, 433–434, 434–440.

14. Ibid. In the Official Records beginning with page 432, there are 24 pages of correspondence and testimony provided by Preble and other officers under his command.

15. Welles, *Diary*, 1:141.

16. Welles to Preble, 20 September 1862, ORN I, 1:434. *Life of Maffitt*, 383.

17. Ibid., 383, 411.

18. Porter, *Naval History*, 626.

19. Journal of Maffitt, ORN I, 1:767.

20. Owsley, *Florida*, 42.

21. Journal of Maffitt, ORN I, 1:768. Owsley, *Florida*, 46.

22. Ibid.

23. Ibid., 44; Journal of Maffitt, ORN I, 1:769.

24. *Life of Maffitt*, 136–137; Owsley, *Florida*, 45.

25. Journal of Maffitt, ORN I, 2:667.

26. Mallory to Maffitt, 25 October 1862, ORN I, 1:762–763.

27. Journal of Maffitt, ORN I, 2:667–668; Boykin, *Florida*, 137–138.

28. Ibid.

29. Emmons to Hitchcock, 12 March 1863, ORN I, 2:30–31.

30. The original journal of the *Florida* was thrown overboard from a blockade runner attempting to enter Charleston, South Caro-

lina. The Official Records covering the cruise of the *Florida* between January 13, 1863 and April 30, 1863, is taken from the rough journal kept by Maffitt. This was loaned to the Navy Department along with other papers by his widow. Boykin, *Florida*, 139–140; *The New York Herald* exclaimed, "Another scourge of the deep is let loose," while *The Richmond Dispatch* issued mocking congratulations for Yankee shipowners on "the bright prospect that lies ahead for their merchantmen."

8. THE HUNTER IS LOOSE

1. Journal of Maffitt, ORN I, 2:668. Boykin, *Florida*, 141.

2. Schufeldt to Seward (enclosure), 21 January 1863, ORN I, 2:47–49, which was the statement of Captain John Brown concerning the destruction of the *Estelle* by the *Florida*. See also Owsley, *Florida*, 50–51.

3. Helm to Benjamin, 26 January 1863, ORN I, 2:641, 668.

4. *Life of Maffitt*, 274; Boykin, *Florida*, 147.

5. Schufeldt to Seward, 21 January 1863, ORN I, 2:47–48. Owsley, *Florida*, 51.

6. Journal of Maffitt, ORN I, 2:668.

7. Schufeldt to Seward, 24 January 1863, ORN I, 2:49–51. Owsley, *Florida*, 52.

8. Officers to Maffitt, 23 January 1863, ORN I, 2:640, also journal of Maffitt, 668.

9. Welles to Wilkes, 23 January 1863, Wilkes to Welles, 24 January 1863, Wilkes to Ridgely, Ronckendorf, and Stevens, 24, 25 January 1863, all in ORN I, 2:54–58. The cruise of the *Alabama* is covered in later chapters.

10. Journal of Maffitt, ORN I, 2:669.

11. Correspondence of Wilkes and Stevens regarding the search and chase of the *Florida*, in ORN I, 2:67–70.

12. Ibid; also, journal of Maffitt, 669; Owsley, *Florida*, 54–55; Stevens to Wilkes, 9 February 1863, ORN I, 2:69–70.

13. Boykin, *Florida*, 156; journal of Maffitt, ORN I, 2:669.

14. Ibid., 670. The *Jacob Bell* was one of the few fast clipper ships captured by the *Florida*. For more insight into the extreme clipper ships see Octavious T. Howe and Frederick G. Matthews, *American Clipper Ships, 1833–1858*, 2 Vols., (New York: Dover, 1886, reprint). For Jacob Bell, see ORN I:289–291.

15. *Life of Maffitt*, 274–275; journal of Maffitt, ORN I, 2:670.

16. Ibid.

17. G. Terry Sinclair, "The Eventful

Cruise of the Florida," *Century Magazine*, July, 1988.

18. Journal of Maffitt, ORN I, 2:670.

19. Ibid.; Eytinge to Welles, 19 February 1863, and Baldwin to Welles, 20 February 1863, both in ORN I, 2:92–93.

20. Journal of Maffitt, ORN I, 2:670. Owsley, *Florida*, 57 cites Seward to Adams, 23 March 1863, Post Records London, State Department, Records of Foreign Posts, Record Group 84, National Archives, Washington, D.C.

21. Stuart L. Bernath, *Squall Across the Atlantic* (Berkeley and Los Angeles: University of California Press, 1970), 63–79. Although the *Peterhoff* carried arms intended for Confederate use, her papers were clearly consigned to a neutral owner in a neutral port. For this reason, the *Peterhoff's* voyage was decreed lawful — four years and two months after the ship had been seized by Wilkes as a prize.

22. Journal of Maffitt, ORN I, 2:671, 676–677. Frederick C. Matthews, *American Merchant Ships* (Salem, Mass.: Marine Research Society, 1931–1932), 2:214–215, hereinafter cited as Matthews, *Merchant Ships*.

23. Boykin, *Florida*, 179; journal of Maffitt, ORN I, 2:677.

24. Ibid., 671.

25. Ibid., 671, 677–678; *Life of Maffitt*, 281; Owsley, *Florida*, 61–62. The *Lapwing* was renamed the Oreto II by Maffitt, but he was inconsistent in his own correspondence regarding the ship's name change.

26. Journal of Maffitt, ORN I, 2:672; log of *Lapwing*, and Maffitt to Mallory, 11 May 1863, ORN I, 2:648–650, 678.

27. Journal of Maffitt, ibid., 672.

28. Ibid., 671; Boykin, *Florida*, 183–184. Statement of Master George F. Brown to U.S. Consul Adamson, ORN I, 2:204–205.

29. Statement of Master Jesse F. Potter to Adamson, ORN I, 2:205–206; journal of Maffitt, ORN I, 2:673.

30. Ibid.

31. Leal to Maffitt, log of the *Florida*, ORN I, 2:643–644, 676; *Life of Maffitt*.

32. Log of *Lapwing*, ORN I, 2:679; Owsley, *Florida*, 68–69; Matthews, *Merchant Ships*, 2:73.

9. DARING BEYOND THE POINT OF MARTIAL PRUDENCE

1. Boykin, *Florida*, 134.

2. Read to Maffitt, 6 May 1863, Read to Mallory, 19 October 1864, ORN I, 2:644, 655.

3. Ibid., 190; Maffitt to Read, 6 May 1863, Ibid., 645; Boykin, *Florida*, 190.

4. Boykin, *Florida*, 196–197.

5. Jim Dan Hill, *Sea Dogs of the Sixties* (Minneapolis: University of Minnesota Press, 1935), 182, hereinafter cited as Hill, *Sea Dogs*; Owsley, *Florida*, 79; *The New York Times*, 29 June 1863.

6. Read to Mallory, 19 October 1864, ORN I, 2:655.

7. Ibid., 654–656.

8. Hill, *Sea Dogs*, 183; Edmund A. Souder and Co. to Welles, 13 June 1863, ORN I, 2:273–274.

9. Boykin, *Florida*, 200.

10. Teague to E. A. Souder and Co., 13 June 1863, ORN I, 2:274; Hill, *Sea Dogs*, 184; Boykin, *Florida*, 200.

11. Welles, *Diary*, 1:327.

12. Welles to Paulding, 13 June 1863, ORN I, 2:275. A review of 40 pages of correspondence in the Official Records provides testimony to the chaos created by Read's adventures along the northeastern coast and Welles' erratic messages in attempting to cope with the problem.

13. Ibid., 276.

14. By An Officer of the United States Navy, "The Cruise of the Clarence-Tacony-Archer" (*Maryland Historical Magazine*, 1915), 10:46. It is not understood why this author wished to remain anonymous; his article seems to agree with other material written about Read's cruise.

15. Boykin, *Florida*, 206.

16. Read to Mallory, 19 October 1864, ORN I, 2:656; Owsley, *Florida*, 82.

17. Read to Mallory, 19 October 1864, ORN I, 2:656: Boykin, *Florida*, 210; Owsley, *Florida*, 82–83.

18. Read to Mallory, 19 October 1864, ORN I, 2:656; Owsley, *Florida*, 83.

19. Ibid.

20. See also *The New York Times*, 29 June 1863.

21. Hill, *Sea Dogs*, 185; Owsley, *Florida*, 83–84.

22. Read to Mallory, 19 October 1864, ORN I, 2:656–657; Hill, *Sea Dogs*, 188–189.

23. Read to Mallory, 19 October 1864, ORN I, 2:657.

24. Ibid.

25. Clarence Hale, "The Capture of the Caleb Cushing" (Maine Historical Society, 1904), Series I, Vol. 1, 203, hereinafter cited as Hale, "Caleb Cushing."

26. Ibid.

27. Owsley, *Florida*, 89; Jewett to Chase,

June 27, 1863, ORN I, 2:323.

28. Hale, "Caleb Cushing," 197–198.

29. Jewett to Chase, 27 June 1863, ORN I, 2:323; Hale, "Caleb Cushing," 198–199.

30. Boykin, *Florida*, 218. Read later wrote that his final shot consisted of deck chain and broken kettles, although one disgusted Northern volunteer claimed that as the cheese landed on the deck, he had exclaimed, "Lord, now they fire stink pots at us, like the Chinese!"

31. Jewett to Chase, 27 June 1863, ORN I, 2:324.

32. Porter, *Naval History*, 814.

10. CATCHING THE CLIPPERS

1. Mallory to Maffitt, 6 May 1863, ORN I, 2:658.

2. Souza to Maffitt, 8 May 1863, ibid., 646.

3. Souza to Maffitt, 9 May 1863, ibid., 647–648; *Life of Maffitt*, 292–294; Owsley, *Florida*, 65–66.

4. Owsley, *Florida*, 65.

5. Adamson to Seward, 27 May 1863 and 10 June 1863, ORN I, 1:217–221, 263–264; *Life of Maffitt*, 295.

6. Baldwin to Welles, 23 July 1863, ORN I, 1:407–408; log of *Florida*, ibid., 679–680; Owsley, *Florida*, 69.

7. Log of *Florida*, ORN I, 2:680.

8. Maffitt to Mallory, 27 July 1863, ORN I, 2:652–654; Adamson to Seward, 10 June 1863, ibid., 263–264; *Life of Maffitt*, 297; Howe and Matthews, 2:587–594.

9. Dudley to Welles, 11 August 1863, ORN I, 2:423, also Maffitt to Mallory, 27 July 1863, ibid. 653. *Life of Maffitt*, 298; Owsley, *Florida*, 70; Howe and Matthews, 2:509–511.

10. Maffitt to Mallory, 7 July 1863, ORN I, 2:653; *Life of Maffitt*, 298–299; Howe and Matthews, 1:32.

11. Mallory to Maffitt, 7 August 1863, ORN I, 2:657–658; *Life of Maffitt*, 299–300; Owsley, *Florida*, 71–72.

12. *Life of Maffitt*, 298–299; Boykin, *Florida*, 222.

13. Maffitt to Mallory, 7 July 1863, ORN I, 2:653–654.

14. Miller to Welles, 9 July 1863, ORN I, 2:383–384; see also, 385, 653.

15. Maffitt to Mallory, 7 July 1863, ORN I, 2:653; Boykin, *Florida*, 224–225; Owsley, *Florida*, 73–74.

16. Welles to Montgomery, 10 July 1863, ORN I, 2:385.

17. Ord to Maffitt, 16 July 1863, ORN I, 2:650–652.

18. Maffitt to Mallory, 7 July 1863, ORN I, 2:653–654; Boykin, *Florida*, 225–228; Owsley, *Florida*, 74–75.

19. Maffitt to Mallory, September 1863, ORN I, 2:659–660; *Life of Maffitt*, 309; Owsley, *Florida*, 75.

20. Maffitt to Mallory, September 1863, ORN I, 2:653–654.

21. Maffitt to Slidell, 18 August 1863, ibid., 658–659; Owsley, *Florida*, 75–76.

22. Owsley, *Florida*, 76; Howe and Matthews, 1:9–11. After losing the Anglo Saxon, Cavarly gave up sailing and joined the Pacific Mail Steamship Company. Ironically, after the war Maffitt joined the same company and both became prominent captains.

23. Maffitt to Mallory, September 1863, ORN I, 2:659–660.

24. Maury to Maffitt, 9 September 1863 and 11 September 1863, ORN I, 2:660–661.

25. Barron to Barney, 5 January 1864, ibid., 661.

26. Papers Relating To the Treaty of Washington, Geneva Arbitration, 4 vols. (Washington, 1872), 3:19, 28, hereinafter cited as "Alabama Claims."

27. Ibid., 64–66.

11. THE STRANGE CASE OF THE ALEXANDRA

1. Bulloch, *Secret Service*, 1:352.

2. Frank J. Merli, "Crown Versus Cruiser: The Curious Case of the *Alexandra*," *Civil War History* 9, No. 2 (June 1863); hereinafter cited as Merli, "Alexandra." The best studies on the Alexandra appear in the works of Richard I. Lester, Frank J. Merli, and Warren F. Spencer. Bulloch was well aware of the trial but never appeared to fully understand the significance of the ruling as it related to policy changes that interrupted his shipbuilding program. At the time of the trial, Bulloch was in the midst of building ironclads. He tended to blame the change in the policy of the British Foreign Office on the changing fortunes of the Confederate armies at Gettysburg and Vicksburg. In reality, the change in policy preventing Confederate cruiser–building was the direct result of the failure of the British courts to change the interpretation of the Foreign Enlistment Act. In essence, the Act was not effectively protecting the neutrality of Great Britain. What British courts could not accomplish through the interpretation of her laws, British policy could change and did change — to the credit to Lord John Russell.

3. Ibid, 168–169.

4. Ibid, 169.

5. Ibid, 170.

6. Richard I. Lester, *Confederate Financing and Purchasing in Great Britain* (Charlottesville, University Press of Virginia, 1975), 94–95, hereinafter cited as Lester.

7. Ibid, 95.

8. Ibid. By comparison, the *Florida* was 700 tons and the *Alabama* 1,050 tons.

9. Bulloch, *Secret Service*, 1:332–333.

10. A crimp was an individual who for a fee supplied sailors to a ship needing a crew. This was usually accomplished by getting the sailor drunk or drugged and delivering the unconscious body to the client.

11. Bulloch, *Secret Service*, 1:338–340.

12. Ibid, 341–343. Bulloch's record for selecting people was impeccable, the only exception being Yonge.

13. Lester, 95–96. Merli, "Alexandra," 173.

14. Lester, 96. Merli, "Alexandra," 174.

15. Lester, 96.

16. Flag–Officer Samuel Barron was in Paris awaiting the completion of the ironclads, some of which were smaller corvettes. His mission was to take command of this fleet when ready for sea and descend upon the blockade, rip it apart, and proceed up the northeastern U.S. coast for the purpose of holding the major cities under tribute. Another side of the strategy involved recapturing New Orleans and reopening the Mississippi. Problems associated with all of this strategy was the deep draft of some of the heavier ironclads and the difficulty of operation in the shoals and over the bars along the coast. Complicating the success of such a mission was the need to cross the Atlantic Ocean, make recoaling stops, and deal with storms and seas entirely new to this class of vessel.

17. Lester, 97–101. The *Pampero* was also known as the *Canton*. Another ironclad known either as No. 61 or the "Scottish Sea Monster" was being built at the same time by Lieutenant North at the Glasgow Shipyards of the Thomsons.

18. Horace White, *Fossett's: A Record of Two Centuries of Engineering* (Bromborough, Cheshire, 1958), 49–50; Lester, 96–97.

12. INTERLUDE AT BREST

1. Boykin, *Florida*, 231–232.

2. Owsley, *Florida*, 92.

3. Boykin, *Florida*, 232–233.

4. Winslow to Welles, 18 September 1863, ORN I, 2:458–459; Owsley, *Florida*, 93.

5. Owsley, *Florida*, 93–94.

6. Boykin, *Florida*, 234–235.

7. Winslow to Welles, 18 September 1863, ORN I, 2:458–459; Owsley, *Florida*, 94–95.

8. Owsley, *Florida*, 94–95.

9. Winslow to Welles, 18 September 1863, ORN I, 2:458–459. This correspondence lists the number of seamen disembarked at Brest as seventy-five. Bulloch, *Secret Service*, 1:180, confirms this total of seventy-five, giving as a reason that the term of enlistment had expired.

10. Cleveland to Welles, 17 September 1863, ORN I, 2:457–458. Spencer, 167; Owsley, *Florida*, 98–99.

11. Bulloch, *Sercret Service*, 1:180–181; Owsley, *Florida*, 100.

12. *Liverpool Daily Post*, September 17, 1863 in Owsley, *Florida*, 100.

13. Owsley, *Florida*, p. 101.

14. Dayton to Winslow, 14 November 1863, ORN I, 2:496; Bulloch, *Secret Service*, 1:182; Owsley, *Florida*, 101–102.

15. Bulloch, *Secret Service*, 1:182.

16. Barron to Barney, 5 January 1864, ORN I, 2:661; Barron to Morris, ibid., 662; Owsley, *Florida*, 102–103. The senior Confederate naval officer in Europe was Barron. His real mission was to take command to the ironclad fleet being built in Britain and France. He never got beyond administrative work.

17. Scharf, 792.

18. The policy of the French government toward the Confederacy changed drastically between the time the Florida entered Brest and the time it sailed. Because of the increased diplomatic difficulties following the trial of the *Alexandra*, the Confederates had looked to France for support in building a navy. At first, Napoleon III gave his encouragement, but he soon discovered that all the Confederate naval activity had been transferred to France, and he began to realize that he was supporting a losing cause. As Great Britain had done, Napoleon quickly altered his policy toward the South and took steps to protect French neutrality. This change in policy was partially influenced by expansion interests in Mexico and the Polish war in Europe.

19. Morris to Barron, 31 January, 1 February, 9 February, ORN I, 2:663–664.

20. Winslow to Welles, 18 September and 3 December 1863, ORN I, 2:458–459, 509–510.

21. Owsley, *Florida*, 105–106; abstract log of the *Florida*, ORN I, 2:680. The following June, Winslow offered a similar challenge to Semmes of the *Alabama*. Semmes accepted the challenge and lost his ship.

22. Winslow to Welles, 30 October 1863, ORN I, 2:479–480; Owsley, *Florida*, 107.

23. Winslow to Welles, 7 November 1863, I, 2:494.

24. Winslow to Welles, 3 December 1863, ORN I, 2:509–510; Dayton to Winslow, 30 November 1863, ibid., 510–511. The *Rappahannock* was formerly the *Victor* of the Royal Navy. The Confederates inspecting the vessel prior to its purchase gave it a superficial evaluation. It proved to be in poor condition. See Chapter 23.

25. Winslow to Welles, 16 January 1864, ORN I, 2:586; ibid., 19 February 1864, 606–607.

13. THE FLORIDA UNDER MORRIS

1. Morris to Barron, 9 February 1864, ORN I, 2:663–664.

2. Ibid., 18 February, 664–665.

3. Ibid., p. 65; log of the *Florida*, 681–682.

4. Owsley, *Florida*, 111–112.

5. Preble to Welles, 28 February 1864, ORN I, 2:614–615.

6. Morris to Barron, 29 February, 1864, ibid., 665–666. See also Morris to Castelbrance and Castelbrance to Morris, 28 February, 666.

7. Preble to Welles, 1 March 1864, ibid., 622–623.

8. Welles to Preble, 31 March 1864, ibid., 636.

9. Log of the *Florida*, ibid., 682.

10. Morris to Castelbrance, 29 February 1864, ibid., 666–667.

11. Preble to Welles, 1 March 1864, ORN I, 2:622–623; log of the *Florida*, ibid., 682.

12. Ibid.; Preble to Welles, 7 March 1864, ibid., 625–626.

13. Log of the *Florida*, ibid., 683; Morris to Mallory, 29 April 1864, ORN I, 3:609. When merchant ships experienced difficulty in obtaining cargoes, guano became the last resort. Most of it came from the Chinchas Islands off the coast of Peru, which were covered with hundreds of feet of dried bird excrement deposited throughout the centuries. Chinese coolies worked these deposits by hand, and the islands were often covered by a yellow haze raised by the dust of hundreds of picks and shovels. The fertilizer had become so popular that dozens of ships would often hover around the islands awaiting their turn to load.

14. Log of *Florida*, ORN I, 3:643.

15. Owsley, *Florida*, 116.

16. Ibid., 116–117; Morris to Hoole, 29 April, and to Mallory, 12 May 1864, ORN I, 3:610, 611.

17. Lardner to Welles, 10 May, 6 June 1864, ORN I, 3:27–28, 45–46.

18. Morris to Averett, and to Mallory, 12 May 1864, ibid., 610, 611.

19. Morris to Mallory, 12 May 1864, ibid., 611.

20. Morris to Mallory, 21 June 1864, ibid., 617–618.

21. Ibid.

22. Quinn to Morris, 15 June 1864, ibid., 614.

23. Morris to Hope, 19 June 1864, ibid., 615.

24. Morris to Munro, 21 June 1864, ibid., 618.

25. Mallory to Morris, 2 June 1864, ibid., 612–613; Morris to Mallory, 27 June and 2 July, ibid., 620–621.

26. Log of *Florida*, ORN I, 3:645; Owsley, *Florida*, 124.

27. Morris to Mallory, 2 July 1864, ORN I, 3:621–622.

28. Owsley, *Florida*, 125–126.

29. Earlier, Maffitt had relieved an engineer named W. F. Jackson for incompetence. The man who signed on at Bermuda is believed to be a different Jackson.

30. Morris to Mallory, 13 July 1864, ORN I, 3:623; log of *Florida*, 645; *Alabama* Claims, 3:583.

31. Ibid.

32. Ibid.

33. Ibid.

34. Ibid.

35. Ibid., 623–624, 645–646.

36. Paulding to Welles, 12 July 1864, ORN I, 3:103; Gibbs to Welles, 18 July 1864, ibid., 109; Morris to Mallory, 13 July 1864, ibid., 623–624.

37. Ibid., 623–624.

38. Ibid.

39. Ibid., 624–625; Owsley, *Florida*, 129–130.

40. See Welles' dispatches in ORN I, 3:100–124.

41. Ibid., 114–116.

42. Ibid., 117, 118.

43. Drayton to Welles, 3 July 1864, ORN I, 3:93; Welles to Steedman, 23 July 1864, ibid., 125; Welles to Drayton, ibid.; Drayton to Welles, 5 September 1864, ibid., 199–200.

44. Owsley, *Florida*, 133–134.

45. Ibid., 134.

46. Ibid.

47. Ibid., 135.

48. Captures of the *Tallahassee*, ORN I, 3:703–704.

14. THE TALLAHASSEE AND THE CHICKAMAUGA

1. Royce G. Shingleton, *John Taylor Wood, Sea Ghost of the Confederacy* (Athens, Ga.: University of Georgia, 1976), 118–120, hereinafter cited as Shingleton, *Wood*. Shingleton's book on Wood's career provides the most comprehensive coverage on the cruise of the Tallahassee.

2. Clary to Welles, 9 September 1864, ORN I, 3:183–184. The intent of Clary's communication was to warn Welles of the unusual speed of the vessel.

3. Mallory to Bulloch, 22 Feburary 1863, ORN II, 2:268–269; Shingleton, *Wood*, 121.

4. *Dictionary of American Biography*, s.v. "Wood, John Taylor."

5. Shingleton, *Wood*, 122–123.

6. *Battles and Leaders*, I:692, 717.

7. John Taylor Wood, "The *Tallahassee's* Dash Into New York Waters," Century Magazine 56, July, 1898, 409, hereinafter cited as Wood, "*Tallahassee's* Dash." The Mound was part of Fort Fisher's outer fortifications and was named for its appearance.

8. Ibid., 410.

9. Ibid.

10. Shingleton, *Wood*, 126–127.

11. Wood to Mallory, 31 August 1864, ORN I, 3:701–703.

12. Shingleton, *Wood*, 128–129.

13. List of Captures, ORN I, 3:703–704.

14. Wood, "*Tallahassee's* Dash," 411.

15. Shingleton, *Wood*, 130; List of Captures, ORN I, 3:703–704.

16. Wood, "*Tallahassee's* Dash," 413.

17. Ibid.

18. Ibid., 412–414; List of Captures, ORN I, 3:703–704.

19. Welles, *Diary*, 2:102, 105, 110–111.

20. Wood to Mallory, 31 August 1864, ORN I, 3:701–703; Wood, "*Tallahassee's* Dash," 411; Shingleton, *Wood*, 136.

21. Wood to Mallory, 31 August 1864, ORN I, 3:701–703; Wood to Mallory, 6 September 1864, ibid., 705–706; Wood, "*Tallahassee's* Dash," 414.

22. Shingleton, *Wood*, 137–138.

23. Wood to Mallory, 31 August 1864, ORN I, 3:701–703; MacDonnell to Wood, 19 August 1864, ibid., 705; Shingleton, *Wood*, 138.

24. See Welles correspondence to numerous commanders in ORN I, 3:159, 178. Brit-ish correspondence covering Wood's stop at Halifax is generally covered in ORN I, 3:704–710. For Wood's return to sea, Wood, "Tallahassee's Dash," 414–416.

25. MacDonnell to Cardwell, 23 August and 31 August 1864, ORN I, 3:707–709.

26. Vance to Mallory, 3 January 1865, ORA I, 2, 46:1156–1158; Mallory to Vance, 28 January 1865, IV, 3:1057; Whiting to Mallory, 6 October 1864, I, 10:774–775. See also Tom H. Wells, *The Confederate Navy: A Study in Organization* (Tuscaloosa: University of Alabama Press, 1971), 45, hereinafter cited as Wells, *Conferederate Navy*.

27. Cruise of the *Olustee*, ORN I, 3:836; Shingleton, *Wood*, 143.

28. John Wilkinson, *The Narrative of a Blockade Runner* (New York: Sheldon and Company, 1877) 227–251, hereinafter cited as Wilkinson's Narrative.

29. Brown to Sands, 29 and 30 October 1864, ORN I, 3:309–311.

30. Journal of the *Chickamauga*, ORN I, 3:712.

31. Welles to Porter, 4 and 5 November 1864, ORN I, 3:318.

32. Journal of the *Chickamauga*, ORN I, 3:712–713.

33. Wilkinson's Narrative, 219–221.

34. Journal of the *Chickamauga*, ORN I, 3:713–714.

35. Wilkinson's Narrative, 227–251.

36. Lester, 104–105. While in Liverpool, the ship acquired the name *Amelia*, and became known as "the ship of seven names." There is no record that she ever sailed under that name, nor is there a record of her appellation after the sale to Japan. In 1867, she was converted to a Japanese merchantman and sailed as the brig *Haya Maro*. Two years later, on June 17, 1869, she struck a rock and sank en route from Yokohoma to Hioge–Kobe. Shingleton, *Wood*, 143.

37. Ibid., 206.

15. NEVER TRUST THE ENEMY

1. Collins to Welles, 30 September, 14 November 1864, ORN I, 3:248, 256–257.

2. Wilson to da Silva Gomes, and da Silva Gomes to Wilson, 5 October 1864, and Morris to Barron, 13 October 1864, ibid., 252–254, 631–632.

3. Ibid.

4. Ibid.

5. Owsley, *Florida*, 139–140.

6. Ibid., 140.

7. Ibid., 140–141.

8. Porter to Welles, 20 February, 1865, ORN I, 3:637; Collins to Welles, 31 October 1864, ibid., 255–256.

9. Ibid.

10. Ibid., 255.

11. Morris to Barron, 7 October 1864, ibid., 632.

12. Macebo to da Silva Gomes, 7 October 1864, ibid., 640–641.

13. Ibid., 258–259.

14. Morris to Barron, 13 October 1864, ORN I, 3:633; Morris to da Silva Gomes, 8 October and 11 October 1864, ibid., 634–636; Dwyer to Morris, 13 October 1864, ibid., 636; Taylor to Morris, 8 October 1864, ibid.

15. Collins to Welles, 14 November 1864, ibid., 258.

16. Beardsley to Collins, 31 October 1863, ibid., 258.

17. No record exists of the *Florida*'s next destination, but it has been speculated that Bahia was intended to be the last stop before Morris rounded Cape Horn in pursuit of the whaling fleet in the Pacific. This later became the mission of the CSS *Shenandoah*, specifically put to sea to fill the void created by the loss of the *Florida* in fulfilling this objective.

18. Beardsley to Collins, 31 October 1864, ORN I, 3:259–260; Owsley, *Florida*, 145–146.

19. Welles to Porter, 18 November 1864, and Collins to Porter, 20 November 1864, ORN I, 3:263; Porter to Morris, 20 February 1865, ibid., 637–638.

20. Collins to Welles, 25 December 1864, ibid., 266–267.

21. Porter to Morris, 20 February 1865, ibid., 638–639; Owsley, *Florida*, 147.

22. Bulloch, *Secret Service*, 2:101.

23. Various correspondence in ORN I, 3:274–276.

24. Breese to Porter, 22 November 1864, Porter to Baker, 24 November 1864; Porter to Baker, 24 November 1864, and Porter to Welles, 28 November 1864, ibid., 274–276.

25. Baker to Porter, 28 November 1864, ibid., 277.

26. Barloza da Silva to Seward, 12 December, and Seward to Barloza da Silva, 26 December 1864, ibid., 282–287. There is no indication in the records to explain why the Brazilian government would still be attempting to recover the *Florida* two weeks after she had sunk. It must be assumed that Brazil had not been informed.

27. Ibid, 286.

28. Ibid, 285–287.

29. Owsley, *Florida*, 147–148.

30. Finding of the court of enquiry in the case of the sinking of the prize steamer *Florida*, ORN I, 3:280.

31. Owsley, *Florida*, 149–150.

32. Ibid.

33. Ibid., 151–152.

34. Ibid., 150–151; Collins to Welles, 16 December 1864, ORN I, 3:266; court martial charges against Collins, ibid., 268.

35. Extract from court martial of Collins, ibid., 268–269.

36. Welles to Godon, 28 October 1865; Godon to Welles, 28 June 1866, 13 July 1866, and 25 August 1866, ibid., 289–292.

37. Welles to Collins, 17 September 1866, ibid., 269.

38. Alabama Claims, Vol. 3, 583–590.

39. Robert G. Albion and Jennie Barres Pope, *Sea Lanes in Wartime*, (New York: W.W. Norton and Company 1942) 172, hereinafter cited as *Sea Lanes*; Owsley, *Florida*, 161.

40. Ibid., 162; *Sea Lanes*, 148–173; Dalzell, 237–248; Owsley, *King Cotton*, 554–555.

16. THE MYSTERIOUS NO. 290

1. Spencer, 15–17; Bulloch, *Secret Service*, 1:59–60; *Dictionary of American Biography*, s.v. "Bulloch, James Dunwoody," Summersell, *Alabama*, 8–9.

2. Bulloch, *Secret Service*, 1:60–61; Summersell, *Alabama*, 9; Bulloch to Mallory, 13 August 1861, ORN II, 2:83–87.

3. Bulloch, *Secret Service*, 1:56; Summersell, *Alabama*, 9; Semmes, SA, 420.

4. Note: The *Nashville* was rated at 1,200 tons, but her principal purpose of design was to carry cargo and passengers.

5. Bulloch, *Secret Service*, 1:56; Summersell, *Alabama*, 9; Semmes, SA, 420.

6. Bulloch, *Secret Service*, 1:62; Summersell, *Alabama*, 12; Bulloch to Mallory, 11 August 1862, ORN II, 2:236.

7. Bulloch to Mallory, 13 August 1861, ORN II, 2:83–87.

8. Summersell, *Alabama*, 12; Bulloch, *Secret Service*, 1:102.

9. Ibid., 1: 227, 229; Summersell, *Alabama*, 12.

10. Bulloch, *Secret Service*, 1:229–230.

11. Ibid., 1:237; Summersell, *Alabama*, 13.

12. Ibid., 13; Bulloch to Yonge, 28 July 1862, and Bulloch to Butcher, 30 July 1862, ORN I, 1:772–774; Bulloch, *Secret Service*,

1:231, 233, 238.

13. Summersell, *Alabama*, 14; Spencer, 49–52; Semmes to Mallory, 15 June 1862, Mallory to Bulloch, 20 April and 3 May 1862, ORN II, 2:186–187, 190; Mallory to Bulloch, 29 May 1862, ORN II, 2:205. Semmes, SA, 386–388.

14. Spencer, 50; Dudley to Collector of Customs, 9 July 1862, ORN II, 2:378–380; Bulloch, *Secret Service*, 1:249–253; Summersell, *Alabama*, 14.

15. Bulloch, *Secret Service*, 1:238.

16. Ibid., 1:238–239; Summersell, *Alabama*, 14; Bulloch to Mallory, 11 August and 10 September, 1862, both in ORN II, 2:235–239, 263–265; Spencer, 50, 55.

17. Ibid., 50; Summersell, *Alabama*, 14–15; Bulloch, *Secret Service*, 1: 239–240; Dalzell, 132–133.

18. Spencer, 55–56; Dalzell, 133; Summersell, *Alabama*, 15.

19. Bulloch *Secret Service*, 1:242; Bulloch to Mallory, 10 September 1862, ORN II, 2:264.

20. Bulloch, *Secret Service*, 1:243.

21. Spencer, 57; Bulloch, *Secret Service*, 1:253. Note: The *Bahama* had also been the tender for the *Florida*.

22. Bulloch to Mallory, 11 August 1862, ORN II, 2:235–239. Note: Bulloch was intelligent and perceptive. Neither Semmes nor anyone else who wrote about the cruisers gave Bulloch proper credit. In a way, Bulloch was forced to write his own memoirs to avoid his personal oblivion. Of all the memoirs written, his were the most thorough and openly honest. By uncomplainingly doing the difficult job he was given by Mallory, Commander Bulloch earned the sole distinction of being the most effective overseas agent for a losing cause [Spencer, 58].

23. Semmes to North, 8 June 1862, ORN I, 1:771; Semmes, SA, 416–417; Arthur Sinclair, *Two Years On the Alabama* (Boston: Lee and Shepard, 1896), 297–338 bios, and 343–352, list of officers and crew, hereinafter cited as Sinclair, *Two Years*; Spencer, 58–59.

24. Even Arthur Sinclair in his *Two Years on the Alabama* fails to list Yonge in his roster appended to the back of his memoirs.

25. Semmes, SA, 402–403.

26. Bulloch, *Secret Service*, 1:255–257; Bulloch to Mallory, 10 September 1862, ORN II, 2:263–265; Summersell, *Alabama*, 16; Journal of *Alabama*, ORN I, 1:783–784. Note: The *Florida* did not leave Mobile until January 17, 1863.

17. "LOTS OF PRIZE MONEY"

1. W. Adolphe Roberts, *Semmes of the Alabama* (New York: Bobbs and Merrill Company, 1938), 26, hereinafter cited as Roberts, *Semmes*; Summersell, *Alabama*, 23.

2. Semmes, SA, 412; Dalzell, 136.

3. Semmes, SA, 412; journal of *Alabama*, ORN I, 1:784–785; Summersell, *Alabama*, 23.

4. Ibid., 28–29; Sinclair, *Two Years*, 290–292; Roberts, *Semmes*, 47; Delaney, 128; Semmes, SA, 416–418.

5. Sinclair, *Two Years*, 292–295; Summersell, *Alabama*, 29.

6. Sinclair, *Two Years*, 296–299.

7. Ibid., 299–300.

8. Ibid., 302–303.

9. Ibid., 304–306.

10. Ibid., 307–308.

11. Ibid., 307–311.

12. Ibid., 311–315.

13. Ibid., 318–322.

14. Ibid., 325–326.

15. Semmes, SA, 419.

16. Summersell, *Alabama*, 35–36.

17. Ibid., 36–37; journal of *Alabama*, ORN I, 1:787; Edward Boykin, *Ghost Ship of the Confederacy* (New York: Funk and Wagnalls, 1957), 188–191, hereinafter cited as Boykin, *Alabama*; Semmes, SA, 423–425; Sinclair, *Two Years*, 25–27; Hoole, 59–60; Kell, *Recollections*, 189; Delaney, 117–118.

18. Journal of *Alabama*, ORN I, 1:787; Semmes, SA, 423–424; Boykin, *Alabama*, 189–190; Summersell, *Alabama*, 36.

19. Semmes, SA, 423–424; journal of *Alabama*, ORN I, 1:787; Sinclair, *Two Years*, 26; Charles G. Summersell, *The Journal of George Townley Fullam, Boarding Officer of the Confederate Sea Raider Alabama* (Tuscaloosa: University of Alabama Press, 1973), 16–17, hereinafter cited as Summersell, *Fullam*; Boykin, *Alabama*, 191. Note: Although prize money never was awarded, the crew of the *Alabama* carefully recorded with constant hope the value of every ship and cargo destroyed. Prize money was the continual center of conversation in both the wardroom and the forecastle.

20. Ibid., 26.

21. Ibid., 191; journal of *Alabama*, ORN I, 1:788; Sinclair, *Two Years*, 26–27; Semmes, SA, 423–428. Kell, *Recollections*, 189; Delaney, 117–118; Summersell, *Alabama*, 36.

22. Summersell, *Fullam*, 18; journal of *Alabama*, ORN I, 1:788; Semmes, SA, 428–430.

23. Ibid., 429; journal of *Alabama*, ORN I, 1:788; Summersell, *Fullam*, 18.

24. Semmes, SA, 429.

25. Ibid., 431.

26. Ibid., 433; journal of the *Alabama*, ORN I, 1:788; Summersell, *Fullam*, 19. Note: The total claims filed for the burning of the *Ocean Rover* were $167,670, which included both those of the owners and those of the insurance companies.

27. Ibid., 19–20; journal of *Alabama*, ORN I, 1:788–789; Semmes, SA, 434–435; Summersell, *Alabama*, 37–38. Note: The *Alert* was the same vessel on which Richard Henry Dana, Jr., served as seaman in the mid-1830s. He later wrote of these adventures in his narrative of the sea, *Two Years Before the Mast*, an American literary classic.

28. Journal of Alabama, ORN I, 1:789; Summersell, *Fullam*, 21.

29. Ibid.

30. Ibid., 22–23; journal of *Alabama*, ORN I, 1:789–790; Semmes, SA, 438.

31. Ibid., 439–440; journal of *Alabama*, ORN I, 1:789–790; Summersell, *Fullam*, 22–23

32. Alabama Claims, 3:591.

33. Journal of *Alabama*, ORN I, 1:790; Semmes, SA, 440–441; Summersell, *Fullam*, 23–24.

34. Ibid., 24–25; journal of the *Alabama*, ORN I, 1:790; Semmes, SA, 442; Alabama Claims, 3:594.

35. Journal of the *Alabama*, ORN I, 1:790–791; Summersell, *Fullam*, 25–27; Semmes, SA, 442–444.

36. Ibid., 444.

37. Ibid., 446–448; Summersell, *Fullam*, 27; Summersell, *Alabama*, 38.

18. NEW ENGLAND SHUDDERS

1. Semmes, SA, 453–455; Sinclair, *Two Years*, 24; Summersell, *Alabama*, 39.

2. Journal of *Alabama*, ORN I, 1:792–793.

3. Semmes, SA, 458–459; Summersell, *Fullam*, 31–32.

4. Ibid., 29–30; Semmes, SA, 458–459; Owsley, *King Cotton*, 148–150.

5. Summersell, *Alabama*, 39; Alabama Claims, 3:595; Summersell, *Fullam*, 30–33.

6. Ibid., 31.

7. Ibid., 32–33; Journal of Alabama, ORN I, 1:460.

8. Semmes, SA, 460–461.

9. Ibid., 461–462; journal of *Alabama*, ORN I, 1:794–795.

10. Journal of *Alabama*, ORN I, 1:462, Summersell, *Fullam*, 33–34.

11. Ibid., 34–36; journal of *Alabama*, ORN I, 1:780, 794–795; Semmes, SA, 463–467; Roberts, *Semmes*, 108–109; Bulloch to Mallory, 7 November 1862, ORN II, 2:294–295.

12. Summersell, *Fullam*, 35; Semmes, SA, 465–466. White drowned when the *Alabama* sank. He could not swim but would have been saved had he spoken up.

13. Ibid., 468; journal of *Alabama*, ORN I, 1:795–796; Summersell, *Fullam*, 37.

14. Semmes, SA, 467; Summersell, *Alabama*, 41–42.

15. Craven to Upton, 29 September 1862, ORN I, 1:489.

16. Pickering to Welles, 6 October 1862, ORN I, 1:490.

17. J. D. Jones to Welles, 16 October 1862, ibid., 508.

18. Welles, *Diary*, 1:175; Welles to S. P. Lee, and Welles to Wilkes, 19 October 1862, ORN I, 1:509–510, 510–511.

19. Journal of *Alabama*, ORN I, 1:796.

20. Ibid., 797–799; Summersell, *Fullam*, 40–41; Semmes, SA, 481–487. This *Lafayette* was the first of two ships having the same name captured by the *Alabama*. The second ship was a bark designated by Fullam as *Lafayette #2*. It was captured April 15, 1863.

21. Journal of *Alabama*, ORN I, 1:799–800.

22. Summersell, *Fullam*, 41–42.

23. Ibid., 42–44; journal of *Alabama*, ORN I, 1:800–802; Semmes, SA, 484–487.

24. Ibid., 485–487.

25. Ibid., 491–492; Summersell, *Fullam*, 45.

26. Ibid., 47; journal of *Alabama*, ORN I, 1:802; Summersell, *Alabama*, 43; Alabama Claims, 3:593.

27. Journal of *Alabama*, ORN I, 1:803–804; Semmes, SA, 494–495.

28. Ibid., 496; Summersell, *Fullam*, 48.

29. Porter, *Naval History*, 643; Semmes, SA, 495–496; Kell, *Recollections*, 195–196; Summersell, *Alabama*, 43.

30. Semmes, SA, 509–510.

31. Ibid, 510–511.

32. Ibid., 511–513; Roberts, *Semmes*, 120. Note: "Old Beeswax" was a nickname given Semmes by the crew and referred to his sharply pointed mustaches. Semmes exercised a policy different from the United States Navy by forbidding his officers the use of alcoholic beverages while on board ship.

33. Ibid., 120–121; journal of *Alabama*,

ORN I, 1:805–806; Semmes, SA, 514–515. Note: Of the many ships pursuing the Alabama, only three ever found her: the USS *Hatteras*, which she sank; the USS *Kearsarge*, which sank her; and the USS *San Jacinto*, from whose guns she escaped.

34. Ronckendorff to Welles, 21 November 1862, ORN I, 1:549–550; Boykin, *Alabama*, 246.

35. Semmes, SA, 516–517; journal of *Alabama*, ORN I, 1:806; Summersell, *Fullam*, 56–57.

36. Semmes, SA, 519.

37. Ibid.

38. Ibid., 524–525; Dalzell, 140. Summersell, *Fullam*, 46.

19. FROM GALVESTON TO BAHIA

1. Journal of Alabama, ORN I, 1:808; Summersell, *Fullam*, 58–59; Semmes, SA, 523.

2. Summersell, *Alabama*, 44–45.

3. Semmes, SA, 529; Sinclair, *Two Years*, 53–57.

4. Summersell, *Alabama*, 45; Summersell, *Fullam*, 63.

5. Ibid., 62–63; Sinclair, *Two Years*, 58; Semmes, SA, 534.

6. Ibid., 532–535; Dalzell, 142–143; Summersell, *Fullam*, 60–66; Sinclair, *Two Years*, 56–59; Summersell, *Alabama*, 45; journal of the *Alabama*, ORN I, 1:780, 782, 810–812.

7. Ibid., 811.

8. Kell, *Recollections*, 204–205.

9. Semmes, SA, 538–540; Sinclair, *Two Years*, 61–64; journal of the *Alabama*, ORN I, 1:814–817.

10. Ibid., 721; Semmes, SA, 541.

11. Ibid., 542–544; journal of Alabama, ORN I, 2:721; Sinclair, *Two Years*, 68–69; Kell, *Recollections*, 208–209.

12. Summersell, *Fullam*, 71–72; journal of *Alabama*, ORN I, 2:721–722.

13. Ibid., 722; Semmes, SA, 545–549; Summersell, *Alabama*, 46; Summersell, *Fullam*, 72.

14. Ibid., 74–75; Hoole, 70–73. Kell valued the *Hatteras* at $160,000.

15. Summersell, *Alabama*, 46; Blake to Welles, 21 January 1863, ORN I, 2:18–20; Summersell, *Fullam*, 72.

16. Ibid., 76–78.

17. Blake to Welles, 27 January 1863, ORN I, 2:22.

18. Semmes, SA, 555–559; Hoole, 70–73; Sinclair, *Two Years*, 73–74; Summersell, *Fullam*, 80–81.

19. Sinclair, *Two Years*, 76.

20. Semmes, SA, 559. Summersell, *Fullam*, 82–83. Other records list the number of sailors lost at Kingston as seven, but the Union records list nine names.

21. Ibid., 82–83; journal of *Alabama*, ORN I, 2:724–725; Semmes, SA, 565–566.

22. Ibid., 568–574; journal of *Alabama* ORN I, 2:724–725; Summersell, *Fullam*, 84.

23. Ibid., 86–87; journal of Alabama, ORN I, 1:726. Semmes discontinued the practice of placing the masters of prizes in irons after the capture of the *Ariel* and allowed them to mess in the steerages.

24. Semmes, SA, 576–577.

25. Ibid., 577–580; Howe and Matthews, 1:228–231; Summersell, *Fullam*, 88–89. 28; journal of *Alabama*, ORN I, 2:728–729.

26. Ibid., 729–730.

27. Ibid., 730–732; Semmes, SA, 584–586; Summersell, *Fullam*, 93.

28. Ibid., 94–95; Semmes, SA, 587; journal of the *Alabama*, ORN I, 2:733–734.

29. Ibid., 734; Sinclair, *Two Years*, 92.

30. Journal of *Alabama*, ORN I, 2:735; Semmes, SA, 589–590; Summersell, *Fullam*, 97–100.

31. Ibid., 97–98.

32. Journal of *Alabama*, ORN I, 2:736–740; Summersell, *Alabama*, 50–51; Semmes, SA, 596–602.

33. Ibid., 603.

34. Ibid., 603–604; Summersell, *Alabama*, 50–51; journal of *Alabama*, ORN I, 2:740–741.

35. Ibid. 740.

36. Ibid., 741; Summersell, Fullam, 107–108; Semmes, SA, 611. Semmes wrote that he had now captured more whalers than were taken by Commodore David Porter in the frigate USS *Essex* when Porter cruised the Pacific fighting the British in the War of 1812. At the time, Porter was credited with a great achievement. His action set the precedent for the present Confederate war on commerce.

37. Journal of Alabama, ORN I, 2:741–742.

38. Ibid., 742; Semmes, SA, 613; Summersell, *Fullam*, 109–111.

39. Ibid.; journal of *Alabama*, ORN I, 2:742–743; William H. Rowe, *The Maritime History of Maine* (New York: 1948), 315–319; Kell, *Recollections*, 216–218; Semmes, SA, 612–613; Semmes to Mallory, 12 May 1863, ORN I, 2:683–685. Kell appraised the *Sea Lark* for $550,000, far above the $342,917 claimed by the owners.

20. CAPE TOWN CAPER

1. Semmes, SA, 616–617.
2. Sinclair, *Two Years*, 116–117.
3. Semmes, SA, 618–619; journal of *Alabama*, ORN I, 2:744–745.
4. Ibid., 745–746; Semmes, SA, 620–621; Summersell, *Fullam*, 115–116; Sinclair, *Two Years*, 120.
5. Semmes, SA, 621–622; journal of the *Alabama*, ORN I, 2:746–747.
6. Ibid., 745–747; Semmes, SA, 621–623; Summersell, *Fullam*, 117–118; *Alabama Claims*, 3:596.
7. Journal of *Alabama*, ORN I, 2:747–748. Sinclair, *Two Years*, 122–123.
8. Howe and Matthews, 2:656–658; Summersell, *Fullam*, 119–120; journal of *Alabama*, ORN I, 2:748–749.
9. Ibid., 750; Semmes, SA, 626–627; Summersell, *Fullam*, 120–121.
10. Ibid., 121–122; journal of *Alabama*, ORN I, 2:750–751.
11. Semmes to Low, 21 June 1863, Semmes to Mallory, 5 August 1863, all in ORN I, 2:688–690, 751–752; Semmes, SA, 627–628; Hoole, 78–81; Sinclair, *Two Years*, 133–135.
12. Semmes, SA, 628–630.
13. Ibid.; Baldwin to Welles, 23 July, and 2, 4, and 17 August 1863, ORN I, 2:407–409, 417–418, 426–427.
14. Semmes, SA, 630–631; journal of *Alabama*, ORN I, 2:753–754; Sinclair, *Two Years*, 127; Summersell, *Fullam*, 124–125.
15. Semmes, SA, 632–633.
16. Ibid., 634–635; journal of *Alabama*, ORN I, 2:754–755; Roberts, *Semmes*, 165–166; Summersell, *Fullam*, 126–127.
17. Ibid., 127; Baldwin to Welles, 17 August 1863, ORN I, 2:426–427; Semmes, SA, 635–636.
18. Journal of *Alabama*, ORN I, 2:758.
19. Ibid., 758–759; Semmes, SA, 640–641. Sinclair, *Two Years*, 140–142; Edna and Frank Bradlow, *Here Comes the Alabama: The Career of the Confederate Raider* (Cape Town: A.A. Balkema, 1958), 56–57, hereinafter Bradlow and Bradlow.
20. Semmes, SA, 648–649; Hoole, 82–83, 90–93; journal of *Alabama*, ransom bond of *Santee*, Low to Barron, March 1864, all in ORN I, 2:691–692, 718, 719, 759.
21. Ibid., 759; Summersell, *Fullam*, 132–133.
22. Semmes, SA, 649–652; Bradlow and Bradlow, 59–63.
23. Ibid., 59–63, 115; Summersell, *Alabama*, 58; Sinclair, *Two Years*, 145–149.

24. Bradlow and Bradlow, 69.
25. Semmes, SA, 653–659, 666–669; Sinclair *Two Years*, 158–159; Summersell, *Fullam*, 142.
26. Ibid., 136; B. W. Walker to Secretary of British Admiralty, 19 August 1863, ORN I, 2:697–699.
27. Walker to Wodehouse, and Wodehouse to Walker, 7 August through 11 August 1863, all in ORN I, 2:699–702.
28. Summersell, *Fullam*, 142–143; Hoole, 88–89; journal of *Alabama*, ORN I, 2:762–763; Sinclair, *Two Years*, 156–159; Semmes, SA, 666–669.
29. Ibid.; Summersell, *Alabama*, 60.
30. Summersell, *Fullam*, 143; Sinclair, *Two Years*, 159; journal of the *Alabama*, ORN I, 2:762–763.
31. Ibid., 765; Semmes, SA, 667–669.
32. Ibid., 668–669; B. W. Walker to the Secretary of the Admiralty, 17 September 1863, ORN I: 2:702–703.
33. Sinclair, *Two Years*, 164; journal of the *Alabama*, ORN I, 2:766; Semmes, SA, 670–671.
34. Ibid., 667–668; Boykin, *Alabama*, 316–318.
35. Journal of *Alabama*, ORN I, 2:767–768, 774–775.

21. AN AGING GREYHOUND

1. Journal of *Alabama*, ORN I, 2:777–778. Semmes, SA, 686–687; Summersell, *Fullam*, 147–148.
2. Ibid., 147; journal of *Alabama*, ORN I, 2:778–779.
3. Ibid., 779; Semmes, SA, 688–689; Sinclair, *Two Years*, 171; *Alabama Claims*, 3:597; Summersell, *Fullam*, 151–152.
4. Ibid., 153–155; journal of *Alabama*, ORN I, 2:780; Semmes, SA, 691–692; Howe and Matthews, 718–722.
5. Semmes, SA, p. 692.
6. Howe and Matthews, 718–722; *Alabama Claims*, 3:600.
7. Journal of *Alabama*, ORN I, 2:780–781; Semmes, SA, 693–695; Summersell, *Fullam*, 156–157.
8. McDougal to Welles, 9 December 1863, ORN I, 2: 560–561. The *Contest's* first mate, James D. Babcock, had served on the Pacific Mail Steamship Company's *Ariel* when captured and bonded by Semmes on December 7, 1862.
9. Ibid.
10. Summersell, *Fullam*, 156–159; Howe and Matthews, 1:103–107.

11. Sinclair, *Two Years*, 183.

12. Ibid., 184–191; journal of *Alabama*, ORN I, 2:784–789; Semmes, SA, 698–706; Summersell, *Fullam*, 163–164.

13. Sinclair, *Two Years*, 196, 200–201; Semmes, SA, 708–709.

14. McDougal to Welles, 23 July, 9 December 1863, and 24 January 1864, ORN I: 2:393–394, 560–561, 591–592.

15. Journal of *Alabama*, ORN I, 2:791–792; Semmes, SA, 714–715.

16. Ibid., 715; Summersell, *Alabama*, 67.

17. Journal of *Alabama*, ORN 1, 2:792–793; Summersell, *Fullam*, 166–169; Semmes, SA, 716–719.

18. Ibid., 718–719; Summersell, *Fullam*, 168–169.

19. Ibid., 169.

20. Ibid, 169–170.

21. Ibid., 170–171; Semmes, SA, 720–721. The inconsistencies in the Confederate's evaluation of their prizes continued with the appraisal of the *Sonora* at $46,545 and the *Highlander* at $75,965. Claims filed for the *Sonora* amounted to $89,044.44 and those for the *Highlander* totalled $191,171. Of the latter, the court allowed $62,402 for loss of freight although the ship was in ballast at the time of its capture. See *Alabama* Claims, 3:601.

22. Journal of *Alabama*, ORN I, 2:793.

23. Ibid. 794–795.

24. Semmes, SA, 723.

25. Ibid., 722–724; journal of *Alabama*, ORN I, 2:795.

26. Ibid., 2:803; Sinclair, *Two Years*, 227–228.

27. Walker to Low, 27 December 1863, Low to Wodehouse, 28 December 1863, Bulloch to Mallory, 2 February 1865, all in ORN II, 2:799–803; Hoole, 98–104.

28. Semmes, SA, 739–742.

29. Ibid., 742–743; Hoole, 105–107; Dalzell, 150–152; Summersell, *Alabama*, 70–71.

30. Journal of Alabama, ORN I, 2:806. Semmes, SA, 744–745.

31. Ibid., 747.

32. Delaney, *Kell*, 218–219; Sinclair, *Two Years*, 243; journal of *Alabama*, ORN I, 3:671; Summersell, *Fullam*, 183.

33. Ibid., 184–185; journal of *Alabama*, I, 3:672.

34. Ibid., 673–676; Semmes, SA, 750–751.

35. Journal of *Alabama*, ORN I, 3:676–677.

36. Ibid.

22. THE KEARSARGE AND THE ALABAMA

1. For the best biography on Winslow, see John M. Ellicott, *The Life of John Ancrum Winslow Rear Admiral, United States Navy* (New York: G. P. Putnam's Sons, 1905), hereinafter cited as Ellicott, *Winslow*; statistical data, ORN II, 1:118–119.

2. Winslow to Welles, 13 June 1864, Dayton to Seward, 13 June 1864, ORN I, 3:50–52; Hill, *Sea Dogs*, 212–214; Boykin, *Alabama*, 348.

3. Journal of *Alabama*, ORN I, 3:677; Summersell, *Alabama*, 74; Semmes, SA, 751–752; Dalzell, 162; Sinclair, *Two Years*, 259: Sinclair stated that Semmes was unaware of the defective powder; Porter, *Naval History*, 650, and List of Officers and Crew of *Kearsarge* and *Alabama*, 655–656; Kell, Recollections, 245–246.

4. Ibid.; Semmes to Bonfils, 14 June 1864, Bonfils to Slidell, 18 June 1864, in ORN I, 3:647–648; Semmes, SA, 752–753.

5. Journal of *Alabama*, ORN I, 3:677.

6. Summersell, *Fullam*, 192. The chronometers were later sold and proceeds distributed among the survivors of the fight.

7. During the War of 1812, Captain Philip Broke commanding the British frigate *Shannon* invited Captain James Lawrence of the American frigate *Chesapeake* to "meet and try the fortunes of our respective flags" off Boston harbor. There had not been a prearranged naval battle since that time.

8. Kell, Recollections, 261; Delaney, *Kell*, 216–220; Semmes, SA, 752–754; Sinclair, *Two Years*, 247–249; Summersell, *Alabama*, 76; Summersell, *Fullam*, 192–193.

9. Ibid., 193; Sinclair, *Two Years*, 254–256; Boykin, *Alabama*, 355–357.

10. Semmes, SA, 757–758, 763–764; Summersell, *Fullam*, 195.

11. Semmes, SA, 756.

12. Ellicott, *Winslow*, 213; Summersell, *Fullam*, 193.

13. Ibid., 193–194; Kell, *Recollections*, 246–247; Sinclair, *Two Years*, 256–257. Summersell, *Alabama*, 77.

14. Semmes, SA, 761–762.

15. Ibid., 757–763; Among the many accounts covering the battle are the following: Semmes to Barron, Armstrong to Barron, Slidell to Semmes, all 21 June 1864, Barron to Mallory, 22, 27 June 1864, Slidell to Benjamin, 20 June 1864, and *Kearsarge* log, 14–21 June 1864, Dayton to Seward 13 June 1864, all in ORN 1, 3:649–641, 677, 51–52, 64–65, 77–78; Sinclair, *Two Years*, 267–290; Soley,

206–208; Boykin, *Alabama*, 355–375; Roberts, *Semmes*, 195–211; Kell, *Recollections*, 249–251; Delaney, *Kell*, 167–178; Summersell, *Fullam*, 191–196; Summersell, *Alabama*, 76–90.

16. Ibid., 84; Roberts, *Semmes*, 209–210; Boykin, *Alabama*, 372–373; Kell; *Recollections*, 249.

17. Ibid., 249–250.

18. Sinclair, *Two Years*, 262.

19. Hill, *Sea Dogs*, 219; Boykin, *Alabama*, 376.

20. Ibid., 270; Kell, *Recollections*, 250–251; Roberts, *Semmes*, 210; Sinclair, *Two Years*, 279–280.

21. Ibid., 270; Summersell, *Fullam*, 195; Summersell, *Alabama*, 84.

22. Kell, *Recollections*, 251; Sinclair, *Two Years*. 280; Boykin, *Alabama*, 377. Hill, *Sea Dogs*, 219; Roberts, *Semmes*, 210–211.

23. Winslow to Welles, 21 June 1864, Welles to Winslow, 6 July, 8 July, and 12 July 1864, Adams to Winslow, 13 July 1864, Winslow to Welles, 30 July 1864, all in ORN I, 3:65, 72–78.

24. Slidell to Semmes, 21 June 1864, Semmes to Slidell, 1 July 1864, Semmes to Barron, 5 July 1864, Winslow to Welles, 20 June 1864, 21 June 1864, ORN I, 3:654–664, 59–65; Summersell, *Fullam*, 195–196; Roberts, *Semmes*, 211.

25. Bulloch, *Secret Service*, I:286.

26. Lancaster to London *Daily News*, 27 June 1864, Davis to Lancaster, 1 March 1865, ORN I, 3:665–669; Semmes, SA, 777–786.

27. Welles to Winslow, ORN I, 3:74; Hill, *Sea Dogs*, 222.

28. Summersell, *Alabama*, 91; Semmes, SA, 788–789.

29. Ibid., 789–790; Kell, *Recollections*, 255–264.

30. Ibid., 268–272; Mallory to Semmes, 15 February 1865, Mitchell to Semmes, 19 February 1865, ORN I, 12:183–187; Semmes, SA, 790–823.

31. Ibid., 268–272; Welles, *Diary*, 2: 410, 436, 457, 467, 471–477; Roberts, *Semmes*, 249–251; Elizabeth Bethel, ed. "The Prison Diary of Raphael Semmes," *Journal of Southern History* 22, (November 1956): 502 and passim; John A. Bolles, "Why Semmes Was Not Tried," *Atlantic Monthly*, July 1872, 88–97, and August 1872, 148–156.

23. THE CSS GEORGIA AND THE CSS RAPPAHANNOCK

1. Frank J. Merli, Great Britain and the Confederate Navy (Bloomington: Indiana University Press, 1970), 127–33, hereinafter, Merli, *Great Britain*; Lester, 24–25, 180–181; Spencer, 127. The three best biographies on Maury in order of importance are: Frances Leigh Williams, *Matthew Fontaine Maury: Scientist of the Sea* (New Brunswick, N.J.: Rutgers University Press, 1963) hereinafter, Williams; Jaquelin Ambler Caskie, *Life and Letters of Matthew Fontaine Maury* (Richmond:1928); and Patricia Jahn, *Scientists of the Civil War: Matthew Fontaine Maury and Joseph Henry* (New York: 1961), hereinafter, Jahn.

2. Spencer, 128–129; A.B.C. Whipple, *The Challenge* (New York: William Morrow & Company, 1987), 85–96. Maury also wrote the *Physical Geography of the Sea* and other school texts. These further established his credentials as a scientist and his authority as a marine biologist.

3. Spencer, 130; Williams, 372.

4. Ibid., 396–398; Jahn, 204.

5. Williams, 402; Mallory to Bulloch, 20 September 1862, ORN II, 2:270.

6. Ibid, 2:260. Bulloch's comments are based on his memory and not on documents.

7. Spencer, 138 cites M. F. Maury to Marin Jansen, Confidential, 20 December 1862, Maury Papers, vol. 17.

8. Spencer, 138–139; Lester, 77–78; Williams, 407–408; Richard C. Todd, *Confederate Finance* (Athens: University of Georgia Press, 1954), 182, 185, hereinafter cited as Todd. Spencer cites M. F. Maury to R. D. Minor, 21 April 1863, Maury Papers, vol. 18.

9. Spencer, 239, n. 26; Alabama Claims, 1:367; Bulloch to Mallory, 25 November 1863, Financial Report, ORN II, 2:522; Lester, 77.

10. Spencer, 139, 239, n. 27–28.

11. Spencer, 139–140, 239 n. 29; M. F. Maury to R. D. Minor, 21 April 1863, Maury Papers, vol. 18.

12. The other seven Confederate officers were Lt. John H. Ingraham and Passed Midshipman John T. Walker of South Carolina, Midshipman James Morris Morgan of Louisiana, Paymaster R. W. Curtis of Arkansas, Surgeon Thomas J. Wheedon of Maryland, Lt. Smith and Chief Engineer Pearson. See Sharf, *History of the Confederate States Navy: Register of Officers*, 803.

13. Alabama Claims, 3:108–109; 281; Lester, 79.

14. Ibid., 141; Alabama Claims, 3:108–109; Spencer, 140, 240, n. 32.

15. Ibid., 217; ORN II, 2:263; Scharf, 803–804.

16. ORN I, 2:811–818.

17. Maury to Barron, 27 December 1863,

and Barron to Maury, 19 January 1864, ORN I, 2:809, 810.

18. The best record of the uneventful cruise of the *Georgia* resides in ORN I, 2:811–818. By following the log, it is apparent that Maury had little mobility under sail and spent many days doing little more than drifting.

19. Spencer, 142, 240, n. 37, 38.

20. Lester, 218–219; ORN I, 3:698.

21. Ibid., 81; Bulloch, *Secret Service,* 2:262; Merli, Great Britain, 219–220; Williams, 410.

22. Ibid., 410; Spencer, 143.

23. Morse to Adams, 28 November 1863, ORN I, 2:505–506.

24. Merli, *Great Britain,* 222; Bulloch, *Secret Service;* 2:266; Spencer, 143.

25. Dayton to Winslow, 30 November, 1863 and 18 February, 1864, Dayton to Seward, 26 January 1864, ORN I, 2:510–511, 605; Lynn M. Case and Warren F. Spencer, *The United States and France: Civil War Diplomacy* (Philadelphia: University of Pennsylvania Press, 1970), 500–509.

26. Count de Chasseloup-Laubat statement of policy, Barron to Campbell, 28 January 1864, Barron to Evans, 29 January 1864, Barron to Mallory, 22 Janurary and February 1864, ORN I, 2:608, 810, 819 and II, 2:575, 580.

27. Preble to Welles, 23 January 1864, Bulloch to Mallory, 14 April 1864, ORN I, 2:590, II, 2:624–625; Spencer, 180.

28. Ibid.; Mallory to Barron, 25 April 1864, ORN II, 2:629–630.

29. Fauntleroy to Barron, 22 March 1864, ORN I, 2:820–821.

30. Ibid.

31. Ibid., April 1864, 3:684–685.

32. Slidell to Benjamin, 16 March 1864, 2, 5, 12 and 21 May 1864, all in ORN II, 3:1064, 1109, 1114, 1118–1119. Fauntleroy to Commissaire of Marine, 1 May 1864, 1110–1111, Barron to Fauntleroy, 16 May 1864, ORN I, 3:691.

33. For details on Fauntleroy's difficulties at Calais, see his correspondence in ORN I, 3:685–691. The incident involving the French vessel *Nil* is summarized in the award of 200 francs plus court costs. See also Spencer, 183.

34. Slidell to Drouyn de Lhuys, 9 June 1864, Slidell to Duke de Persigny, 17 June 1864, and Fauntleroy to Barron, 8 July 1864, all in ibid, 691–694.

35. Fauntleroy to Barron, with correspondence beginning 8 July and ending 19 October 1864, all in ORN I, 3:694–701.

24. THE SEA KING

1. Mallory to Bulloch, 18 July 1864, ORN II, 2:687.

2. Bulloch, *Secret Service,* 2:112–121.

3. Ibid., 2:125.

4. Mallory to Bulloch, 19 August 1964, Bulloch to Mallory, 29 September 1864, ORN II, 2:707–709, 728.

5. Bulloch, *Secret Service,* 2:125, 133; Spencer, 198.

6. Bulloch to Mallory, 6 October 1864, ORN II, 2:728–730.

7. James D. Horan, ed., *CSS Shenandoah; The Memoirs of Lieutenant James I. Waddell* (New York: Crown Publishers, 1960), 66–71, hereinafter cited as Waddell's Memoirs. Horan's treatment of Waddell's memoirs contains many editorial errors; however, the memoirs themselves have useful historical value and are cited where applicable.

8. Bulloch to Mallory, 20 October 1864, ORN II, 2:236–237; Bulloch, *Secret Service,* 2:131–132.

9. Ibid., 2:131–134.

10. Ibid., 2:134–135.

11. Two previous works covering the cruise of the CSS *Shenandoah* are Murray Morgan's *Dixie Raider, The Saga of the CSS Shenandoah* (New York: E.P. Dutton and Comapany, 1948), 18–19, hereinafter cited as Morgan, *Dixie Raider,* and Stanley F. Horn's *Gallant Rebel* (New Brunswick,N.J.: Rutgers University Press, 1947), 30–31, hereinafter cited as Horn, *Gallant Rebel,* both of which are drawn upon for background information and mainly represent unqualified sources.

12. Bulloch to Waddell and Barron to Waddell, 5 October 1864, ORN I, 3:749–756.

13. Craven to Welles, 31 October 1864, Craven to Adams, 10 October 1864, Moran to Craven, 11 October 1864 and Dudley to Craven, 11 October 1864, all in ORN I, 3:341–344; Morgan, *Dixie Raider,* 30–31.

14. Moran to Craven, 11 October 1864, ORN I,2:343–344.

15. Horn, *Gallant Rebel,* 33–34.

25. A ROUGH START

1. John Grimball, "Career of the Shenandoah," *Southern Historical Society Papers,* XXV, 117, hereinafter cited as Grimball. The article was first published in the *Sunday News,* Charleston, S.C., February 3, 1895. Morgan, *Dixie Raider,* 33.

2. Waddell's Memoirs, 91.

3. Ibid, 92.

4. Horn, *Gallant Rebel,* 43–44.

5. Morgan, *Dixie Raider,* 36–37.

6. Bulloch to Waddell, 5 October 1864, I, 3:752. Waddell's Memoirs, 94; John T. Mason, "The Last of the Confederate Cruisers," *Century Magazine*, August, 1898, Vol. 56, 602, hereinafter cited as Mason.

7. Mason, 602. Murray, *Dixie Raider*, 39.

8. Waddell in his memoirs counted 23 in the crew, but his report to Bulloch dated 25 January 1865, ORN I, 3:759–760, stated that he started the cruise with 20 enlistees and 22 officers. Whichever count is accurate, it is certain that the vessel was shorthanded. See also William C. Whittle, "The Cruise of the Shenandoah," *Southern Historical Society Papers*, Vol. 35, 1907, p. 243, 244, hereinafter cited as Whittle, Cruise.

9. Ibid., 244; Mason, 602.

10. List of Officers, ORN I, 3:785. Waddell's Memoirs, 94.

11. Whittle, Cruise, 245; Horn, *Gallant Rebel*, 49–50.

12. Waddell's Memoirs, 95–96. Bulloch's official measurements of the Shenandoah were: "She is 1160 tons, classed A-1 for fourteen years at Lloyds; frames, beams, etc., of iron but planked from keel to gunwale with East India teak. She is a full-rigged ship with rolling top sails, has plenty of accommodations for officers of all grades. Her 'tween decks' are 7 ft. 6 in. with large air ports. Her engines are direct acting with two cylinders 47 inches in diameter, 2 ft. 9 in. stroke, nominal horsepower 220 but indicating 850 horsepower and she has a lifting screw. The log of the ship shows her to be a fast sailer under canvas for with her screw up she has made 330 miles in 24 hours." For Waddell's description of the vessel, see his memoirs, 98.

13. Waddell's Memoirs, 99–102.

14. *Lining's Journal*, Museum of the Confederacy, Richmond, Virginia, hereinafter cited as Lining. The *Journal* does not contain page numbers and cites will be by date, 19 October 1864.

15. Log of the Shenandoah, ORN I, 3:785; Waddell's Memoirs, 103–104; Morgan, *Dixie Raider*, 45–46.

16. Bulloch to Waddell, 5 October 1864, ORN 1, 3:752.

17. Waddell's Memoirs, 104.

18. Cornelius E. Hunt, *The Shenandoah, or the Last Confederate Cruiser*, (New York: C.W. Carleton & Co., 1868) 31, hereinafter cited as Hunt; Morgan, *Dixie Raider*, 52–53.

19. Lining, 30 October 1864; Morgan, *Dixie Raider*, 54. Both Whittle and Mason disagree on the number of men who joined the raider's crew. See Whittle, Cruise, 245, and Mason, 603.

20. Shenandoah's log, ORN I, 3:786. Waddell's Memoirs, 107; Whittle, Cruise, 245–246; Horn, *Gallant Rebel*, 73–74; Hunt, 35–39.

21. Ibid., 39–42; Waddell's Memoirs, 109;

22. Shenandoah's log, ORN I, 3:786; Morgan, *Dixie Raider*, 64–65; Lining, 9 November 1864

23. Horn, *Gallant Rebel*, 80–81; Mason, 605; Waddell's Memoirs. 110.

24. Ibid., 111. Hunt, 44. Horn, *Gallant Rebel*, 82–83.

25. Lining, 12 November 1864; Morgan, *Dixie Raider*, 68.

26. Ibid., 68–69; Waddell's log, ORN I, 3:803; Lining, 12 Novemnber 1864; Whittle, Cruise, 246

27. Morgan, Dixie Raider, 68–69.

28. Ibid., 71.

29. Waddell's log, ORN I, 3:804.

30. Morgan, *Dixie Raider*, 55–56, 73–74; Bulloch, *Secret Service*, 2:173–174.

31. Morgan, *Dixie Raider*, 74.

32. Bulloch, *Secret Service*, 2:173.

33. Clark to Welles, and Libbey to Clark, ORN I, 3:400–403.

26. TO THE OTHER SIDE OF THE WORLD

1. Mason, 605; Hunt, *Shenandoah*, 56–58; Whittle, Cruise, 247–248; Horn, Gallant Rebel, 90; Morgan, *Dixie Raider*, 78–80.

2. Waddell's Memoirs, 113; Waddell's log, ORN I, 3:787, 804.

3. Waddell's Memoirs, 113; Rodgers to Welles, 5 and 9 January 1865, ORN I, 3:403–406.

4. Lining, December 29, 1864; Hunt, *Shenandoah*, 73–75; Mason, 605; Whittle, Cruise, 248–249.

5. Ibid., 249; Waddell's Memoirs, 119–120; Waddell's log, ORN I, 3:807; Morgan, *Dixie Raider*, 109–111.

6. Lining, 6 January 1865; Hunt, *Shenandoah*, 87–89.

7. Mason, 606; Morgan, *Dixie Rebel*, 121–122.

8. Lining, January 25, 1865.

9. Morgan, *Dixie Raider*, 123–124.

10. Waddell's log, ORN I, 3:809; Whittle, Cruise, 249.

11. Francis to Waddell, 26 January 1865, ORN I, 3:761–762.

12. Morgan, *Dixie Raider*, 131–132; *Alabama* Claims, 3:117–119.

13. Ibid., 3:118.

14. Waddell's Memoirs, 130–131; Waddell's journal, ORN I, 3:810, 811; Mason, 606;

Grimball, 122; Morgan, *Dixie Raider*, 132.

15. Standish to Waddell, 1 February 1865, ORN I, 3:766.

16. Waddell's Log, ibid., 812.

17. Waddell's Log, ibid., 811; Hunt, *Shenandoah*, 101–102.

18. Grimball, 1222; Lyttleton to Waddell, 6 February, 1865, ORN I, 3:810.

19. Waddell's journal, ibid.; Mason, 606; Waddell's Memoirs, 131.

20. Ibid., 132.

21. Francis to Waddell, Standish to Beaver, and Waddell to Francis, 14 February 1865, all in ORN I, 3:769–771.

22. Ibid.

23. Morgan, *Dixie Raider*, 140–141.

24. Waddell to Francis, Francis to Waddell, 15 February 1865, ORN I, 3:771–772.

25. Case of the Australian government versus the CSS *Shenandoah*, ibid., 773–774.

26. Francis to Waddell, 15 February, and Waddell to Francis, 16 February 1865, ibid., 772–774; Waddell's Memoirs, 135.

27. *Alabama* Claims, 3:122–130. The foregoing is documented in the *Argument of the United States during the Geneva Tribunal*; Morgan, *Dixie Raider*, 148–150; Horn, *Gallant Rebel*, 138–142.

28. Hunt, *Shenandoah*, 113–115.

29. Waddell's Memoirs, 137.

30. Morgan, *Dixie Raider*, 151–155.

27. ARCTIC NIGHTMARE

1. Waddell's journal, ORN I, 3:815; Hunt, *Shenandoah*, 117–118.

2. Whittle, *Cruise*, 251; Waddell's Memoirs, 143–144.

3. Ibid., 144–145; log of the *Shenandoah* and Waddell's journal, both in ORN I, 3:788, 815; Hunt, Shenandoah, 119–125.

4. Waddell's journal, ORN I, 3:816.

5. Ibid., 816–820; Hunt, *Shenandoah*, 130–138. In addition to the cited references, the complete story of the Shenadoah's visit to Ponape is also described in Morgan, *Dixie Raider*, 171–187, and in Horn, *Gallant Rebel*, 162–176.

6. Waddell's Memoirs, 153–155; log of *Shenandoah*, ORN I, 3:788–789.

7. Waddell's journal, ibid., 3:822–823.

8. Log of the Shenandoah, ORN I, 3:789. Whittle, *Cruise*, 252; Mason, 608, states that 15 men joined the ship's company, including two mates.

9. Hunt, *Shenandoah*, 154–167; Morgan, *Dixie Raider*, 195–199.

10. Waddell to Whittle, 29 May 1865, ORN I, 3:775.

11. Log of the Shenandoah, ORN I, 3:790; 825; Mason, 608.

12. Morgan, *Dixie Raider*, 212–213.

13. Log of the *Shenandoah*, ORN I, 3:790; *Alabama* Claims, 3: 603, 607; Hunt, *Shenandoah*, 169–171.

14. Waddell's Journal, ORN I, 3:825; Morgan, *Dixie Raider*, 213–214; Whittle, *Cruise*, 252–253.

15. Waddell crossed the international dateline twice during this period, thereby creating two entries for June 22. During this time, the crew could work in daylight for nearly 24 hours.

16. Waddell's Memoirs, 164–165; Hunt, *Shenandoah*, 173–175; Waddell's journal, ORN I, 3:825–826.

17. Ibid., 826–827; Mason, 609.

18. Hunt, *Shenandoah*, 178–182.

19. Morgan, *Dixie Raider*, 221.

20. Waddell's Memoirs, 166–167; Whittle, *Cruise*, 253. Whittle wrote: "We felt that the South had sustained great reverses, but at no time did we feel a more imperative duty to prosecute our work with vigor."

21. Hunt, *Shenandoah*, 184.

22. Waddell's Journal, ORN I, 3:827–828.

23. Hunt, *Shenandoah*, 191–193.

24. Waddell's journal, ORN I, 3:828; Waddell's Memoirs, 167–168.

25. Morgan, *Dixie Raider*, 234.

26. Ibid, 236.

27. Waddell's Memoirs, 168–169.

28. Waddell's Memoirs, 169–170; Hunt, *Shenandoah*, 202–203.

29. Ibid., 199–202; Mason, 609.

30. Waddell's Memoirs, 169–171; *Alabama* Claims, 3:133, 602–609; Hunt, *Shenandoah*, 203–206; Waddell's journal, ORN I, 3:791.

31. Ibid., 830. The *Shenandoah* reached her deepest penetration north on June 29, 1865, to 66 × 44′ N.

32. McDougal to Welles, 29 July 1865 and List of Captures by the Shenandoah, ORN I, 3:569, 792.

28. CRUISER WITHOUT A COUNTRY

1. Waddell's Journal, ORN I, 3:831.

2. Waddell's Memoirs, 175.

3. James to McCullough, 20 July 1865, ORN I, 3:588.

4. McDougal to Welles, 23 July 1865, ORN I, 3:571.

5. Morgan, *Dixie Raider*, 257–259.

6. Waddell's Memoirs, 175.

7. Hunt, *Shenandoah*, 218; Lining, Au-

gust 2, 1865; Grimball, 124–125; Whittle, Cruise, 254–255.

8. Log of the Shenandoah, ORN I, 3:791; Waddell's Memoirs, 176.

9. Whittle, Cruise, 255; Waddell's Memoirs, 176–177.

10. Waddell's journal, ORN I, 3:832; Hunt, *Shenandoah*, 222–223.

11. Hunt, *Shenandoah*, 224, 226.

12. Ibid., 292–293. Both petitions are in ORN I, 3:779–782. See also Mason, 609–610; Morgan, *Dixie Raider*, 277–282. Whittle, an occasional critic of Waddell, wrote nothing of the incident.

13. ORN I, 3:782–783.

14. Lining, October 2, 1865.

15. Hunt, *Shenandoah*, 232. Hunt wrote that he "fully agreed" with his brother officers "regarding the conduct of Captain Waddell as unwarranted and ungentlemanly," referring to the letter Waddell wrote denouncing some of the officers as "mutineers."

16. Morgan, *Dixie Raider*, 284–288.

17. Waddell's Memoirs, 179–181; Waddell's journal, ORN I, 3:833–834; Whittle, Cruise, 256; Hunt, *Shenandoah*, 233.

18. Ibid., 233–239; Lining, October 26, 1865; log of Shenandoah, ORN I, 3:792.

19. Waddell's journal, ORN I, 3:834–835; Hunt, *Shenandoah*, 241–242; Mason, 610; Whittle, Cruise, 256.

20. Waddell to Russell, 6 November 1865, ORN I, 3:783–784.

21. Morgan, *Dixie Raider*, 299.

22. Ibid, 300.

23. Ibid.

24. Waddell's Memoirs, 182–183.

25. Whittle, Cruise, 257–258 for extract from the Crown's statement.

26. Ibid. 258; Waddell's Memoirs, 184–185; Waddell's journal, ORN I, 3:835–836; Hunt, *Shenandoah*, 259–260.

27. Morgan, *Dixie Raider*, 308–309.

28. Waddell's Journal, ORN I, 3: 836.

29. Waddell's Memoirs, 47–49.

30. Waddell's Memoirs, 43; Whittle, Cruise, 258.

31. Morgan, *Dixie Raider*, 332; Whittle, Cruise, 258. The flag of the Shenandoah, preserved by Richard L. Maury, CSA, son of Matthew Fontaine Maury, can be seen at the Museum of the Confederacy in Richmond, Virginia.

29. THE ALABAMA CLAIMS

1. *The Official Correspondence on the Claims of the United States in respect to the Alabama*, Published by Earl Russell (London, 1867), 147, hereinafter cited as Russell's Correspondence.

2. *Papers relating to Foreign Affairs accompanying the Annual Message of the President to the First Session Thirty-ninth Congress*, Part I, (Washington, 1866), 565.

3. Russell's Correspondence, 165.

4. Ibid., 166.

5. Ibid., 223.

6. Thomas Willing Balch, *The Alabama Arbitration* (Philadelphia: Allen, Lane and Scott, 1900), 74, n. 43, hereinafter cited as Balch.

7. G. V. Fox, *Narrative of the Mission to Russia, in 1866, of the Honorable Gustavus Vasa Fox* (New York: D. Appleton & Co.,1873), 48, 49.

8. Montague Bernard, *A Historical Account of the Neutrality of Great Britain During the American Civil War* (London: Longman's, Green, Reader and Dyer, 1870), 483; *Papers Relating to Foreign Affairs Accompanying the Annual Message of the President to the Second Session*, Fortieth Congress (Washington, Government Printing Office, 1868), pt. 1, 45.

9. Balch, 95.

10. *Appendix to the Congressional Globe: Containing Speeches, Important State Papers and the Laws of the First Session, Forty-first Congress* (Washington: Government Printing Office, 1869), 21–26; "Speech of Hon. Charles Sumner on the Johnson-Clarendon Treaty for the Settlement of Claims, delivered in the U.S. Senate" (Washington: Congressional Globe, 1869).

11. Dalzell, 231.

12. *Correspondence Concerning Claims Against Great Britain*, vol. 3, (Washington: Government Printing Office, 1870), 786–787.

13. Ibid., volume 4, 3–4.

14. Ibid, volume 6, 15–18.

15. Alabama Claims, 1:9; J. C. Bancroft Davis, *Mr. Fish and the Alabama Claims, A Chapter in Diplomatic History* (Boston and New York: Houghton, Mifflin Company 1892), 70, hereinafter cited as Davis, *Mr. Fish and the Alabama Claims.*

16. Claims of British subjects involved losses of merchant vessels, cargos and personal property captured or seized by the United States navy as suspected contraband destined for the Confederacy.

17. Alabama Claims, 1:12, 14, 207.

18. Caleb Cushing, *The Treaty of Washington, Its Negotiation, Execution and the Discussion Relating Thereto* (New York:

Harper and Brothers, 1873) 26, 78–94, hereinafter cited as Cushing, *Treaty*.

    19. *Alabama* Claims, 4:14, 16.

    20. Ibid., 1:185, 4:4–5.

    21. Ibid., 2:434, 593–604; Davis, *Mr. Fish and the Alabama Claims*, 74–82, 89–96.

    22. Balch, 125.

    23. Ibid., 126; *Alabama* Claims, 4:21.

    24. Ibid., 4:8, 15-48, 49, 230–544; Cushing, *Treaty*, 126-149.

    25. Ibid., 126-128. Dalzell, 234–235.

    26. *Alabama* Claims, 1:14, 207.

    27. Dalzell, 235.

Other Sources

Manuscripts and Unpublished Documents

Stephen R. Mallory Diary, Southern Historical Collection, University of North Carolina
Library, Chapel Hill, N.C.

Periodicals

Alta California
Cape Town *Argus*
Charleston *Mercury*
Hunt's Merchant Magazine
Liverpool *Daily Post*
Liverpool *Mercury*
London *Globe*
London *Herald*
London *Index*
London *Post*
London *Telegraph*
London *Times*
Mobile *Tribune*
New Orleans *True Delta*
New York *Herald*
New York Times
New York *Tribune*
Pall Mall Gazette
Richmond *Dispatch*
Richmond *Enquirer*
Richmond *Examiner*
Tory Herald

Index